Documents of American Social Welfare History

Documents of American Social Welfare History

Vincent E. Faherty

University of Southern Maine

Bassim Hamadeh, CEO and Publisher
Amy Smith, Project Editor
Cassie Carey, Production Editor
Jess Estrella, Senior Graphic Designer
Alisa Munoz, Licensing Coordinator
Natalie Piccotti, Director of Marketing
Kassie Graves, Vice President of Editorial
Jamie Giganti, Director of Academic Publishing

Copyright © 2019 by Vincent E. Faherty. All rights reserved. No part of this publication may be reprinted, reproduced, transmitted, or utilized in any form or by any electronic, mechanical, or other means, now known or hereafter invented, including photocopying, microfilming, and recording, or in any information retrieval system without the written permission of Cognella, Inc. For inquiries regarding permissions, translations, foreign rights, audio rights, and any other forms of reproduction, please contact the Cognella Licensing Department at rights@cognella.com.

Trademark Notice: Product or corporate names may be trademarks or registered trademarks, and are used only for identification and explanation without intent to infringe.

Cover image copyright © 2013 Depositphotos/pashabo, copyright © 2015 iStockphoto LP/CastaldoStudio.

Printed in the United States of America.

ISBN: 978-1-5165-2280-4 (pbk) / 978-1-5165-2281-1 (br)

Dedication

First, and most importantly, I dedicate this work to my amazing wife, Angela, for her constant support and encouragement during the completion of this manuscript and to the members of my immediate family—my oldest son, Vincent; his wife, Laura; and their two darling daughters, Stella Victoria and Lydia Charlotte; and my youngest son, David; and his new bride, Elizabeth. Thank you all for your patience in the face of my countless distracted moments when we were together and for your unquestioning support as I raced against deadlines to finalize this work. I could not, quite literally, have done it without each and every one of you.

Brief Contents

Preface   xxiii

Chapter 1
The Beginnings: Christopher Columbus   1

Chapter 2
Early Views of Poverty: *Elizabethan Poor Laws* Introduced into the American Colonies, circa 1700   11

Chapter 3
America's Foundational Documents: The *Constitution of the United States* (1787) and the *Bill of Rights* (1789)   21

Chapter 4
The Life of a Slave: Frederick Douglass's *Narrative of the Life of Frederick Douglass, An American Slave* (1845)   31

Chapter 5
An Exposure of Racism: Harriet Beecher Stowe's *Uncle Tom's Cabin: Life Among the Lowly* (1852)   41

Chapter 6
Setback for Equality: *The Dred Scott Decision (Scott v. Sandford)* (1857)   51

Chapter 7
The Call for Freedom and Equality: The *Emancipation Proclamation* (1863)   61

Chapter 8
Reaction to Equality for All: The *Organization and Principles of the Ku Klux Klan* (1868)   73

Chapter 9
The Oppression of Native Americans: Helen Hunt Jackson's *A Century of Dishonor* (1881)   85

Chapter 10
Prejudice and Discrimination Continues: *The Chinese Exclusion Act*, PL 47–126 (1882)   95

Chapter 11
Urban Poverty: Jacob Riis's *How the Other Half Lives: Studies Among the Tenements of New York* (1890)   107

Chapter 12
Racial Segregation Continued: *Plessy v. Ferguson*, 163 U.S. 537 (1896)   119

Chapter 13
Two Views of Racism: Booker T. Washington's *Up from Slavery* (1901) and W.E.B. Du Bois's *The Souls of Black Folk* (1903)   129

Chapter 14
Food Health and Safety: Upton Sinclair's *The Jungle* (1906)   143

Chapter 15
The Settlement House Movement: Jane Addams's *Twenty Years at Hull House* (1910)   155

Chapter 16
Voting Equality for Women: The *19th Amendment to the Constitution of the United States* (1920)   167

Chapter 17
The Era of Forced Sterilizations: *Buck v. Bell*, 274 U.S. 200 (1927)   177

Chapter 18
Confronting the Great Depression: The New Deal and *The Social Security Act* (1935)   189

Chapter 19
Rural Poverty and Displacement: John Steinbeck's *The Grapes of Wrath* (1939)   203

Chapter 20
The Japanese Relocation Order: *Executive Order 9066* (1942)   215

Chapter 21
Small Steps for Racial Equality: Integration of the Armed Services, *Executive Order 9981* (1948)   227

Chapter 22
Separate and Not Equal: *Brown v. Board of Education of Topeka* (1954)   239

Chapter 23
Oppression of Migrant Workers: *Harvest of Shame* (1960)   251

Chapter 24
Songs of Protest: "This Land Is Your Land," "Blowin' in the Wind," "I Ain't Marching Anymore," "Eve of Destruction," and "We Shall Overcome" (1940–1964)   263

Chapter 25
The War on Poverty: *Economic Opportunity Act*, PL 88–452 (1964)   279

Chapter 26
Discrimination Further Challenged: The *Civil Rights Act* (1964) and the *Voting Rights Act* (1965)   293

Chapter 27
Equality in Juvenile Justice: *In re Gault*, 387 U.S. 1 (1967)   307

Chapter 28
Legal Access to Abortion: *Roe v. Wade*, 410 U.S. 113 (1973)   321

Chapter 29
Adoption and Foster Care for Native Americans: *Indian Child Welfare Act*, PL 95–608 (1978)   335

Chapter 30
Modern Welfare Reform: *Personal Responsibility and Work Opportunity Reconciliation Act*, PL 104–193 (1996)   347

Chapter 31
Modern Health Care Reform: The *Patient Protection and Affordable Care Act* (2010) and Recent Developments (2018)   359

Appendix   371

Index   373

Detailed Contents

Preface   xxiii
   Deduction vs. Induction   xxiii
   A Practical Definition of Social Welfare   xxvi
   Purpose and Measurable Learning Objectives   xxvi
   Types of Primary Historical Documents   xxvii
   Relationship of Social Welfare History and Social Policy Development   xxviii
   Structure of Each Chapter   xxviii
   A Special Note Regarding the Linkage to Relevant Social Welfare History Section   xxix
   Analytical Model: Linkage of Social Welfare History Event and Primary Document   xxx
   Recommendations for Classroom Use   xxx
   Consistency with the 2015 *Educational Policy and Accreditation Standards* (EPAs) of the Council on Social Work Education (CSWE)   xxxi
   Acknowledgments   xxxii

Chapter 1
The Beginnings: Christopher Columbus   1

---

   1. A. Christopher Columbus Describes Native Peoples, 1492   1
   Introduction   1
   Primary Text Material   3
      The Journal of Christopher Columbus   3
   1. B. Eyewitness Account of Spanish Cruelty Toward Native Peoples, 1552   4
   Introduction   4
   Linkage to Social Welfare History   5
   Primary Text Material   6
      A Brief Account of the Destruction of the Indies   6
   Timeline of General Events in History, the Humanities,

and Science During This Period (1492–1600)   7
Additional Selected References   10
Questions for Further Research and Discussion   9

Chapter 2
Early Views of Poverty: *Elizabethan Poor Laws* Introduced into the American Colonies, circa 1700   11

Introduction   11
Linkage to Social Welfare History (1600–1750)   15
Primary Text Material   16
  The Elizabethan Poor Law [43 Eliz. Cap. 2. 7, A.D. 1601]   16
Timeline of General Events in History, the Humanities, and Science During This Period (1600–1750)   18
Questions for Further Research and Discussion   19
Additional Selected References   20

Chapter 3
America's Foundational Documents: The *Constitution of the United States* (1787) and the *Bill of Rights* (1789)   21

Introduction   21
Linkage to Social Welfare History (1750–1800)   25
Primary Text Material   26
  The Constitution of the United States of America (1787)   26
  The Preamble to the Bill of Rights (1789)   27
Timeline of General Events in History, the Humanities, and Science During This Period (1750–1800)   28
Questions for Further Research and Discussion   29
Additional Selected References   30

Chapter 4
The Life of a Slave: Frederick Douglass's *Narrative of the Life of Frederick Douglass, An American Slave* (1845)   31

Introduction   31
Linkage to Social Welfare History (1800–1850)   33
Primary Text Material   36
  Douglass, F. (1845). *Narrative of the Life of Frederick Douglass, An American Slave. Written by Himself.* Boston: Anti-Slavery Office, No. 25 Cornhill. Chapter 2.   36

Timeline of General Events in History, the Humanities, and Science During This Period (1800–1850)   38
Questions for Further Research and Discussion   39
Additional Selected References   39

Chapter 5
An Exposure of Racism: Harriet Beecher Stowe's *Uncle Tom's Cabin: Life Among the Lowly* (1852)   41

Introduction   41
Linkage to Social Welfare History (1850–1875)   43
Primary Text Material   46
  Uncle Tom's Cabin   46
Timeline of General Events in History, the Humanities, and Science During This Period (1850–1875)   47
Questions for Further Research and Discussion   49
Additional Selected References   49

Chapter 6
Setback for Equality: *The Dred Scott Decision (Scott v. Sandford)* (1857)   51

Introduction   51
Linkage to Social Welfare History (1850–1875)   54
Primary Text Material   56
  Scott v. Sandford, 60 U.S. 393 (1856)   56
Timeline of General Events in History, the Humanities and Science During This Period (1850–1875)   57
Questions for Further Research and Discussion   58
Additional Selected References   59

Chapter 7
The Call for Freedom and Equality: The *Emancipation Proclamation* (1863)   61

Introduction   61
Linkage to Social Welfare History (1850–1875)   65
Primary Text Material   67
  The Emancipation Proclamation (January 1, 1863)   67
Timeline of General Events in History, the Humanities, and Science During This Period (1850–1875)   69
Questions for Further Research and Discussion   70
Additional Selected References   71

Chapter 8
Reaction to Equality for All: The *Organization and Principles of the Ku Klux Klan* (1868)   73

Introduction   73
Linkage to Social Welfare History (1850–1875)   76
Primary Text Material   78
  Organization and Principles of the Ku Klux Klan   78
Timeline of General Events in History, the Humanities, and Science During This Period (1850–1875)   80
Questions for Further Research and Discussion   82
Additional Selected References   82

Chapter 9
The Oppression of Native Americans: Helen Hunt Jackson's *A Century of Dishonor* (1881)   85

Introduction   85
Linkage to Social Welfare History (1875–1900)   88
Primary Text Material   91
  Jackson, H. H. (1889). *A century of dishonor: A sketch of the United States government's dealings with some Indian tribes.* Boston: Roberts Brothers.   91
Timeline of General Events in History, the Humanities, and Science During This Period (1875–1900)   92
Questions for Further Research and Discussion   93
Additional Selected References   94

Chapter 10
Prejudice and Discrimination Continues: *The Chinese Exclusion Act*, PL 47–126 (1882)   95

Introduction   95
Linkage to Social Welfare History (1875–1900)   99
Primary Text Material   102
  Chinese Exclusion Act (1882)   102
Timeline of General Events in History, the Humanities, and Science During This Period (1875–1900)   102
Questions for Further Research and Discussion   104
Additional Selected References   104

Chapter 11
Urban Poverty: Jacob Riis's *How the Other Half Lives: Studies Among the Tenements of New York* (1890)   107

Introduction   107
Linkage to Social Welfare History (1875–1900)   111
Primary Text Material   114
   Riis, J. A. (1890). *How the other half lives: Studies among the tenements of New York*. New York: Charles Scribner's Sons.   114
Timeline of General Events in History, the Humanities, and Science During This Period (1875–1900)   115
Questions for Further Research and Discussion   116
Additional Selected References   117

Chapter 12
Racial Segregation Continued: *Plessy v. Ferguson*, 163 U.S. 537 (1896)   119

Introduction   119
Linkage to Social Welfare History (1875–1900)   122
Primary Text Material   125
   U.S. Supreme Court *Plessy v. Ferguson*, 163 U.S. 537 (1896)   125
   Mr. Justice Harlan Dissenting   126
Timeline of General Events in History, the Humanities, and Science During This Period (1875–1900)   126
Questions for Further Research and Discussion   127
Additional Selected References   128

Chapter 13
Two Views of Racism: Booker T. Washington's *Up from Slavery* (1901) and W.E.B. Du Bois's *The Souls of Black Folk* (1903)   129

Introduction   129
Linkage to Social Welfare History (1900–1925)   133
Primary Text Material   136
   Up from Slavery: An Autobiography by Booker T. Washington (1901)   136
   The Souls of Black Folk: Essays and Sketches by W.E.B. Du Bois (1903)   137
Timeline of General Events in History, the Humanities, and Science During This Period (1900–1925)   139
Questions for Further Research and Discussion   141
Additional Selected References   141

Chapter 14
Food Health and Safety: Upton Sinclair's *The Jungle* (1906)   143

Introduction   143
Linkage to Social Welfare History (1900–1925)   146

Primary Text Material   148
  Upton Sinclair. (1906). *The Jungle.* New York: Doubleday, Page & Co.   148
Timeline of General Events in History, the Humanities, and Science During This Period (1900–1925)   150
Questions for Further Research and Discussion   152
Additional Selected References   153

Chapter 15
The Settlement House Movement: Jane Addams's *Twenty Years at Hull House* (1910)   155

Introduction   155
Linkage to Social Welfare History (1900–1925)   158
Primary Text Material   160
  Twenty Years at Hull House with Autobiographical Notes by Jane Addams (1912)   160
Timeline of General Events in History, the Humanities, and Science During This Period (1900–1925)   162
Questions for Further Research and Discussion   164
Additional Selected References   165

Chapter 16
Voting Equality for Women: The *19th Amendment* to the *Constitution of the United States* (1920)   167

Introduction   167
Linkage to Social Welfare History (1900–1925)   170
Primary Text Material   172
  Declaration of Sentiments and Resolutions, Seneca Falls, New York (July 1848)   172
  Transcript of *19th Amendment to the U.S. Constitution:* Women's Right to Vote *(1920)*   173
Timeline of General Events in History, the Humanities, and Science During This Period (1900–1925)   173
Questions for Further Research and Discussion   175
Additional Selected References   176

Chapter 17
The Era of Forced Sterilizations: *Buck v. Bell,* 274 U.S. 200 (1927)   177

Introduction   177
Linkage to Social Welfare History (1925–1950)   180

Primary Text Material   183
  Buck v. Bell (1927)   183
  Timeline of General Events in History, the Humanities, and Science During This Period (1925–1950)   184
Questions for Further Research and Discussion   186
Additional Selected References   187

Chapter 18
Confronting the Great Depression: The New Deal and *The Social Security Act* (1935)   189

Introduction   189
Linkage to Social Welfare History (1925–1950)   194
Primary Text Material   197
  The Social Security Act (1935)   *197*
  Timeline of General Events in History, the Humanities, and Science During This Period (1925–1950)   198
Questions for Further Research and Discussion   201
Additional Selected References   201

Chapter 19
Rural Poverty and Displacement: John Steinbeck's *The Grapes of Wrath* (1939)   203

Introduction   203
Linkage to Social Welfare History (1925–1950)   206
Primary Text Material   209
  The Grapes of Wrath   209
  Timeline of General Events in History, the Humanities, and Science During This Period (1925–1950)   211
Questions for Further Research and Discussion   213
Additional Selected References   214

Chapter 20
The Japanese Relocation Order: *Executive Order 9066* (1942)   215

Introduction   215
Linkage to Social Welfare History (1925–1950)   219
Primary Text Material   222
  Portions of the Transcript of *Executive Order 9066:* Resulting in the Relocation of Japanese (1942)   222
  Timeline of General Events in History, the Humanities, and Science During

This Period (1925–1950)   223
Questions for Further Research and Discussion   225
Additional Selected References   226

Chapter 21
Small Steps for Racial Equality: Integration of the Armed Services, *Executive Order 9981* (1948)   227

Introduction   227
Linkage to Social Welfare History (1925–1950)   230
Primary Text Material   233
  Transcript of *Executive Order 9981:* Desegregation of the Armed Forces (1948)   233
Timeline of General Events in History, the Humanities, and Science During This Period (1925–1950)   234
Questions for Further Research and Discussion   237
Additional Selected References   237

Chapter 22
Separate and Not Equal: *Brown v. Board of Education of Topeka* (1954)   239

Introduction   239
Linkage to Social Welfare History (1950–1975)   242
Primary Text Material   245
  Brown v. Board of Education (1954)   245
Timeline of General Events in History, the Humanities, and Science During This Period (1950–1975)   246
Questions for Further Research and Discussion   248
Additional Selected References   249

Chapter 23
Oppression of Migrant Workers: *Harvest of Shame* (1960)   251

Introduction   251
Linkage to Social Welfare History (1950–1975)   254
Primary Text Material   257
  Harvest of Shame (1960)   257
Timeline of General Events in History, the Humanities, and Science During This Period (1950–1975)   258
Questions for Further Research and Discussion   261
Additional Selected References   262

Chapter 24
Songs of Protest: "This Land Is Your Land," "Blowin' in the Wind," "I Ain't Marching Anymore," "Eve of Destruction," and "We Shall Overcome" (1940–1964)   263

Introduction   263
Linkage to Social Welfare History (1950–1975)   268
Primary Text Material   272
  "This Land Is Your Land"   272
  "Blowin' in the Wind"   272
  "I Ain't Marching Anymore"   272
  "Eve of Destruction"   272
  "We Shall Overcome"   273
Timeline of General Events in History, the Humanities, and Science During This Period (1950–1975)   273
Questions for Further Research and Discussion   276
Additional Selected References   277

Chapter 25
The War on Poverty: *Economic Opportunity Act*, PL 88–452 (1964)   279

Introduction   279
Linkage to Social Welfare History (1950–1975)   284
Primary Text Material   287
  The Economic Opportunity Act of 1964   287
Timeline of General Events in History, the Humanities, and Science During This Period (1950–1975)   288
Questions for Further Research and Discussion   291
Additional Selected References   292

Chapter 26
Discrimination Further Challenged: The *Civil Rights Act* (1964) and the *Voting Rights Act* (1965)   293

Introduction   293
Linkage to Social Welfare History (1950–1975)   297
Primary Text Material   301
  The *Civil Rights Act* of 1964   301
  The Voting Rights Act of 1965   302
Timeline of General Events in History, the Humanities, and Science During This Period (1950–1975)   302
Questions for Further Research and Discussion   305
Additional Selected References   305

Chapter 27
Equality in Juvenile Justice: *In re Gault*, 387 U.S. 1 (1967)   307

  Introduction   307
  Linkage to Social Welfare History (1950–1975)   311
  Primary Text Material   314
    In re Gault (1967)   314
  Timeline of General Events in History, the Humanities, and Science During This Period (1950–1975)   316
Questions for Further Research and Discussion   319
Additional Selected References   319

Chapter 28
Legal Access to Abortion: *Roe v. Wade*, 410 U.S. 113 (1973)   321

  Introduction   321
  Linkage to Social Welfare History (1950–1975)   324
  Primary Text Material   327
    Roe v. Wade (1973)   327
  Timeline of General Events in History, the Humanities, and Science During This Period (1950–1975)   329
Questions for Further Research and Discussion   332
Additional Selected References   333

Chapter 29
Adoption and Foster Care for Native Americans: *Indian Child Welfare Act*, PL 95–608 (1978)   335

  Introduction   335
  Linkage to Social Welfare History (1975–2000)   339
  Primary Text Material   341
    Indian Child Welfare Act (1978)   341
  Timeline of General Events in History, the Humanities, and Science During This Period (1975–2000)   343
Questions for Further Research and Discussion   345
Additional Selected References   346

Chapter 30
Modern Welfare Reform: *Personal Responsibility and Work Opportunity Reconciliation Act*, PL 104–193 (1996)   347

  Introduction   347

Linkage to Social Welfare History (1975–2000)   351
Primary Text Material   353
   Personal Responsibility and Work Opportunity Reconciliation Act (1996)   353
Timeline of General Events in History, the Humanities, and Science During This Period (1975–2000)   355
Questions for Further Research and Discussion   357
Additional Selected References   358

Chapter 31
Modern Health Care Reform: The *Patient Protection and Affordable Care Act* (2010) and Recent Developments (2018)   359

Introduction   359
Linkage to Social Welfare History (2000–2018)   364
Primary Text Material   366
   Patient Protection and Affordable Care Act (2010)   366
Timeline of General Events in History, the Humanities, and Science During This Period (2000–2018)   367
Questions for Further Research and Discussion   368
Additional Selected References   369

Appendix   371
Analytical Model: Linkage of Social Welfare History Event and Primary Document   371

Index   373

Preface

Welcome to *Documents of American Social Welfare History*, a book obviously about social welfare history, but I want to forewarn you that this is not your "typical" history book. In other words, if you are looking for a standard treatment of major historical events and notable people in our nation's past, as well as overlapping themes or patterns of historical significance, all wrapped up in chapters that follow an orderly sequence, then this book may disappoint you. There are many excellent and clearly referenced history books on the market that follow that model and realize those goals, and they do so admirably. So, this author decided that there did not exist any pressing need for another social welfare history book that would only duplicate existing resources.

Documents of American Social Welfare History uses an uncommon approach. Each chapter presents an historic primary document or documents that played a significant role as the American social welfare system evolved and then invites you—the active, not passive, learner/participant—to study its message carefully and then expand your knowledge by pursuing further historical research related to that primary document. In the most straightforward terms, *Documents of American Social Welfare History* employs an *inductive*, rather than a *deductive*, approach to teaching and learning social welfare history.

Deduction vs. Induction

In the daily exercise of human reasoning—that is, how we humans make most decisions in our lives—two distinct processes of thought are possible: We can use either a deductive or an inductive tactic. For example, if you came to a corner on a busy urban street and you wanted to cross, you would probably have silently running in your mind the basic principle that green means go, and red means stop. Operating, then, on that unspoken principle, you would decide whether to start walking across the street depending on if the traffic light facing you was green or red. In this example, you would be moving reasonably from a general principle and applying that general principle to a specific reality—that is, the color of the traffic light. So, to progress from either a principle, theory, or definition down to a specific example, case, or situation would be a real-life example of deductive reasoning. If you looked at a regional weather map on television and saw an image of a large dark cloud with rain markings covering your local area, it would be reasonable (logical) for you to grab your rain gear and assume that it was raining in your neighborhood even before you looked out a window. Again, to progress from the "big picture" (i.e., the regional weather map) down to the "little picture" (i.e., your distinct neighborhood) is an example of deductive reasoning. This type of reasoning, however, is not an example of a tested, scientific process because, in distinct situations, the general theory or big picture may not truly apply to the specific circumstance. Although it may be cloudy and raining over your geographic region on that weather map, it also might be cloudy with no rain at this exact moment outside your house. In spite of the impreciseness of a deductive reasoning process, you still would be quite rational to carry with you a raincoat and an umbrella. In this situation, obviously, it would help to have additional information.

The inductive process of making logical decisions in our lives, then, functions in the opposite manner. An inductive type of reasoning flows upward, so to speak, from a specific example or case to some overarching principle or assumption. To use the same scenarios as above, this is how an inductive process works: If you were planning to drive from the suburbs into the downtown area of an urban center and, looking out of your window, saw heavy rain in your neighborhood, you would be completely logical if you packed rain gear in your car before you left because you assumed it would be raining downtown also. It would help your decision, certainly, if you had access to more information about the weather forecast for the downtown area, but even without it, you would be logical to assume it is raining there. Your reasoning process in this situation is inductive because you went from the individual situation (i.e., your own suburban neighborhood) and moved to the larger geographic area (i.e., the entire downtown urban area).

Similarly (to use a silly example), if your city managers decided one evening to change the color pattern of green and red traffic signals to purple and white traffic signals but failed to inform the public, you would be naturally confused as you stood on the corner and stared at the changing purple and white traffic lights, not knowing when to cross. In this admittedly unlikely situation, you would need additional information before you dared to cross the street. You could quickly learn the new color system, however, by perhaps waiting for several traffic signal cycles and watching what other pedestrians do or observing when cars slow down and stop. Here you would be using an inductive process because you are moving from individual cases (i.e., what cars do in reaction to the white and purple traffic signals) up to a general principle (i.e., now purple means stop, and white means go).

In both of the previous examples, you could logically proceed if you had some additional information that adds to the information you gained from this one specific situation of looking outside your window or gazing on a purple-and-white color scheme for traffic signals. To summarize: A deductive process of reasoning flows downward from some overall assumption to a precise example or situation, whereas an inductive reasoning process moves upward from a specific example to a universal principle. Neither process is error-free, and that is why we have a better (but still not perfect) decision-making process called the scientific method in Western society.

In the structured educational environments of colleges and universities, most instructors you encounter in the classroom and most books you use in your formal studies will be based upon the deductive method of instruction. As a general rule, the instructor has assigned readings from a textbook containing chapters that include definitions of terms, statements of prior research findings on the subject of that chapter, perhaps some explanatory descriptions of processes, and a series of explicit examples or applications of the presented materials. You, the student, are asked to review the chapter or chapters and come prepared to ask questions for clarification and probably be open to discussing further what you have gained from the readings. The instructor, then, in the classroom may summarize the new material, add additional examples or applications, elicit any questions you may have, and then engage the class members in an active discussion of the topic. With some variations to allow for individual instructors' use of other teaching strategies, such as role playing, debates, guest speakers, or media presentations, this process describes a classic deductive method of teaching that occurs in probably 95% of all classrooms across the nation.

There is another method—an inductive approach—that takes place in mainly law schools, especially during the first two years of study, and in many graduate business school courses. In these situations, the students are not assigned to read textbook chapters of theoretical material but are instead assigned to read fact-filled *cases* that, for law students, consist of verbatim transcripts of past court decisions and, for business students, consist of a real or simulated organizational problem that needs to be resolved. Similarly, students are expected to review the case material very meticulously before class. The instructors in law and business, when employing such a case method approach, use their classroom time quite differently. They do not typically lecture or provide summaries or examples; rather, they primarily try to engage the students actively and draw out from them relevant theories, patterns, or action plans by asking directed questions and providing suggestive prompts when needed. Essentially, the inductive method of teaching and learning requires students to be active participants in the classroom processes and to broaden their vision beyond the specific case, which serves only as the foundation for further exploration and discovery.

As stated earlier, *Documents of American Social Welfare History* presents an inductive approach to the study of the history of the social welfare system in our nation. Each chapter contains one or two selections from primary documents that highlight, in this author's estimation, a notable event or process in that history. Unlike other history books that follow a deductive approach, *Documents of American Social Welfare History* does not cover every significant social welfare historical event, movement, or personality. There are gaps, admittedly, in the chronological flow of the chapters through time because an inductive approach to learning assumes that the specific cases are the beginning, not the end, of a discovery process. Part of your task, as a student, will be to study the primary document carefully then step away, as if you are looking through a camera that rises up and away from a street scene in a Hollywood or television movie, so that you have a wider and more comprehensive view of the overall context in which the scene is taking place.

Thus, as an active and engaged learner in the inductive process, you will, hopefully, explore beyond the actual historical case by conducting further reading and research on the topic discussed in each chapter. This additional exploratory process that you pursue will help integrate the individual chapters with one another and open up the broader environment in which those primary documents were composed.

A Practical Definition of Social Welfare

Because this is a history of American social welfare book, it is essential that we all agree on terminology. The words *history* and *American* are fairly obvious (though, admittedly, the United States is technically North America as distinct from Canada and both Central and South America), but the phrase *social welfare* does need some clarification. In most Introduction to Sociology classes, the instructors as well as the sociology textbooks typically present the idea that American society exists on a foundation consisting of four distinct pillars or towers or supports: the *family* unit, the *economic* system, the *political* system, and the *organized religion* establishment. From this perspective, then, these three final pillars sustain the entire basic family group by providing it with an economic system that furnishes jobs and usable financial resources; stable governmental structures that offer safety, security, and equality to individual communities; and, finally, the opportunity to worship a supreme being voluntarily, without coercion, and freely according to one's own religious heritage or to not worship at all as a personal choice.

As far as that explanation goes, it is a generally helpful way to comprehend the complex structures and processes found in a modern, industrialized democratic society. However, to truly understand where the social welfare components fit into this four-legged societal structure—and where social workers, psychologists, other human service workers, as well as doctors and educators actually work and apply their professional skills—it is necessary to add a fifth "leg" to that image of a society. This fifth support, then, is the social welfare establishment. Thus, when the family unit breaks down through separation, abuse, etc.; when the economy falters and does not provide adequate financial support; when the political system is dysfunctional and does not supply safety, stability, and equal treatment for all; and when the religious establishment fails to adequately meet the spiritual and emotional needs of individuals, that is when the social welfare system commences.

In a very practical sense, the social welfare system can be accessed when all of the other foundational supports of society totally fail or provide only inadequate responses for whatever reason. Social welfare, for the purposes of this text, then, is generally defined as *the composite of all the organized goods and services provided under either public, nonprofit, and proprietary auspices and designed to promote health, prosperity, and well-being to individuals, groups, and communities.*

Purpose and Measurable Learning Objectives

The overall purpose of *Documents of American Social Welfare History* is to approach the exploration of social welfare history inductively, with a textbook that draws on appropriate primary documents and is relevant for the professional education of students of social work and other human services disciplines. The following concrete objectives, then, flow from this ultimate purpose and can be measured by a series of educational assignments that are based on these primary documents and selected by the instructors of a course. With the assistance of this book and by the end of an introductory course, or section of a course, devoted to American social welfare history, a student-learner should be able to:

1. *Understand* the interlocking nature of social welfare history in the development of social policies and programs in the United States
2. *Discuss* the role that selected primary historical documents played in the continuing development, whether positive or negative, of elements of the American social welfare system
3. *Engage* in further independent exploration and research on other historical events and movements that occurred during the creation of selected primary historical documents
4. *Demonstrate* an appreciation for the unique perspective that can be gained by utilizing the inductive method of instruction to study historical documentary material

Types of Primary Historical Documents

In historical research, a primary document is also referred to as an original document, an original source, or, simply, as evidence of some previous occurrence. Primary documents are essentially a type of physical recording that were composed at the time of the event or historical period under study. For the purposes of *Documents of American Social Welfare History*, what is referred to as a *primary document* will consist of one of the following:

a. A piece of federal legislation, such as the *Patient Protection and Affordable Care Act* (ACA), passed in 2010
b. A United States Supreme Court decision, such as *Roe v. Wade*, decided in 1973
c. A notable organizational or governmental decision, such as *Executive Order 9066*, also known as the *Japanese Relocation Order*, signed by President Franklin Roosevelt in 1942
d. Personal letters or journals of prominent individuals, such as Christopher Columbus's account of his first meeting with native peoples in 1492
e. Autobiographies, such as Booker T. Washington's *Up From Slavery*, published in 1901
f. Fictional novels with a social agenda, such as Upton Sinclair's *The Jungle*, published in 1906
g. Journalistic disclosures of some societal issue, such as Jacob Riis's *How the Other Half Lives: Studies Among the Tenements of New York*, published in 1890

h. Creative musical compositions, such as the songs protesting poverty, segregation, and war that were written between 1940 and 1967, such as Bob Dylan's "Blowin' in the Wind"

Relationship of Social Welfare History and Social Policy Development

Although it is honorable and beneficial to study history for its own sake, the study of social welfare history achieves another, equally crucial, dimension—namely, it underscores the intimate relationship between the development of a new social welfare policy or program and the immediate historical context and environment in which that change appeared. It would be difficult, for example, to explain the massive federal governmental expansion under the New Deal program of the Roosevelt administration starting in 1936 unless one clearly understood the devastation of individuals, families, and societal institutions resulting from the Stock Market Crash in 1929 and the resulting Great Depression that quickly and stubbornly spread across the nation. Nor can the 1954 Brown v. Board of Education Supreme Court decision be fully comprehended until we acknowledge just how frustrated and politically active members of the African American community were becoming in post-World War II America. Thus, this assumed relationship between social welfare history and social policy and program development can be viewed as an essential component of the formal education of social workers and other human service professionals.

For purposes of discussion and clarification, this author assumes that when we talk about a formal *social policy*, what is meant is either: (1) a formal court decision rendered by a state Court of Appeals or by the United States Supreme Court; (2) a federal law passed by both houses of Congress and signed by the president; or (3) an administrative decision published in some manner by a major organization, such as a state or federal governmental department, a university, a private corporation, a religious entity, a social service agency, or another societal institution. Social workers and other human services professionals, by definition, are committed to changing negative social policies that harm vulnerable groups in society, as well as developing new policies that advance the human condition and society at large. That means, on a totally pragmatic level, that social workers and human service professionals should work cooperatively with other engaged individuals and groups to improve/develop local, state, and federal legislation; state and federal court decisions; and organizational decisions.

Structure of Each Chapter

The internal structure of *Documents of American Social Welfare History* consists of the following sections of content for each chapter:

> **Introduction** – Provides a general historical and contextual overview of the primary document discussed.

- **Linkage to Relevant Social Welfare History** – Furnishes a chronological series of other social welfare historical events occurring within the same general time frame of the primary document under consideration.
- **Internet Sources for the Content of This Introduction** – Cites all of the Internet addresses (i.e., the URLs) that were referenced during the drafting of the Introduction.
- **Primary Text Material** – Presents either selected sections or the entire text of the primary document that is the focus of each chapter.
- **Timeline of Other Events in History, the Humanities, and Science During This Period** – Lists other, more general, historical events that transpired during a designated time period as a way to offer a broader, non–social welfare, context in which the primary document emerged.
- **Questions for Further Research and Discussion** – Provides the student-learner with a number of ideas around which further research and discussion could be centered.
- **Additional Selected References** – Itemizes current and readily available books on the broad topic being studied in each chapter in order to facilitate further exploration.

A Special Note Regarding the Linkage to Relevant Social Welfare History Section

What you will encounter in this section of each chapter is a list of other relevant social welfare history events that transpired during the same time interval, usually in 25-year blocks (e.g., 1900–1925). Consistent with the inductive approach to teaching/learning that was employed during the crafting of *Documents of American Social Welfare History* and described above, you, the student-learner, will be challenged to search through the social welfare events and personalities listed in this section and conclude whether any substantive relationship exists between the event/personality and the primary document that is the focus of each chapter. In other words, those linkages will not be stated definitively, as would occur in a deductive approach to history, but instead will be left to your own further examination and innovation. This underlines the reality that an inductive methodology is essentially a journey of self-discovery.

To assist you in this endeavor, this author offers a three-level model of analysis you can employ to draw conclusions about a relationship between a specific social welfare historical event and a corresponding primary document. Perhaps it will clarify the situation if you could conceive of this analytical model as a three-dimensional chess board on which the players could move their pieces left or right, front or back, and even up or down. What would emerge would be a highly intricate pattern of chess pieces arranged in three possible levels and from three distinct perspectives.

This analytical model involves a subjective process of responding to questions regarding each of three dimensions: *timing*, *direction*, and *outcome*.

> ### Analytical Model: Linkage of Social Welfare History Event and Primary Document
>
> **Relevant Social Welfare History Event:**
>
> **Primary Document:**
>
> Timing: Did the social welfare historical event occur
> before _____ or
> after _____ the primary document was composed?
>
> Direction: Between the event and the primary document, was there a
> direct relationship (i.e., strong, obvious) _____ or
> indirect relationship (i.e., weak, unforeseen) _____ or
> tangential relationship (i.e., virtually nonexistent, vague) _____ or
> non-relationship (i.e., not logically present) _____?
>
> Effect: Considering the outcome of the relationship between the historical event and the primary document, was that outcome, in your judgement,
> positive (i.e., constructive, enhancing, progressive) _____ or
> negative (i.e., harmful, damaging, regressive) _____ or
> neutral (i.e., indistinct, detached, balanced) _____?
>
> **Comments:**
>
> This is, obviously, only a suggested analytical model. You as a student-learner are encouraged to develop your own alternative model with which to evaluate any possible linkage between social welfare historical events and selected primary historical documents relevant to social welfare history. If so desired, a copy of this analytical model can be accessed in Appendix 1 of this book for future use.

Recommendations for Classroom Use

For instructors using *Documents of American Social Welfare History* either as a primary or secondary text, there are several recommendations designed to assist you in your teaching efforts. First, you will notice immediately that only relatively short sections of most of the primary documents are provided in the text. Generally speaking, this was done to keep the length of the book at a reasonable level, thereby keeping publication costs down to a minimum for the sake of the students who are the ultimate consumers. You will note further, however, that placed at the end of every primary document is an Internet URL that links directly to the entire manuscript of the primary document itself. Furthermore, with several of the primary documents, there are also Internet URLs provided that link to other media sites containing more detailed information about the topic being discussed in the chapter. You are encouraged to assign your students to read further into the primary documentary material and to access the additional media material on the Internet for learning purposes.

Second, similarly for production cost purposes, as well as due to copyright restrictions, there are only a limited number of images and pictures in each chapter. Given this reality, a valuable oral presentation or written paper that you assign to your students might be to search the Internet for additional images and pictures that capture the essence of the historical events and personalities being discussed in each chapter. The website images.google.com offers thousands of free Internet images on a wide variety of subjects that, if used solely for noncommercial classroom purposes, avoids any copyright limitations.

Third, because *Documents of American Social Welfare History* is structured as an inductive, rather than deductive, teaching/learning instrument, be aware that your students may have to be reinforced as the semester progresses in their roles as active learners whose knowledge will advance only if they expand their efforts beyond the specific primary document under discussion. This self-discovery component of the inductive method is, perhaps, its most valuable asset and should lead to exciting classroom discussions and written reports.

Fourth, if you choose to add media presentations to the classroom, or as assignments, there are many episodes in the Public Broadcasting System's (PBS) historical series *American Experience* that are relevant to much of the material in *Documents of American Social Welfare History*. In this series, for example, there are documentaries that encompass events and individuals such as the Pilgrims, the abolitionists, the Gilded Age, the Orphan Trains, John Brown's Holy War, the Scopes "Monkey" Trial, the Crash of 1929, President Franklin Roosevelt, Eleanor Roosevelt, the civil rights movement (Eyes on the Prize), etc. Unfortunately, only the trailers for these films are accessible by streaming at http://www.pbs.org/wgbh/americanexperience. The full versions must be purchased from PBS or, perhaps, are available through your college/university's media services.

Fifth, although it has been criticized for its overt progressive bias and lack of historical precision, the controversial 2012 film series produced by Oliver Stone, *The Untold History of the United States*, can be beneficial to your students as a convenient visual record of the political, economic, and social forces influencing American society during the time period when many of the primary documents were composed. This 12-episode set of documentaries chronicles the time periods from approximately World War I through the early years of the Barack Obama administration and is available through the streaming services of Netflix. It is suggested, however, that students be alerted to the fact that Stone's approach is controversial and this documentary series has been criticized by commentators on the political right (see https://www.nationalreview.com/2012/11/misremembrance-things-past-charles-c-w-cooke/), the political left (see https://www.thedailybeast.com/oliver-stones-junk-history-of-the-united-states-debunked), and the political center (see http://www.nytimes.com/2012/11/25/magazine/oliver-stone-rewrites-history-again.html).

Consistency with the 2015 *Educational Policy and Accreditation Standards* (EPAs) of the Council on Social Work Education (CSWE)

The historical content contained in *Documents of American Social Welfare History* contributes to students' attainment of several sections in the Educational Policy and

Accreditation Standards (EPAS) of the Council on Social Work Education (CSWE). For example, in Competency 1: Demonstrate Ethical and Professional Behavior, there is the requirement that "... Social workers understand the profession's history, its mission, and the roles and responsibilities of the profession . . . ." Furthermore, Competency 5: Engage in Policy Practice necessitates that "... Social workers understand the history and current structures of social policies and services, the role of policy in service delivery, and the role of practice in policy development . . . ." Competency 5 then continues, "... Social workers recognize and understand the historical, social, cultural, economic, organizational, environmental, and global influences that affect social policy . . . ."

Acknowledgments

I wish to acknowledge the never-ending and warm encouragement offered to me by Kassie Graves, vice president, editorial, at Cognella Inc. Kassie, you have always been so affirming in your reception of my ideas and have also been so positively constructive in your evaluative comments of my work. I have been truly enlightened by every professional encounter with you. I offer a sincere thank you also to Haley Brown, Project Editor; Jess Estrella, Senior Graphic Designer; Cassie Carey, Production Editor; Leah Sheets, associate editor; Dani Skeen, Marketing Specialist; and, Amy Smith, project editor; and to the other thoroughly competent staff at Cognella Inc., all of whom have contributed significantly to the ongoing crafting as well as the final publication and release of this work.

Several of my social work colleagues around the country, notably Retchenda George-Bettisworth at the University of Alaska, Fairbanks, Shannon R. Lane at Sacred Heart University, and three other anonymous reviewers offered their critiques of early drafts of this book. I also commend them for their frank insights and practical suggestions that helped soften the sharp edges of those original drafts. I certainly take full responsibility for the final product, but I know that it is a creation that is brightly polished by their wisdom.

Finally, I acknowledge all of my former social work students with whom I have had the distinct pleasure of interacting with over the years in Utah, Missouri, Iowa, and Maine. Your pursuit of active learning environments in which you can be fully engaged in your own education has challenged me to write this book. My only hope is that this book will accomplish that critical purpose in some small manner.

Vincent E. Faherty
Cape Elizabeth, Maine
April 2018

Chapter 1

The Beginnings

Christopher Columbus

1. A. Christopher Columbus Describes Native Peoples, 1492

Introduction

Admiral Christopher Columbus, acting directly under the royal commission of King Ferdinand and Queen Isabella, the Catholic monarchs of Aragon, Castile, and León in Spain, sailed from Cádiz, Spain, in early 1492. Years before this commission was granted to Columbus, the king and queen had reinstated the Inquisition in Spain and had vigorously tried to spread the Catholic faith by expelling Jews and Muslims from their territories, sparing only those individuals who converted from Judaism (*conversos*) or Islam (*Moriscos*). Thus, it is generally accepted that Ferdinand and Isabella were interested in expanding the faith in other lands and not just conquering new territories across the ocean for their realm.

The monarchs had formally commissioned Admiral Columbus to explore and conquer for Spain the islands and continent that were reported to lie somewhere west of Spain. Columbus and his crew of 120 men, on board three ships—the Niña, the Pinta, and the Santa Maria—sailed west and eventually arrived at a series of islands off what they believed to be Asia. Columbus and his party probably landed first on some island in the modern-day Bahamas, then traveled on to Cuba and to Haiti and to the Dominican Republic, which he called Hispaniola. Soon after landing there, Admiral Columbus took

FIGURE 1.1 Christopher Columbus. This portrait was executed in the first half of the 16th century, after the death of Columbus.

possession of all the islands and declared the lands in the name of his sovereigns, the king and queen. The notary present on the voyage, Rodrigo de Escobedo, duly recorded this action on the island of Hispaniola. The native peoples on the islands, probably members of the Arawak tribe, apparently reacted indifferently and made no notice of this monumental change in their lives and future.

Admiral Columbus reported that the Arawaks they encountered were naked but very friendly. One group who rowed out in canoes and came on board even shouted out to others, "Come and see the men who have come from heavens. Bring them victuals and drink."

He also testified in his *Journal* that ". . . the natives are an inoffensive people, and so desirous to possess anything they saw with us, that they kept swimming off to the ships with whatever they could find, and readily bartered for any article we saw fit to give them in return, even such as broken platters and fragments of glass." Although the Arawak tribes were warlike with each other, Admiral Columbus found them to not be a threat to him and his men because they were unsophisticated in their attitudes and possessed no advanced weaponry. The crew was even allowed to travel freely on land and was willingly guided by the native peoples throughout their forests and villages. Ultimately, however, Columbus was searching for gold that he could send back to the king and queen as compensation for their generosity in funding his expedition. To attain this goal, he is reported to have taken some natives captive, so he could force them to reveal the source of the gold that he mistakenly believed they were hiding. Thus, begins the terrible story of the atrocities committed by these early explorers against the technologically inferior natives. As reliable historical sources report, the Spanish soldiers, over time, were responsible for humiliation, physical beatings, rape, enslavement, and even murder of the Arawak native people.

What follows is an excerpt from Columbus's narrative description of his first encounter with the native population.

Internet Sources for the Content of This Introduction Include:

https://www.smithsonianmag.com/travel/columbus-confusion-about-the-new-world-140132422/
http://exploration.marinersmuseum.org/subject/christopher-columbus/
https://www.thenation.com/article/the-invention-of-christopher-columbus-american-hero/
https://en.wikipedia.org/wiki/christopher_columbus

FIGURE 1.2 Replicas of the caravels Pinta and Niña and the carrack Santa Maria.

Primary Text Material

The Journal of Christopher Columbus

Presently many inhabitants of the island assembled. What follows is in the actual words of the Admiral in his book of the first navigation and discovery of the Indies.

"I," he says, "that we might form great friendship, for I knew that they were a people who could be more easily freed and converted to our holy faith by love than by force, gave to some of them red caps, and glass beads to put round their necks, and many other things of little value, which gave them great pleasure, and made them so much our friends that it was a marvel to see. They afterwards came to the ship's boats where we were, swimming and bringing us parrots, cotton threads in skeins, darts, and many other things; and we exchanged them for other things that we gave them, such as glass beads and small bells. In fine, they took all, and gave what they had with good will. It appeared to me to be a race of people very poor in everything. They are as naked as when their mothers bore them, and so do the women, although I did not see more than one young girl. All I saw were youths, none more than thirty years of age. They are very well made, with very handsome bodies, and very good countenances. Their hair is short and coarse, almost like the hairs of a horse's tail. They wear the hairs brought down to the eyebrows, except a few locks behind, which they wear long and never cut. They paint themselves black, and they are the colour of the Canarians, neither black nor white. Some paint themselves white, others red, and others of what colour they find. Some paint their faces, others the whole body, some only round the eyes, others only on the nose. They neither carry nor know anything of arms, for I showeth them swords, and they took them by the blade and cut themselves through ignorance. They have no iron, their darts being wands without iron, some of them having a fish's tooth at the end, and others being pointed in various ways. They are all of fair stature and size, with good faces, and well made. I saw some with marks of wounds on their bodies, and I made signs to ask what it was, and they gave me to understand that people from other adjacent islands came with the intention of seizing them, and that they defended themselves. I believed, and still believe, that they come here from the mainland to take them prisoners. They should be good servants and intelligent, for I observed that they quickly took in what was said to them, and I believe that they would easily be made Christians, as it appeared to me that they had no religion. I, our Lord being pleased, will take hence, at the time of my departure, six natives for your Highnesses, that they may learn to speak. I saw no beast of any kind except parrots, on this island."

The above is in the words of the Admiral.

From: Full text of Columbus, C. (1493); Cabot, J. (1498); and Corte-Reale, G. (1501). *The journal of Christopher Columbus* (during his first voyage, 1492–1493) and

Continued

> documents relating to the voyages of John Cabot and Gaspar Corte-Real [microform]. Clemens, R., & Markham, C. B. (Trans.). (1893). London: Hakluyt Society.
>
> Source and full text available at https://archive.org/stream/cihm_05312/cihm_05312_djvu.txt.
>
> This media file is in the public domain.
>
> For a more modern and easier-to-read translation of *The journal of Christopher Columbus*, see:
> Columbus, C. (1492). *The journal of Christopher Columbus*. Jane, C. (Trans.). (1968). London: Blond Publishing. Full text available at http://archive.org/stream/cihm_05312#page/15/mode/2up

1. B. Eyewitness Account of Spanish Cruelty Toward Native Peoples, 1552

Introduction

Among other historical developments, this was the period of the Spanish Inquisition, initiated in 1481 by King Ferdinand and Queen Isabella. It is no coincidence that the Spanish soldiers sent with Columbus, both initially and on a continuing replacement basis, were not fresh, young recruits but hardened combat veterans who had been part of the brutal military response against heretics and unbelievers, particularly those Spanish Jews and Muslims who were suspected of having falsely converted to Catholicism but secretly continued to practice Judaism and Islam. It seems inevitable, then, that sanctioned abusive behavior against another set of unbelievers in lands far from home would eventually emerge. Tragically, that is exactly what evolved against the native peoples as witnessed and recorded in gory detail by a young Spanish businessman-turned-priest almost 60 years after Admiral Columbus's initial journey.

Bartolomé de Las Casas was a young civilian merchant who traveled to Hispaniola in 1502 to provide supplies to the Spanish army and the governmental bureaucracy there during the initial years of conquest and colonization. Due to his travels delivering supplies to the various outposts, he personally witnessed the cruelty and physical atrocities committed by the Spanish settlers on the native peoples. Las Casas returned to Spain in 1506 and began a lifelong campaign to highlight the negative aspects of colonization and to advocate for humane treatment of indigenous peoples in conquered lands anywhere. Eventually receiving ordination, first as a Dominican priest and then as a bishop, Las Casas returned several times to the New World in pursuit of his social justice agenda. One of his books, *The Devastation of the Indies, A Brief Account*, published in 1552, provides a gripping, even frightening, account of this crucial period during the early colonization of the Western hemisphere and is viewed, even today, as a classic sociological and anthropological exposé. Some scholars hypothesize that this book even influenced why Protestant England confronted Catholic Spain on its foreign policy in general and especially on its colonial policy.

Although Admiral Columbus's journey west and discovery of America has directly and positively influenced the advancement of human history in so many tangible ways, the full historical record including the negative consequences of exploration and conquest must be acknowledged and studied in present contexts. It appears to many that the discovery of America carried with it disastrous levels of human suffering, religious intolerance to non-Christian belief systems, and cultural insensitivity toward anyone considered "different." Regrettably, many believe that those tendencies continue at some level of national consciousness throughout America, even today.

Internet Sources for the Content of This Introduction Include:

http://justus.anglican.org/resources/bio/203.html

https://www.gilderlehrman.org/history-by-era/american-indians/resources/bartolomé-de-las-casas-debates-subjugation-indians-1550

https://en.wikipedia.org/wiki/bartolomé_de_las_casas

Linkage to Social Welfare History

Because Admiral Christopher Columbus and his companions established the first non-native settlement on what is probably now known as the island shared by Haiti and the Dominican Republic, it would be both inappropriate and inaccurate to search for any formal linkage between his early discoveries and what would become the American social welfare institution. In fact, the land we now call North America had not yet been visited by foreign nations by 1492, except for possible Nordic Vikings explorations along the northeast coast in the 10th century. That is not meant to dismiss any possible tribal structures that the native Arawak Indians had established to care for their dependent children, their aged, and those members experiencing health needs or physical disabilities. History, quite simply, is relatively silent about the community resources available to the native peoples.

What can be linked, in this author's estimation, is the rigid, moralistic value system of Columbus and his compatriots, who viewed the native population as *the others* because they did not look, speak, or act as they did and, therefore, needed to be conquered. This deeply held set of human values apparently led to the massive military occupation of the islands under their control with corresponding abuse and flagrant violations of human liberty in an attempt to forcibly integrate the Arawak Indians into a white, Christian, European-centric world view. This fear of *the other* and the painful attempts at submission and control of individuals and groups who have a different skin color, language, or religion seems be an ongoing element that is imbued in so much of later American society. This is not to assert that Admiral Columbus himself was the initial cause of this rigid value system, but it does allege that what he introduced to the New World was a European

FIGURE 1.3 Christopher Columbus's soldiers torturing Arawak Indians for failing to meet mining quotas.

Primary Text Material

A Brief Account of the Destruction of the Indies

THE CRUELTIES OF THE Spaniards Committed in AMERICA and Of the island of HISPANIOLA

"... The Spaniards first assaulted the innocent sheep, so qualified by the Almighty ... like most cruel tigers, wolves and lions hunger-starved, studying nothing, for the space of forty years, after their first landing, but the massacre of these wretches, whom they have so inhumanely and barbarously butchered and harassed with several kinds of torments, never before known, or heard (of which you shall have some account in the following discourse) that of three millions of persons, which lived in Hispaniola itself, there is at present but the inconsiderable remnant of scarce three hundred . . .

"... the Spaniards ... mounted on generous steeds, well-weaponed with lances and swords, begin to exercise their bloody butcheries and stratagems, and overrunning their cities and towns, spared no age, or sex, nay not so much as women with child, but ripping up their bellies, tore them alive in pieces. They laid wagers among themselves, who should with a sword at one blow cut, or divide a man in two; or which of them should decollate or behead a man, with the greatest *dexterity; nay farther, which should sheath his sword in the bowels of a man with the quickest dispatch and expedition . . .*

"They snatched young babes from the mother's breasts, and then dashed out the brains of those innocents against the rocks; others they cast into rivers scoffing and jeering them, and called upon their bodies when falling with derision, the true testimony of their cruelty, to come to them, and inhumanely exposing others to their merciless swords, together with the mothers that gave them life . . .

"They erected certain Gibbets [gallows], large, but low made, so that their feet almost reached the ground, every one of which was so ordered as to bear thirteen persons in honour and reverence (as they said blasphemously) of our Redeemer and his twelve Apostles, under which they made a fire to burn them to ashes whilst hanging on them . . . The lords and persons of noble extract were usually exposed to this kind of death; they ordered gridirons to be placed and supported with wooden forks, and putting a small fire under them, these miserable wretches by degrees and with loud shrieks and exquisite torments, at last expired. . . ."

Formal title: A brief account of the destruction of the Indies or, a faithful narrative of the horrid and unexampled massacres, butcheries, and all manner of cruelties, that hell and malice could invent, committed by the Popish Spanish Party on the inhabitants of West-India, together with the devastations of several kingdoms in America by fire and sword, for the space of forty and two years, from the time of its first discovery by them.

Source and full text available at http://www.gutenberg.org/cache/epub/20321/pg20321-images.html.

worldview that championed conquest, subjugation, and even annihilation of those who were different for the ultimate purpose of profit. Looking over the history of the United States and its developing social welfare system as it dealt with national issues such as income justice, race relations, and health care, it seems difficult to deny that there is not some semblance of Columbus's value system present today throughout our nation's social welfare system.

Timeline of General Events in History, the Humanities, and Science During This Period (1492–1600)

These general historical events may help you understand more clearly the overall historical context during which the primary documents were created.

- Seven months after he left, Christopher Columbus returns to Spain, provides vivid descriptions of his journey to the "Indies," and exhibits a group of natives he brought with him whom he calls "Indians" (1493).

- Explorer John Cabot reports discovering Vineland in the North Atlantic, the present Newfoundland, Canada (1498).
- Leonardo da Vinci completes the *Mona Lisa* (1506).
- Geography professor Amerigo Vespucci publishes a map of the New World, displaying it as a different continent positioned between Asia and Europe. He names the New World "America" (1507).
- Michelangelo finishes painting the ceiling of the Sistine Chapel in Rome (1512).
- Niccolò Machiavelli writes *The Prince* (1513).
- Martin Luther publicizes his *Ninety-Five Theses* in Germany, thus ushering in the Protestant Reformation (1517).
- The native population in the New World experiences an epidemic of syphilis, probably introduced, along with other diseases, by the soldiers and crew during Columbus's journeys (1521).
- The cacao bean (which produces chocolate) is first brought to Spain by the explorer Hernán Cortés (1523).
- Explorer Jacques Cartier claims the area around Quebec, Montreal, and the Saint Lawrence River Valley for France (1530).
- King Henry VIII is recognized as head of the Church of England (1532).
- Explorer Jacques Cartier claims for France the Canadian territories now known as Quebec, Montreal, and the Saint Lawrence River Valley (1534).
- Journeying north from Mexico, Spanish explorer Hernando de Soto discovers the Mississippi River (1540).
- Spanish explorer Francisco Vázquez de Coronado returns to Spain, dejected after having failed to discover the fabled "Cities of Gold" in the New World (1542).
- Astronomer Nicolaus Copernicus publishes his discovery that the earth and other planets revolve around the sun, contrary to current belief (1543).
- Prince Ivan the Terrible is crowned as the first tsar of all Russia (1547).
- Public libraries are established throughout Timbuktu in present-day Mali, Africa (1548).
- Tobacco, imported from the New World, is welcomed in Europe as a new type of medicine (1550).
- The Spanish establish a new colony in present-day St. Augustine, Florida (1565).
- The British Navy decimates the Spanish Armada in the English Channel, thus assuming dominance in naval power (1588).
- In his publication *A Brief and True Report of the New Found Land of Virginia*, Thomas Harriot publishes vivid and distorted images of the native population drawn by the governor of Roanoke Colony, John White (1593).
- In London, King James I announces his plan to vigorously fight the efforts of the Puritans, who are trying to reform the Church of England (1600).

Sources:

Daniel, C. (1989). *Chronicle of America*. Mt. Kisco, New York: Chronicle Publications.

Mercer, D. (2000). *Millennium year by year*. New York: Dorling Kindersley Publications. Retrieved from https://en.wikipedia.org/wiki/16th_century#events

Questions for Further Research and Discussion

1. Apparently, at his first encounter, Admiral Christopher Columbus viewed the native population as harmless, thereby presenting no immediate threat to him and his men. Do you believe Columbus interpreted friendliness as weakness and lack of material goods as poverty? Expand on your answer with examples.
2. The need to Christianize and impose a Western European/Spanish culture on the indigenous population emerges as a dominant theme throughout Columbus's journal. Could this attitude serve as a precursor to future relationships with these, and other, explorers from Europe?
3. Read further excerpts in Columbus's journal, especially as he narrates his later experiences during his second and third journeys to the New World. Do you sense any change of attitude in Columbus's mind as he deepens his knowledge of this new society he has discovered? Were these attitudes positive, neutral, or negative toward the native population? Finally, do you believe that human nature generally tends to react negatively when one encounters *the other*, especially if they are viewed as harmless, or was this a component unique to Columbus and, perhaps, some other early explorers? Do you sense any remnants of these initial images today in modern society?
4. Conduct further research on other early European explorers to America (e.g., Ferdinand Magellan, Amerigo Vespucci, John Cabot, Giovanni da Verrazzano, Sir Walter Raleigh, and Henry Hudson). Did you discover from their accounts that other explorers also had such destructive opinions about the native peoples they encountered?
5. Read additional excepts of Bartolomé de Las Casas's distressing narrative of the mistreatment of native people in the early days of our nation's history and summarize the ways in which the most basic principles of social justice and social equality were violated.
6. After additional study of these primary documents as well as other secondary historical material, identify major themes or patterns of behavior of the early explorers against the native population. For example, did you find behavior patterns held by these explorers that could be classified as *cultural, political,* or *sexual* in nature? Did you discover any individuals, such as Las Casas, or groups that resisted the brutality against the native peoples and advocated for compassion and acceptance of their differences?

Additional Selected References

Bedini, S. (Ed.). (1992). *The Christopher Columbus encyclopedia*. New York: Simon & Schuster.

Castro, D. (2007). *Another face of empire*. Durham, NC: Duke University Press.

De Vorsey, L., & Parker, J. (Eds.) (1985). *In the wake of Columbus: Islands and controversy*. Detroit: Wayne State University Press.

Fernandez-Armesto, F. (1991). *Columbus*. New York: Oxford University Press.

Flint, V. I. J. (1992). *The imaginative landscape of Christopher Columbus*. Princeton, NJ: Princeton University Press.

Hessler, J. W., De Simone. D., & Van Dueser. C. (2014). *Christopher Columbus book of privileges: 1502, the claiming of a new world*. Delray Beach, Florida, and Washington, DC: Levenger Press in association with the Library of Congress.

Milanich, J. T., & Milbrath, S. (Eds.). (1989). *First encounters: Spanish explorations in the Caribbean and the United States, 1492–1570*. Gainesville: University of Florida Press and the Florida Museum of Natural History.

Phillips, W. D., & Phillips, C. R. (1992). *The worlds of Christopher Columbus*. Cambridge, England: Cambridge University Press.

Sullivan, P. F. (Ed.). (1995). *Indian freedom: The cause of Bartolomé de Las Casas, 1484–1566, A reader*. Kansas City: Sheed and Ward.

Wilford, J. N. (1991). *The mysterious history of Columbus: An exploration of the man, the myth, the legacy*. New York: Knop, distributed by Random House.

Credits

Fig. 1.1: Source: https://commons.wikimedia.org/wiki/File:Portrait_of_a_Man,_Said_to_be_Christopher_Columbus.jpg.

Fig. 1.2: Source: https://commons.wikimedia.org/wiki/File:1893_Nina_Pinta_Santa_Maria_replicas.jpg.

Fig. 1.3: Source: www.ancient-origins.es.

Chapter 2

Early Views of Poverty

Elizabethan Poor Laws Introduced into the American Colonies, circa 1700

Introduction

Religion was a dominant force in the early colonial times before the American Revolution, and occasionally specific religious traditions influenced the organization, and even the very existence, of the distinct colonial territories. The English Anglican Church, for example, clearly dominated life in Virginia; the breakaway Puritan denomination settled in what is now Massachusetts and northern New England; and Catholics flocked to Maryland, which had been established with the stated purpose of offering religious freedom to Catholics. Across the ocean in England, religion also dominated society and guided major English political institutions, especially the monarchy and the Parliament. As later history shows, certain developments in England during this early colonial period, such as the *English Bill of Rights*, did exert a profound effect on how the new colonial society functioned and how the *Elizabethan Poor Laws* influenced its multicultural citizenry.

In the colonies' home country, James II ruled as the King of England from 1685 until he was deposed in what has been termed the Glorious Revolution in 1688. A Roman Catholic, James II advocated strongly for the principle of the *divine right of kings* and tried, unsuccessfully as it turned out, to minimize the authority of the Parliament. He also tried to guarantee religious freedom for Catholics and those Protestant denominations that did not conform with the beliefs and practices of Anglican Church. The final insult to the powerful Tories in Parliament was the birth of a male heir to James, thereby guaranteeing a Catholic succession and canceling the plan for his older daughter, Mary, to return the throne to Protestant control. In 1688, the Parliament quickly convinced a Protestant relative, William of Orange, to return to England

FIGURE 2.1   Queen Elizabeth I ("The Ditchley Portrait") standing on a map of England.

with an army and depose James II, who then fled to France. Emboldened by their new power, the Parliament passed *An Act Declaring the Rights and Liberties of the Subject and Settling the Succession of the Crown* in March 1689. Commonly referred to simply as the *English Bill of Rights*, this law voided the principle of the *divine right of kings* and forcefully proclaimed the rights of individual citizens as expressed through their legitimately elected representatives. Significantly for the American colonies, parts of this legislation, notably those relating to freedom of speech and the admonition against cruel and unusual punishment, clearly served as the philosophical foundation of the *American Bill of Rights*, which are the first 10 amendments to the *United States Constitution* that were enacted more than 100 years later in 1791.

During the reign of Tudor Queen Elizabeth I (1558–1603), who was Henry VIII's daughter with Anne Boleyn, the English Parliament passed the *Elizabethan Poor Laws of 1601*, technically a compilation of several earlier laws affecting the poor. These laws, including the later *Law of Settlement and Removal*, followed the migration of peoples from Europe and were formally introduced throughout the British-settled American colonies, particularly in Massachusetts and Virginia by the beginning of the 18th century. These *Poor Laws of 1601* and the *Law of Settlement and Removal* expressed one of the earliest examples of a public ruling body's acceptance of public responsibility for the economic and social welfare of its vulnerable subjects, notably the aged, the sick, the physically disabled, and abandoned or orphaned children. The unemployed and social outcasts (e.g., vagrants and criminals) were also a focus of concern in these laws, but less so and with a noticeable level of stern oversight and physical control.

FIGURE 2.2 The gang children.

Because many settlers in the American colonies were either indentured servants who served under contract for a specified time or slaves forcibly introduced into society, the effects of the *Elizabethan Poor Laws* were extensive. Blending a mixture of Christian charity as interpreted by the Anglican Church and tax-funded public benevolence, this early social welfare system included the:

1. Expectation that parents were responsible for the welfare of their children, as well as the expectation that adult children were responsible for the welfare of their parents and grandparents
2. Understanding that the parish was responsible only for its own inhabitants, so wanderers and vagrants from other parishes could be denied assistance and forcibly returned to their parish of birth
3. Assignment of older children as apprentices
4. Appointment of an overseer of the poor in each community parish
5. Establishment of a system of *outdoor relief* consisting of direct allocations of food, clothing, heating materials, and, occasionally, cash for those believed to be the "deserving poor" (i.e., the aged, widows, and those with visual physical disabilities)
6. Construction or designation of institutions of *indoor relief* in the form of what eventually became known as almshouses, poor farms, poorhouses, workhouses, orphanages, and hospitals
7. Financing of the various social welfare services by the direct taxation of individuals in each parish

Further information on the *Elizabethan Poor Laws* is available in de Schweinitz, K. (1943). *England's road to social security: From the Statute of Laborers in 1349 to the Beverage Report of 1942.* New York: Barnes & Company.

See also http://www.victorianweb.org/history/poorlaw/elizpl.html.

For a broader discussion of poverty during the Elizabethan era, see http://www.bbc.co.uk/history/british/tudors/poverty_01.shtml.

A half-century later, the *Law of Settlement and Removal* (1662), which is generally discussed in conjunction with the *Elizabethan Poor Laws*, added a geographic restraint on poor individuals to move freely from one parish to another by providing any overseer of the poor with the authority to return any nonlocal poor individual back to his or her home parish. There was even a provision for the payment of a *bounty* to anyone catching a nonlocal ". . . rogue, vagabond, or sturdy Beggar . . . who was travelling through the parish illegally."

Clearly, the *Elizabethan Poor Laws* and the *Law of Settlement and Removal* have reverberated through the centuries and still exert a profound influence on the public attitude toward the American social welfare institution. How else can one explain the enduring concepts of the so-called *worthy* and *unworthy* recipients of social welfare benefits? How else can one understand why so much societal effort is exerted to decide the proper ratio between institutional care (*indoor relief*) from home-based or outpatient services (*outdoor relief*)? Finally, how else can one interpret many local communities' intentions to provide financial and social services for their own immediate residents only rather than for those "outsiders" who come from another community and especially from another country?

- For an interesting view of colonial life, see online the restored colonial village maintained in Williamsburg, Virginia. This open-air museum is accessible at http://www.history.org/Almanack/places/index.cfm. Click on the links to "Community" and "Government" for particularly relevant information.

Internet Sources for the Content of This Introduction Include:

https://socialwelfare.library.vcu.edu/programs/poor-laws/
https://www.britannica.com/event/poor-law
https://www.britannica.com/topic/workhouse
https://www.historyonthenet.com/the-tudors-elizabethan-poor-law-1601/
https://en.wikipedia.org/wiki/act_for_the_relief_of_the_poor_1601
https://en.wikipedia.org/wiki/poor_relief_act_1662
http://economistsview.typepad.com/economistsview/2007/03/the_1601_elizab.html
http://swpust2015.blogspot.com/2016/07/the-elizabethan-poor-law-of-1601-in.html

Linkage to Social Welfare History (1600–1750)

Social welfare historical events for this time period include the following:

- Resulting from episodes of religious persecution of Quakers in England and America, William Penn establishes a Quaker colony that stresses religious tolerance in Philadelphia, Pennsylvania (1680).
- The Mennonite Church in Germantown, Pennsylvania, publicly denounces slavery (1688).
- The Salem Witch Trials begin in Massachusetts (1692).
- The Puritan minister Reverend Cotton Mather publishes *Memorable Providences, Relating to Witchcrafts and Possessions*, arguing for the religious justification to formally try a number of witches in Salem, Massachusetts (1689).
- Samuel Sewall publishes *The Selling of Joseph*, a pamphlet that is notable as the first antislavery text to appear in colonial America (1700).
- The *Triangle Trade* system (i.e., the international slave trade) thrives, linking the export of slaves from West Africa, rum from the West Indies, and crops and manufactured goods between Europe and the American Colonies (1720).
- The Ursuline Sisters, a Catholic religious community of women, launches the first orphanage for girls in New Orleans (1729).
- The Reverend George Whitefield pursues a religious revival along the East Coast that will be known as the Great Awakening of religious fervor among many believers (1739).
- Across South Carolina, the state with the second largest population of African slaves after Virginia, a series of slave insurrections against their owners erupts, resulting in the deaths of and injuries to many slaves. (1739).

Note: For a more reflective and functional use of this list of contemporary social welfare historical events, see Question #6 under the **Questions for Further Research and Discussion** section (below).

Sources:
Daniel, C. (1989). *Chronicle of America*. Mt. Kisco, New York: Chronicle Publications.

Mercer, D. (2000). *Millennium year by year*. New York: Dorling Kindersley Publications. Retrieved from https://socialwelfare.library.vcu.edu/events/1700s/

Primary Text Material

The Elizabethan Poor Law [43 Eliz. Cap. 2. 7, A.D. 1601]

"Be it enacted by the Authority of this present Parliament, That the Churchwardens of every Parish, and four, three or two substantial Householders there, as shall be thought meet, having respect to the Proportion and Greatness of the Same Parish and Parishes, to be nominated yearly in Easter Week, or within one Month after Easter, under the Hand and Seal of two or more Justices of the Peace in the same County, whereof one to be of the Quorum, dwelling in or near the same Parish or Division where the same Parish doth lie, shall be called Overseers of the Poor of the same Parish: And they, or the greater Part of them, shall take order from Time to Time, by, and with the Consent of two or more such Justices of Peace as is aforesaid, for setting to work the Children of all such whose Parents shall not by the said Churchwardens and Overseers, or the greater Part of them be thought able to keep and maintain their Children: And also for setting to work all such Persons, married or unmarried, having no Means to maintain them, and use no ordinary and daily Trade of Life to get their Living by: And also to raise weekly or otherwise (by Taxation of every Inhabitant, Parson, Vicar and other, and of every Occupier of Lands, Houses, Tithes impropriate, Propriations of Tithes, Coal-Mines, or saleable Underwoods in the said Parish, in such competent Sum and Sums of Money as they shall think fit) a convenient Stock of Flax, Hemp, Wool, Thread, Iron, and other necessary Ware and Stuff, to set the Poor on Work : And also competent Sums of Money for and towards the necessary Relief of the Lame, Impotent, Old, Blind, and such other among them being Poor, and not able to work, and also for the putting out of such Children to be apprentices, to be gathered out of the same Parish, according to the Ability of the same Parish, and to do and execute all other Things as well for the disposing of the said Stock, as otherwise concerning the Premisses, as to them shall seem convenient . . ."

". . . VII. And be it further enacted, That the father and grandfather, and the mother and grandmother, and the children of every poor old, blind, lame and impotent person, or other poor person not able to work, being of

sufficient ability, shall, at their own charges, relieve and maintain every such poor person in that manner, and according to that rate, as by the justices of the peace of that county where such sufficient persons dwell, or the greater number of them, at their general quarter-sessions shall be assessed; (2) upon pain of every one of them shall forfeit twenty shillings for every month which they shall fail therein . . ."

Source: Great Britain (1888). *A collection of important English statutes* (3rd ed.). Cambridge, MA: Waterman and Amee.

Source and full text available at http://www.workhouses.org.uk/poorlaws/1601act.shtml.

The Law of Settlement and Removal (1662)

". . . Whereas the necessity, number, and continual increase of the poor . . . through the whole kingdom of England and dominion of Wales is very great and exceeding burdensome . . .; [and] whereas, by reason of some defects in the law, poor people are not restrained from going from one parish to another . . ., to settle themselves in those parishes where there is the best stock, the largest commons, or wastes to build cottages, and the most woods for them to burn and destroy . . . that it shall and may be lawful upon complaint made by the Church wardens or Overseers of the Poor of any Parish to any Justice of the Peace within Forty days after any such Person or Persons coming so to settle . . . to remove and convey such person or persons to such Parish where he or they were last legally settled either as a native Householder Sojourner Apprentice or Servant for the space of forty days at the least unless he or they give sufficient security for the discharge of the said Parish to be allowed by the said Justices."

"And be . . . it enacted . . . that it shall and may be lawful to and for any justice of peace, to whom any rogue, vagabond, or sturdy beggars . . . shall be brought, to reward any person or persons that shall apprehend any rogue, vagabond, or sturdy beggar, by granting unto such person or persons an order or warrant under his hand and seal . . . requiring him to pay such person or persons the sum of 2s. for every rogue, vagabond, or sturdy beggar which shall be so apprehended . . ."

Source and full text available at Section L Act to Relieve the Poor. Retrieved from http://www.constitution.org/sech/sech_114.htm.

Full text also available at www.workhouses.org.uk/poorlaws/1601act.shtml.

Further information on the *Elizabethan Poor Laws* available at http://www.victorianweb.org/history/poorlaw/elizpl.html.

FIGURE 2.3   Punch magazine cartoon from 1843 criticizing the Poor Laws.

Timeline of General Events in History, the Humanities, and Science During This Period (1600–1750)

These general historical events may help you understand more clearly the overall historical context during which the primary documents were created.

- The first recorded astronomical observatory is constructed in Greenwich, England, to determine the precise position of the moon and stars for navigational purposes at sea (1675).
- Christiaan Huygens discovers that light consists of waves that travel through the air at great speeds in straight lines and waves (1678).
- Explorer Robert de La Salle travels the entire length of the Mississippi River and claims the territory for France (1682).

- French King Louis XIV, the Sun King, arrives at his renovated hunting lodge, now the largest palace in Europe, at Versailles, outside of Paris (1682).
- Sir Isaac Newton promulgates the *Law of Gravitation*, concluding that the planets revolve around the sun (1687).
- King William of Orange assumes the English crown after defeating the Catholic King James II (1688).
- The English Parliament promulgates the *Act of Settlement*, which bars Roman Catholics from ever ascending to the English throne (1701).
- English astronomer Edmond Halley discovers that comets travel in elliptical patterns, thus allowing for predictions as to when they will return and pass by earth (1705).
- The *Act of Union* passes, joining Scotland with England and thereby establishing the Kingdom of Great Britain (1707).
- Noted architect Sir Christopher Wren completes the rebuilding of St. Paul's Cathedral in London (1710).
- The first shipment of coffee from the island of Java in Indonesia is delivered to Amsterdam, the capital of the Netherlands (1712).
- French settlers establish the city of New Orleans (1718).
- Author Daniel Defoe publishes *Robinson Crusoe* in London (1719).
- Dutch navigator Jacob Roggeveen discovers Easter Island in the Pacific with its large and mysterious statues facing the ocean (1722).
- Benjamin Franklin publishes *Poor Richard's Almanac*, a collection of weather predictions plus several moral guidelines, such as hard work leads to virtue and wealth (1732).
- Due mainly to immigration and the richness of natural resources, the colonial population exceeds 1 million for the first time (1750).

Sources:

Daniel, C. (1989). *Chronicle of America*. Mt. Kisco, New York: Chronicle Publications.

Mercer, D. (2000). *Millennium year by year*. New York: Dorling Kindersley Publications. Retrieved from https://en.wikipedia.org/wiki/18th_century#events

Questions for Further Research and Discussion

1. By the mid-17th century, the dictates of the *Elizabethan Poor Laws* (1601) and the *Law of Settlement and Removal* (1662) had been implemented throughout most of the American colonies. Explore through further research where and how these principles became imbued into the laws and attitudes of early American colonial society.
2. Following further research focused on the Colonial Period, are you able to find whether social welfare services were available and accessible for African indentured servants or slaves and for native people?
3. Looking specifically at the issue of religious discrimination and social welfare, do you believe that colonists following the Anglican tradition, rather than any

other Protestant tradition or Roman Catholicism, were treated differently when they needed social welfare services? Support your beliefs with historical details.
4. Select one or two of the original 13 American colonies, then explore whether you can discern the presence of *indoor* and *outdoor* relief services in those communities. What about the distinction between *worthy* and *unworthy* poor in how social welfare services were distributed?
5. Following up on #4 (above), did you discover in your research exploration any evidence of the offering of social welfare services by *nonpublic authorities* (i.e., nonprofit or voluntary organizations, whether secular or religious in orientation)?
6. Select three events appearing under the **Linkage to Social Welfare** section (above), conduct further Internet research regarding them, then conclude whether you believe there exists any plausible relationship between the *Elizabethan Poor Laws* and the *Law of Settlement and Removal* and the events you have chosen. Use the analytical model presented in Appendix 1 of this book, or develop your own analytical model, to draw these conclusions.
7. Select one book from the **Additional Selected References** list at the end of this chapter. Briefly read through it, then summarize the main points contained in the book. Identify your own personal reactions to this book.

Additional Selected References

Birtles, S. (1999). *Common land, poor relief, and enclosure: The use of manorial resources in fulfilling parish obligations, 1601–1934. Past & Present.* 165, 74–106

Botelho, L. (2004). *Old age and the English poor law, 1500–1700.* Rochester, NY: Boydell and Brewer.

Day, P. J. (1989). *A new history of social welfare.* Englewood Cliffs, NJ: Prentice Hall.

de Schweinitz, K. (1943). *England's road to social security: From the Statute of Laborers in 1349 to the Beverage Report of 1942.* New York: Barnes & Company.

Herndon, R. W., & Murray, J. E. (2009). *Children bound to labor: The pauper apprentice system in early America.* Ithaca: Cornell University Press.

Mizrahi, T., & Davis, L. E. (Eds.). (2008). *Encyclopedia of social work* (20th ed.). Washington, DC: National Association and Oxford University Press.

Patriquin, L. (2007). *Agrarian capitalism and poor relief in England, 1500–1860: Rethinking the origins of the welfare state.* Basingstoke: Palgrave Macmillan.

Pound, J. (1971). *Poverty and vagrancy in Tudor England.* Harlow: Longman.

Wrightson, K. (1982). *English society, 1580–1680.* New Brunswick, NJ: Rutgers University Press.

Credits

Fig. 2.1: Source: https://commons.wikimedia.org/wiki/File:Queen_Elizabeth_I_(%27The_Ditchley_portrait%27)_by_Marcus_Gheeraerts_the_Younger.jpg.

Fig. 2.2: Source: http://www.victorianweb.org/art/illustration/pinwell/6.html.

Fig. 2.3: Copyright © Punch (CC by 4.0) at https://commons.wikimedia.org/wiki/File:The_%22milk%22_of_poor-law_%22kindness%22_Wellcome_L0003350.jpg.

Chapter 3

America's Foundational Documents

The *Constitution of the United States* (1787)
and the *Bill of Rights* (1789)

Introduction

The first foundational document of the new American experiment was the *Declaration of Independence* that declared the American colonies free from the British Crown's rule on July 4, 1776. Universally acclaimed as a courageous affirmation that basic human rights must never be abridged by any organized power, the second sentence of the *Declaration of Independence* states that principle most directly and comprehensively: "We hold these truths to be self-evident, that all men are created equal, that they are endowed by their Creator with certain inalienable Rights, that among these are Life, Liberty, and the pursuit of Happiness."

One year later in 1777, the *Articles of Confederation* were approved by the Continental Congress during the early days of the American Revolution. As the name implies, this second foundational document stands as a formal agreement to join together as a community of states to pursue a shared goal. The *Articles of Confederation* exist as the first statement of unity among the 13 original states and, as such, predate the more formal *Constitution of the United States* by 10 years. Although important for providing a common name and organizational relationship for the new union of states against Great Britain, the *Articles of Confederation* significantly prevented a strong central government to emerge by insisting on the principle currently referred to as *states' rights*. In doing so, this document set in motion the dynamic tension that exists even today between how federal and state entities accept responsibility for some social problems and the forms in which resources, laws, and programs are available to address those problems.

The third foundational document in our nation's history, the *Constitution of the United States*, endures as the supreme law of the land and dictates how the contemporary central government in Washington is organized and, furthermore, how it relates to the individual states and to the nation's citizens. It was formulated by 55 delegates from the original 13 states (except Rhode Island) at the Constitutional Convention in Philadelphia in 1787. Rhode Island refused to send delegates because it did not want a strong federal government and was apparently content with the weak federal system established in the *Articles of Confederation*. Some of the eminent delegates to the Convention (eventually known as "Framers") included George Washington as president of the Convention, Alexander Hamilton from New York, Benjamin Franklin from Pennsylvania, and James Madison from Virginia. Following the Convention, and for the purpose of assisting the ratification process by the states, Madison, Hamilton and John Jay composed and distributed *The Federalist Papers* as a series of supporting essays in newspapers throughout the 13 states. The *Constitution of the United States* was eventually ratified by all the original states, including Rhode Island, by 1790.

How to deal with the issue of slavery created tension and much debate at the Constitutional Convention because several Northern states had already begun to outlaw slavery, whereas the Southern states were deeply committed to exploiting it for commercial purposes. The dominant argument for slavery's continuance was that it should be a state and not a national decision. In the end, there developed what appears to be an imbalanced compromise for the sake of unity: The slave trade would not be prohibited before 1808; all states agreed to return fugitive slaves to their owners (the infamous "Fugitive Slave Clause" in the document—Article 4, Section 2, Clause 3—which became moot with the passage of the *13th Amendment* in 1865 abolishing slavery); and, for representation and tax purposes, slaves would be counted as only three-fifths of a person.

The *Constitution of the United States* established the basic governmental structure in which is embedded, perhaps, what can be interpreted as a hazy reference to a social welfare system—in, for example, the commitment to *promote the general welfare* and for the new government's ability to *collect taxes* and to *make rules for the government*. Additionally, the principle of a *separation of powers* between the executive, legislative, and judicial branches of the federal government is created in the *Constitution* to avoid any one branch from becoming too powerful. This principle is notable because it will be invoked often in support of later social welfare developments (e.g., *Brown v. Board of Education*, which ended racial segregation of public schools in 1954). The opening phrase of the Constitution—"We, the people"—is iconic and highlights the fact that the United States was created for the benefit of its people and not to simply establish a union of individual states, as had been accomplished in the *Articles of Confederation* 10 years earlier.

For a short YouTube presentation on the *Constitution of the United States*, see https://www.youtube.com/watch?v=OSW15ldEv6w.

The fourth essential document in our nation's early life was crafted just two years after the *Constitution of the United States*. Containing what are the first 10 Amendments to the *Constitution*, this document is collectively referred to simply as the *Bill of Rights*.

FIGURE 3.1 The Constitution of the United States.

Closely related to the original *Constitution of the United States*, which emphasizes order and structure, the *Bill of Rights* champions individual liberty and freedom from control by a government. Madison introduced these additions to limit the powers of the federal government over the states and to protect the citizens' rights to free speech and free association, to a free press, and to a public trial by jury. Essentially, the *Bill of Rights* resolved some of the issues between the Federalists, like Hamilton, who believed in a strong central government and the Anti-Federalists, like Jefferson, who argued for more individual freedom and strong state-based authority. Since the *Bill of Rights* was formally ratified by three-fourths of the states in 1791, the United States Constitution has been amended 17 additional times up to the present day. From the language used, as well as the examples cited, it seems clear that this early Congress designed the *Bill of Rights* to protect the individual against the power of the federal government. This primacy of the individual over governmental excess is an essential element in any effective social welfare endeavor. Tragically, however, the *individual* in this proclamation of a set of *citizens' rights* was still narrowly defined at the end of the 18th century to benefit primarily white male landowners. Women, slaves and former slaves, and children, though they enjoyed the most basic of freedoms, were still essentially excluded from many provisions of this *Bill of Rights*. Within a social welfare context, later federal legislation, Supreme Court decisions, and bureaucratic responses will reduce some, but not all, of these recognized societal

FIGURE 3.2　The Bill of Rights.

injustices. Indeed, the achievement of a fully comprehensive, effective, and accessible social welfare system that can readily respond to the needs of the most vulnerable will continue to be a national work in progress.

It seems clear, even after a casual reading of the *Constitution of the United States* and the *Bill of Rights*, that the issue of social welfare was not addressed either directly or indirectly. Perhaps that apparent omission was due to the simple fact that the concept of social welfare in the American colonies had not clearly emerged and been incorporated into colonial society, even though elements of the *Elizabethan Poor Laws* and the *Law of Settlement* had been institutionalized throughout the colonies by the British in pre-Revolutionary times. Whatever the reason or reasons, perhaps that lapse has influenced current society's lack of enthusiasm to recognize that there do indeed exist national social problems that require serious attention. In other words, those individuals in law and in government who demand a *strict interpretation* of the Constitution may feel justified in denying or minimizing the essential role that should be played by social welfare policies and programs because, in their view, there is no mention of that concept in the text of the *Constitution of the United States*, including the *Bill of Rights*.

Internet Sources for the Content of This Introduction Include:

https://www.whitehouse.gov/1600/constitution
http://www.history.com/topics/constitution
https://www.britannica.com/topic/constitution-of-the-united-states-of-america
https://en.wikipedia.org/wiki/united_states_constitution
https://www.billofrightsinstitute.org/founding-documents/bill-of-rights/
http://www.history.com/topics/bill-of-rights
https://www.britannica.com/topic/bill-of-rights-united-states-constitution
https://en.wikipedia.org/wiki/united_states_bill_of_rights

Linkage to Social Welfare History (1750-1800)

Social welfare historical events for this time period include the following:

- Benjamin Franklin helps create a designated hospital for the care of the insane in Philadelphia (1751).
- Franklin, in his essay *Observations Concerning the Increase of Mankind, Peopling of Countries*, proposes that slavery is not economically sound when compared to the normal free laborer system in England and, furthermore, that education is wasted on Native Americans because of their unruly nature (1751).
- Williamsburg, Virginia, establishes its first public residential mental health facility (1773).
- In what is recognized as the first public social welfare program, the Continental Congress authorizes the payment of a federal pension to all military officers and enlisted men disabled in the Revolutionary War (1776).

- As part of the infamous *Triangle Trade* of goods and people, approximately 100,00 African slaves are sold in the Southern states in the United States and throughout the Caribbean and Brazil (1780).
- Approximately 10,000 slaves are granted freedom after their service in either the American Continental Army or various colonial militias (1782).
- Britain formally recognizes the independence of the 13 former colonies, renamed the United States of America (1783).
- The French Assembly authorizes the *Declaration of the Rights of Man*, thereby emphasizing the principles of human freedom and equality of rights (1789).
- South Carolina opens its first publicly funded orphanage for children in Charleston (1790).
- Thomas Paine publishes *The Rights of Man*, proclaiming that all humans are born free and all have equal rights as citizens (1791).
- Eli Whitney invents the cotton gin, leading to the industrialization of the cotton industry and the need for slave labor throughout the Southern states (1793).
- In Paris, the ruling convention abolishes slavery in all French territories (1794).
- In his publication *Agrarian Justice*, Thomas Paine suggests the implementation of a social insurance program for established European nations as well as for the new American nation (1795).
- Thomas Malthus publishes his *Essay on the Principle of Population*, which warns against uncontrolled population growth because that would slow down the progress toward a utopian society (1798).

Note: For a more reflective and functional use of this list of contemporary social welfare historical events, see Question #3 under the **Questions for Further Research and Discussion** section (below).

Sources:
Daniel, C. (1989). *Chronicle of America*. Mt. Kisco, NY: Chronicle Publications.
Mercer, D. (2000). *Millennium year by year*. New York: Dorling Kindersley Publications. Retrieved from https://socialwelfare.library.vcu.edu/events/1700s/

Primary Text Material

The Constitution of the United States of America (1787)

We the People of the United States, in order to form a more perfect Union, establish Justice, insure domestic Tranquility, provide for the common defence, promote the general Welfare, and secure the Blessings of Liberty to ourselves and our Posterity, do ordain and establish this Constitution for the United States of America.

Article. I. Section. 1.

All legislative Powers herein granted shall be vested in a Congress of the United States, which shall consist of a Senate and House of Representatives. . . .

Section. 8.

The Congress shall have Power To lay and collect Taxes, Duties, Imposts and Excises, to pay the Debts and provide for the common Defence and general Welfare of the United States; but all Duties, Imposts and Excises shall be uniform throughout the United States; . . .

To make Rules for the Government and Regulation of the land and naval Forces;

To provide for calling forth the Militia to execute the Laws of the Union, suppress Insurrections and repel Invasions; . . .

Article. II. Section. 1.

The executive Power shall be vested in a President of the United States of America. He shall hold his Office during the Term of four Years, and, together with the Vice President, chosen for the same Term, be elected, as follows

Article. III. Section. 1.

The judicial Power of the United States shall be vested in one supreme Court, and in such inferior Courts as the Congress may from time to time ordain and establish. . . .

Full text available at http://www.archives.gov/exhibits/charters/constitution_transcript.html.

For a special presentation by the *New York Times* of the full text of the United States Constitution, with annotations at significant sections, see https://www.nytimes.com/interactive/projects/documents/annotated-constitution.

The Preamble to the Bill of Rights (1789)

THE Conventions of a number of the States, having at the time of their adopting the Constitution, expressed a desire, in order to prevent misconstruction or abuse of its powers, that further declaratory and restrictive clauses should be added: . . .

Amendment I. Congress shall make no law respecting an establishment of religion, or prohibiting the free exercise thereof; or abridging the freedom of speech, or of the press; or the right of the people peaceably to assemble, and to petition the Government for a redress of grievances.

Amendment II. A well regulated Militia, being necessary to the security of a free State, the right of the people to keep and bear Arms, shall not be infringed. . . .

Amendment IV. The right of the people to be secure in their persons, houses, papers, and effects, against unreasonable searches and seizures, shall not be violated, and no Warrants shall issue, but upon probable cause, supported by

Continued

Oath or affirmation, and particularly describing the place to be searched, and the persons or things to be seized.

Amendment V. *No person shall be held to answer for a capital, or otherwise infamous crime, unless on a presentment or indictment of a Grand Jury . . . nor shall be compelled in any criminal case to be a witness against himself, nor be deprived of life, liberty, or property, without due process of law; nor shall private property be taken for public use, without just compensation.*

Amendment VI. *In all criminal prosecutions, the accused shall enjoy the right to a speedy and public trial, by an impartial jury of the State and district wherein the crime shall have been committed . . . and to be informed of the nature and cause of the accusation; to be confronted with the witnesses against him; . . .*

Amendment VIII. *Excessive bail shall not be required, nor excessive fines imposed, nor cruel and unusual punishments inflicted.*

Amendment X. *The powers not delegated to the United States by the Constitution, nor prohibited by it to the States, are reserved to the States respectively, or to the people.*

Full text available at http://www.archives.gov/exhibits/charters/bill_of_rights_transcript.html.

This media file is in the public domain.

Timeline of General Events in History, the Humanities, and Science During This Period (1750–1800)

These general historical events may help you understand more clearly the overall historical context during which the primary documents were created.

- The Battle of Bunker Hill, the first major conflict of the American Revolution, resulted in a defeat for the colonists but with major losses by the British (1775).
- Patrick Henry pronounces his famous "Give me liberty or give me death" speech in the Second Virginia Convention in Richmond, Virginia (1775).
- Paul Revere rides into Lexington, Massachusetts, and warns the local militia that "the British are coming!" (1775).
- Thomas Paine publishes his anti-British pamphlet *Common Sense* (1776).
- The *Declaration of Independence* is drafted on July 4 (1776).
- Adam Smith publishes *The Wealth of Nations* (1776).
- The Continental Congress promulgates the *Articles of Confederation and Perpetual Union*, which formally binds the states together into a new united body (1777).
- The British surrender to General George Washington at Yorktown, Virginia, thus ending the American Revolutionary War (1781).
- The City of San Francisco is established by Spanish settlers (1781).

- German astronomer William Herschel discovers a new planet in our solar system that will be named Uranus (1781).
- James Watt introduces the steam engine to the industrial market (1786).
- The *Constitution of the Unites States* is approved (1787).
- Citizens in Paris stormed the Bastille prison, ushering in the French Revolution (1789).
- George Washington is elected as the first president of the United States of America (1789).
- Wolfgang Amadeus Mozart composes *The Magic Flute* (1791).
- French revolutionary Maximilien de Robespierre is elected to the Committee of Public Safety, a position from which he will launch his villainous "Reign of Terror" over French society (1793).
- English doctor Edward Jenner discovers a vaccine to prevent smallpox (1796).
- The United States Congress passes *The Sedition Act*, outlawing any treasonous writings by American citizens (1798).
- French General Napoleon Bonaparte conquers Egypt by defeating the native Muslim Mameluke army (1798).

Sources

Daniel, C. (1989). *Chronicle of America*. Mt. Kisco, NY: Chronicle Publications.

Mercer, D. (2000). *Millennium year by year*. New York: Dorling Kindersley Publications. Retrieved from https://en.wikipedia.org/wiki/18th_century#events

Questions for Further Research and Discussion

1. After exploring the entire texts of the *Constitution of the United States of America* and the *Bill of Rights*, as well as secondary sources relating to these documents, elaborate with specific details three or more of the following six topics:
   a. The issue of *states' rights*, along with its positive and negative consequences
   b. The ability of the federal government to raise *revenue through taxation* rather than through other means
   c. The ability to establish *societal rules* to promote the general welfare of American society, as well as the process under which those rules are made
   d. The introduction of the *separation of powers* between the legislative, judicial, and executive branches of government and how well that division of responsibility has functioned
   e. The principle of the primacy of the *individual* over possible governmental excess and whether that primacy has endured over the centuries
   f. The narrow definition of the *individual* to include only white male landowners and how that distinction has led to discrimination and oppression
2. Based on what you have discovered in Question #1 (a through f above), what are some of the policy and program implications for the American social welfare system?

3. Select three events appearing under the **Linkage to Social Welfare** section (above), conduct further Internet research regarding them, then conclude whether you believe there exists any plausible relationship between the *Constitution of the United States* or the *Bill of Rights* and the events you have chosen. Use the analytical model presented in Appendix 1 of this book, or develop your own analytical model, to draw these conclusions.
4. Select one book from the **Additional Selected References** list at the end of this chapter. Briefly read through it, then summarize the main points contained in the book. Identify your own personal reaction to this book.

Additional Selected References

Amar, A. (1998). *The Bill of Rights: Creation and reconstruction*. New Haven: Yale University Press.

American Historical Association & American Political Science Association. (1988). *This Constitution: From ratification to the Bill of Rights*. Washington, DC: Congressional Quarterly.

Commission on the Bicentennial of the United States Constitution & American Library Association. (1990). *With liberty and justice for all: 1991, the Bill of Rights and beyond*. Washington, DC: The Commission.

Commission on the Bicentennial of the United States Constitution. (1991). *Selected bibliography on the Constitution and the Bill of Rights*. Washington, DC: The Commission.

Conley, P. T., Kaminski, J. P., U.S. Constitution Council of the Thirteen Original States, & University of Wisconsin–Madison. (1992). *The Bill of Rights and the states: The colonial and revolutionary origins of American liberties*. Madison, WI: Madison House.

Goldwin, R. A. (1997). *From parchment to power: How James Madison used the Bill of Rights to save the Constitution*. Washington, DC: AEI Press.

Labunski, R. E. (2006). *James Madison and the struggle for the Bill of Rights*. Oxford: Oxford University Press.

St. John, J. (1990). *A child of fortune: A correspondent's report on the ratification of the U.S. Constitution and battle for a Bill of Rights*. Ottawa, IL: Jameson Books.

Schwartz, B. (1971). *The Bill of Rights: A documentary history*. New York: Chelsea House Publishers.

Zink, J. (2014). James Wilson versus the Bill of Rights: Progress, popular sovereignty, and the idea of the U.S. Constitution. *Political Research Quarterly, 67*(2), 253–265. Retrieved from http://www.jstor.org.ursus-proxy-1.ursus.maine.edu/stable/24371781

Credits

Fig. 3.1: Source: https://commons.wikimedia.org/wiki/File:Constitution_of_the_United_States,_page_1.jpg.

Fig. 3.2: Source: https://commons.wikimedia.org/wiki/File:Bill_of_Rights_Pg1of1_AC.jpg.

Chapter 4

The Life of a Slave

Frederick Douglass's *Narrative of the Life of Frederick Douglass, An American Slave* (1845)

Introduction

Born into slavery in eastern Maryland at the beginning of the 19th century, Frederick Douglass ultimately became one of the most famous civil rights advocates in American history. He not only spoke out against slavery through the abolitionist movement, but he also championed women's rights and equality of Native Americans and immigrants.

Douglass was born to a slave woman and a white father and initially named Frederick Augustus. His father was probably the slave master or one of the white masters, whom he never knew nor spoke about. His early years were spent mostly with his maternal grandparents and other relatives, and he was eventually sold in his teenage years to various landowners, as were other slaves at the time. Extreme physical beatings, psychological humiliations, and meager food rations were targeted daily toward Douglass and the other slaves by one notorious slave master, Edward Covey. Douglass escaped Covey's plantation in 1838, fled to New York City, and eventually settled in New Bedford, Massachusetts, which had a large free African American community. While in Bedford, Douglass married Anna Murray, the African American woman who helped him flee by providing him with money and forged identity papers that categorized him as a freed African American. Upon his marriage, Frederick Augustus officially adopted the surname of "Douglass," which was a reference to a character in Sir Walter Scott's 1810 narrative poem, *Lady of the Lake*. Douglass and his wife joined an African American church, and he became active in antislavery events, which is where he first met William Garrison, the white leader in the abolitionist movement.

Douglass taught himself to read and write and eventually became a noted and prolific orator on slavery and a range of social injustice issues.

FIGURE 4.1 Frederick Douglass.

In fact, his public speaking competency was so apparent and widely appreciated that many supporters could hardly believe that he had been born and raised as a slave. While living in Rochester, New York, later in his career, Douglass edited the highly influential abolitionist newspaper *The North Star*, which was then changed to *Frederick Douglass' Paper* and finally renamed *The Douglass Monthly*. These publications, plus his public performances as a gifted and strong-minded orator, solidified his reputation both nationally and internationally. Douglass also published three autobiographies: *Narrative of the Life of Frederick Douglass, An American Slave* (1845), which chronicled in vivid language his early life as a slave and two other self-reflections about his later years; *My Bondage and My Freedom* (1855); and *The Life and Times of Frederick Douglass* (1881). These works are considered classics in the "slave narratives" literary tradition.

As one of the few men and the only African American man to attend the 1848 Seneca Falls Convention, which was the first formal women's rights assembly, Douglass publicly supported Elizabeth Cady Stanton when she proposed at that meeting that women should have the right to vote. Years later, after the Civil War, when the *15th Amendment* to the *United States Constitution* was passed and granted freed African American men the right to vote, Douglass supported it as a realistic first step to universal suffrage. Stanton opposed the amendment because it excluded women, leading to a breach in her relationship with Douglass.

Douglass also was initially allied with the legendary abolitionist John Brown but eventually distanced himself from Brown's radical antigovernment behavior, especially his 1859 raid on the military installation at Harpers Ferry. Fearing that such violent actions would negatively change the growing public opinion against slavery, Douglass assumed that the full emancipation of slaves in the South would be delayed.

During the Civil War, Douglass helped recruit African Americans for military service in the Union Army and is reported to have served at least twice as advisor to President Abraham Lincoln on racial matters. After the Civil War, in the early 1870s, Douglass moved to Washington, DC and edited the *New National Era*, a reconstituted abolitionist newspaper that now was devoted to covering Reconstruction throughout the South as well as the broad African American community in the greater Washington, DC area. He was an understandably harsh critic of the first Ku Klux Klan organization and other nativist groups that continued the degradation and dominance over African Americans during Reconstruction through lynching and other terrorist acts that damaged voting rights, public education, religion, housing, employment, and virtually every aspect of everyday living. These abuses continued even after the formal period of Reconstruction and evolved legislatively into the infamous Jim Crow laws mandating segregation of the races from the 1890s up through the mid-20th century. Approaching these problems positively, Douglass also advocated publicly for more educational opportunities and better employment prospects for African Americans, as well as equal voting rights for all.

During his career, Douglass traveled widely through Africa and Europe, where he spoke out against slavery and injustice wherever he witnessed it. He visited Ireland at the beginning of the Great Famine there in 1845 and supported Daniel O'Connell, the noted Irish Nationalist who championed the emancipation of Ireland from the dominance of Great Britain as the result of the *Act of Union*. In his later years during the 1870s, Douglass also endorsed the Irish Home Rule movement directed by Charles Stewart Parnell.

After the death of his wife, Anna, Douglass married Helen Pitts, his white secretary, with whom he had two children. As can be predicted, this marriage was extremely controversial at the time and serves today, perhaps, as one notable example of the complicated mixed racial heritage of modern America.

Sometimes referred to as "the most photographed African American in the 19th century," Douglass stands tall as a recognized leader in the antislavery movement as well as a variety of other progressive causes. His numerous literary works, as well as his notable accomplishments during his life, serve as rich primary documentary evidence of how one person's vision can influence society and national social policy decades after one's death, even to the present day. It can be assumed, certainly, that Douglass's memory is still influential in recent social justice movements, such as the Civil Rights Movement, Black History Month, the Black Lives Matter Movement, etc.

Internet Sources for the Content of This Introduction Include:

https://www.pbs.org/wgbh/aia/part4/4p1539.html
http://www.history.com/topics/black-history/frederick-douglass
https://www.nps.gov/frdo/learn/historyculture/frederickdouglass.htm
http://docsouth.unc.edu/neh/douglass/bio.html
http://www.americaslibrary.gov/aa/douglass/aa_douglass_subj.html
https://en.wikipedia.org/wiki/frederick_douglass

Linkage to Social Welfare History (1800–1850)

Social welfare historical events for this time period include the following:

- Great Britain abolishes the slave trade (1807).
- Importation of any new slaves into the United States is banned (1807).
- Using methods that would be classified today as "macro practice," the New York Society for the Prevention of Pauperism is founded with the goal of eliminating poverty (1817).

FIGURE 4.2   Image from an abolitionist pamphlet.

- Thomas Gallaudet and Laurent Clerc establish the first American school for the deaf in Hartford, Connecticut (1817).
- The United States Congress passes the *Revolutionary War Pension Act*, which provides a monetary pension to all Revolutionary War veterans (1818).

- Freed slaves from America establish a new colony in Liberia, West Africa (1822).
- The Bureau of Indian Affairs is created within the Department of War with a mission to manage treaty negotiations, Indian schools, and all trading procedures with Indian tribes (1824).
- The American Society for the Promotion of Temperance is founded (1826).
- Thomas "Daddy" Rice, a New York comedian, introduces a new character in his minstrel show: Jim Crow, an absurd and offensive caricature of an African American that quickly catches on with many in the white community and endures (1828).
- President Andrew Jackson signs *The Indian Removal Act*, which forcibly transports all Native American tribes westward, away from white-populated areas, and grants them land rights and some financial assistance (1830).
- Nat Turner, the slave who led a failed rebellion that killed a number of whites and African Americans, writes *The Confessions of Nat Turner: The Leader of the Late Insurrection in Southampton, Virginia* (1831).
- Massachusetts enacts the first known legislation protecting children who work in factories by requiring them to attend school at least three months every year (1836).
- Charles Dickens publishes *Oliver Twist*, a socially critical novel about children raised in a London poorhouse, widely recognized today as one of the early depictions of child abuse and neglect (1837).
- The United States Army oversees the forced relocation of almost 20,000 Cherokee Native Americans from their homelands in the southeastern states to an Indian territory west of the Mississippi River. This journey became known in popular culture as *The Trail of Tears* because reportedly more than 4,000 Cherokees perished along the way due to exposure, disease, and exhaustion (1838).
- Robert Purvis, a noted abolitionist, helps to initiate *The Underground Railroad*, a network of private homes, churches, and organizations that facilitate a way for escaped slaves to travel north to freedom (1838).
- Mental health advocate Dorothea Dix exposes to the Massachusetts legislature the inhumane conditions in the state's insane asylum and publicly appeals for institutional reform (1843).
- Former slave Sojourner Truth begins to publicly support the abolitionist movement by lecturing across the nation (1843).
- In New York City, the New York Association for Improving the Condition of the Poor is established. This early social service organization will eventually evolve into the Charity Organization Society, which will develop the formal "case method" of social service delivery (1843).
- The Irish potato crop is devastated by a longstanding blight that begins the *Great Irish Famine*, in which more than 1 million Irish peasants die and 2 million more immigrate to the United States, Canada, and Australia (1845).
- Newspaper editor John L. O'Sullivan introduces a concept that will dictate national policy for decades: that the United States has a *Manifest Destiny* from God to annex and control all territory in North America (1845).

- Elizabeth Cady Stanton and Lucretia Mott organize the *Seneca Falls Convention*, which champions universal suffrage and other women's rights (1848).
- Karl Marx and Friedrich Engels publish *The Communist Manifesto*, which calls for workers of the world to unite against the oppressive class power system in society (1848).
- Philosopher Henry David Thoreau publishes *Civil Disobedience*, a discourse on the need to resist unjust governmental actions such as slavery, the oppression of native people, and war (1849).

Note: For a more reflective and functional use of this list of contemporary social welfare historical events, see Question #6 under the **Questions for Further Research and Discussion** section (below).

Sources:

Daniel, C. (1989). *Chronicle of America*. Mt. Kisco, NY: Chronicle Publications.

Mercer, D. (2000). *Millennium year by year*. New York: Dorling Kindersley Publications. Retrieved from https://socialwelfare.library.vcu.edu/events/1800-1850/

Primary Text Material

Douglass, F. (1845). *Narrative of the Life of Frederick Douglass, An American Slave.* **Written by Himself. Boston: Anti-Slavery Office, No. 25 Cornhill. Chapter 2.**

"... *Here, too, the slaves of all the other farms received their monthly allowance of food, and their yearly clothing. The men and women slaves received, as their monthly allowance of food, eight pounds of pork, or its equivalent in fish, and one bushel of corn meal. Their yearly clothing consisted of two coarse linen shirts, one pair of linen trousers, like the shirts, one jacket, one pair of trousers for winter, made of coarse negro cloth, one pair of stockings, and one pair of shoes; the whole of which could not have cost more than seven dollars. The allowance of the slave children was given to their mothers, or the old women having the care of them. The children unable to work in the field had neither shoes, stockings, jackets, nor trousers, given to them; their clothing consisted of two coarse linen shirts per year. When these failed them, they went naked until the next allowance-day. Children from seven to ten years old, of both sexes, almost naked, might be seen at all seasons of the year.*

There were no beds given the slaves, unless one coarse blanket be considered such, and none but the men and women had these. This, however, is not considered a very great privation. They find less difficulty from the want of beds, than from the want of time to sleep; for when their day's work in the field is done, the most of them having their washing, mending, and cooking to do, and having few or none of the ordinary facilities for doing either of these, very many of their sleeping hours are consumed in preparing for the field the coming day; and when this is done, old and young, male and female, married and single, drop down side by side, on one common bed,—the cold, damp floor,—each covering himself or herself with their miserable blankets; and here they sleep till they are summoned to the field by the driver's horn. At the sound of this, all must rise, and be off to the field. There must be no halting; everyone must be at his or her post; and woe betides them who hear not this morning summons to the field; for if they are not awakened by the sense of hearing, they are by the sense of feeling: no age nor sex finds any favor. Mr. Severe, the overseer, used to stand by the door of the quarter, armed with a large hickory stick and heavy cowskin, ready to whip anyone who was so unfortunate as not to hear, or, from any other cause, was prevented from being ready to start for the field at the sound of the horn.

Mr. Severe was rightly named: he was a cruel man. I have seen him whip a woman, causing the blood to run half an hour at the time; and this, too, in the midst of her crying children, pleading for their mother's release. He seemed to take pleasure in manifesting his fiendish barbarity. Added to his cruelty, he was a profane swearer. It was enough to chill the blood and stiffen the hair of an ordinary man to hear him talk. Scarce a sentence escaped him but that was commenced or concluded by some horrid oath. The field was the place to witness his cruelty and profanity. His presence made it both the field of blood and of blasphemy. From the rising till the going down of the sun, he was cursing, raving, cutting, and slashing among the slaves of the field, in the most frightful manner. His career was short. He died very soon after I went to Colonel Lloyd's; and he died as he lived, uttering, with his dying groans, bitter curses and horrid oaths. His death was regarded by the slaves as the result of a merciful providence . . ."

Source and full text available at http://www.gutenberg.org/files/23/23-h/23-h.htm.

For further information about the life of Frederick Douglass, see the National Park Services site at https://www.nps.gov/frdo/learn/historyculture/frederickdouglass.htm.

For direct access to his diary during his 1886 tour of Africa and Europe, his personal and official letters, and other papers of Frederick Douglass, see https://www.loc.gov/collections/frederick-douglass-papers/about-this-collection/.

For a National Public Radio report on Frederick Douglass's charge that slave owners used hunger as a weapon to manage and dominate their slaves, see http://www.npr.org/sections/thesalt/2017/02/10/514385071/frederick-douglass-on-how-slave-owners-used-food-as-a-weapon-of-control.

For access to digital copies of the *New National Era,* see http://chroniclingamerica.loc.gov/lccn/sn84026753/.

Timeline of General Events in History, the Humanities, and Science During This Period (1800–1850)

These general historical events may help you understand more clearly the overall historical context during which the primary document was created.

- The Kingdom of Great Britain joins with the Kingdom of Ireland to form the new Great Britain (1800).
- Ludwig von Beethoven performs his *Moonlight Sonata* for the first time (1802).
- The United States doubles its size with the land mass acquired through the Louisiana Purchase from France (1803).
- Bonaparte Napoleon is crowned emperor (1805).
- The Lewis and Clark expedition completes its voyage to the Pacific Ocean (1805).
- Noah Webster publishes his dictionary of the English language, which is used in America (1806).
- The controversial Elgin Marbles, removed by Lord Elgin from the Parthenon in Athens, are publicly displayed for the first time in London (1812).
- The University of Berlin is founded and serves as a model of modern universities (1812).
- Jane Austen publishes *Pride and Prejudice* (1813).
- Napoleon is defeated by the British duke of Wellington at the Battle of Waterloo (1815).
- Mary Shelley publishes *Frankenstein* in London (1818).
- The United States annexes Florida from Spain (1819).
- Congress passes the *Missouri Compromise*, which allows for one free state (Maine) to be admitted into the Union and one slave state (Missouri) to be admitted (1820).
- President James Monroe announces his *Monroe Doctrine*, which prohibits any European monarchies from colonizing any land in the New World and from interfering with any country in the Western hemisphere (1823).
- The Erie Canal is completed, thus connecting the Great Lakes with the Atlantic Ocean (1825).
- John Quincy Adams is elected president of the United States (1825).
- James Fenimore Cooper publishes *The Last of the Mohicans*, a novel about America's frontier history (1826).
- Noah Webster publishes *The American Dictionary of the English Language*, his effort to establish America's independence from Great Britain in the use of language (1828).
- Joseph Smith publishes *The Book of Mormon* and establishes the Church of the Latter-day Saints (1830).
- Samuel Morse develops the Morse Code, which revolutionizes communications across distances (1836).
- In France, Louis Daguerre invents the daguerreotype, a method of producing white-and-black photographic images from copper plates (1837).

- The Gold Rush launches in California, leading to a massive westward migration (1849).

Questions for Further Research and Discussion

1. After delving deeper into Frederick Douglass's published works and papers, document his specific accomplishments as part of the general abolitionist movement to eradicate slavery.
2. What were some notable achievements by Douglass within the area of universal suffrage for women?
3. How precisely did Douglass involve himself in the area of full social equality for the Native American tribes in the 19th century?
4. Douglass traveled widely through Europe and Africa during his many public speaking engagements. Can you find examples of how he challenged the practice of human slavery in Africa and how he championed the right of the Irish to be free from British subjugation?
5. From your perceived understanding of Douglass's "moral compass," what explicit social justice issues today in the 21st century could you project that he would pursue? How do you think he would rank those issues?
6. Select three events appearing under the **Linkage to Social Welfare** section (above), conduct further Internet research regarding them, then conclude whether you believe there exists any plausible relationship between the *Narrative of the Life of Frederick Douglass, An American Slave* and the events you have chosen. Use the analytical model presented in Appendix 1 of this book, or develop your own analytical model, to draw these conclusions.
7. Select one book from the **Additional Selected References** list at the end of this chapter. Briefly read through it, then summarize the main points contained in the book. Identify your own personal reaction to this book.

Additional Selected References

Buccola, N. (2012). *The political thought of Frederick Douglass: In pursuit of American liberty.* New York: New York University Press.

Chaffin, T. (2014). *Giant's causeway: Frederick Douglass's Irish odyssey and the making of an American visionary.* Charlottesville, VA: University of Virginia Press.

Chesebrough, D. B. (1998). *Frederick Douglass: Oratory from slavery.* Westport, CT: Greenwood Press.

Colaiaco, J.A. (2006). *Frederick Douglass and the fourth of July.* New York: Palgrave Macmillan.

Lawson, B. E., & Kirkland, F. M. (Eds.). (1999). *Frederick Douglass: A critical reader.* Malden, MA: Blackwell Publishers.

Leer, M. S. (Ed.). (2009). *The Cambridge companion to Frederick Douglass*. Cambridge, MA: Cambridge University Press.

Levine, R. S. (2016). *The lives of Frederick Douglass*. Cambridge, MA: Harvard University Press.

McFeely, W. S. (1991). *Frederick Douglass*. New York: W. W. Norton.

Myers, P. C. (2008). *Frederick Douglass: Race and the rebirth of American liberalism*. Lawrence, KS: University Press of Kansas.

Oakes, J. (2007). *The radical and the Republican: Frederick Douglass, Abraham Lincoln, and the triumph of antislavery politics*. New York: W. W. Norton.

Credits

Fig. 4.1: Source: https://www.oercommons.org/courseware/module/15465/overview.

Fig. 4.2: Source: http://justpamphlet.com/flyer-pamphlet/pamphlets-leaflet-printing-history/.

Chapter 5

An Exposure of Racism

Harriet Beecher Stowe's *Uncle Tom's Cabin: Life Among the Lowly* (1852)

Introduction

Harriet Beecher Stowe was born into a deeply religious family in Litchfield, Connecticut, in 1811. Her father was an ordained minister who raised his children in an environment that enforced high moral values, love for education, and deep respect for all human life. Educated in a classical liberal arts and sciences tradition at the Hartford Women's Seminary, headed by her older sister, Catherine, Stowe studied a curriculum that was traditionally offered to only males at that time. Early in her own education, Stowe knew she wanted to become a professional writer. She would eventually author numerous newspaper articles, several children's books, as well as biographies and works on religion and family life.

After moving with her family to Ohio in 1832, Stowe witnessed several physical conflicts between freed African Americans and Irish immigrants and heard graphic proslavery sentiments expressed by many native-born Americans. She eventually married Calvin Stowe, who was a prominent abolitionist university professor, and both of them participated in helping escaped slaves navigate through the Ohio "stations" on the *Underground Railroad* to freedom. The Stowe family ultimately moved to Brunswick, Maine, where Calvin accepted a teaching position at Bowdoin College. While in Maine, Stowe suffered the death of her infant son, Samuel, and that tragedy, according

FIGURE 5.1 Portrait of Harriet Beecher Stowe.

to some historians, influenced her to write *Uncle Tom's Cabin* because she was then able to identify with the pain and loss that slaves experience all their lives. Others attribute the novel more to Stowe's resistance to the recently enacted federal legislation, *The Fugitive Slave Act* (1850), which required the return of all freed slaves to their rightful owners.

Uncle Tom's Cabin vaulted Stowe into national and international prominence in 1852 and remains one of the most readable, poignant, and explicit documentations of the horrors of human slavery. What makes Stowe all the more notable as an author is the fact that she exerted such a force on society at a time when women had little influence on social issues or public policy, especially on such a sensitive issue as slavery in the mid-19th century. Her goal in writing *Uncle Tom's Cabin* was to instruct Northerners about the appalling harmful effects of slavery on human beings and to enlighten Southerners as to the viciousness of their culture that allowed slavery to endure.

Predictably, Stowe's novel contributed to an expansion of the abolitionist movement all throughout the Northern states, whereas resistance was swift and widespread throughout the South. The literary response to *Uncle Tom's Cabin* by those who either actively supported slavery or were at least neutral on the issue is classified into a unique genre of texts known as either "anti-Tom literature" or, more generally, as "plantation literature," which had existed for decades before in the South. Within this niche are those works that portrayed a folksy, carefree atmosphere on the antebellum Southern plantations with contented slaves who accepted freely their lot in life. Other works dismissed *Uncle Tom's Cabin* as merely an irrelevant example of children's literature and some even aggressively discredited Stowe herself. Because she admittedly spent very little time in the South during her life, many critics charged that she was insensitive to the unique culture of the South and to its distinctive strengths and challenges.

One example of the plantation literature, *Planter's Northern Bride*, by Caroline Lee Hentz, is a direct, frontal attack on the abolitionist movement itself and was written, ironically, by a Northern white woman who was an acquaintance of Stowe's. Other novels in this plantation

FIGURE 5.2 Painting of Uncle Tom and Little Eva.

literature genre include: *The Swallow Barn*, by John Pendleton Kennedy; *In Ole Virginia*, by Thomas Nelson Page; *The Sword and the Distaff*, by William Gilmore Simms; *Little Eva, The Flower of the South*, by Philip Cozans; *"Uncle Tom's Cabin" Contrasted with Buckingham Hall, the Planter's Home*, by Robert Criswell; *Aunt Phillis's Cabin; Or, Southern Life as It Is*, by Mary Henderson Eastman; and *The Marbeau Cousins*, by Harry Stillwell Edwards.

Although *Uncle Tom's Cabin* pointedly delivered a robust call for social justice for African Americans, the book also enshrined a number of unfortunate racial stereotypes that continue even into modern times—images such as the always smiling, portly Mammy; the loyal Uncle Tom who suffers in silence and never complains about his white owners; the cute but senseless "pickaninny" children; or the Simon Legree character whose very name engenders the picture of avarice, cruelty, and evil. The notorious "N-word" is also liberally applied whenever the slaves are referenced in general terms, and when slaves are addressed directly, it is always with their first names, unlike the white characters who are referred to as Mr., Mrs., and Miss.

Further indication that slavery was such a critical issue throughout American society, especially throughout the Northern states, was the use of popular literature to display how this devastating policy affected both slaves and non-slaves. Indeed, *Uncle Tom's Cabin* is viewed by many historians as one of the most powerful and influential literary works that did positively influence social policy in America—and perhaps was even an indirect spark that led to the Civil War a decade later. This fictional narrative was not just a condemnation of slavery and an espousal of the abolitionist movement; it was also a portrait that championed the power of Christianity, the ultimate goodness of people, and the frustrating ineptitude of law as a moral guide for society.

+ For further information on Harriet Beecher Stowe and an interactive tour of the Harriet Beecher Stowe Center in Hartford, Connecticut, see https://www.harrietbeecherstowecenter.org.

Internet Sources for the Content of This Introduction Include:

http://www.nytimes.com/learning/general/onthisday/bday/0614.html
http://www.historynet.com/harriet-beecher-stowe
http://utc.iath.virginia.edu/interpret/exhibits/hedrick/hedrick.html
http://www.history.com/topics/harriet-beecher-stowe
http://www.nytimes.com/learning/general/onthisday/bday/0614.html
https://en.wikipedia.org/wiki/harriet_beecher_stowe
https://en.wikipedia.org/wiki/uncle_tom%27s_cabin

Linkage to Social Welfare History (1850–1875)

Social welfare historical events for this time period include the following:

+ The Reverend Charles Loring Brace, founder of the Children's Aid Society in New York City, begins sending seemingly-abandoned street children westward to farm families in

what is now the Midwest. This practice is commonly known as sending "orphan trains" and is, technically, a precursor to modern foster care and adoption services (1852).
- The Know-Nothing Party (officially the Order of the Star-Spangled Banner), a violent, nativist, anti-immigrant, anti-Roman Catholic, and racist organization, holds its annual convention in New York City (1854).
- The federal government establishes the Government Hospital for the Insane (presently known as St. Elizabeth's Hospital in Washington, DC), which represents the first public federal institution opened for mental health purposes (1855).
- In Congress, South Carolina Congressional Representative Preston Brooks ruthlessly beats Massachusetts Senator Charles Sumner with his walking stick after Sumner's speech against slavery (1856).
- In Paris, Louis Pasteur discovers airborne bacteria as the cause of infections (1856).
- The U.S. Supreme Court issues the *Dred Scott Decision*, declaring that no African American descended from slaves has a right to citizenship (1857). This decision was effectively invalidated by the passage the *13th* and *14th Amendments* to the *United States Constitution* a few years later, after the Civil War.
- The Young Women's Christian Association (YWCA) opens its first boarding house for single women in New York City (1858).
- Radical abolitionist John Brown is hanged in Charleston, West Virginia, for murder, treason, and inciting insurrection after his attack on a federal armory in Harpers Ferry, West Virginia (1859).
- South Carolina secedes from the Union on the issue of slavery, provoking other states to form a Confederacy of border and Southern states (1860).
- Dorothea Dix, the noted mental health reformer, is appointed as the superintendent of the female nurses for the Union Army (1861).
- Ohio passes the first state law that requires the removal of children from all county poorhouses and their placement in more suitable accommodations (1861).
- President Abraham Lincoln issues the *Emancipation Proclamation*, granting freedom to all slaves in all the Confederate states (1863).
- Massachusetts formally organizes the first two African American armed units, the Massachusetts 54th and 55th regiments, to participate in the Civil War. The units were segregated by race from other white units and led by white officers (1863).
- New York City experiences bloody antidraft riots implemented mostly by poor Irish immigrants who were angered because wealthy young men were able to purchase their exemptions from military service. In the melee, African American neighborhoods are looted and burned and an orphanage for African American children is destroyed (1863).
- Austrian monk and botanist Gregor Mendel discovers specific genetic laws governing the inheritance of human characteristics (1865).
- The United States War Department launches the Freedmen's Bureau to support freed slaves with financial assistance, jobs, education, relocation services, family reunification services, and legal benefits (1865).

- The *13th Amendment* to the *United States Constitution* is enacted, formally abolishing slavery throughout the nation (1865).
- A new secret society named the Ku Klux Klan is formed in Pulaski, Tennessee, by former Confederate soldiers to terrorize freed slaves. This organization quickly spreads throughout many Southern states (1865).
- With the Civil War over, the United States Army turns its attention to the growing "Indian problem" by initiating the building of a string of military forts from North and South Dakota down to the Texas border. These military establishments are poised to be the first line of defense for settlers against the resident Native American tribes, most of whom resist the government's expanding appropriation of their lands (1866).
- The United States Congress passes the *Reconstruction Act*, which appoints military governors over regions throughout the former Confederate states. These governors possess full authority over local voter eligibility rules, can remove local officials if necessary, and can impose martial law during any acts of resistance or terrorism (1867).
- The federal government establishes the United States Department of Education (1867).
- In London, Karl Marx publishes *Das Kapital*, predicting the self-destruction of capitalism and the rise of a government of the proletariat (1867).
- Following a period of ratification, the *14th Amendment* to the *United States Constitution* is passed, declaring that all freed slaves have the right to vote in national and local elections. Many women are unhappy with the wording of this amendment because it still excludes women from the right to vote (1868).
- Noted Progressive leaders Elizabeth Cady Stanton and Susan B. Anthony launch a new journal, *Revolution*, that advocates for universal suffrage and other women's rights (1868).
- The belligerent racist group, the Ku Klux Klan, publishes its *Organization and Principles of the Ku Klux Klan* (1868).
- The United States Congress approves the *15th Amendment to the United States Constitution*, which, in effect, orders all states to allow African American men the right to vote and never prohibit anyone to vote based on race, color, and previous servitude (1869). However, through the use of devices such as poll takes, literary tests, physical inaccessibility to polling places, and intimidation, African Americans do not fully gain the right to vote until the passage of the *Voting Rights Act* of 1965.
- A new secret organization, the *Noble Order of the Knights of Labor*, is formed to champion workers' rights in any dispute with management, therein establishing the first trade union movement (1869).
- Anthony and Stanton inaugurate the National Woman Suffrage Association, whose mission is to advocate for voting rights for all women (1869).
- A hostile United States Congress refuses to reauthorize the Freedmen's Bureau, and it is abruptly abolished (1872).

- Dr. Stephen Smith founds the American Public Health Association (1872).
- Reverend Brace publishes *The Dangerous Classes of New York and Twenty Years' Work Among Them* (1872).
- The Women's Christian Temperance Union (WCTU) is instituted in Cleveland, Ohio (1874).
- The New York Society for the Prevention of Cruelty to Children is inaugurated in New York City (1875).

Note: For a more reflective and functional use of this list of contemporary social welfare historical events, see Question #5 under the **Questions for Further Research and Discussion** section (below).

Sources:
Daniel, C. (1989). *Chronicle of America*. Mt. Kisco, NY: Chronicle Publications.
Mercer, D. (2000). *Millennium year by year*. New York: Dorling Kindersley Publications. Retrieved from https://socialwelfare.library.vcu.edu/events/1851-1900/

Primary Text Material

Uncle Tom's Cabin

The following excerpt from *Uncle Tom's Cabin* contains a short dialogue between Mr. Shelby, Tom's owner, and Shelby's friend, Mr. Haley, during which Haley expresses an interest in buying some of Shelby's slaves. Note, especially, their belief that slaves can be easily bought, sold, and traded as if they were mere animal livestock.

". . . *What on earth can you want with the child?*" said Shelby.

"*Why, I've got a friend that's going into this yer branch of the business—wants to buy up handsome boys to raise for the market. Fancy articles entirely—sell for waiters, and so on, to rich 'uns, that can pay for handsome 'uns. It sets off one of yer great places—a real handsome boy to open door, wait, and tend. They fetch a good sum; and this little devil is such a comical, musical concern, he's just the article!*'

"*I would rather not sell him,*" said Mr. Shelby, thoughtfully; "*the fact is, sir, I'm a humane man, and I hate to take the boy from his mother, sir.*"

"*O, you do?—La! yes—something of that ar natur. I understand, perfectly. It is mighty onpleasant getting on with women, sometimes, I al'ays hates these yer screechin,' screamin' times. They are mighty onpleasant; but, as I manages business, I generally avoids 'em, sir. Now, what if you get the girl off for a day, or a week, or so; then the thing's done quietly,—all over before she comes home. Your wife might get her some ear-rings or a new gown, or some such truck, to make up with her.*"

"*I'm afraid not.*"

> *"Lor bless ye, yes! These critters ain't like white folks, you know; they gets over things, only manage right. Now, they say,"* said Haley, assuming a candid and confidential air, *"that this kind o' trade is hardening to the feelings; but I never found it so. Fact is, I never could do things up the way some fellers manage the business. I've seen 'em as would pull a woman's child out of her arms, and set him up to sell, and she screechin' like mad all the time;—very bad policy—damages the article—makes 'em quite unfit for service sometimes. I knew a real handsome gal once, in Orleans, as was entirely ruined by this sort o' handling. The fellow that was trading for her didn't want her baby; and she was one of your real high sort, when her blood was up. I tell you, she squeezed up her child in her arms, and talked, and went on real awful. It kinder makes my blood run cold to think of 't; and when they carried off the child, and locked her up, she jest [. . .] went ravin' mad, and died in a week. Clear waste, sir, of a thousand dollars, just for want of management,—there's where 't is. It's always best to do the humane thing, sir; that's been my experience."* And the trader leaned back in his chair, and folded his arm, with an air of virtuous decision, apparently considering himself a second Wilberforce. . . ."
>
> [Note: William Wilberforce was an early 19th-century English politician who led the movement to abolish the slave trade throughout the British Empire, which finally occurred three days before his death in 1833.]
>
> Excerpt from: Stowe, H. B. (1852). *Uncle Tom's cabin: Life among the lowly.* Boston: John P. Jewitt. iBook's version.
>
> Source and full text available at http://www.gutenberg.org/ebooks/203?msg=welcome_stranger#2HCH0045.

Timeline of General Events in History, the Humanities, and Science During This Period (1850–1875)

These general historical events may help you understand more clearly the overall historical context during which the primary document was created.

- The notable phrase, "Go West, young man, go West," coined by Indiana newspaper editor John L. Soule, captures many people's imagination and helps the westward expansion of the nation (1851).
- Isaac Singer invents the modern sewing machine (1851).
- Illinois Senate candidates Abraham Lincoln and Stephen Douglas engage in a pre-election debate that will become known as the *Lincoln–Douglas Debates*, during which Lincoln delivers his celebrated antislavery appraisal that "a house divided against itself cannot stand" (1858).

- In London, Charles Darwin publishes *The Origin of the Species*, which overturns current theory by proclaiming the human race evolved from a common ancestor (1859).
- Abraham Lincoln is elected president of the United States (1860).
- The Pony Express begins, eventually linking the East Coast with the West Coast with mail delivery in approximately 10 days (1860).
- Fort Sumter, in Charleston, South Carolina, is bombarded and captured by Confederate troops, which leads to the outbreak of the Civil War (1861).
- Victor Hugo publishes *Les Misérables* in Paris (1862).
- President Lincoln delivers his legendary *Gettysburg Address* at a Pennsylvania battlefield, in which he implores "that the nation shall, under God, have a new birth of freedom, and that the government of the people, by the people, and for the people, shall not perish from the earth" (1863).
- Lewis Carroll, a pseudonym for Charles Dodgson, publishes *Alice in Wonderland* (1865).
- The Civil War ends with the surrender of General Robert E. Lee to General Ulysses S. Grant at the Appomattox, Virginia, courthouse, leaving the country profoundly divided over the issue of slavery (1865).
- President Abraham Lincoln is assassinated by John Wilkes Booth at Ford's Theatre in Washington, DC (1865).
- Alexander Gardner publishes a compilation of photographs, in austere black and white, chronicling the many of the horrors of the Civil War in his book, *Gardner's Photographic Sketch Book of the War* (1866). A selection of these prints and further information about Gardner can be accessed at http://rmc.library.cornell.edu/7milVol/images.html.
- After a multiyear support campaign, Secretary of State William Seward convinces the United States Congress to authorize the purchase of Alaska from Russia (1867).
- Swedish chemical engineer Alfred Nobel invents a safe alternative to gun powder called dynamite (1867).
- Leo Tolstoy publishes *War and Peace* in St. Petersburg, Russia (1867).
- The first transcontinental railroad from New York to San Francisco is completed when the rails are joined at Promontory Point, Utah (1869).
- Work is completed on the Suez Canal in Egypt, connecting the Mediterranean Sea with the Red Sea (1869).
- Victor Emmanuel II enters Rome and declares it to be the new capital of a united Italy (1870).
- Giuseppe Verdi presents his opera, *Aida*, for the first time at the Italian theatre in Cairo, Egypt (1871).
- Adventure writer Jules Verne publishes *Around the World in 80 Days* in Paris (1872).
- The first American national park, Yellowstone National Park, is created in California (1879).

Sources:

Daniel, C. (1989). *Chronicle of America*. Mt. Kisco, NY: Chronicle Publications.
Events of the 1800s. Retrieved from https://en.wikipedia.org/wiki/19th_century
Mercer, D. (2000). *Millennium year by year*. New York: Dorling Kindersley Publications.

Questions for Further Research and Discussion

1. Study closely the fictional characters, both African American and white, portrayed in *Uncle Tom's Cabin* and discuss whether these images have endured as stereotypes of individual personalities within both communities. Cite examples and specific scene references. Do you believe that the negative images/stereotypes in *Uncle Tom's Cabin* have affected in any manner the structures or processes involved in the modern social welfare system in the United States? If yes, how so?
2. After reading further sections of *Uncle Tom's Cabin*, do you gain a sense of what it feels like, day to day, to be enslaved by some absolute owner? Describe those sensations as they would affect you personally.
3. Following further research, catalog the intense reactions, both positive and negative, throughout both the North and the South following the publication of *Uncle Tom's Cabin*.
4. Study one or two examples of the plantation literature that arose in response to *Uncle Tom's Cabin*, and discuss the counterarguments presented that challenged Harriet Beecher Stowe's main arguments against slavery.
5. Select three events appearing under the **Linkage to Social Welfare** section (above), conduct further Internet research regarding them, then conclude whether you believe there exists any plausible relationship between *Uncle Tom's Cabin* and the events you have chosen. Use the analytical model presented in Appendix 1 of this book, or develop your own analytical model, to draw these conclusions.
6. Select one book from the **Additional Selected References** list at the end of this chapter. Briefly read through it, then summarize the main points contained in the book. Identify your own personal reaction to this book.

Additional Selected References

Ammons, E. (Ed.). (2007). *Harriet Beecher Stowe's Uncle Tom's cabin: A casebook*. New York: Oxford University Press.
Donovan, J. (1991). *Uncle Tom's cabin: Evil, affliction, and redemptive love*. Boston: Twayne.
Gardner, A. (1865–1866). *Gardner's photographic sketch book of the war*. Washington, DC: Philp & Solomons.
Gates, H. L., & Robbins, H. (Eds.). (2006). *The annotated Uncle Tom's cabin*. New York: W. W. Norton.

Griesing, A. (2013). *Harriet Beecher Stowe's "Uncle Tom's cabin": The creation and influence of a masterpiece.* Hamburg: Anchor Academic Publishing.

Hochman, B. (2011). *"Uncle Tom's cabin" and the reading revolution.* Amherst: University of Massachusetts Press.

Jordan-Lake, J. (2005). *Whitewashing "Uncle Tom's cabin": Nineteenth-century women novelists respond to Stowe.* Nashville, TN: Vanderbilt University Press.

Morgan, J. (2007). *"Uncle Tom's cabin" as visual culture.* Columbia, MO: University of Missouri Press.

Rosenthal, D. J. (2003). *Routledge literary sourcebook on Harriet Beecher Stowe's "Uncle Tom's cabin."* Florence, KY: Routledge/Taylor & Francis Group.

Weinstein, C. (2004). *The Cambridge companion to Harriet Beecher Stowe.* Cambridge: Cambridge University Press.

Credits

Fig. 5.1: Source: https://commons.wikimedia.org/wiki/File:Harriet_Beecher_Stowe_by_Francis_Holl.JPG.

Fig. 5.2: Source: https://commons.wikimedia.org/wiki/File%3AEdwin_Longsden_Long_-_Uncle_Tom_and_Little_Eva.JPG.

Chapter 6

Setback for Equality

The Dred Scott Decision (Scott v. Sandford) (1857)

Introduction

By the middle of the 19th century, the institution of slavery was under assault, especially from individuals and groups in the Northeast and in the those newly admitted midwestern states and territories that declared themselves to be "free" and intentionally beyond the reaches of legal enslavement. Inevitably, there arose situations in which the "free" and "slave" areas of the United States would clash on the issue of jurisdiction over court decisions involving slaves. Although it had generally been possible to buy oneself out of slavery or to be freed out of generosity by one's owners, it had never been tested in the courts whether a slave possessed any rights under the *United States Constitution*. This question became more controversial if a slave owner moved with his slaves to a free state or territory where slavery was prohibited by local law. One person in slavery, Dred Scott, served as the catalyst for that controversy to begin and to be settled, at least for a time, until the Civil War raised the issue once more.

Born into slavery sometime during the late 1790s, Scott initially was part of the Alabama plantation owned by Peter Blow. When the Blow family moved to St. Louis, Missouri, Scott was sold to a United States Army medical officer, Dr. John Emerson, sometime in the early 1830s. At that time, both Alabama and Missouri were considered slave states. Over the next nine years, Scott went with Dr. Emerson as he was reassigned to several free states and territories—the state of Illinois and the territory of Wyoming before it became a state. While in the Wyoming territory, Scott married a fellow slave, Harriet Robinson.

The Army eventually transferred Dr. Emerson back to Missouri, and when he died, Emerson's wife placed Scott out with several local families as a slave. Helped financially by some abolitionist friends, Scott first sought to buy his, his wife's, and their two daughters' freedom from Mrs. Emerson, but she refused the offer. In 1847, Scott then filed a petition for their freedom in the St. Louis

FIGURE 6.1 Photograph of Dred Scott taken around the time of his court case.

Circuit Court. He argued that because he had lived for nine years as a free man, it would be wrong to impose slave status on him once again. The discussion in court centered around two conflicting rights: the right to be a free under the *United States Constitution* versus the right that owners possess over their legally purchased property. This first trial ended on a legal technicality, and the case was retried a second time in 1850 with a decision to free the Scotts on the principle of "once free, always free." Mrs. Emerson, intending to protect her property rights, appealed to the Missouri Supreme Court, which reversed the lower court decision in 1852. That decision underscored the fact that Missouri was a slave state and, furthermore, that slaves were legally considered property. A further complicating factor in the 1850s was the incendiary nature of the topic of slavery and the growing emergence of the abolitionist movement across the United States.

As their next tactic, the Scotts petitioned the United States Supreme Court to overturn the Missouri Supreme Court decision. Technically, the Supreme Court case is identified as *Scott v. Sandford*, though it is known more colloquially as simply the *Dred Scott Decision*. Sandford is Mrs. Emerson's brother, John Sandford, in whose name the Supreme Court case was filed because he was legally in control of the Emerson estate at the time.

The Scotts lost on a 7–2 decision in 1857. The Supreme Court declared that no one born a slave could ever be a citizen, no matter where they lived, because they were merely "property" and, therefore, could never have any standing to sue in a federal court. It should be noted that the Chief Justice of the United States Supreme Court, Roger Taney, was a former Maryland slave owner and the majority of Supreme Court justices hearing the case were from proslavery states. To further illustrate the vileness and inhumanity of the decision, Chief Judge Taney, in the text of the opinion, accentuated his belief that African slaves were never intended by the Founding Fathers to be included in the *United States Declaration of Independence* because they were not "people," only "property." There was also an insinuation in the opinion that slavery itself was constitutionally protected.

Once the *Dred Scott Decision* was publicized, there surged widespread denunciation in the North and joyful acceptance across the South. Most historians agree that the *Dred Scott Decision* influenced the growth of the antislavery Republican Party, contributed to the election of Abraham Lincoln as president of the United States, and undoubtedly hastened the march toward the Civil War.

Ironically, Mrs. Emerson later married a famous abolitionist, eventually changed her attitude toward slavery, and transferred the Scotts back to Scott's original owners, the Blow family, who immediately freed them from their servitude. Scott himself was thus able to live as a free man for the last 18 months of his life before dying of tuberculosis in 1858.

At this time, Abraham Lincoln was an emerging leader in the Republican Party, and he used the *Dred Scott Decision* as a focal point with his opponent during the celebrated *Lincoln–Douglas Debates* in 1858. Today, the *Dred Scott Decision* is universally judged to be one of the worst Supreme Court Decisions in American history. It was essentially annulled with the passage of the *14th Amendment* to the *Constitution of the United States* in 1868, which clarified and expanded citizenship to include all former male slaves and their male descendants.

With the Civil War still a number of years away, the United States found itself split by two geographic realities: the slave states throughout the South and the free states in the North, Midwest, and West. Once the Supreme Court rendered its historic *Dred Scott Decision*, the most serious effect was to open up the entire country—in both slave and free states—to an intrinsic support for slavery. Thus, for a time after the *Dred Scott Decision*, any escaped slave living in a free state could no longer feel safe from capture and return because slaves, no matter where they resided, no longer had rights under the law as did non-slaves. This change impacted not just the Southern states but also the entire nation.

Society was further divided by the disparate ideologies of the two political parties, with most members of the Democratic Party adamantly proslavery and most members of the Republican Party antislavery. Our nation existed, at this point in its short history, as a "house divided," a biblical phrase originally appearing in the *New Testament* in Mark 3:24 and repeated by Senate candidate Abraham Lincoln in 1858 during the Republican Convention in Illinois.

Although effectively repealed 12 years later with the passage *14th Amendment*, this Supreme Court decision tragically still evokes bitter memories within the African American community today and remains an embarrassment to the historical legacy of the United States Supreme Court.

- For further information on the *Dred Scott Decision*, see the website of the Old Courthouse of the St. Louis First Circuit, managed today by the National Parks Service, where the Scotts initially sued for their freedom, available at https://www.nps.gov/jeff/planyourvisit/dredscott.htm.
- See also the *Dred Scott Case Collection* of primary and secondary materials maintained by Washington University in St. Louis at http://digital.wustl.edu/dredscott/.

Internet Sources for the Content of This Introduction Include:

https://www.pbs.org/wgbh/aia/part4/4p2932.html
http://www.history.com/topics/black-history/dred-scott-case
https://www.oyez.org/cases/1850-1900/60us393
https://www.britannica.com/event/dred-scott-decision
http://www.historynet.com/dred-scott
https://en.wikipedia.org/wiki/dred_scott_v._sandford
https://web.archive.org/web/20070930201342/http://www.historynet.com/magazines/civil_war_times/3037746.html

Linkage to Social Welfare History (1850–1875)

Social welfare historical events for this time period include the following:

- The Reverend Charles Loring Brace, founder of the Children's Aid Society in New York City, begins sending seemingly-abandoned street children westward to farm families in what is now the Midwest. This practice is commonly known as sending "orphan trains" and is, technically, a precursor to modern foster care and adoption services (1852).
- Harriet Beecher Stowe publishes *Uncle Tom's Cabin: Life Among the Lowly* as an innovative confrontation to widespread slavery in the South (1852).
- The Know-Nothing Party (officially the Order of the Star-Spangled Banner), a violent, nativist, anti-immigrant, anti-Roman Catholic, and racist organization, holds its annual convention in New York City (1854).
- The federal government establishes the Government Hospital for the Insane (presently known as St. Elizabeth's Hospital in Washington, DC), which represents the first public federal institution opened for mental health purposes (1855).
- In Congress, South Carolina Congressional Representative Preston Brooks ruthlessly beats Massachusetts Senator Charles Sumner with his walking stick after Sumner's speech against slavery (1856).
- In Paris, Louis Pasteur discovers airborne bacteria as the cause of infections (1856).
- The Young Women's Christian Association (YWCA) opens its first boarding house for single women in New York City (1858).
- Radical abolitionist John Brown is hanged in Charleston, West Virginia, for murder, treason, and inciting insurrection after his attack on a federal armory in Harpers Ferry, West Virginia (1859).
- South Carolina secedes from the Union on the issue of slavery, provoking other states to form a Confederacy of border and Southern states (1860).
- Dorothea Dix, the noted mental health reformer, is appointed as the superintendent of the female nurses for the Union Army (1861).
- Ohio passes the first state law that requires the removal of children from all county poorhouses and their placement in more suitable accommodations (1861).
- President Abraham Lincoln issues the *Emancipation Proclamation*, granting freedom to all slaves in all the Confederate states (1863).
- Massachusetts formally organizes the first two African American armed units, the Massachusetts 54th and 55th regiments, to participate in the Civil War. The units were segregated by race from other white units and led by white officers (1863).
- New York City experiences bloody antidraft riots implemented mostly by poor Irish immigrants who were angered because wealthy young men were able to purchase their exemptions from military service. In the melee, African American neighborhoods are looted and burned and an orphanage for African American children is destroyed (1863).

- Austrian monk and botanist Gregor Mendel discovers specific genetic laws governing the inheritance of human characteristics (1865).
- The United States War Department launches the Freedmen's Bureau to support freed slaves with financial assistance, jobs, education, relocation services, family reunification services, and legal benefits (1865).
- The *13th Amendment* to the *United States Constitution* is enacted, formally abolishing slavery throughout the nation (1865).
- A new secret society named the Ku Klux Klan is formed in Pulaski, Tennessee, by former Confederate soldiers to terrorize freed slaves. This organization quickly spreads throughout many Southern states (1865).
- With the Civil War over, the United States Army turns its attention to the growing "Indian problem" by initiating the building of a string of military forts from North and South Dakota down to the Texas border. These military establishments are poised to be the first line of defense for settlers against the resident Native American tribes, most of whom resist the government's expanding appropriation of their lands (1866).
- The United States Congress passes the *Reconstruction Act*, which appoints military governors over regions throughout the former Confederate states. These governors possess full authority over local voter eligibility rules, can remove local officials if necessary, and can impose martial law during any acts of resistance or terrorism (1867).
- The federal government establishes the United States Department of Education (1867).
- In London, Karl Marx publishes *Das Kapital*, predicting the self-destruction of capitalism and the rise of a government of the proletariat (1867).
- Following a period of ratification, the *14th Amendment* to the *United States Constitution* is passed, declaring that all freed slaves have the right to vote in national and local elections. Many women are unhappy with the wording of this amendment because it still excludes women from the right to vote (1868).
- Noted Progressive leaders Elizabeth Cady Stanton and Susan B. Anthony launch a new journal, *Revolution*, that advocates for universal suffrage and other women's rights (1868).
- The belligerent racist group, the Ku Klux Klan, publishes its *Organization and Principles of the Ku Klux Klan* (1868).
- The United States Congress approves the *15th Amendment to the United States Constitution*, which, in effect, orders all states to allow African American men the right to vote and never prohibit anyone to vote based on race, color, and previous servitude (1869). However, through the use of devices such as poll takes, literary tests, physical inaccessibility to polling places, and intimidation, African Americans do not fully gain the right to vote until the passage of the *Voting Rights Act* of 1965.
- A new secret organization, the *Noble Order of the Knights of Labor*, is formed to champion workers' rights in any dispute with management, therein establishing the first trade union movement (1869).

- Anthony and Stanton inaugurate the National Woman Suffrage Association, whose mission is to advocate for voting rights for all women (1869).
- A hostile United States Congress refuses to reauthorize the Freedmen's Bureau, and it is abruptly abolished (1872).
- Dr. Stephen Smith founds the American Public Health Association (1872).
- Reverend Brace publishes *The Dangerous Classes of New York and Twenty Years' Work Among Them* (1872).
- The Women's Christian Temperance Union (WCTU) is instituted in Cleveland, Ohio (1874).
- The New York Society for the Prevention of Cruelty to Children is inaugurated in New York City (1875).

Note: For a more reflective and functional use of this list of contemporary social welfare historical events, see Question #5 under the **Questions for Further Research and Discussion** section (below).

Sources:

Daniel, C. (1989). *Chronicle of America*. Mt. Kisco, NY: Chronicle Publications.

Mercer, D. (2000). *Millennium year by year*. New York: Dorling Kindersley Publications.

Social welfare developments 1850–1875. (2011). Retrieved from https://socialwelfare.library.vcu.edu/events/1851-1900/

Primary Text Material

Scott v. Sandford, 60 U.S. 393 (1856)

"[. . .]

4. A free negro of the African race, whose ancestors were brought to this country and sold as slaves, is not a "citizen" within the meaning of the Constitution of the United States.

5. When the Constitution was adopted, they were not regarded in any of the States as members of the community which constituted the State, and were not numbered among its "people or citizens." Consequently, the special rights and immunities guaranteed to citizens do not apply to them. And not being "citizens" within the meaning of the Constitution, they are not entitled to sue in that character in a court of the United States, and the Circuit Court has not jurisdiction in such a suit.

6. The only two clauses in the Constitution which point to this race treat them as persons whom it was morally lawfully to deal in as articles of property and to hold as slaves.

> 7. Since the adoption of the Constitution of the United States, no State can by any subsequent law make a foreigner or any other description of persons citizens of the United States, nor entitle them to the rights and privileges secured to citizens by that instrument. . . ."
>
> Source and full text available at https://supreme.justia.com/cases/federal/us/60/393/.
>
> See also http://www.pbs.org/wgbh/aia/part4/4h2933.html.
>
> For additional primary documentary material, see also http://www.loc.gov/rr/program/bib/ourdocs/DredScott.html.

Timeline of General Events in History, the Humanities and Science During This Period (1850–1875)

These general historical events may help you understand more clearly the overall historical context during which the primary document was created.

- The notable phrase, "Go West, young man, go West," coined by Indiana newspaper editor John L. Soule, captures many people's imagination and helps the westward expansion of the nation (1851).
- Isaac Singer invents the modern sewing machine (1851).
- Illinois Senate candidates Abraham Lincoln and Stephen Douglas engage in a pre-election debate that will become known as the *Lincoln–Douglas Debates*, during which Lincoln delivers his celebrated antislavery appraisal that "a house divided against itself cannot stand" (1858).
- In London, Charles Darwin publishes *The Origin of the Species*, which overturns current theory by proclaiming the human race evolved from a common ancestor (1859).
- Abraham Lincoln is elected president of the United States (1860).
- The Pony Express begins, eventually linking the East Coast with the West Coast with mail delivery in approximately 10 days (1860).
- Fort Sumter, in Charleston, South Carolina, is bombarded and captured by Confederate troops, which leads to the outbreak of the Civil War (1861).
- Victor Hugo publishes *Les Misérables* in Paris (1862).
- President Lincoln delivers his legendary *Gettysburg Address* at a Pennsylvania battlefield, in which he implores "that the nation shall, under God, have a new birth of freedom, and that the government of the people, by the people, and for the people, shall not perish from the earth" (1863).
- Lewis Carroll, a pseudonym for Charles Dodgson, publishes *Alice in Wonderland* (1865).

- The Civil War ends with the surrender of General Robert E. Lee to General Ulysses S. Grant at the Appomattox, Virginia, courthouse, leaving the country profoundly divided over the issue of slavery (1865).
- President Abraham Lincoln is assassinated by John Wilkes Booth at Ford's Theatre in Washington, DC (1865).
- After a multiyear support campaign, Secretary of the Interior William Seward convinces the United States Congress to authorize the purchase of Alaska from Russia (1867).
- Alexander Gardner publishes a compilation of photographs, in austere black and white, chronicling the many of the horrors of the Civil War in his book, *Gardner's Photographic Sketch Book of the War* (1866). A selection of these prints and further information about Gardner can be accessed at http://rmc.library.cornell.edu/7milVol/images.html.
- After a multiyear support campaign, Secretary of State William Seward convinces the United States Congress to authorize the purchase of Alaska from Russia (1867).
- Swedish chemical engineer Alfred Nobel invents a safe alternative to gun powder called dynamite (1867).
- Leo Tolstoy publishes *War and Peace* in St. Petersburg, Russia (1867).
- The first transcontinental railroad from New York to San Francisco is completed when the rails are joined at Promontory Point, Utah (1869).
- Work is completed on the Suez Canal in Egypt, connecting the Mediterranean Sea with the Red Sea (1869).
- Victor Emmanuel II enters Rome and declares it to be the new capital of a united Italy (1870).
- Giuseppe Verdi presents his opera, *Aida*, for the first time at the Italian theatre in Cairo, Egypt (1871).
- Adventure writer Jules Verne publishes *Around the World in 80 Days* in Paris (1872).
- The first American national park, Yellowstone National Park, is created in California (1872).

Sources:

Daniel, C. (1989). *Chronicle of America*. Mt. Kisco, NY: Chronicle Publications.

Events of the 1800s. https://en.wikipedia.org/wiki/19th_century

Mercer, D. (2000). *Millennium year by year*. New York: Dorling Kindersley Publications.

Questions for Further Research and Discussion

1. Study the full text of *Scott v. Sandford*, and list the exact words and phrases used to describe slaves, slave owners, property owners, and the concept of slavery itself.

2. Conduct online research of newspaper articles and editorials published at the time of the *Dred Scott Decision*, and summarize the reactions to this contemporary Supreme Court decision. Were the historical reactions positive, negative, or neutral?
3. Study other United States Supreme Court decisions made between the years 1825 and 1875. Do you see any patterns in the judges' rulings during that period that might explain the particular outcome of the *Dred Scott Decision*?
4. Conduct an Internet search for the phrase *Dred Scott Decision*, and report on any recent (i.e., 20th and 21st century) references to this epic court decision. In what contexts were those later references made?
5. Select three events appearing under the **Linkage to Social Welfare** section (above), conduct further Internet research regarding them, then conclude whether you believe there exists any plausible relationship between the *Dred Scott Decision* and the events you have chosen. Use the analytical model presented in Appendix 1 of this book, or develop your own analytical model, to draw these conclusions.
6. Select one book from the **Additional Selected References** list at the end of this chapter. Briefly read through it, then summarize the main points contained in the book. Identify your own personal reaction to this book.

Additional Selected References

Cromwell, S. (2009). *Dred Scott v. Sandford: A slave's case for freedom and citizenship.* Minneapolis: Compass Point Books.

Ehrlich, W. (1979). *They have no rights: Dred Scott's struggle for freedom.* Westport, CT: Greenwood Press.

Fehenbacher, D. E. (1978). *The Dred Scott case: Its significance in American law and politics.* New York: Oxford University Press.

Fehrenbacher, D. E. (1981). *Slavery, law, and politics: The Dred Scott case in historical perspective.* New York: Oxford University Press.

Finkelman, P. (1997). *Dred Scott v. Sandford: A brief history with documents.* Boston: Bedford Books.

Konig, D. T., Finkelman, P., & Bracey, C.A. (Eds.). (2010). *The Dred Scott case: Historical and contemporary perspectives on ace and law.* Athens: Ohio University Press.

Maltz, E. M. (2007). *Dred Scott and the politics of slavery.* Lawrence, KS: University Press of Kansas.

McPherson, J. M. (1988). *Battle cry of freedom: The Civil War era.* New York: Oxford University Press.

Ratner, L. A., & Teeter, D. L. (2003). *Fanatics and fire-eaters: Newspapers and the coming of the Civil War.* Urbana, IL: University of Illinois Press.

Schweikart, L. (2010). *Seven events that made America America: And proved that the founding fathers were right all along.* New York: Sentinel.

Swain, G. (2004). *Dred and Harriet Scott: A family's struggle for freedom*. Saint Paul, MN: Borealis Books.

Tushnet, M. (2008). *I dissent: Great opposing opinions in landmark Supreme Court cases*. Boston: Beacon Press.

Urofsky, M. I. (2012). *Supreme decisions: Great constitutional cases and their impact*. Boulder, CO: Westview Press.

Wilson, C. M. (1973). *The Dred Scott decision*. Philadelphia: Auerbach Publishers.

Credit

Fig. 6.1: Source: https://commons.wikimedia.org/wiki/File:Dred_Scott_photograph_(circa_1857).jpg.

Chapter 7

The Call for Freedom and Equality

The *Emancipation Proclamation* (1863)

Introduction

During the time some federal legislators were focusing on the initiation of public support for higher education, the Civil War erupted in full force. Between 1861 and 1863, the Union garrison at Fort Sumter, South Carolina, was attacked; the Battle of Bull Run, Virginia, was fought; the innovative ironclad warships, the *Monitor* and the *Merrimac*, battled to a draw off Hampton Roads, Virginia; and the bloodiest battle of the war at Antietam, Maryland, ended in a technical victory for the Union Army commanded by General George McClellan. Following this Union Army victory, President Lincoln issued a warning to the Confederate states that if they continued to rebel, then he would issue an *executive order* that would free all people enslaved throughout the nation. No encouraging response evolved from the Confederate leaders, so on January 1, 1863, President Lincoln released the *Emancipation Proclamation* in Washington, DC.

The border states of Delaware, Kentucky, Maryland, and Missouri, even though they allowed slavery to exist, were exempted from the *Emancipation Proclamation* because they were not, technically, in rebellion against the Union and had not formally seceded. Also exempted were areas in several Confederate states that had already been defeated and occupied by the Union Army, as well as the areas in Virginia that were designated as West Virginia. The Confederate states that were directly and immediately affected included: Alabama, Arkansas, Florida, Georgia, most of Louisiana, North Carolina, South Carolina, and Texas.

Although the *Emancipation Proclamation* did change the official status from "enslaved" to "free" for approximately 3 million individuals, it did not legally abolish slavery as a societal institution. That progressive reality would have to await the passage of the *13th Amendment* to the *Constitution of the United States* two years later in 1865.

The foundational principle of the *Emancipation Proclamation* was not the inherent evil of slavery, as one might expect. Instead, it was based upon the fact that that the Union Army, as it advanced through the Confederate states, had the right to seize any property that was materially beneficial to the enemy—that is, the Confederate Army. As commander in chief of the Union Army, President Lincoln, in turn, had a right to formally acknowledge the existence of that wartime principle. Because the Confederate states considered slaves as mere "property," it was only logical, then, that they could be seized and their future determined solely by the Union Army. This was an ironic twist on the South's adherence to their slave-as-property judgment.

It was rumored that as a disincentive to freed slaves to join the Union Army, Confederate military officers threatened to outright kill any freed slave who was captured wearing a Union Army uniform. This speculation was apparently confirmed during the so-called *Fort Pillow Massacre* in 1864. This Tennessee military installation was being defended by a Union Army company consisting of 350 African American soldiers and 200 white soldiers. The Battle of Fort Pillow, approximately 45 miles north of Memphis, Tennessee, was a particularly savage affair and has continued to be controversial in historical accounts even to the present day. The Union garrison in the fort was overrun by a superior force of Confederate cavalry, and surviving Union witnesses attest to the charge that the Confederate victors purposely massacred most of the African American troops after the battle was won and a surrender had been communicated. Although numbers differ according to several accounts, it appears that approximately 300 Union soldiers perished after the surrender was announced, 80% of whom were African American.

FIGURE 7.1   Portrait of the first reading of the Emancipation Proclamation by President Lincoln.

Controversy still rages among Northern and Southern historians about some of the facts regarding this incident.

President Lincoln faced significant resistance both before and after the passage of his *executive order*. Individuals throughout the Northern states, surprisingly perhaps, opposed the movement to free the slaves for several reasons: First, the abolition of slavery was not included in the *Constitution of the United States*; second, once freed, too many African Americans would move to Northern states and compete unfairly for jobs and resources; and finally, there would exist a danger that freed slaves would retaliate against white communities by going on a rampage of illegal activity.

In retrospect, it may be hard to conceive that such an iconic statement opposing slavery, as the *Emancipation Proclamation* is, could be opposed. Indeed, it was disputed, both before and after its passage, throughout both the Union and the Confederate states.

There were several conflicting forces at work during this period that showed how complex the issue of slavery was in the United States. Some opposed President Lincoln because they were pacifists against all wars; others feared social disintegration due to the sudden shock to the Southern economic and social systems; still others worried about jobs and resources in the face of a predicted migration of freed slaves into Northern states. In carefully worded terms that alluded to some of these contrary motives, the Illinois State Legislature issued a formal statement in opposition to the *Emancipation Proclamation* shortly after its announcement in 1863. They declared that it would lead to widespread insurrection and judged it to be an "uneffaceable (sic) disgrace to the American people."

[Full text of the Illinois state legislators' formal statement available at http://edale1.home.mindspring.com/Resolution%20of%20the%20Illinois%20Legislature%20in%20Opposition%20to%20the%20Emancipation%20Proclamation.htm.]

During these early years of the Civil War, President Lincoln continued his campaign against the existence of slavery throughout the Confederacy and, spurred by recent Union victories on the battlefield, was emboldened to announce the *Emancipation Proclamation* in January 1863. The fact that this intense focus on dismantling slavery occurred at the end of the first two years of hostilities serves to highlight the historical assumption that it was indeed slavery, and not simply states' rights, that was the major cause underlying the Civil War. A strong and vocal abolitionist movement in the North, as well as a progressive antislavery House of Representatives, influenced President Lincoln to, in effect, disregard the earlier *Dred Scott Decision* and declare that slaves were indeed "persons" and worthy of being freed from involuntary servitude. For a more complete timeline and details regarding Civil War events during this period, see http://memory.loc.gov/ammem/cwphtml/tl1861.html.

Given the social context of this period, problems of racism and a pervasive white ethnocentrism prevailed throughout the United States. In addition to overt hostility toward African Americans and Native Americans, many in society also subjugated immigrant Mexicans and Chinese in punitive ways, even as these groups vividly helped to build the infrastructure of an expanding nation. Furthermore, it would be overly optimistic to presume that all people living in the Northern states were solidly antislavery in their beliefs

FIGURE 7.2   Photo of a celebration of the Emancipation Proclamation in Massachusetts.

and/or actions. Many of those who formally opposed slavery as an institution because of its fundamental premise of forced servitude still assumed that slaves would function at a lower status in society upon gaining their freedom. In this view, African Americans, as well as any other non-white minority group, should be afforded basic Christian charity and fellowship, but because they lacked education, functional work, and necessary personality traits, they should not be accorded full-scale citizenship right away. Indeed, as history will show, it took almost a century longer for the process of full integration of African Americans to even begin—with the desegregation of the military by President Harry Truman in 1948, followed shortly by the desegregation of public education in *Brown vs. Board of Education* in 1954 and the broader *Civil Rights Movement* of the 1960s. Thus, it should not come as a surprise that President Lincoln met with some formal resistance to his *Emancipation Proclamation* in some Northern state legislatures.

Internet Sources for the Content of This Introduction Include:
https://www.pbs.org/wgbh/aia/part4/4h1549.html
http://www.history.com/topics/american-civil-war/emancipation-proclamation
https://www.archives.gov/exhibits/featured-documents/emancipation-proclamation
https://www.civilwar.org/learn/articles/10-facts-emancipation-proclamation
http://www.ushistory.org/us/34a.asp

http://www.american-historama.org/1860-1865-civil-war-era/emancipation-proclamation.htm
https://www.britannica.com/event/emancipation-proclamation
http://www.encyclopedia.com/history/united-states-and-canada/us-history/emancipation-proclamation
https://en.wikipedia.org/wiki/emancipation_proclamation

Linkage to Social Welfare History (1850–1875)

Social welfare historical events for this time period include the following:

- The Reverend Charles Loring Brace, founder of the Children's Aid Society in New York City, begins sending seemingly-abandoned street children westward to farm families in what is now the Midwest. This practice is commonly known as sending "orphan trains" and is, technically, a precursor to modern foster care and adoption services (1852).
- Harriet Beecher Stowe publishes *Uncle Tom's Cabin: Life Among the Lowly* as an innovative confrontation to widespread slavery in the South (1852).
- The Know-Nothing Party (officially the Order of the Star-Spangled Banner), a violent, nativist, anti-immigrant, anti-Roman Catholic, and racist organization, holds its annual convention in New York City (1854).
- The federal government establishes the Government Hospital for the Insane (presently known as St. Elizabeth's Hospital in Washington, DC), which represents the first public federal institution opened for mental health purposes (1855).
- In Congress, South Carolina Congressional Representative Preston Brooks ruthlessly beats Massachusetts Senator Charles Sumner with his walking stick after Sumner's speech against slavery (1856).
- In Paris, Louis Pasteur discovers airborne bacteria as the cause of infections (1856).
- The U.S. Supreme Court issues the *Dred Scott Decision*, declaring that no African American descended from slaves has a right to citizenship (1857). This decision was effectively invalidated by the passage the *13th* and *14th Amendments* to the *United States Constitution* a few years later, after the Civil War.
- The Young Women's Christian Association (YWCA) opens its first boarding house for single women in New York City (1858).
- Radical abolitionist John Brown is hanged in Charleston, West Virginia, for murder, treason, and inciting insurrection after his attack on a federal armory in Harpers Ferry, West Virginia (1859).
- South Carolina secedes from the Union on the issue of slavery, provoking other states to form a Confederacy of border and Southern states (1860).
- Dorothea Dix, the noted mental health reformer, is appointed as the superintendent of the female nurses for the Union Army (1861).
- Ohio passes the first state law that requires the removal of children from all county poorhouses and their placement in more suitable accommodations (1861).

- Massachusetts formally organizes the first two African American armed units, the Massachusetts 54th and 55th regiments, to participate in the Civil War. The units were segregated by race from other white units and led by white officers (1863).
- New York City experiences bloody antidraft riots implemented mostly by poor Irish immigrants who were angered because wealthy young men were able to purchase their exemptions from military service. In the melee, African American neighborhoods are looted and burned and an orphanage for African American children is destroyed (1863).
- Austrian monk and botanist Gregor Mendel discovers specific genetic laws governing the inheritance of human characteristics (1865).
- The United States War Department launches the Freedmen's Bureau to support freed slaves with financial assistance, jobs, education, relocation services, family reunification services, and legal benefits (1865).
- The *13th Amendment* to the *United States Constitution* is enacted, formally abolishing slavery throughout the nation (1865).
- A new secret society named the Ku Klux Klan is formed in Pulaski, Tennessee, by former Confederate soldiers to terrorize freed slaves. This organization quickly spreads throughout many Southern states (1865).
- With the Civil War over, the United States Army turns its attention to the growing "Indian problem" by initiating the building of a string of military forts from North and South Dakota down to the Texas border. These military establishments are poised to be the first line of defense for settlers against the resident Native American tribes, most of whom resist the government's expanding appropriation of their lands (1866).
- The United States Congress passes the *Reconstruction Act*, which appoints military governors over regions throughout the former Confederate states. These governors possess full authority over local voter eligibility rules, can remove local officials if necessary, and can impose martial law during any acts of resistance or terrorism (1867).
- The federal government establishes the United States Department of Education (1867).
- In London, Karl Marx publishes *Das Kapital*, predicting the self-destruction of capitalism and the rise of a government of the proletariat (1867).
- Following a period of ratification, the *14th Amendment* to the *United States Constitution* is passed, declaring that all freed slaves have the right to vote in national and local elections. Many women are unhappy with the wording of this amendment because it still excludes women from the right to vote (1868).
- Noted Progressive leaders Elizabeth Cady Stanton and Susan B. Anthony launch a new journal, *Revolution*, that advocates for universal suffrage and other women's rights (1868).
- The belligerent racist group, the Ku Klux Klan, publishes its *Organization and Principles of the Ku Klux Klan* (1868).

- The United States Congress approves the *15th Amendment to the United States Constitution*, which, in effect, orders all states to allow African American men the right to vote and never prohibit anyone to vote based on race, color, and previous servitude (1869). However, through the use of devices such as poll takes, literary tests, physical inaccessibility to polling places, and intimidation, African Americans do not fully gain the right to vote until the passage of the *Voting Rights Act* of 1965.
- A new secret organization, the *Noble Order of the Knights of Labor*, is formed to champion workers' rights in any dispute with management, therein establishing the first trade union movement (1869).
- Anthony and Stanton inaugurate the National Woman Suffrage Association, whose mission is to advocate for voting rights for all women (1869).
- A hostile United States Congress refuses to reauthorize the Freedmen's Bureau, and it is abruptly abolished (1872).
- Dr. Stephen Smith founds the American Public Health Association (1872).
- Reverend Brace publishes *The Dangerous Classes of New York and Twenty Years' Work Among Them* (1872).
- The Women's Christian Temperance Union (WCTU) is instituted in Cleveland, Ohio (1874).
- The New York Society for the Prevention of Cruelty to Children is inaugurated in New York City (1875).

Note: For a more reflective and functional use of this list of contemporary social welfare historical events, see Question #5 under the **Questions for Further Research and Discussion** section (below).

Sources:

Daniel, C. (1989). *Chronicle of America*. Mt. Kisco, NY: Chronicle Publications.

Mercer, D. (2000). *Millennium year by year*. New York: Dorling Kindersley Publications.

Social welfare developments 1850–1900. (2011). Retrieved from https://socialwelfare.library.vcu.edu/events/1851-1900/

Primary Text Material

The Emancipation Proclamation (January 1, 1863)

"By the President of the United States of America:
A Proclamation.
Whereas, on the twenty-second day of September, in the year of our Lord one thousand eight hundred and sixty-two, a proclamation was issued by the

Continued

President of the United States, containing, among other things, the following, to wit:

That on the first day of January, in the year of our Lord one thousand eight hundred and sixty-three, all persons held as slaves within any State or designated part of a State, the people whereof shall then be in rebellion against the United States, shall be then, thenceforward, and forever free; and the Executive Government of the United States, including the military and naval authority thereof, will recognize and maintain the freedom of such persons, and will do no act or acts to repress such persons, or any of them, in any efforts they may make for their actual freedom. . . .

Now, therefore I, Abraham Lincoln, President of the United States, by virtue of the power in me vested as Commander-in-Chief, of the Army and Navy of the United States in time of actual armed rebellion against the authority and government of the United States, and as a fit and necessary war measure for suppressing said rebellion, do, on this first day of January, in the year of our Lord one thousand eight hundred and sixty-three, and in accordance with my purpose so to do publicly proclaimed for the full period of one hundred days, from the day first above mentioned, order and designate as the States and parts of States wherein the people thereof respectively, are this day in rebellion against the United States. . . .

And by virtue of the power, and for the purpose aforesaid, I do order and declare that all persons held as slaves within said designated States, and parts of States, are, and henceforward shall be free; and that the Executive government of the United States, including the military and naval authorities thereof, will recognize and maintain the freedom of said persons.

And I hereby enjoin upon the people so declared to be free to abstain from all violence, unless in necessary self-defense; and I recommend to them that, in all cases when allowed, they labor faithfully for reasonable wages.

And I further declare and make known, that such persons of suitable condition, will be received into the armed service of the United States to garrison forts, positions, stations, and other places, and to man vessels of all sorts in said service.

And upon this act, sincerely believed to be an act of justice, warranted by the Constitution, upon military necessity, I invoke the considerate judgment of mankind, and the gracious favor of Almighty God.

In witness whereof, I have hereunto set my hand and caused the seal of the United States to be affixed.

Done at the City of Washington, this first day of January, in the year of our Lord one thousand eight hundred and sixty-three, and of the Independence of the United States of America the eighty-seventh.

By the President: ABRAHAM LINCOLN

WILLIAM H. SEWARD, Secretary of State."

Source and full text available at https://www.archives.gov/exhibits/featured-documents/emancipation-proclamation.

Timeline of General Events in History, the Humanities, and Science During This Period (1850–1875)

These general historical events may help you understand more clearly the overall historical context during which the primary document was created.

- The notable phrase, "Go West, young man, go West," coined by Indiana newspaper editor John L. Soule, captures many people's imagination and helps the westward expansion of the nation (1851).
- Isaac Singer invents the modern sewing machine (1851).
- Illinois Senate candidates Abraham Lincoln and Stephen Douglas engage in a pre-election debate that will become known as the *Lincoln–Douglas Debates*, during which Lincoln delivers his celebrated antislavery appraisal that "a house divided against itself cannot stand" (1858).
- In London, Charles Darwin publishes *The Origin of the Species*, which overturns current theory by proclaiming the human race has evolved from a common ancestor (1858).
- Abraham Lincoln is elected president of the United States (1860).
- The Pony Express begins, eventually linking the East Coast with the West Coast with mail delivery in approximately 10 days (1860).
- Fort Sumter, in Charleston, South Carolina, is bombarded and captured by Confederate troops, which leads to the outbreak of the Civil War (1861).
- Victor Hugo publishes *Les Misérables* in Paris (1862).
- President Lincoln delivers his legendary *Gettysburg Address* at a Pennsylvania battlefield, in which he implores "that the nation shall, under God, have a new birth of freedom, and that the government of the people, by the people, and for the people, shall not perish from the earth" (1863).
- Lewis Carroll, a pseudonym for Charles Dodgson, publishes *Alice in Wonderland* (1865).
- The Civil War ends with the surrender of General Robert E. Lee to General Ulysses S. Grant at the Appomattox, Virginia, courthouse, leaving the country profoundly divided over the issue of slavery (1865).
- President Abraham Lincoln is assassinated by John Wilkes Booth at Ford's Theatre in Washington, DC (1865).
- Alexander Gardner publishes a compilation of photographs, in austere black and white, chronicling the many of the horrors of the Civil War in his book, *Gardner's Photographic Sketch Book of the War* (1866). A selection of these prints and further information about Gardner can be accessed at http://rmc.library.cornell.edu/7milVol/images.html.
- After a multiyear support campaign, Secretary of the Interior William Seward, convinces the United States Congress to authorize the purchase of Alaska from Russia (1867).
- Swedish chemical engineer Alfred Nobel invents a safe alternative to gun powder called dynamite (1867).

- Leo Tolstoy publishes *War and Peace* in St. Petersburg, Russia (1867).
- The first transcontinental railroad from New York to San Francisco is completed when the rails are joined at Promontory Point, Utah (1869).
- Work is completed on the Suez Canal in Egypt, connecting the Mediterranean Sea with the Red Sea (1869).
- Victor Emmanuel II enters Rome and declares it to be the new capital of a united Italy (1870).
- Giuseppe Verdi presents his opera, *Aida*, for the first time at the Italian theatre in Cairo, Egypt (1871).
- Adventure writer Jules Verne publishes *Around the World in 80 Days* in Paris (1872).
- The first American national park, Yellowstone National Park, is created in California (1872).

Sources:

Daniel, C. (1989). *Chronicle of America*. Mt. Kisco, NY: Chronicle Publications.
Events of the 1800s. Retrieved from https://en.wikipedia.org/wiki/19th_century
Mercer, D. (2000). *Millennium year by year*. New York: Dorling Kindersley Publications.

Questions for Further Research and Discussion

1. Following further Internet research, report on the approximate number of slaves who found freedom after the *Emancipation Proclamation* and then volunteered for service in the Union Army. Report also on the challenges they faced in reaching the Union Army lines and enlisting for service.
2. Try to access other primary sources (e.g., newspaper editorials, interviews with public officials and community leaders, letters to the editor, etc.) published between 1863 to 1864 on the subject of slavery. From this material, determine how widespread and intense the resistance to President Lincoln's *Emancipation Proclamation* was. If you do discover evidence of negative reactions, can you detect any patterns or trends in those sentiments?
3. Read the full text of the above-referenced Illinois State Legislature's resistance to the *Emancipation Proclamation* (available at http://edale1.home.mindspring.com/Resolution%20of%20the%20Illinois%20Legislature%20in%20Opposition%20to%20the%20Emancipation%20Proclamation.htm), and search for similar statements in online newspaper articles and editorials published at the time. Then summarize the various counterarguments raised against the *Emancipation Proclamation*, and note any common themes that emerge.
4. After additional research into the events at the Battle of Fort Pillow, Tennessee, in 1864, list the competing historical evidence on whether African American

soldiers were purposely massacred after the surrender was declared or, instead, they tragically died during their defense of the fort during a military encounter. What primary evidentiary evidence exists regarding this incident?
5. Select three events appearing under the **Linkage to Social Welfare section** (above), conduct further Internet research regarding them, then conclude whether you believe there exists any plausible relationship between the *Emancipation Proclamation* and the events you have chosen. Use the analytical model presented in Appendix 1 of this book, or develop your own analytical model, to draw these conclusions.
6. Select one book from the **Additional Selected References** list at the end of this chapter. Briefly read through it, then summarize the main points contained in the book. Identify your own personal reaction to this book.

Additional Selected References

Brewster, T. (2014). *Lincoln's gamble: The tumultuous six months that gave America the Emancipation Proclamation and changed the course of the Civil War*. New York: Scribner.

Carnahan, B. M. (2007). *Act of justice: Lincoln's Emancipation Proclamation and the law of war*. Lexington: University Press of Kentucky.

Egerton, D. R. (2016). *Thunder at the gates: The black Civil War regiments that redeemed America*. New York: Basic Books.

Fradin, D. B. (2008). *The Emancipation Proclamation*. New York: Marshall Cavendish Benchmark.

Franklin, J. H. (1963). *The Emancipation Proclamation*. Garden City, NY: Doubleday.

Guelzo, A. C. (2004). *Lincoln's Emancipation Proclamation: The end of slavery in America*. New York: Simon & Schuster.

Holzer, H., Medford, E. G., & Williams, F. J. (2006). *The Emancipation Proclamation: Three views (social, political, iconographic)*. Baton Rouge: Louisiana State University Press.

Masur, L. P. (2012). *Lincoln's hundred days: The Emancipation Proclamation and the war for the Union*. Cambridge, MA: Belknap Press of Harvard University Press.

Ward, A. (2005). *River run red: The Fort Pillow Massacre in the American Civil War*. New York: Viking Press.

Young, R. (1994). *The Emancipation Proclamation: Why Lincoln really freed the slaves*. New York: Dillon Press.

Credits

Fig. 7.1: Source: https://commons.wikimedia.org/wiki/File%3AEmancipation_proclamation.jpg.

Fig. 7.2: Source: https://psmag.com/social-justice/desperate-efforts-to-re-unite-during-reconstruction.

Chapter 8

Reaction to Equality for All

The *Organization and Principles of the Ku Klux Klan* (1868)

Introduction

It is generally believed that in 1865, former Confederate soldiers in Pulaski, Tennessee, launched the Ku Klux Klan as a local social club. Its goal was to resist the Reconstruction policies that were imposed over the South by the Republican majority in Congress following the end of the Civil War, especially in the federal government's commitment to freedom and equality for former slaves. The original Ku Klux Klan group soon multiplied across the Southern states and morphed into a terrorist organization that violently opposed the education, voting rights, and economic development of freed slaves. Overall, this earliest Ku Klux Klan assemblage was a loosely organized regional entity with local units exerting autonomous management of their activities. Similar groups that also championed white supremacy and resistance to Republican Party control sprouted up and joined in parallel strategies including secret meetings, hidden identification, and the wearing of masks and hoods.

Although no official records were kept, indications are that the membership of the Ku Klux Klan tended to include a wide variety of types: ex-Confederate soldiers and militia; poor unemployed whites and white farmers; Democratic politicians aligned against the Republican majority in Congress; wealthy plantation owners who had lost their supply of cheap labor; members of the professional class, such as doctors, lawyers, and religious ministers; small business owners; and even local police officials. Operating as vigilante groups at night, the Ku Klux Klan's signature burning cross and hooded garments were designed specifically to terrify African Americans and their supporters. The Ku Klux Klan operated during these early years as independent bands of troublemakers who incited riots; assassinated African Americans and white Republicans; burned churches, homes, and public buildings; and generally spread terror throughout Southern society.

The origin and meaning of the name Ku Klux Klan is unknown, and several distinct explanations endure. The most commonly held belief is that the name is derived from the Greek word *kyklos*, meaning "circle," which has no beginning and no end. To this was then added the word *klan*, derived from the Scottish word *clan*. Indeed, there are many 20th-century photos of Ku Klux Klan members meeting in a circle around a burning cross in a deserted field. One other interesting explanation is from the anonymous author, a self-proclaimed former Ku Klux Klan member, of a short book *The Oaths, Signs, Ceremonies, and Objects of the Ku Klux Klan: A Full Exposé* (1868). In this book, the author claims that the name comes from the three clicks that take place when an unloaded rifle is fully cocked and then discharged, which was a password-type procedure used when Klan members approached a secret meeting in the woods. In this author's own words:

FIGURE 8.1 Mississippi Ku Klux Klan members in the disguises in which they were captured.

> ". . . when a Brother approaches the spot where a band is assembled, the sentinels, always concealed, challenge him by bringing their rifles to a full cock. That operation, as everyone knows, produces two sounds or clicks, one when the hammer reaches the half cock, and the other when it comes to the full cock. These sounds or clicks are represented by "Ku-Klux." The "Klan" is the sound of the hammer on the nipple of the piece when the trigger is pulled, and the hammer snapped . . ."

Source and full text available at https://www.gutenberg.org/files/26105/26105-h/26105-h.htm.

The original Ku Klux Klan eventually dissolved by the late 1870s when the Democratic Party controlled the Southern states and the Reconstruction policies were overturned. As a national organization, it was reincarnated and progressed through two additional historical periods still proclaiming its dual purposes: to sustain white supremacy and to keep America "pure" of contamination. The second appearance of the Ku Klux Klan at the beginning of the 20th century followed the publication of the notoriously prejudiced book *The Clansman*, by Thomas Dixon in 1905, and the resulting racist film *Birth of a Nation*, by D. W. Griffith in 1915. Coincidentally, this second reincarnation of the Ku Klux Klan also appeared during the time of the Supreme Court's *Plessy v. Ferguson* decision in 1896, which formally legalized the doctrine of *separate but equal*, a decision that undoubtedly cheered on the forces of segregation. In the early 20th century, the Ku Klux Klan achieved a better-organized national presence by supporting the infamous *Jim Crow* legislation throughout the South and by expanding its hatred to Catholics, Jews, immigrants from southern Europe, trade unions, and any member of the Republican party. In its third revival in the 1950s, the Ku Klux Klan quickly reacted to the United States Supreme Court's decision *Brown v. Board of Education* in 1954, which declared that the principle of *separate but equal* was unconstitutional when applied to the public education of African American children. In this latest restoration, the Ku Klux Klan as a national organization continued through the Civil Rights Movement of the 1960s and is currently still functional, though less visibly so. In an attempt to attain some public respectability today, the organization has adopted the new name of the Church of the National Knights of the Ku Klux Klan, complete with a website and musical anthem, where it states that its mission is to safeguard America from communism, foster Christianity, and defend white superiority in a troubled world.

At the same time that the Ku Klux Klan was beginning to spread throughout the former Confederate states, Congress also sought to extend to all freed slaves the same rights guaranteed to anyone else born in the United States. The *1866 Civil Rights Act* was the continuation of the *Emancipation Proclamation* of President Abraham Lincoln in the struggle to eradicate slavery and force the acceptance of equality without regard to race, color, or previous status of servitude. Several pieces of anti-Ku Klux Klan legislation were passed in succeeding decades throughout the 19th century and, more recently, major Civil Rights legislation, such as the *Civil Rights Act* and the *Voting Rights Act* that became laws in 1964 and 1965, respectively. Still, resistance to full equality for all citizens of any color or nationality remains unfulfilled across society. Tragically, the remnants of the Ku Klux Klan and other hateful organizations continue to retain their corrosive influence, however subtle, over modern American culture.

- For further information about the Church of the National Knights of the Ku Klux Klan, see http://cnkkkk.net.
- For further information about one of the current operations of the Church of the National Knights of the Ku Klux Klan, see the Southern Poverty Law Center link at https://www.splcenter.org/fighting-hate/extremist-files/group/church-national-knights-ku-klux-klan.
- See also, *Klansville, U.S.A.*, a film about the Ku Klux Klan in North Carolina, accessible at http://www.pbs.org/wgbh/americanexperience/films/klansville/.
- For a glimpse into the secret codes and language used currently by the Ku Klux Klan, see https://www.splcenter.org/fighting-hate/extremist-files/ideology/ku-klux-klan.
- For a detailed plot and character description of the D. W. Griffith's racist movie *The Birth of a Nation*, see http://www.filmsite.org/birt.html. This film is also available for rental, in DVD format, through Netflix (https://dvd.netflix.com/Movie/309264).

Internet Sources for the Content of This Introduction Include:

https://www.splcenter.org/fighting-hate/extremist-files/ideology/ku-klux-klan
http://www.history.com/topics/ku-klux-klan
https://www.britannica.com/topic/ku-klux-klan
http://www.pbs.org/wgbh/americanexperience/features/grant-kkk/
https://www.pbs.org/wnet/jimcrow/stories_events_kkk.html

http://www.slate.com/articles/news_and_politics/history/2016/03/how_a_detachment_of_u_s_army_soldiers_smoked_out_the_original_ku_klux_klan.html
https://en.wikipedia.org/wiki/ku_klux_klan

Linkage to Social Welfare History (1850–1875)

Social welfare historical events for this time period include the following:

- The Reverend Charles Loring Brace, founder of the Children's Aid Society in New York City, begins sending seemingly-abandoned street children westward to farm families in what is now the Midwest. This practice is commonly known as sending "orphan trains" and is, technically, a precursor to modern foster care and adoption services (1852).
- Harriet Beecher Stowe publishes *Uncle Tom's Cabin: Life Among the Lowly* as an innovative confrontation to widespread slavery in the South (1852).
- The Know-Nothing Party (officially the Order of the Star-Spangled Banner), a violent, nativist, anti-immigrant, anti-Roman Catholic, and racist organization, holds its annual convention in New York City (1854).
- The federal government establishes the Government Hospital for the Insane (presently known as St. Elizabeth's Hospital in Washington, DC), which represents the first public federal institution opened for mental health purposes (1855).
- In Congress, South Carolina Congressional Representative Preston Brooks ruthlessly beats Massachusetts Senator Charles Sumner with his walking stick after Sumner's speech against slavery (1856).
- In Paris, Louis Pasteur discovers airborne bacteria as the cause of infections (1856).
- The U.S. Supreme Court issues the *Dred Scott Decision*, declaring that no African American descended from slaves has a right to citizenship (1857). This decision was effectively invalidated by the passage the *13th* and *14th Amendments* to the *United States Constitution* a few years later, after the Civil War.
- The Young Women's Christian Association (YWCA) opens its first boarding house for single women in New York City (1858).
- Radical abolitionist John Brown is hanged in Charleston, West Virginia, for murder, treason, and inciting insurrection after his attack on a federal armory in Harpers Ferry, West Virginia (1859).
- South Carolina secedes from the Union on the issue of slavery, provoking other states to form a Confederacy of border and Southern states (1860).
- Dorothea Dix, the noted mental health reformer, is appointed as the superintendent of the female nurses for the Union Army (1861).
- Ohio passes the first state law that requires the removal of children from all county poorhouses and their placement in more suitable accommodations (1861).
- President Abraham Lincoln issues the *Emancipation Proclamation*, granting freedom to all slaves in all the Confederate states (1863).

- Massachusetts formally organizes the first two African American armed units, the Massachusetts 54th and 55th regiments, to participate in the Civil War. The units were segregated by race from other white units and led by white officers (1863).
- New York City experiences bloody antidraft riots implemented mostly by poor Irish immigrants who were angered because wealthy young men were able to purchase their exemptions from military service. In the melee, African American neighborhoods are looted and burned and an orphanage for African American children is destroyed (1863).
- Austrian monk and botanist Gregor Mendel discovers specific genetic laws governing the inheritance of human characteristics (1865).
- The United States War Department launches the Freedmen's Bureau to support freed slaves with financial assistance, jobs, education, relocation services, family reunification services, and legal benefits (1865).
- The *13th Amendment* to the *United States Constitution* is enacted, formally abolishing slavery throughout the nation (1865).
- A new secret society named the Ku Klux Klan is formed in Pulaski, Tennessee, by former confederate soldiers to terrorize freed slaves. This organization quickly spreads throughout many Southern states (1865).
- With the Civil War over, the United States Army turns its attention to the growing "Indian problem" by initiating the building of a string of military forts from North and South Dakota down to the Texas border. These military establishments are poised to be the first line of defense for settlers against the resident Native American tribes, most of whom resist the government's expanding appropriation of their lands (1866).
- The United States Congress passes the *Reconstruction Act*, which appoints military governors over regions throughout the former confederate states. These governors possess full authority over local voter eligibility rules, can remove local officials if necessary, and can impose martial law during any acts of resistance or terrorism (1867).
- The federal government establishes the United States Department of Education (1867).
- In London, Karl Marx publishes *Das Kapital*, predicting the self-destruction of capitalism and the rise of a government of the proletariat (1867).
- Following a period of ratification, the *14th Amendment* to the *United States Constitution* is passed, declaring that all freed slaves have the right to vote in national and local elections. Many women are unhappy with the wording of this amendment because it still excludes women from the right to vote (1868).
- Noted Progressive leaders Elizabeth Cady Stanton and Susan B. Anthony launch a new journal, *Revolution*, that advocates for universal suffrage and other women's rights (1868).
- The United States Congress approves the *15th Amendment to the United States Constitution*, which, in effect, orders all states to allow African American men the right to vote and never prohibit anyone to vote based on race, color, and previous

servitude (1869). However, through the use of devices such as poll takes, literary tests, physical inaccessibility to polling places, and intimidation, African Americans do not fully gain the right to vote until the passage of the *Voting Rights Act* of 1965.
- A new secret organization, the *Noble Order of the Knights of Labor*, is formed to champion workers' rights in any dispute with management, therein establishing the first trade union movement (1869).
- Anthony and Stanton inaugurate the National Woman Suffrage Association, whose mission is to advocate for voting rights for all women (1869).
- A hostile United States Congress refuses to reauthorize the Freedmen's Bureau, and it is abruptly abolished (1872).
- Dr. Stephen Smith founds the American Public Health Association (1872).
- Reverend Brace publishes *The Dangerous Classes of New York and Twenty Years' Work Among Them* (1872).
- The Women's Christian Temperance Union (WCTU) is instituted in Cleveland, Ohio (1874).
- The New York Society for the Prevention of Cruelty to Children is inaugurated in New York City (1875).

Note: For a more reflective and functional use of this list of contemporary social welfare historical events, see Question #6 under the Questions for Further Research and Discussion section (below).

Sources:
Daniel, C. (1989). *Chronicle of America*. Mt. Kisco, NY: Chronicle Publications.
Mercer, D. (2000). *Millennium year by year*. New York: Dorling Kindersley Publications.
Social welfare developments 1850–1900. (2011). Retrieved from https://socialwelfare.library.vcu.edu/events/1851-1900/

Primary Text Material

What follows are materials published in 1868 that show the first Ku Klux Klan's attempt to formulate a mission statement, an initiation oath, and a set of questions to be asked of all new applicants.

[Note: The use of three asterisks *** in the material below signifies that the specific name of the local Ku Klux Klan chapter would be inserted during the initiation rites.]

Organization and Principles of the Ku Klux Klan

"...Character and Objects of the Order
This is an institution of chivalry, humanity, mercy, and patriotism; embodying in its genius and its principles all that is chivalric in conduct, noble in

sentiment, generous in manhood, and patriotic in purpose; its peculiar objects being:

First, to protect the weak, the innocent, and the defenseless from the indignities, wrongs, and outrages of the lawless, the violent, and the brutal; to relieve the injured and oppressed; to succor the suffering and unfortunate, and especially the widows and orphans of Confederate soldiers.

Second, to protect and defend the Constitution of the United States, and all laws passed in conformity thereto, and to protect the states and the people thereof from all invasion from any source whatever.

Third, to aid and assist in the execution of all constitutional laws, and to protect the people from unlawful seizure and from trial, except by their peers in conformity to the laws of the land. . .

Initiation Oath and Selected Questions To Be Asked Candidates

"I — solemnly swear or affirm that I will never reveal any thing that I may this day (or night) learn concerning the Order of the * * *, and that I will true answer make to such interrogatories as may be put to me touching my competency for admission into the same. So help me God."

INTERROGATORIES TO BE ASKED:

1st. Have you ever been rejected, upon application for membership in the * * *, or have you ever been expelled from the same?

2nd. Are you now, or have you ever been a member of the Radical Republican Party, or either of the organizations known as the "Loyal League" and the "Grand Army of the Republic"?

3rd. Are you opposed to the principles and policy of the Radical Party, and to the Loyal League, and the Grand Army of the Republic, so far as you are informed of the character and purposes of those organizations?

4. Did you belong to the Federal Army during the late war, and fight against the South during the existence of the same?

5. Are you opposed to Negro equality both social and political?

6. Are you in favor of a white man's government in this country?

7. Are you in favor of constitutional liberty, and a government of equitable laws instead of a government of violence and oppression?

8. Are you in favor of maintaining the constitutional rights of the South?

9. Are you in favor of the reenfranchisement and emancipation of the white men of the South, and the restitution of the Southern people to all their rights, alike proprietary, civil, and political?

10. Do you believe in the inalienable right of self-preservation of the people against the exercise of arbitrary and unlicensed power"?

Source: Fleming, W. (Ed.). (1905). *Ku Klux Klan: Its origin, growth, and disbandment.* New York: Neale Publishing Company.

Source and full text available at https://www.gutenberg.org/files/31819/31819-h/31819-h.htm.

FIGURE 8.2   Ku Klux Klan parade in Washington, DC.

Timeline of General Events in History, the Humanities, and Science During This Period (1850–1875)

These general historical events may help you understand more clearly the overall historical context during which the primary document was created.

- The notable phrase, "Go West, young man, go West," coined by Indiana newspaper editor John L. Soule, captures many people's imagination and helps the westward expansion of the nation (1851).
- Isaac Singer invents the modern sewing machine (1851).
- Illinois Senate candidates Abraham Lincoln and Stephen Douglas engage in a pre-election debate that will become known as the *Lincoln–Douglas Debates*, during which Lincoln delivers his celebrated antislavery appraisal that "a house divided against itself cannot stand" (1858).
- In London, Charles Darwin publishes *The Origin of the Species*, which overturns current theory by proclaiming the human race has evolved from a common ancestor (1858).
- Abraham Lincoln is elected president of the United States (1860).

- The Pony Express begins, eventually linking the East Coast with the West Coast with mail delivery in approximately 10 days (1860).
- Fort Sumter, in Charleston, South Carolina, is bombarded and captured by Confederate troops, which leads to the outbreak of the Civil War (1861).
- Victor Hugo publishes *Les Misérables* in Paris (1862).
- President Lincoln delivers his legendary *Gettysburg Address* at a Pennsylvania battlefield, in which he implores "that the nation shall, under God, have a new birth of freedom, and that the government of the people, by the people, and for the people, shall not perish from the earth" (1863).
- Lewis Carroll, a pseudonym for Charles Dodgson, publishes *Alice in Wonderland* (1865).
- The Civil War ends with the surrender of General Robert E. Lee to General Ulysses S. Grant at the Appomattox, Virginia, courthouse, leaving the country profoundly divided over the issue of slavery (1865).
- President Abraham Lincoln is assassinated by John Wilkes Booth at Ford's Theatre in Washington, DC (1865).
- Alexander Gardner publishes a compilation of photographs, in austere black and white, chronicling the many of the horrors of the Civil War in his book, *Gardner's Photographic Sketch Book of the War* (1866). A selection of these prints and further information about Gardner can be accessed at http://rmc.library.cornell.edu/7milVol/images.html.
- After a multiyear support campaign, Secretary of the Interior William Seward convinces the United States Congress to authorize the purchase of Alaska from Russia (1867).
- Swedish chemical engineer Alfred Nobel invents a safe alternative to gun powder called dynamite (1867).
- Leo Tolstoy publishes *War and Peace* in St. Petersburg, Russia (1867).
- The first transcontinental railroad from New York to San Francisco is completed when the rails are joined at Promontory Point, Utah (1869).
- Work is completed on the Suez Canal in Egypt, connecting the Mediterranean Sea with the Red Sea (1869).
- Victor Emmanuel II enters Rome and declares it to be the new capital of a united Italy (1870).
- Giuseppe Verdi presents his opera, *Aida*, for the first time at the Italian theatre in Cairo, Egypt (1871).
- Adventure writer Jules Verne publishes *Around the World in 80 Days* in Paris (1872).
- The first American national park, Yellowstone National Park, is created in California (1872).

Sources:
Daniel, C. (1989). *Chronicle of America*. Mt. Kisco, NY: Chronicle Publications.
Events of the 1800s. Retrieved from https://en.wikipedia.org/wiki/19th_century
Mercer, D. (2000). *Millennium year by year*. New York: Dorling Kindersley Publications.

Questions for Further Research and Discussion

1. Following further research into the organizing principles of the Ku Klux Klan, during its initial phase and then during its subsequent two revivals, did you find evidence that it tried to hide its true nature by appealing to chivalry, mercy, and patriotism? Summarize what you discovered.
2. Focus on the first revival of the Ku Klux Klan after 1915, and report, with specific examples, on its particularly violent actions during that period.
3. Focus on the second revival of the Ku Klux Klan after 1954, and report, with specific examples, on its overt and covert activities during that period.
4. Focus on the current (i.e., 21st-century) operations of the Ku Klux Klan organization and report, with specific examples, on its name change, its public image, and its range of activities.
5. If you are a Netflix customer, access the 1915 film *The Birth of a Nation* and list all the racist images and language used to portray African Americans during this time period.
6. Select three events appearing under the **Linkage to Social Welfare** section (above), conduct further Internet research regarding them, then conclude whether you believe there exists any plausible relationship between the *Organization and Principles of the Ku Klux Klan* and the events you have chosen. Use the analytical model presented in Appendix 1 of this book, or develop your own analytical model, to draw these conclusions.
7. Select one book from the **Additional Selected References** list at the end of this chapter. Briefly read through it, then summarize the main points contained in the book. Identify your own personal reaction to this book.

Additional Selected References

Chalmers, D. M. (1987). *Hooded Americanism: The history of the Ku Klux Klan* (3rd ed.). Durham, NC: Duke University Press.

Dixon, T., & Clark, T. (1970). *The Clansman: An historical romance of the Ku Klux Klan*. Lexington: University Press of Kentucky.

Ingalls, Robert P. (1979). *Hoods: The story of the Ku Klux Klan*. New York: G.P. Putnam's Sons.

Martinez, J. M. (2007). *Carpetbaggers, cavalry, and the Ku Klux Klan: Exposing the invisible empire during Reconstruction*. New York: Rowman & Littlefield.

McVeigh, R. (2009). *The rise of the Ku Klux Klan: Right-wing movements and national politics*. Minneapolis: University of Minnesota Press.

Mecklin, J. M. (2006). *The Ku Klux Klan: A study of the American mind*. Unknown: Home Farm Books.

Newton, M., & Newton, J. S. (1991). *The Ku Klux Klan: An encyclopedia*. New York: Garland Publishing/Oxford University Press.

O'Neil, P. M. (2016). Ku Klux Klan. In S. Bronner (Ed.), *Encyclopedia of American studies*. Baltimore, MD: Johns Hopkins University Press. Available at: http://eas-ref.press.jhu.edu/view?aid=640

Trelease, A. W. (1995). *White terror: The Ku Klux Klan conspiracy and Southern Reconstruction*. Baton Rouge: Louisiana State University Press.

Tourgee, A. (1989). *The invisible empire*. Baton Rouge: Louisiana State University Press. (Original work printed 1880)

Wade, W. C. (1987). *The fiery cross: The Ku Klux Klan in America*. New York: Simon & Schuster.

Credits

Fig. 8.1: Source: https://m-staging.timeline.com/stories/fargo-gets-it-right-after-every-war-comes-a-crime-wave.

Fig. 8.2: Source: https://commons.wikimedia.org/wiki/File:The_Ku_Klux_Klan_on_parade_down_Pennsylvania_Avenue,_1928_-_NARA_-_541885.jpg.

Chapter 9

The Oppression of Native Americans
Helen Hunt Jackson's *A Century of Dishonor* (1881)

Introduction

The author was born Helen Fiske in Amherst, Massachusetts, in 1831 to her parents, Deborah Vinal Fiske and Nathan Fiske, an Amherst College professor and Calvinist minister. Both parents died by the time Jackson was a teenager, but she was well cared for and able to receive an excellent classical education at the Ipswich Female Seminary in Massachusetts and the Abbot Institute in New York. In 1853, Jackson married Edward Hunt, a United States Army officer, with whom she had two sons, one of whom died in childbirth and the other of whom died as a young child from diphtheria. She faced more tragedy with the death of her husband in an accident in 1863.

Jackson always loved writing and literature, so following the loss of her entire immediate family, she started attending local writers support groups. From those experiences, she started writing poems and children's books to support herself. During this time, she became a prolific writer who received wide positive notoriety for her creative works. For health reasons, Jackson moved to Colorado and eventually married her second husband, William Jackson, a wealthy local banker and railroad executive. During these years, Jackson maintained her friendship with several notable authors, including Emily Dickenson, Ralph Waldo Emerson, Harriet Beecher Stowe, and Oliver Wendell Holmes.

Through a chance encounter in Boston at a meeting of the Indian Commission in 1879, Chief Standing Bear, the leader of the Ponca tribe, captivated Jackson with his depiction of the appalling living conditions of his people. The Chief expounded on the fact that such a predicament for his tribe, as well as other Native American tribes, was due primarily to the federal government's intrusion into native lands, as well as their violation of existing treaties. Concentrating explicitly on his own tribe, Chief Standing Bear illustrated how the

FIGURE 9.1 Photographic image of Helen Hunt Jackson.

Poncas had been forcibly removed from their native lands in Nebraska and driven to a reservation in Indian territory, in present-day Oklahoma. During the trek there and after they arrived, the Ponca people suffered from disease, inadequate and poor quality food, unsanitary housing, and harsh climate changes. These hardships foisted upon his people were, according to Chief Standing Bear, due to the unfair treatment at the hands of the government Indian agents and local judges who were accommodating to the movement to clear Indian tribal members from their native lands so that newly arrived white settlers could build their farms, towns, and businesses.

Compelled by this new knowledge, Jackson launched herself into a new activist crusade and began to raise money, circulate petitions, and write letters in support of Native American rights. She began to investigate the facts surrounding the living conditions of native tribes and interviewed government officials and tribal members, which led to a series of published reports, public lectures, and attempts to influence state and local legislation.

Throughout this period, Jackson found the time to publish the seminal work of her life, *A Century of Dishonor*, in 1881, a gripping narrative of the plight on Native Americans in late 19th-century America. The book centered on seven native tribes—the Cherokee, Cheyenne, Delaware, Nez Perce, Ponca, Sioux, and Winnebago—and chronicled three gruesome massacres of Native Americans by whites. Using her own resources, Jackson sent a copy of *A Century of Dishonor* to each member of Congress with a note written in red ink that stated the following quote attributed to Benjamin Franklin: "Look upon your hands: They are stained with the blood of your relations" (see http://www.thewildwest.org/cowboys/wildwestlegendarywomen/204-helenhuntjackson).

Sadly, but perhaps predictably, *A Century of Dishonor* did not immediately change many minds. Some dismissed her work because, in their opinion, it contained only anecdotal data and did not present clearly and convincingly broad patterns of behavior that could prove any willful intention to harm Native Americans. Others, such as President Theodore Roosevelt, remained unconvinced because he firmly believed in the strict compliance of existing federal laws regarding land rights for Native American tribes. It must be noted that during the last decades of the 19th century, America was expanding westward in population and territorial acquisition. America, according to popular tradition, had a Manifest Destiny to expand its land mass and to colonize the ever-expanding frontier. The Native American tribes were mostly viewed as impediments to progress. They were mere savages, not yet fully Christianized, and incapable of integrating into the cultural heritage of the rest of America.

Soon after, Jackson moved to California for health reasons, and she began to study the conditions of Native Americans living in the series of Indian missions there. When Spain ruled the California territory, Native Americans throughout the Southwest were protected by official grants of lands surrounding the Indian missions, which were established to Christianize them. After the Mexican-American war, these missions were secularized by the federal government and the Native Americans lost their protected land rights. Jackson soon discovered that their present predicament basically mirrored the experiences of other Native American tribes throughout the Western United States. This led her to write her second most-known creative work in 1884, *Ramona*, which is a fictional novel about a mixed-race Native American orphan who endures discrimination and persecution in California. Jackson died in 1885 and is reported to have implored President Grover Cleveland on her deathbed to take up the cause of the oppressed Native American peoples across America.

It was Jackson's hope that she could do for Native Americans what her friend, Harriet Beecher Stowe, did for African Americans in her 1852 novel *Uncle Tom's Cabin*. Unfortunately, that never materialized during her life, nor did she personally witness any

FIGURE 9.2   A 19th-century photograph of three Nez Perce Indians.

significant legislative changes toward Native American rights. Partly due to the influence of her advocacy, however, the *Dawes Act*, the first federal law to address the issue of land rights of Native Americans, was passed by Congress in 1887.

Although it is undisputed that *A Century of Dishonor* did little to change prevailing attitudes toward Native Americans in the late 19th century, it was not a pointless effort. To subsequent generations, Jackson's work is viewed as iconic and the very first attempt to graphically represent the subjugation and ongoing oppression of Native American tribes. She deplored the fact that Native American people living on reservations across America were the least educated, the most poorly housed, the sickest, and the most unemployed and that they were subjected, on a day-to-day basis, to more cruelty than any other group of citizens in this nation.

- For a short overview of Helen Hunt Jackson's life, see https://www.youtube.com/watch?v=GWWMfUl8MNE.

Internet Sources for the Content of This Introduction Include:

http://www.nanations.com/century-of-dishonor.htm
https://en.wikipedia.org/wiki/a_century_of_dishonor
https://www.britannica.com/biography/helen-hunt-jackson
http://www.cogreatwomen.org/project/helen-hunt-jackson/
http://www.thewildwest.org/cowboys/wildwestlegendarywomen/204-helenhuntjackson
https://www.civilwarwomenblog.com/helen-hunt-jackson/
http://www.coloradovirtuallibrary.org/digital-colorado/colorado-histories/beginnings/helen-hunt-jackson-author-and-indian-advocate/
https://en.wikipedia.org/wiki/helen_hunt_jackson

Linkage to Social Welfare History (1875–1900)

Social welfare historical events for this time period include the following:

- General George Custer, along with 275 troopers of the Seventh Cavalry Regiment, are defeated at Little Bighorn in the Dakota territory by Cheyenne and Sioux Indians, led by Chiefs Crazy Horse and Sitting Bull, thus halting the government's drive to return all Cheyenne and Sioux to their reservations (1876).
- Reconstruction formally ends with the withdrawal of all federal troops from Southern states (1877).
- Ten members of the Molly Maguires, an early trade union organization dedicated to improving working conditions in the mining industry, are hanged for murder based on suspect testimony of infiltrators hired by the Pinkerton National Detective Agency (1877).
- The Charity Organization Society (COS), using a model of delivering social services by the individual case method, is formally established in Buffalo, New York (1877).

- In London, the Reverend William Booth formally launches the Salvation Army organization (1878).
- In Pennsylvania, Henry Pratt establishes the Carlisle School, the first boarding school program whose goal is to teach Native American children how to speak correct English and fully integrate into the dominant white society. The children are provided with uniforms, assigned new Europeanized names, and forbidden to speak their native languages (1879).
- Over the past 10 years, approximately 120,000 Chinese immigrants arrive in California, most of whom are men lured by jobs in the mining and railroad industries (1880).
- Milton George organizes the National Farmers Alliance in Chicago to advocate for farm families (1880).
- Booker T. Washington opens the Tuskegee Institute in Alabama as a school for the training of African Americans in the industrial arts (1881).
- Inspired by the work of the Internal Red Cross, Clara Barton founds the American Red Cross organization (1881).
- The American Federation of Labor (AFL), at its first national convention when it was stilled named the Federation of Organized Trades and Labor Unions of the United States and Canada, calls for the prohibition of any type of labor for children younger than 14 years of age (1881).
- To quell unrest in the white community over foreigners taking low-level jobs, the *Chinese Exclusion Act*, restricting the immigration and naturalization of Chinese nationals for 10 years, becomes federal law (1882).
- Congress passes the *Immigration Act*, a federal law that charges a tax on all immigrants and bars from admission anyone poor or with a criminal background (1882).
- William Sumner publishes *What Social Classes Owe to Each Other*, a work that applies the natural selection theory of Charles Darwin to social classes and roles (1883).
- Labor leader Samuel Gompers promotes state legislation to prohibit the manufacture of cigars in tenements where thousands of young children work (1883).
- In a group of cases known as the *Civil Rights Cases*, the United States Supreme Court rules that the *14th Amendment*, which mandates the equal treatment for all citizens, does not apply to any privately-owned businesses, such as restaurants, hotels, or railroads, thus ushering in the infamous Jim Crow laws across the South (1883).
- A new drug, cocaine, is introduced by the pharmaceutical industry for use as a local anesthetic (1884).
- Anti-Chinese sentiment erupts into deadly race riots in Rock Springs, the Wyoming Territory, and Tacoma and Seattle in Washington (1885).
- The Haymarket Square labor rally in Chicago ends in violence (1886).
- Defeated Apache leader Geronimo surrenders to Army General Nelson Miles in Arizona (1886).

- *The Dawes Act*, allocating private ownership of land to Indians on federal reservations, is enacted as a law (1887).
- Jane Addams and Ellen Gates Starr open the first settlement house, Hull House, in Chicago, incorporating the use of community-based macro practice as a means of social service delivery (1889).
- Journalist Jacob Riis publishes *How the Other Half Lives*, a devastating pictorial exposé of the poor living in New York City's Lower East Side (1890).
- The infamous *Wounded Knee Massacre* occurs, during which United States Army troops slaughter approximately 150 men, women, and children of the Lakota tribe due to a tragic miscommunication (1890).
- Ellis Island, in New York Harbor, opens to process the escalating surge of immigrants (1892).
- At its National Convention, the Democratic Party includes in its party platform a call for the prohibition of all child labor for children younger than 15 years of age (1892).
- Coca-Cola, advertised as an elixir, and reportedly containing small amounts of cocaine, is introduced (1886).
- President William Harrison reveals the *Treaty of Annexation of Hawaii* (1893).
- In Colorado, women are granted the right to vote in state and local elections (1893).
- Czech composer Antonin Dvorak concludes his *Symphony No. 9, New World Symphony*, a work influenced by African American and Native American melodies, in New York City (1893).
- Pro-American businesses leaders, aided by a company of United States Marines, depose Hawaiian Queen Lili'uokalani and declare the islands an independent republic (1894).
- Labor leader Eugene Debs and the American Railway Union call a national strike and boycott against the Pullman Company and the federal government (1894).
- Booker T. Washington delivers what will be known as *The Atlanta Compromise Speech*, which extols the benefits of education and vocational training for African Americans (1895).
- The United States Supreme Court decides, in *Plessy v. Ferguson*, that segregation of state public facilities is allowed, thereby introducing the principles of separate but equal and white supremacy (1896).
- Prostitution is legalized in the French Quarter section of New Orleans (1897).
- The federal government formally annexes Hawaii with the public support and encouragement of Sanford Ballard Dole and other American business leaders (1898).
- Maud Ballington Booth and Ballington Booth inaugurate the Volunteers of America in New York City (1896).
- Economist Thorstein Veblen publishes *The Theory of the Leisure Class*, an anticapitalistic indictment of wealthy society across America (1899).
- W.E.B. Du Bois publishes *The Philadelphia Negro*, warning about the dangers of what he termed the "color line" in America (1899).

- In Chicago, Jane Addams and Julia Lathrop help introduce the first juvenile court, where dependent, neglected, and delinquent children and adolescents are treated with rehabilitation rather than with punishment, as occurred in adult courts (1899).

Note: For a more reflective and functional use of this list of contemporary social welfare historical events, see Question #5 under the **Questions for Further Research and Discussion** section (below).

Sources:

Daniel, C. (1989). *Chronicle of America*. Mt. Kisco, NY: Chronicle Publications.

Mercer, D. (2000). *Millennium year by year.* New York: Dorling Kindersley Publications.

Social welfare developments 1851–1900. (2011). Retrieved from https://socialwelfare.library.vcu.edu/events/1851-1900/

Primary Text Material

Jackson, H. H. (1889). *A century of dishonor: A sketch of the United States government's dealings with some Indian tribes.* **Boston: Roberts Brothers.**

"... *The question of the honorableness of the United States' dealings with the Indians turns largely on a much disputed and little understood point. What was the nature of the Indians' right to the country in which they were living when the continent of North America was discovered? Between the theory of some sentimentalists that the Indians were the real owners of the soil, and the theory of some politicians that they had no right of ownership whatever in it, there are innumerable grades and confusions of opinion. The only authority on the point must be the view and usage as accepted by the great discovering Powers at the time of discovery, and afterward in their disposition of the lands discovered ...*

Each discovering Power might regulate the relations between herself and the Indians; but as to the existence of the Indians' "right of occupancy," there was absolute unanimity among them. That there should have been unanimity regarding any one thing between them, is remarkable. It is impossible for us to realize what a sudden invitation to greed and discord lay in this fair, beautiful, unclaimed continent—eight millions of square miles of land—more than twice the size of all Europe itself. What a lure to-day would such another new continent prove! The fighting over it would be as fierce now as the fighting was then, and the "right of occupancy" of the natives would stand small chance of such unanimous recognition as the four Great Powers [England, France, Spain, and Portugal] then justly gave it ... (p.10)

Continued

> *However great perplexity and difficulty there may be in the details of any and every plan possible for doing at this late day anything like justice to the Indian, however hard it may be for good statesmen and good men to agree upon the things that ought to be done, there certainly is, or ought to be, no perplexity whatever, no difficulty whatever, in agreeing upon certain things that ought not to be done, and which must cease to be done before the first steps can be taken toward righting the wrongs, curing the ills, and wiping out the disgrace to us of the present condition of our Indians.*
>
> *Cheating, robbing, breaking promises—these three are clearly things which must cease to be done. One more thing, also, and that is the refusal of the protection of the law to the Indian's rights of property, "of life, liberty, and the pursuit of happiness."*
>
> *When these four things have ceased to be done, time, statesmanship, philanthropy, and Christianity can slowly and surely do the rest. Till these four things have ceased to be done, statesmanship and philanthropy alike must work in vain, and even Christianity can reap but small harvest . . ."* (p. 337)
>
> Source and full text available at http://www.gutenberg.org/files/50560/50560-h/50560-h.htm#Page_324.

Timeline of General Events in History, the Humanities, and Science During This Period (1875–1900)

These general historical events may help you understand more clearly the overall historical context during which the primary document was created.

- At the Centennial Exhibition in Philadelphia, Alexander Graham Bell demonstrates his latest invention, the telephone (1876).
- Mark Twain publishes *Tom Sawyer* (1876).
- Thomas Edison applies for a patent on his latest invention, which he calls the phonograph (1877).
- Thomas Edison demonstrates his successful innovation called the electric light (1879).
- The first geological survey of the Grand Canyon and the Colorado River is completed (1881).
- Jesse James, the popular outlaw who robbed banks and hijacked trains, is shot dead by his cousin Bob Ford in St. Joseph, Missouri (1882).
- Hiram Maxim invents a repeating machine gun capable of firing 600 bullets per minute (1884).
- Mark Twain publishes *The Adventures of Huckleberry Finn* (1884).
- The Statue of Liberty, a gift from the French government, is dedicated in New York Harbor (1886).

- The *Sherman Antitrust Act*, designed to prevent business monopolies that hurt the consumer, is enacted into law (1890).
- In a break from both the Democratic and Republican parties, the Populist Party platform, developed by farmers in the South and West, is publicly announced (1892).
- John Philip Sousa introduces a "new sound" for marching bands (1892).
- The World Columbian Exposition, commemorating the 400th anniversary of Christopher Columbus's voyage, opens in Chicago and showcases the latest technology (1893).
- William Jennings Bryan delivers his *Cross of Gold* speech, in which he promotes both gold and silver as legal tender in American monetary policy (1896).
- Based on the *New York Journal's* cartoon, The Yellow Kid, the phrase *yellow journalism* is coined to describe highly sensationalized journalism (1896).
- *New York Sun* Editor Francis Church responds to a letter from young Virginia O' Hanlon by affirming, "Yes, Virginia, there is a Santa Claus" (1897).
- The Spanish-American War commences, following the sinking of the battleship Maine in the harbor in Havana, Cuba (1898).
- Colonel Theodore Roosevelt leads his Rough Riders, including some African Americans troopers, to victory at San Juan Hill in Santiago, Cuba (1898).
- Scott Joplin publishes the *Maple Leaf Rag* and adds to the popularity of ragtime music (1899).

Sources:

Daniel, C. (1989). *Chronicle of America*. Mt. Kisco, NY: Chronicle Publications.
Events of the 1800s. Retrieved from https://en.wikipedia.org/wiki/19th_century
Mercer, D. (2000). *Millennium year by year*. New York: Dorling Kindersley Publications.

Questions for Further Research and Discussion

1. There are seven individual Native American tribes highlighted in *A Century of Dishonor*. Choose one of these native tribes, read the entire account, and summarize what occurred. Did you discover any underlying themes that emerged? If so, identify those themes. Did you encounter any specific facts that surprised you? If so, identify those facts.
2. *A Century of Dishonor* also recounts the horrors of three incidents involving massacres of native peoples by whites: the *Conestoga Massacre*, the *Gnadenhütten Massacre*, and the *Massacre of Apaches in the Arizona Territory*. Choose one of these incidents, read the entire account, and summarize what occurred. Did you discover any underlying themes that emerged? If so, identify those themes. Did you encounter any specific facts that surprised you? If so, identify those facts.

3. Read sections of Helen Hunt Jackson's novel *Ramona* (available online at http://www.gutenberg.org/files/2802/2802-h/2802-h.htm). Then summarize your impressions of this fictional work and describe what life would be like for a mixed-race Native American orphan girl in late-19th-century California.
4. Following further research on the Internet, can you find any more recent references to *A Century of Dishonor*, especially during the Civil Rights Movement of the 1960s and later?
5. Select three events appearing under the **Linkage to Social Welfare** section (above), conduct further Internet research regarding them, then conclude whether you believe there exists any plausible relationship between *A Century of Dishonor* and the events you have chosen. Use the analytical model presented in Appendix 1 of this book, or develop your own analytical model, to draw these conclusions.
6. Select 1 book from the **Additional Selected References** list at the end of this chapter. Briefly read through it, then summarize the main points contained in the book. Identify your own personal reaction to this book.

Additional Selected References

Banning, E. I. (1973). *Helen Hunt Jackson*. New York: Vanguard Press.
May, A. (1987). *Helen Hunt Jackson: A lonely voice of conscience*. San Francisco: Chronicle Books.
Odell, R. (1939). *Helen Hunt Jackson*. New York: D. Appleton-Century Co.
Phillips, K. (2003). *Helen Hunt Jackson: A literary life*. Berkeley, CA: University of California Press.
Sherer Mathes, V. (1992). *Helen Hunt Jackson and her Indian reform legacy*. Austin, TX: University of Texas Press.
Sherer Mathes, V. (Ed.). (1998). *Indian reform letters of Helen Hunt Jackson, 1879–1885*. Norman, OK: University of Oklahoma Press.
Starr, K. (1985). *Inventing the dream: California through the Progressive Era*. New York: Oxford University Press.
Thayer, F. S. (1886). *A tribute to Helen Hunt Jackson*. Denver: Frank S. Thayer. Public domain copy available at https://books.google.com/books?id=NtIrAQAAMAAJ&printsec=frontcover&source=gbs_ge_summary_r&cad=0#v=onepage&q&f=false
Torr, J. D. (2003). *Westward expansion*. San Diego: Greenhaven Press.
Webb O'Dell, R. (1939). *Helen Hunt Jackson*. New York: Appleton-Century.
West, M. I. (Ed.). (2002). *Westward to a high mountain: Selected Colorado writings of Helen Hunt Jackson*. Palmer Lake, CO: Filter Press.
Wilkins, E. T., Wilkins, J. W., & Boyer, P. S. (1971). *Notable American women: 1607–1950*. Cambridge, MA: Harvard University Press.

Credits

Fig. 9.1: Source: https://www.flickr.com/photos/internetarchivebookimages/14758067876/.
Fig. 9.2: Source: https://commons.wikimedia.org/wiki/File:Chief_Joseph_Group_Photo.png.

Chapter 10

Prejudice and Discrimination Continues

The Chinese Exclusion Act, PL 47–126 (1882)

Introduction

One of the long-term consequences of the Gold Rush in California, starting in 1848, was the expansive growth in the number of immigrants from China, who streamed to the West Coast of the United States in search of opportunity and employment. In the very early days following the discovery of gold, these new Chinese immigrants were not publically accepted but merely tolerated and mostly left alone to pursue their dreams. Once the flow of gold lessened and competition arose for new mining sites and for the jobs that accompanied the gold mining trade, the immigrant Chinese community suffered overt prejudice and discrimination. Many relocated to urban centers such as Los Angeles and San Francisco, where they took menial jobs in restaurants and commercial laundries. Others, however, accepted employment in the railroad industry. In fact, they were actively recruited through the 1860s to help construct the planned transcontinental railroad that would connect the western states and territories with the midwestern and eastern states.

Spurred on by massive federal funding, the Central Pacific Railroad construction crews pushed east from Sacramento, California, and the Union Pacific Railroad thrust westward in expanding its rail lines from Omaha, Nebraska. The Central Pacific Railroad hired mostly Chinese immigrants, whereas the Union Pacific Railroad drew most of its workers from newly arrived Irish and other European immigrants. The two railroad companies met at Promontory Summit, Utah, on May 10, 1869, and thus began the first connected transportation system across the United States that joined the East Coast to the West Coast.

FIGURE 10.1 Chinese immigration to America: Sketch on board the steamship Alaska, bound for San Francisco.

The crucial role that Chinese immigrants played in that successful venture eastward and westward cannot be stressed too much, even though it was barely recognized by most at the time and even today is scarcely celebrated. By 1868, there were an estimated 12,000 Chinese immigrants employed by the Central Pacific Railroad, and they comprised 80% of the construction workforce. With that large number of workers employed, clearly, they did not function only as cooks, but rather they filled the full range of physical construction jobs, some of which were quite dangerous. They blasted solid rock with black powder dynamite charges, laid wood ties and steel tracks, and, armed with only a pick and a shovel, dug tunnels and irrigation ditches through the notoriously rugged Sierra Nevada mountain range in California and Nevada. A number died and others were seriously injured during this undertaking, but virtually all of the Chinese immigrants proved themselves to be industrious, resourceful, and productive employees. Once completed, the transcontinental railroad facilitated the movement of other immigrant groups from the East Coast to new communities in the Midwest and West, thus helping the expansion of the United States.

Prejudice and discrimination, however, surrounded the Chinese immigrants in the railroad industry and elsewhere throughout California. On the railroads, they were typically paid less than the white workers, excluded from full citizenship by California law at the time, forced to pay state taxes, and they had no official standing in courts to address any grievances. In urban areas, the Chinese tended to cluster in certain neighborhoods, giving rise to the "Chinatown" areas that still exist in urban America. In the last half of the 18th century, the Chinatown areas were viewed by the native-born Americans as filled with young, single males who frequented houses of prostitution, smoked opium, gambled, and ate exotic foods.

The economic instability of these times fueled the growing resentment against Chinese immigrants, who were viewed by native-born Americans as racial inferiors, inept "coolies" willing to work for less and, therefore, responsible for any perceived or real decline in the available job market. Others were offended on moral grounds because they viewed the Chinese immigrants as sinful individuals who spurned the Christian religion and its inherent value system. Still others challenged Chinese immigrants for purely racial reasons: They threatened to defile the "purity" of the native-born American population by their presence and potential for interracial marriage. On the other side, a number of business leaders were willing to overlook these deficiencies in Chinese immigrants because they were, at least, a willing and cheap source of unskilled labor.

It was this toxic and contradictory environment that led directly and indirectly to the passage of the *Chinese Exclusion Act* in 1882. The act ordered a 10-year moratorium on the entry into the United States of any unskilled or skilled Chinese immigrant laborer. An exception was allowed for Chinese diplomats and other government officials, students for the term of their education, and wealthy businessmen seeking contacts with American enterprises. Chinese immigrants already residing in the United States were ordered to apply for a certificate that attested to their status as a resident of the United States. Finally, no person of Chinese ancestry could ever become an American citizen, according to the *Chinese Exclusion Act*.

Although the term of the law was a specified 10 years, it could be continued by a simple vote in Congress.

FIGURE 10.2   A Skeleton in His Closet.

Note: Editorial cartoon "A Skeleton in His Closet." Uncle Sam holding a "Protest against Russian exclusion of Jewish Americans" paper and looking in shock at a Chinese skeleton labeled "American exclusion of Chinese" in his closet.

In 1882, President Chester Arthur signed into law the *Chinese Exclusion Act*, the first example in American history of restricting immigration to any group based solely on national identity. China immediately condemned the law as a harmful development that would obstruct positive diplomatic relations between the two nations and its citizens. The Congress and the president had made their decision, however, and thus began a series of strained relations between China and the United States that exists even to the present day.

Predictably, the spirit of the *Chinese Exclusion Act* was continued in the passage of the *Geary Act* 10 years later in 1892 and then made permanent in 1902. Further laws restricted the immigration of Chinese nationals through the 1920s, culminating in the *National Origins Act* in 1929. This federal law limited all immigration to 150,000 per year and fully excluded all Asian nationals, not just Chinese, because their race was considered to be "inferior." In 1943, that law was repealed by the *Magnuson Act*, which was passed only because China was viewed as a bulwark against Japan and, thus, a valuable ally of the United States during World War II. Even in this 1943 repeal, however, only 105 Chinese immigrants were allowed to enter the United States each year. Finally, all immigration restrictions based on national identity was repealed in the *Immigration Act* signed into law by President Lyndon Johnson in 1965.

The future regarding general immigration restriction remains uncertain, however, at the time of this writing. In 2017, President Donald Trump began a process to explore the exclusion of all immigrants from specified countries in the Middle East whose populations are primarily Muslim, though that attempt has been mitigated somewhat by the courts. Furthermore, in 2018, the Trump administration embarked on a policy of rigorously limiting immigration in general and securing the nation's borders against undocumented individuals and families who are often escaping crime, terror, and poverty in their home countries. Thus, the immigration question continues to be fluid in this nation.

- The indispensable contribution of Chinese immigrants to the successful completion of the transcontinental railroad is comprehensively chronicled by the Central Pacific Railroad History Museum, whose website can be accessed at http://cprr.org/museum/chinese.html.
- See also the 2015 PBS-sponsored short film *The Chinese Builders of Gold Mountain*, produced by Nimbus Films, which shows the contribution of Chinese immigrant labor to the California gold mining and wine-making enterprises as well as their involvement in the completion of the transcontinental railroad, available at http://vids.kvie.org/video/2365472420/.

Internet Sources for the Content of This Introduction Include:

http://ocp.hul.harvard.edu/immigration/railroads.html
http://ocp.hul.harvard.edu/immigration/exclusion.html

https://history.state.gov/milestones/1866-1898/chinese-immigration
https://www.loc.gov/rr/program/bib/ourdocs/chinese.html
https://www.loc.gov/teachers/classroommaterials/presentationsandactivities/presentations/immigration/chinese6.html
http://www.npr.org/sections/codeswitch/2017/05/05/527091890/the-135-year-bridge-between-the-chinese-exclusion-act-and-a-proposed-travel-ban
https://en.wikipedia.org/wiki/chinese_exclusion_act

Linkage to Social Welfare History (1875-1900)

Social welfare historical events for this time period include the following:

- General George Custer, along with 275 troopers of the Seventh Cavalry Regiment, are defeated at Little Bighorn in the Dakota territory by Cheyenne and Sioux Indians, led by Chiefs Crazy Horse and Sitting Bull, thus halting the government's drive to return all Cheyenne and Sioux to their reservations (1876).
- Reconstruction formally ends with the withdrawal of all federal troops from Southern states (1877).
- Ten members of the Molly Maguires, an early trade union organization dedicated to improving working conditions in the mining industry, are hanged for murder based on suspect testimony of infiltrators hired by the Pinkerton National Detective Agency (1877).
- The Charity Organization Society (COS), using a model of delivering social services by the individual case method, is formally established in Buffalo, New York (1877).
- In London, the Reverend William Booth formally launches the Salvation Army organization (1878).
- In Pennsylvania, Henry Pratt establishes the Carlisle School, the first boarding school program whose goal is to teach Native American children how to speak correct English and fully integrate into the dominant white society. The children are provided with uniforms, assigned new Europeanized names, and forbidden to speak their native languages (1879).
- Over the past 10 years, approximately 120,000 Chinese immigrants arrive in California, most of whom are men lured by jobs in the mining and railroad industries (1880).
- Milton George organizes the National Farmers Alliance in Chicago to advocate for farm families (1880).
- Booker T. Washington opens the Tuskegee Institute in Alabama as a school for the training of African Americans in the industrial arts (1881).
- Helen Hunt Jackson publishes *A Century of Dishonor*, which documents the persecution endured by seven Indian tribes in 19th-century America, mostly due to actions by public officials (1881).

- Inspired by the work of the Internal Red Cross, Clara Barton founds the American Red Cross organization (1881).
- The American Federation of Labor (AFL), at its first national convention when it was still named the Federation of Organized Trades and Labor Unions of the United States and Canada, calls for the prohibition of any type of labor for children younger than 14 years of age (1881).
- Congress passes the *Immigration Act*, a federal law that charges a tax on all immigrants and bars from admission anyone poor or with a criminal background (1882).
- William Sumner publishes *What Social Classes Owe to Each Other*, a work that applies the natural selection theory of Charles Darwin to social classes and roles (1883).
- Labor leader Samuel Gompers promotes state legislation to prohibit the manufacture of cigars in tenements where thousands of young children work (1883).
- In a group of cases known as the *Civil Rights Cases*, the United States Supreme Court rules that the *14th Amendment*, which mandates the equal treatment for all citizens, does not apply to any privately-owned businesses, such as restaurants, hotels, or railroads, thus ushering in the infamous Jim Crow laws across the South (1883).
- A new drug, cocaine, is introduced by the pharmaceutical industry for use as a local anesthetic (1884).
- Anti-Chinese sentiment erupts into deadly race riots in Rock Springs, the Wyoming Territory, and Tacoma and Seattle in Washington (1885).
- The Haymarket Square labor rally in Chicago ends in violence (1886).
- Defeated Apache leader Geronimo surrenders to Army General Nelson Miles in Arizona (1886).
- *The Dawes Act*, allocating private ownership of land to Indians on federal reservations, is enacted as a law (1887).
- Jane Addams and Ellen Gates Starr open the first settlement house, Hull House, in Chicago, incorporating the use of community-based macro practice as a means of social service delivery (1889).
- Journalist Jacob Riis publishes *How the Other Half Lives*, a devastating pictorial exposé of the poor living in New York City's Lower East Side (1890).
- The infamous *Wounded Knee Massacre* occurs, during which United States Army troops slaughter approximately 150 men, women, and children of the Lakota tribe due to a tragic miscommunication (1890).
- Ellis Island, in New York Harbor, opens to process the escalating surge of immigrants (1892).
- At its National Convention, the Democratic Party includes in its party platform a call for the prohibition of all child labor for children younger than 15 years of age (1892).
- Coca-Cola, advertised as an elixir, and reportedly containing small amounts of cocaine, is introduced (1892).

- President William Harrison reveals the *Treaty of Annexation of Hawaii* (1893).
- In Colorado, women are granted the right to vote in state and local elections (1893).
- Czech composer Antonin Dvorak concludes his *Symphony No. 9, New World Symphony*, a work influenced by African American and Native American melodies, in New York City (1893).
- Pro-American businesses leaders, aided by a company of United States Marines, depose Hawaiian Queen Lili'uokalani and declare the islands an independent republic (1894).
- Labor leader Eugene Debs and the American Railway Union call a national strike and boycott against the Pullman Company and the federal government (1894).
- Booker T. Washington delivers what will be known as *The Atlanta Compromise Speech*, which extols the benefits of education and vocational training for African Americans (1895).
- The United States Supreme Court decides, in *Plessy v. Ferguson*, that segregation of state public facilities is allowed, thereby introducing the principles of separate but equal and white supremacy (1896).
- Prostitution is legalized in the French Quarter section of New Orleans (1897).
- The federal government formally annexes Hawaii with the public support and encouragement of Sanford Ballard Dole and other American business leaders (1898).
- Maud Ballington Booth and Ballington Booth inaugurate the Volunteers of America in New York City (1896).
- Economist Thorstein Veblen publishes *The Theory of the Leisure Class*, an anti-capitalistic indictment of wealthy society across America (1899).
- W.E.B. Du Bois publishes *The Philadelphia Negro*, warning about the dangers of what he termed the "color line" in America (1899).
- In Chicago, Jane Addams and Julia Lathrop helped introduce the first juvenile court, where dependent, neglected, and delinquent children and adolescents are treated with rehabilitation rather than with punishment, as occurred in adult courts (1899).

Note: For a more reflective and functional use of this list of contemporary social welfare historical events, see Question #5 under the **Questions for Further Research and Discussion** section (below).

Sources:

Daniel, C. (1989). *Chronicle of America*. Mt. Kisco, NY: Chronicle Publications.
Mercer, D. (2000). *Millennium year by year*. New York: Dorling Kindersley Publications.
Social welfare developments 1851–1900. (2011). Retrieved from https://socialwelfare.library.vcu.edu/events/1851-1900/

Primary Text Material

Chinese Exclusion Act (1882)

"An Act to execute certain treaty stipulations relating to Chinese.

Whereas in the opinion of the Government of the United States the coming of Chinese laborers to this country endangers the good order of certain localities within the territory thereof: Therefore,

Be it enacted by the Senate and House of Representatives of the United States of America in Congress assembled, That from and after the expiration of ninety days next after the passage of this act, and until the expiration of ten years next after the passage of this act, the coming of Chinese laborers to the United States be, and the same is hereby, suspended; and during such suspension it shall not be lawful for any Chinese laborer to come, or having so come after the expiration of said ninety days to remain within the United States.

SEC. 2. That the master of any vessel who shall knowingly bring within the United States on such vessel, and land or permit to be landed, any Chinese laborer, from any foreign port or place, shall be deemed guilty of a misdemeanor, and on conviction thereof shall be punished by a fine of not more than five hundred dollars for each and every such Chinese laborer so brought, and maybe also imprisoned for a term not exceeding one year . . .

. . . SEC. 14. That hereafter no State court or court of the United States shall admit Chinese to citizenship; and all laws in conflict with this act are hereby repealed.

SEC. 15. That the words "Chinese laborers", wherever used in this act shall be construed to mean both skilled and unskilled laborers and Chinese employed in mining . . ."

Source and full text available at https://www.ourdocuments.gov/doc.php?flash=false&doc=47&page=transcript.

Timeline of General Events in History, the Humanities, and Science During This Period (1875–1900)

These general historical events may help you understand more clearly the overall historical context during which the primary document was created.

- At the Centennial Exhibition in Philadelphia, Alexander Graham Bell demonstrates his latest invention, the telephone (1876).
- Mark Twain publishes *Tom Sawyer* (1876).
- Thomas Edison applies for a patent on his latest invention, which he calls the phonograph (1877).

- A vast track of land encompassing parts of Colorado and Wyoming is formally dedicated as the first national preserve and named Yellowstone National Park (1879).
- Thomas Edison demonstrates his successful innovation called the electric light (1879).
- The first geological survey of the Grand Canyon and the Colorado River is completed (1881).
- Jesse James, the popular outlaw who robbed banks and hijacked trains, is shot dead by his cousin Bob Ford in St. Joseph, Missouri (1882).
- Hiram Maxim invents a repeating machine gun capable of firing 600 bullets per minute (1884).
- Mark Twain publishes The Adventures of Huckleberry Finn (1884).
- The Statue of Liberty, a gift from the French government, is dedicated in New York Harbor (1886).
- The *Sherman Antitrust Act*, designed to prevent business monopolies that hurt the consumer, is enacted into law (1890).
- In a break from both the Democratic and Republican parties, the Populist Party platform, developed by farmers in the South and West, is publically announced (1892).
- John Philip Sousa introduces a "new sound" for marching bands (1892).
- The World Columbian Exposition, commemorating the 400th anniversary of Christopher Columbus's voyage, opens in Chicago and showcases the latest technology (1893).
- William Jennings Bryan delivers his Cross of Gold speech, in which he promotes both gold and silver as legal tender in American monetary policy (1896).
- Based on the *New York Journal's* cartoon, The Yellow Kid, the phrase *yellow journalism* is coined to describe highly sensationalized journalism (1896;).
- *New York Sun* Editor Francis Church responds to a letter from young Virginia O' Hanlon by affirming, "Yes, Virginia, there is a Santa Claus" (1897).
- The Spanish-American War commences, following the sinking of the battleship Maine in the harbor in Havana, Cuba (1898).
- Colonel Theodore Roosevelt leads his Rough Riders, including some African Americans troopers, to victory at San Juan Hill in Santiago, Cuba (1898).
- Scott Joplin publishes the *Maple Leaf Rag* and adds to the popularity of ragtime music (1899).

Sources:

Daniel, C. (1989). *Chronicle of America*. Mt. Kisco, NY: Chronicle Publications.

Events of the 1800s. Retrieved from https://en.wikipedia.org/wiki/19th_century

Mercer, D. (2000). *Millennium year by year*. New York: Dorling Kindersley Publications.

Questions for Further Research and Discussion

1. Read the entire text of the *Chinese Exclusion Act*, and list all the words, phrases, and full sentences that express the prejudice and discrimination that existed in society during that period of American history.
2. Explore further on the Internet the various types of support that Chinese immigrants provided both to the state of California and to the entire nation during this period. Summarize the results of your further research.
3. Conduct an Internet search for the editorials and news articles published in major urban newspapers after the passage of the *Chinese Exclusion Act* on May 6, 1882, then summarize your findings. Did you uncover any noticeable trends or patterns of response?
4. Based on the primary documentary material presented here, as well as other material you discover, what federal policy or policies do you believe should have been developed or changed at that time? Describe those policies in detail. Recall that a policy can be either *legislative* (i.e., a law), *judicial* (i.e., a court decision), or *administrative* (i.e., an executive or organizational policy) in nature.
5. Select three events appearing under the **Linkage to Social Welfare** section (above), conduct further Internet research regarding them, then conclude whether you believe there exists any plausible relationship between the *Chinese Exclusion Act* and the events you have chosen. Use the analytical model presented in Appendix 1 of this book, or develop your own analytical model, to draw these conclusions.
6. Select one book from the **Additional Selected References** list at the end of this chapter. Briefly read through it, then summarize the main points contained in the book. Identify your own personal reaction to this book.

Additional Selected References

Chan, S. (Ed.). (1991). *Entry denied: Exclusion and the Chinese community in America, 1882–1943*. Philadelphia: Temple University Press.

Chang, I. (2003) *The Chinese in America: A narrative history*. New York: Penguin Books.

Gold, M. (2012). *Forbidden citizens: Chinese exclusion and the U.S. Congress: A legislative history*. Alexandria, VA: TheCapital.Net.

Gyory, A. (1998). *Closing the gate: Race, politics, and the Chinese Exclusion Act*. Chapel Hill, NC: University of North Carolina Press.

Hsu, M. Y. (2015). *The good immigrants: How the yellow peril became the model minority*. Princeton, NJ: Princeton University Press.

Hu, S., & Dong, J. (Eds.). (2010). *The rocky road to liberty: A documented history of Chinese immigration and exclusion*. Saratoga, CA: Javin Press.

Miller, S. C. (1969). *The unwelcome immigrant: The American image of the Chinese, 1785–1882*. Berkeley: University of California Press.

Moody, J. (1921). *The railroad builders: A chronicle of the welding of the states.* New Haven: Yale University Press.

Railton, B. (2013). *The Chinese Exclusion Act: What it can teach us about America.* New York: Palgrave Macmillan.

Roleff, T. L. (2004). *Immigration.* San Diego, CA: Greenhaven Press.

Steiner, S. (1979). *Fusang: The Chinese who built America: The railroad men.* New York: Harper & Row.

Wong, K. S., & Chan, S. (Eds.). (1998). *Claiming America: Constructing Chinese American identities during the Exclusion Era.* Philadelphia: Temple University Press.

Yung, J., Chang, G. H., & Lai, H. M. (2006). *Chinese American voices: From the gold rush to the present.* Berkeley: University of California Press.

Credits

Fig. 10.1: Source: https://img.haikudeck.com/mi/C65CD9DD-DB86-4613-90DB-EC5AABEEA6C7.jpg.

Fig. 10.2: Source: https://commons.wikimedia.org/wiki/File:ChineseExclusionSkeletonCartoon.jpg.

Chapter 11

Urban Poverty

Jacob Riis's *How the Other Half Lives: Studies Among the Tenements of New York* (1890)

Introduction

Jacob Riis was born in 1849 in Denmark and immigrated to the United States in 1870. He was trained as a carpenter, but upon arrival in New York, he struggled for several years in various cities to find stable work. Reportedly, he worked at various times as a carpenter, farmer, ironworker, bricklayer, salesman, and community newspaper reporter. During these early years, he was often unemployed, hungry, and homeless, which forced him to live, at times, on the streets of the Lower East Side of Manhattan in New York City. Riis lived in the infamous Five Points neighborhood, an intersection that radiated off into a maze of alleys and side streets, made famous in the fictional and romanticized Hollywood production *Gangs of New York*, directed by Martin Scorsese in 2002.

As a result of these early experiences, Riis literally inhabited the surroundings that he would expose in the future. These distressing personal experiences with poverty proved to be indispensable to his sense of moral outrage at the shocking and demoralizing conditions that poor immigrants were forced to live under.

Riis eventually landed steady work in New York City as a police reporter for the *New-York Tribune* in 1884 and, a few years later, a general reporter for *The Evening Sun*. In his initial role as a police reporter, Riis was assigned to the crime-ridden and dilapidated Lower East Side neighborhood, the landing place of most immigrants seeking a new life in America. Early demonstrating a crisp and gifted writing ability, Riis excelled in his new career and sensitively described in print and image the appalling life circumstances of the urban poor. Along with the horror shown, Riis was able to portray the very humanity

FIGURE 11.1 Jacob Riis.

of people surviving in poverty as well as their bravery and self-reliance against intolerable odds.

In addition to his narrative competency, Riis was one of the first to incorporate flash photography into his journalistic work, a new technology that allowed him to record his subjects inside their dwellings or outside in low light and at night. He also pioneered the use of half-tone reproduction, a photographic process that employs the use of dots of varying sizes and spacing and generates printed images in shades of gray ranging from near-white to total black. This technique heightened the credibility of his photos, which gave rise to a recognition that shockingly graphic printed images could be an agent for social change.

Influenced by the writings of Charles Dickens in England, Riis believed that environmental factors, such as derelict housing, unsanitary living conditions, and the lack of opportunity for work contributed to the presence of poverty and crime, not the fact that some people were intentionally lazy and lawless. Children especially, Riis claimed, could escape the fate of their trapped parents if they had access to parks, playgrounds, and open spaces, like the seashore.

Riis's writings and photographs led to journal articles, interviews, public lectures, and the eventual compilation of his work in the book *How the Other Half Lives: Studies Among the Tenements of New York*, published in 1890. Immediate praise and adulation ensued. The future President Theodore Roosevelt, then the head of the Police Commission in New York City, reportedly contacted Riis with this message: "I have read your book and I have come to help." Soon after, Roosevelt accompanied Riis on a night tour of a slum neighborhood and was so moved by what he witnessed that he worked with New York City officials on legislation to improve the conditions in tenement neighborhoods.

Regrettably, Riis appears also to be a product of his time and place in 19th-century American history—a time when many espoused a belief in what has been termed *scientific racism*. Substantial scientific interest during this period was devoted to investigating phenomena such as the influence of cranial size on intelligence, the practice of eugenics as a means of "purifying" the human race, and the penchant to classify the different races in hierarchical order. Thus, there existed a very small gap between objective scientific inquiry and a belief in the superiority of the white Nordic race with the resultant conviction that other, non-white races or ethnic groups were substantively different and intellectually inferior. This is not to assert that Riis was a racist. Some of the narrative material accompanying his photos, however, does hint that he seems to harbor some

FIGURE 11.2 Children sleeping on Mulberry Street.

racial and ethnic stereotypes even when he is displaying the horrific conditions in the slum tenements. For example, at the beginning of Chapter 5, titled "The Italians in New York" in *How the Other Half Lives*, Riis writes:

> "... The Italian comes in at the bottom [of immigrants], and in the generation that came over the sea he stays there. In the slums he is welcomed as a tenant who "makes less trouble" than the contentious Irishman or the order-loving German, that is to say: is content to live in a pig-sty.... His ignorance and unconquerable suspicion of strangers dig the pit into which he falls. He not only knows no word of English, but he does not know enough to learn..." (pp. 49–50)

His description of African American residents in Chapter 13, titled "The Color Line in New York," also seems somewhat insensitive and prejudicial when he writes:

> "... As a matter of fact the colored man takes in New York, without a struggle, the lower level of menial service for which his past traditions and natural love of ease perhaps as yet fit him best. Even the colored barber is rapidly getting to be a thing of the past. Along the shore, at any unskilled labor, he works unmolested; but he does not appear to prefer the job..." (p. 150)

Other ethnic groups are similarly described in stereotypical language, in spite of the fact that Riis is unwavering in his condemnation of landlords and corrupt city officials who have abused the immigrants and the African American descendants of individuals formerly enslaved.

Finally, Riis is recognized as the precursor to the group of "muckrakers" who were active during the first few decades of the 20th century in America. In this context, a muckraker is an investigative journalist or author who stirred up the dirt or muck that coated society due to the manipulation and corruption of individuals. Noted muckrakers during the Progressive Era in American history were: Lincoln Steffens, whose 1904 book *The Shame of Cities* exposed corruption and incompetence in metropolitan government; Ida Tarbell, who uncovered the monopolistic grip of John D. Rockefeller over the oil industry in her 1904 book *The History of the Standard Oil Company*; and Upton Sinclair, who in 1906 shocked most Americans with his graphic exposé of the contamination and danger in the Chicago meat-packing industry in his novel *The Jungle*.

+ For a more extensive view of other of Riis's photographs displaying the tragic results of poverty, see http://www.museumsyndicate.com/artist.php?artist=930.

FIGURE 11.3   Bandit's Roost (59 1/2 Mulberry Street in New York City).

- See also the website of the International Center on Photography at https://www.icp.org/browse/archive/constituents/jacob-riis?all/all/all/all/all/0.

Internet Sources for the Content of This Introduction Include:

https://petapixel.com/2013/06/16/how-the-other-half-lives-photographs-of-nycs-underbelly-in-the-1890s/
https://www.britannica.com/biography/jacob-riis
https://www.nps.gov/gate/learn/historyculture/jacob-riis-biography.htm
https://www.biography.com/people/jacob-riis
http://www.nyharborparks.org/visit/jari.html
https://en.wikipedia.org/wiki/jacob_riis

Linkage to Social Welfare History (1875–1900)

Social welfare historical events for this time period include the following:

- General George Custer, along with 275 troopers of the Seventh Cavalry Regiment, are defeated at Little Bighorn in the Dakota territory by Cheyenne and Sioux Indians, led by Chiefs Crazy Horse and Sitting Bull, thus halting the government's drive to return all Cheyenne and Sioux to their reservations (1876).
- Reconstruction formally ends with the withdrawal of all federal troops from Southern states (1877).
- Ten members of the Molly Maguires, an early trade union organization dedicated to improving working conditions in the mining industry, are hanged for murder based on suspect testimony of infiltrators hired by the Pinkerton National Detective Agency (1877).
- The Charity Organization Society (COS), using a model of delivering social services by the individual case method, is formally established in Buffalo, New York (1877).
- In London, the Reverend William Booth formally launches the Salvation Army organization (1878).
- In Pennsylvania, Henry Pratt establishes the Carlisle School, the first boarding school program whose goal is to teach Native American children how to speak correct English and fully integrate into the dominant white society. The children are provided with uniforms, assigned new Europeanized names, and forbidden to speak their native languages (1879).
- Over the past 10 years, approximately 120,000 Chinese immigrants arrive in California, most of whom are men lured by jobs in the mining and railroad industries (1880).
- Milton George organizes the National Farmers Alliance in Chicago to advocate for farm families (1880).
- Booker T. Washington opens the Tuskegee Institute in Alabama as a school for the training of African Americans in the industrial arts (1881).

- Helen Hunt Jackson publishes *A Century of Dishonor*, which documents the persecution endured by seven Indian tribes in 19th-century America, mostly due to actions by public officials (1881).
- Inspired by the work of the Internal Red Cross, Clara Barton founds the American Red Cross organization (1881).
- The American Federation of Labor (AFL), at its first national convention when it was stilled named the Federation of Organized Trades and Labor Unions of the United States and Canada, calls for the prohibition of any type of labor for children younger than 14 years of age (1881).
- To quell unrest in the white community over foreigners taking low-level jobs, the *Chinese Exclusion Act*, restricting the immigration and naturalization of Chinese nationals for 10 years, becomes federal law (1882).
- Congress passes the *Immigration Act*, a federal law that charges a tax on all immigrants and bars from admission anyone poor or with a criminal background (1882).
- William Sumner publishes *What Social Classes Owe to Each Other*, a work that applies the natural selection theory of Charles Darwin to social classes and roles (1883).
- Labor leader Samuel Gompers promotes state legislation to prohibit the manufacture of cigars in tenements where thousands of young children work (1883).
- In a group of cases known as the *Civil Rights Cases*, the United States Supreme Court rules that the *14th Amendment*, which mandates the equal treatment for all citizens, does not apply to any privately-owned businesses, such as restaurants, hotels, or railroads, thus ushering in the infamous Jim Crow laws across the South (1883).
- A new drug, cocaine, is introduced by the pharmaceutical industry for use as a local anesthetic (1884).
- Anti-Chinese sentiment erupts into deadly race riots in Rock Springs, the Wyoming Territory, and Tacoma and Seattle in Washington (1885).
- The Haymarket Square labor rally in Chicago ends in violence (1886).
- Defeated Apache leader Geronimo surrenders to Army General Nelson Miles in Arizona (1886).
- *The Dawes Act*, allocating private ownership of land to Indians on federal reservations, is enacted as a law (1887).
- Jane Addams and Ellen Gates Starr open the first settlement house, Hull House, in Chicago, incorporating the use of community-based macro practice as a means of social service delivery (1889).
- The infamous *Wounded Knee Massacre* occurs, during which United States Army troops slaughter approximately 150 men, women, and children of the Lakota tribe due to a tragic miscommunication (1890).
- Ellis Island, in New York Harbor, opens to process the escalating surge of immigrants (1892).

- At its National Convention, the Democratic Party includes in its party platform a call for the prohibition of all child labor for children younger than 15 years of age (1892).
- Coca-Cola, advertised as an elixir, reportedly containing small amounts of cocaine, is introduced (1892).
- President William Harrison reveals the *Treaty of Annexation of Hawaii* (1893).
- In Colorado, women are granted the right to vote in state and local elections (1893).
- Czech composer Antonin Dvorak concludes his *Symphony No. 9, New World Symphony*, a work influenced by African American and Native American melodies, in New York City (1893).
- Pro-American businesses leaders, aided by a company of United States Marines, depose Hawaiian Queen Lili'uokalani and declare the islands an independent republic (1894).
- Labor leader Eugene Debs and the American Railway Union call a national strike and boycott against the Pullman Company and the federal government (1894).
- Booker T. Washington delivers what will be known as *The Atlanta Compromise Speech,* which extols the benefits of education and vocational training for African Americans (1895).
- The United States Supreme Court decides, in *Plessy v. Ferguson*, that segregation of state public facilities is allowed, thereby introducing the principles of separate but equal and white supremacy (1896).
- Prostitution is legalized in the French Quarter section of New Orleans (1897).
- The federal government formally annexes Hawaii with the public support and encouragement of Sanford Ballard Dole and other American business leaders (1898).
- Maud Ballington Booth and Ballington Booth inaugurate the Volunteers of America in New York City (1896).
- Economist Thorstein Veblen publishes *The Theory of the Leisure Class*, an anti-capitalistic indictment of wealthy society across America (1899).
- W.E.B. Du Bois publishes *The Philadelphia Negro*, warning about the dangers of what he termed the "color line" in America (1899).
- In Chicago, Jane Addams and Julia Lathrop helped introduce the first juvenile court, where dependent, neglected, and delinquent children and adolescents are treated with rehabilitation rather than with punishment, as occurred in adult courts (1899).

Note: For a more reflective and functional use of this list of contemporary social welfare historical events, see Question #5 under the **Questions for Further Research and Discussion** section (below).

Sources:

Daniel, C. (1989). *Chronicle of America*. Mt. Kisco, NY: Chronicle Publications.

Mercer, D. (2000). *Millennium year by year*. New York: Dorling Kindersley Publications.

Social welfare developments 1851–1900. (2011). Retrieved from https://socialwelfare.library.vcu.edu/events/1851-1900/

Primary Text Material

Riis, J. A. (1890). *How the other half lives: Studies among the tenements of New York.* New York: Charles Scribner's Sons.

"... It is ten years and over, now, since that line divided New York's population evenly. To-day three-fourths of its people live in the tenements, and the nineteenth century drift of the population to the cities is sending ever-increasing multitudes to crowd them. The fifteen thousand tenant houses that were the despair of the sanitarian in the past generation have swelled into thirty-seven thousand, and more than twelve hundred thousand persons call them home. The one way out he saw—rapid transit to the suburbs—has brought no relief. We know now that there is no way out; that the 'system' that was the evil offspring of public neglect and private greed has come to stay, a storm-centre forever of our civilization. Nothing is left but to make the best of a bad bargain.

What the tenements are and how they grow to what they are, we shall see hereafter. The story is dark enough, drawn from the plain public records, to send a chill to any heart. If it shall appear that the sufferings and the sins of the "other half," and the evil they breed, are but as a just punishment upon the community that gave it no other choice, it will be because that is the truth. The boundary line lies there because, while the forces for good on one side vastly outweigh the bad—it were not well otherwise—in the tenements all the influences make for evil; because they are the hot-beds of the epidemics that carry death to rich and poor alike; the nurseries of pauperism and crime that fill our jails and police courts; that throw off a scum of forty thousand human wrecks to the island asylums and workhouses year by year; that turned out in the last eight years around half million beggars to prey upon our charities; that maintain a standing army of ten thousand tramps with all that that implies; because, above all, they touch the family life with deadly moral contagion. This is their worst crime, inseparable from the system. That we have to own it the child of our own wrong does not excuse it, even though it gives it claim upon our utmost patience and tenderest charity..." (pp. 3-4)

Source and full text available at https://www.gutenberg.org/files/45502/45502-h/45502-h.htm.

Timeline of General Events in History, the Humanities, and Science During This Period (1875–1900)

These general historical events may help you understand more clearly the overall historical context during which the primary document was created.

- At the Centennial Exhibition in Philadelphia, Alexander Graham Bell demonstrates his latest invention, the telephone (1876).
- Mark Twain publishes *Tom Sawyer* (1876).
- Thomas Edison applies for a patent on his latest invention, which he calls the phonograph (1877).
- Thomas Edison demonstrates his successful innovation called the electric light (1879).
- The first geological survey of the Grand Canyon and the Colorado River is completed (1881).
- Jesse James, the popular outlaw who robbed banks and hijacked trains, is shot dead by his cousin Bob Ford in St. Joseph, Missouri (1882).
- Hiram Maxim invents a repeating machine gun capable of firing 600 bullets per minute (1884).
- Mark Twain publishes *The Adventures of Huckleberry Finn* (1884).
- The Statue of Liberty, a gift from the French government, is dedicated in New York Harbor (1886).
- The *Sherman Antitrust Act*, designed to prevent business monopolies that hurt the consumer, is enacted into law (1890).
- In a break from both the Democratic and Republican parties, the Populist Party platform, developed by farmers in the South and West, is publically announced (1892).
- John Philip Sousa introduces a "new sound" for marching bands (1892).
- The World Columbian Exposition, commemorating the 400th anniversary of Christopher Columbus's voyage, opens in Chicago and showcases the latest technology (1893).
- William Jennings Bryan delivers his Cross of Gold speech, in which he promotes both gold and silver as legal tender in American monetary policy (1896).
- Based on the *New York Journal's* cartoon, The Yellow Kid, the phrase *yellow journalism* coined to describe highly sensationalized journalism (1896).
- *New York Sun* Editor Francis Church responds to a letter from young Virginia O'Hanlon by affirming, "Yes, Virginia, there is a Santa Claus" (1897).
- The Spanish-American War commences, following the sinking of the battleship Maine in the harbor in Havana, Cuba (1898).
- Colonel Theodore Roosevelt leads his Rough Riders, including some African Americans troopers, to victory at San Juan Hill in Santiago, Cuba (1898).
- Scott Joplin publishes the *Maple Leaf Rag* and adds to the popularity of ragtime music (1899).

Sources:

Daniel, C. (1989). *Chronicle of America*. Mt. Kisco, NY: Chronicle Publications.
Events of the 1800s. Retrieved from https://en.wikipedia.org/wiki/19th_century
Mercer, D. (2000). *Millennium year by year*. New York: Dorling Kindersley Publications.

Questions for Further Research and Discussion

1. Review carefully the array of Jacob Riis's photographs at sites such as http://www.museumsyndicate.com/artist.php?artist=930 and https://www.icp.org/browse/archive/constituents/jacob-riis?all/all/all/all/0. Then choose five photographs that you believe especially capture the image of late-19th-century urban poverty. Summarize, using very specific words and phrases, what you see in these five photographs.

2. Read more extensively the narrative parts of several chapters in Riis's *How the Other Half Lives*, especially the introductions to his chapters. Can you discern any patterns or themes that emerge from Riis's narrative descriptions? Summarize any that you discover.

3. Conduct a more general Internet research on the investigative journalists, known as the muckrakers, who published during the first decades of the 20th century. Choose one muckraker and examine her or his original works in greater detail. Then summarize what you have discovered, emphasizing the issue that the muckraker wrote about and how influential the final work was in addressing that issue. You will be able to access the full text of most works published during this period at http://www.gutenberg.org/ebooks/.

4. Based on the black-and-white photographs of people living in urban poverty as captured by Riis, as well as other material you discover, what federal policy or policies do you believe should have been developed or changed at that time? Describe those policies in detail. Recall that a policy could be either *legislative* (i.e., a law), *judicial* (i.e., a court decision), or *administrative* (i.e., an executive or organizational policy) in nature.

5. Select three events appearing under the **Linkage to Social Welfare** section (above), conduct further Internet research regarding them, then conclude whether you believe there exists any plausible relationship between the photographs of Jacob Riis and the events you have chosen. Use the analytical model presented in Appendix 1 of this book, or develop your own analytical model, to draw these conclusions.

6. Select one book from the **Additional Selected References** list at the end of this chapter. Briefly read through it, then summarize the main points contained in the book. Identify your own personal reaction to this book.

Additional Selected References

Alland, A. (1993). *Jacob A. Riis: Photographer and citizen*. Millerton, NY: Aperture.

Dowling, R. M. (2008) *Slumming in New York: From the waterfront to mythic Harlem*. Evanston, IL: University of Illinois Press.

Fried, L., & Fierst, J. (1977). *Jacob A. Riis: A reference guide*. Boston: G.K. Hall.

Gandaal, K. (1997). *The virtues and the vicious: Jacob Riis, Stephen Crane, and the spectacle of the slum*. New York: Oxford University Press.

Pascal, J. B. (2005). *Jacob Riis: Reporter and reformer*. New York: Oxford University Press.

Sandler, M. W. (2005). *America through the lens: Photographers who changed the nation*. New York: Henry Holt and Co.

Stange, M. (1989). *Symbols of ideal life: Social documentary photography in America, 1890–1915*. Cambridge: Cambridge University Press.

Swienty, T. (2008). *The other half: The life of Jacob Riis and the world of immigrant America* (A. Buk-Swienty, Trans.) New York: W. W. Norton & Company.

Unrau, H. D., & United States. (1981). *Historic structure report, Jacob Riis Park Historic District, historical data, Gateway National Recreation Area New Jersey, New York, package no. 109*. Denver, CO: Denver Service Center, Branch of Historic Preservation, Mid-Atlantic/North Atlantic Team, National Park Service, U.S. Dept. of the Interior.

Ware, L. (1938). Jacob A. Riis: *Police reporter, reformer, useful citizen*. New York: Appleton-Century.

Yochelson, B., Riis, J. A., & Czitrom, D. J. (2007). *Rediscovering Jacob Riis: Exposure journalism and photography in turn-of-the-century*. New York: New Press.

Credits

Fig. 11.1: Source: https://commons.wikimedia.org/wiki/File:Jacob_Riis_3.jpg.

Fig. 11.2: Source: https://commons.wikimedia.org/wiki/File:Riischildren.jpg.

Fig. 11.3: Source: https://commons.wikimedia.org/wiki/File:Bandit%27s_Roost_by_Jacob_Riis.jpeg.

Chapter 12

Racial Segregation Continued

Plessy v. Ferguson, 163 U.S. 537 (1896)

Introduction

The period in American history after the end of the Civil War from 1865 until the election of Rutherford B. Hayes in 1877 is considered the Reconstruction Period, during which the Southern states were largely forced to accept the new reality of absolute equality of rights for all African Americans. It is critical to note that in the mid- and late-19th century, the Republican Party was considered to be progressive on the issue of civil rights, whereas the Democratic Party was rigidly proslavery and pro-Confederacy. During this era, federal troops occupied key areas of the Southern states and provided control over former Confederate practices and institutions, as well as new organizations, such as the Freedmen's Bureau, furnishing concrete help and services to African Americans in areas such as education, employment, housing, and legal situations.

It was in this societal context following the end of Reconstruction that the State of Louisiana passed the *Separate Car Act* (1890), which mandated separate railroad cars in the State of Louisiana for the "white and colored races." This law further stipulated that the segregated railroad cars must have equal facilities in them and both whites and non-whites could not use the car assigned to the other race. In New Orleans, a multiracial group of professionals established the Citizens' Committee to challenge the constitutionality of that law, especially because the language of the law did not clearly define either who was "white" and who was "colored." The Committee enlisted the help of a mixed-race individual, Homer Plessy, a local shoemaker who was seven-eighths white and, therefore, easily passed for white in social situations. The lawyer who defended Plessy was noted civil rights activist Albion Tourgée. The goal was to put forth a test case that would engender public reaction and,

The Daily Picayune of June 9, 1892, took note when Homer Plessy violated Louisiana's Separate Car Act in an effort to test the law.

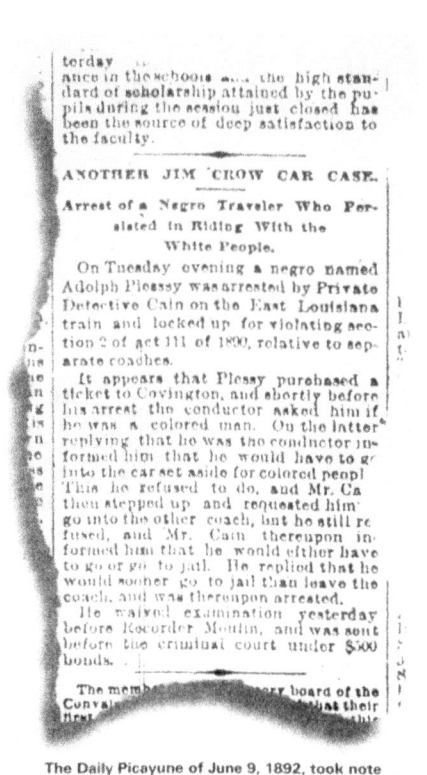

FIGURE 12.1   Newspaper article reporting the arrest of Homer Adolph Plessy for violation of railway segregation law.
NOTE: There are no known photographs of Homer Plessy.

hopefully, dismantle the original legislation. In 1892, Plessy bought a first-class railway ticket on the East Louisiana Railway for travel within Louisiana, and after the Citizens' Committee notified the railway company who Plessy was and what would happen, he purposely sat in a "whites-only" railroad car at the New Orleans station. When ordered by the conductor to leave, he refused and was arrested and soon convicted in a Louisiana District Court by Judge John Ferguson of violating Louisiana law. Plessy immediately challenged Judge Ferguson's decision to the Louisiana Supreme Court, but that court promptly affirmed the lower court decision.

Plessy and the Citizens' Committee then appealed the case to the United States Supreme Court, arguing that any law requiring the segregation of the races on public railways violated both the *13th Amendment* to the *Constitution of the United States*, which abolished slavery, and the *14th Amendment*, which guaranteed "equal protection" rights to all races. In 1896, United States Supreme Court Justice Henry Brown, writing for the majority, upheld the lower court decisions and declared that slavery was not being reintroduced by the original statute and that, furthermore, the *14th Amendment* pertained only to legal rights, such as voting, and did not apply to social rights, such as riding in a railroad car. Justice Brown also remarked that the *14th Amendment* was not intended to abolish the distinctions between the races nor to compel the "comingling" of the races in any social setting. The one lone dissenter, Justice John Marshall Harlan, argued valiantly that the *Constitution of the United States* protects all persons equally and does not confer any privileged status on one race over any other. Justice Harlan went on to note that the *Constitution of the United States* was "color blind" and declared that the Court was just as wrong in this decision as an earlier Court was in the *Dred Scott Decision* in 1857. Unfortunately, *Plessy v. Ferguson* continued the spirit behind the *Dred Scott Decision* (1857), which temporarily legalized slavery and served as the controlling principle in all subsequent cases involving racial separation until *Brown v. Board of Education* in 1954.

Although the Supreme Court decision itself did not use the explicit phrase "separate but equal," *Plessy v. Ferguson* did provide constitutional support for later laws and behaviors that validated the segregation of the races and did literally introduce into American society the concepts of *white supremacy* and *separate but equal*. During this period and for decades later, though some Louisiana railroad cars may have provided equal features for both races, other social entities—such as schools, hospitals, churches, public restrooms, theaters, business waiting rooms, even water fountains—clearly did not have equal facilities for both races.

Plessy v. Ferguson wiped out most of the legislative and social victories that African Americans gained during the brief period of the Reconstruction in the South. During these remarkable 12 years, the Republican Party was able to use the force of the United States Army and new social institutions, such as the Freedmen's Bureau, to advance a political agenda that pursued justice and equality for African Americans in education, housing, employment opportunities, voting rights, and elected political office. Northern religious missionaries, teachers, political consultants, and businessmen streamed south to assist these efforts, and they were vilified by many Southerners as "carpetbaggers." Similarly, those few Southern businessmen who saw opportunities in an equal society and supported the Reconstruction ventures were maligned as "skalawags." By 1878, however, the Democratic Party, dominated by Southern segregationists, gained legislative influence over the nation. President Hayes withdrew the United States Army from Southern states and dismantled the Freedmen's Bureau, and the nation entered a grueling period of Jim Crow legislation and social behavior. The nation witnessed the rise of armed white militias throughout the South whose only intent was to terrorize the African American community into submission. Tragically, the long campaign to restrict the civil and social rights of African Americans began again with a vengeance.

FIGURE 12.2 Albion Tourgée, the lawyer who defended Homer Plessy.

Ten years after *Plessy v. Ferguson*, a group of concerned African Americans from 14 states met in Niagara Falls, New York, to oppose racial segregation and to advocate for equality of rights for all. Led by prominent African American leaders W.E.B. Du Bois and William Trotter, the group became known as the Niagara Movement and eventually morphed into the National Association for the Advancement of Colored People (NAACP), which continues today to fight racism and to seek social justice and equality for all. Perhaps the most ironic legacy of *Plessy v. Ferguson* is the nonprofit organization established by the descendants of the individuals involved. In 2009, Keith Plessy and Phoebe Ferguson, descendants of Homer Plessy and Judge John Ferguson, started the Plessy and Ferguson Foundation with an emphasis on the *and* rather than *versus*. The Foundation's mission is to teach the history of the Supreme Court case and to facilitate dialogue about civil rights in communities. The Foundation's website is accessible at http://www.plessyandferguson.org/?page_id=16.

Internet Sources for the Content of This Introduction Include:

https://www.pbs.org/wnet/supremecourt/antebellum/landmark_plessy.html
https://www.britannica.com/event/plessy-v-ferguson
https://www.casebriefs.com/blog/law/constitutional-law/constitutional-law-keyed-to-stone/equality-and-the-constitution/plessy-v-ferguson-3/2/
https://en.wikipedia.org/wiki/plessy_v._ferguson
http://www.history.com/topics/black-history/plessy-v-ferguson
https://www.thoughtco.com/plessy-v-ferguson-1773294

Linkage to Social Welfare History (1875–1900)

Social welfare historical events for this time period include the following:

- General George Custer, along with 275 troopers of the Seventh Cavalry Regiment, are defeated at Little Bighorn in the Dakota territory by Cheyenne and Sioux Indians, led by Chiefs Crazy Horse and Sitting Bull, thus halting the government's drive to return all Cheyenne and Sioux to their reservations (1876).
- Reconstruction formally ends with the withdrawal of all federal troops from Southern states (1877).
- Ten members of the Molly Maguires, an early trade union organization dedicated to improving working conditions in the mining industry, are hanged for murder based on suspect testimony of infiltrators hired by the Pinkerton National Detective Agency (1877).
- The Charity Organization Society (COS), using a model of delivering social services by the individual case method, is formally established in Buffalo, New York (1877).
- In London, the Reverend William Booth formally launches the Salvation Army organization (1878).
- In Pennsylvania, Henry Pratt establishes the Carlisle School, the first boarding school program whose goal is to teach Native American children how to speak correct English and fully integrate into the dominant white society. The children are provided with uniforms, assigned new Europeanized names, and forbidden to speak their native languages (1879).
- Over the past 10 years, approximately 120,000 Chinese immigrants arrive in California, most of whom are men lured by jobs in the mining and railroad industries (1880).
- Milton George organizes the National Farmers Alliance in Chicago to advocate for farm families (1880).
- Booker T. Washington opens the Tuskegee Institute in Alabama as a school for the training of African Americans in the industrial arts (1881).

- Helen Hunt Jackson publishes *A Century of Dishonor*, which documents the persecution endured by seven Indian tribes in 19th-century America, mostly due to actions by public officials (1881).
- Inspired by the work of the Internal Red Cross, Clara Barton founds the American Red Cross organization (1881).
- The American Federation of Labor (AFL), at its first national convention when it was stilled named the Federation of Organized Trades and Labor Unions of the United States and Canada, calls for the prohibition of any type of labor for children younger than 14 years of age (1881).
- To quell unrest in the white community over foreigners taking low-level jobs, the *Chinese Exclusion Act*, restricting the immigration and naturalization of Chinese nationals for 10 years, becomes federal law (1882).
- Congress passes the *Immigration Act*, a federal law that charges a tax on all immigrants and bars from admission anyone poor or with a criminal background (1882).
- William Sumner publishes *What Social Classes Owe to Each Other*, a work that applies the natural selection theory of Charles Darwin to social classes and roles (1883).
- Labor leader Samuel Gompers promotes state legislation to prohibit the manufacture of cigars in tenements where thousands of young children work (1883).
- In a group of cases known as the *Civil Rights Cases*, the United States Supreme Court rules that the *14th Amendment*, which mandates the equal treatment for all citizens, does not apply to any privately-owned businesses, such as restaurants, hotels, or railroads, thus ushering in the infamous Jim Crow laws across the South (1883).
- A new drug, cocaine, is introduced by the pharmaceutical industry for use as a local anesthetic (1884).
- Anti-Chinese sentiment erupts into deadly race riots in Rock Springs, the Wyoming Territory, and Tacoma and Seattle in Washington (1885).
- The Haymarket Square labor rally in Chicago ends in violence (1886).
- Defeated Apache leader Geronimo surrenders to Army General Nelson Miles in Arizona (1886).
- *The Dawes Act*, allocating private ownership of land to Indians on federal reservations, is enacted as a law (1887).
- Jane Addams and Ellen Gates Starr open the first settlement house, Hull House, in Chicago, incorporating the use of community-based macro practice as a means of social service delivery (1889).
- Journalist Jacob Riis publishes *How the Other Half Lives*, a devastating pictorial exposé of the poor living in New York City's Lower East Side (1890).
- The infamous *Wounded Knee Massacre* occurs, during which United States Army troops slaughter approximately 150 men, women, and children of the Lakota tribe due to a tragic miscommunication (1890).

- Ellis Island, in New York Harbor, opens to process the escalating surge of immigrants (1892).
- At its National Convention, the Democratic Party includes in its party platform a call for the prohibition of all child labor for children younger than 15 years of age (1892).
- Coca-Cola, advertised as an elixir, reportedly containing small amounts of cocaine, is introduced (1892).
- President William Harrison reveals the *Treaty of Annexation of Hawaii* (1893).
- In Colorado, women are granted the right to vote in state and local elections (1893).
- Czech composer Antonin Dvorak concludes his *Symphony No. 9, New World Symphony*, a work influenced by African American and Native American melodies, in New York City (1893).
- Pro-American businesses leaders, aided by a company of United States Marines, depose Hawaiian Queen Lili'uokalani and declare the islands an independent republic (1894).
- Labor leader Eugene Debs and the American Railway Union call a national strike and boycott against the Pullman Company and the federal government (1894).
- Booker T. Washington delivers what will be known as *The Atlanta Compromise Speech*, which extols the benefits of education and vocational training for African Americans (1895).
- Prostitution is legalized in the French Quarter section of New Orleans (1897).
- The federal government formally annexes Hawaii with the public support and encouragement of Sanford Ballard Dole and other American business leaders (1898).
- Maud Ballington Booth and Ballington Booth inaugurate the Volunteers of America in New York City (1896).
- Economist Thorstein Veblen publishes *The Theory of the Leisure Class*, an anticapitalistic indictment of wealthy society across America (1899).
- W.E.B. Du Bois publishes *The Philadelphia Negro*, warning about the dangers of what he termed the "color line" in America (1899).
- In Chicago, Jane Addams and Julia Lathrop helped introduce the first juvenile court, where dependent, neglected, and delinquent children and adolescents are treated with rehabilitation rather than with punishment, as occurred in adult courts (1899).

Note: For a more reflective and functional use of this list of contemporary social welfare historical events, see Question #5 under the **Questions for Further Research and Discussion** section (below).

Sources:
Daniel, C. (1989). *Chronicle of America*. Mt. Kisco, NY: Chronicle Publications.
Mercer, D. (2000). *Millennium year by year*. New York: Dorling Kindersley Publications.

Social welfare developments 1851–1900. (2011). Retrieved from
https://socialwelfare.library.vcu.edu/events/1851-1900/

Primary Text Material

U.S. Supreme Court
Plessy v. Ferguson, 163 U.S. 537 (1896)

"... petitioner was required by the conductor, under penalty of ejection from said train and imprisonment, to vacate said coach, and occupy another seat, in a coach assigned by said company for persons not of the white race, and for no other reason than that petitioner was of the colored race; that, upon petitioner's refusal to comply with such order, he was, with the aid of a police officer, forcibly ejected from said coach, and hurried off to, and imprisoned in, the parish jail of New Orleans, and there held to answer a charge made by such officer to the effect that he was guilty of having criminally violated an act of the general assembly of the state, approved July 10, 1890, in such case made and provided..."

"... This case turns upon the constitutionality of an act of the general assembly of the state of Louisiana, passed in 1890, providing for separate railway carriages for the white and colored races..."

"... The constitutionality of this act is attacked upon the ground that it conflicts both with the thirteenth amendment of the constitution, abolishing slavery, and the fourteenth amendment, which prohibits certain restrictive legislation on the part of the states.

1. That it does not conflict with the thirteenth amendment, which abolished slavery and involuntary servitude, except a punishment for crime, is too clear for argument..."

"... 2. By the fourteenth amendment, all persons born or naturalized in the United States, and subject to the jurisdiction thereof, are made citizens of the United States and of the state wherein they reside; and the states are forbidden from making or enforcing any law which shall abridge the privileges or immunities of citizens of the United States, or shall deprive any person of life, liberty, or property without due process of law, or deny to any person within their jurisdiction the equal protection of the laws..."

"... The distinction between laws interfering with the political equality of the negro and those requiring the separation of the two races in schools, theaters, and railway carriages has been frequently drawn by this court..."

"... We consider the underlying fallacy of the plaintiff's argument to consist in the assumption that the enforced separation of the two races stamps the colored race with a badge of inferiority. If this be so, it is not by reason of anything found in the act, but solely because the colored race chooses to put that construction upon it..."

Continued

Mr. Justice Harlan Dissenting

"The white race deems itself to be the dominant race in this country. And so it is, in prestige, in achievements, in education, in wealth, and in power. So, I doubt not, it will continue to be for all time, if it remains true to its great heritage, and holds fast to the principles of constitutional liberty. But in view of the constitution, in the eye of the law, there is in this country no superior, dominant, ruling class of citizens. There is no caste here. Our constitution is color-blind, and neither knows nor tolerates classes among citizens. In respect of civil rights, all citizens are equal before the law. The humblest is the peer of the most powerful. The law regards man as man, and takes no account of his surroundings or of his color when his civil rights as guaranteed by the supreme law of the land are involved. It is therefore to be regretted that this high tribunal, the final expositor of the fundamental law of the land, has reached the conclusion that it is competent for a state to regulate the enjoyment by citizens of their civil rights solely upon the basis of race.

In my opinion, the judgment this day rendered will, in time, prove to be quite as pernicious as the decision made by this tribunal in the Dred Scott Case . . ."

Source and full text available at https://www.ourdocuments.gov/doc.php?flash=false&doc=52&page=transcript.

FIGURE 12.3 Supreme Court Justice John Marshall Harlan.

Timeline of General Events in History, the Humanities, and Science During This Period (1875–1900)

These general historical events may help you understand more clearly the overall historical context during which the primary document was created.

- At the Centennial Exhibition in Philadelphia, Alexander Graham Bell demonstrates his latest invention, the telephone (1876).
- Mark Twain publishes *Tom Sawyer* (1876).
- Thomas Edison applies for a patent on his latest invention, which he calls the phonograph (1877).
- Thomas Edison demonstrates his successful innovation called the electric light (1879).
- The first geological survey of the Grand Canyon and the Colorado River is completed (1881).
- Jesse James, the popular outlaw who robbed banks and hijacked trains, is shot dead by his cousin Bob Ford in St. Joseph, Missouri (1882).

- Hiram Maxim invents a repeating machine gun capable of firing 600 bullets per minute (1884).
- Mark Twain publishes *The Adventures of Huckleberry Finn* (1884).
- The Statue of Liberty, a gift from the French government, is dedicated in New York Harbor (1886).
- The *Sherman Anti5rust Act*, designed to prevent business monopolies that hurt the consumer, is enacted into law (1890).
- In a break from both the Democratic and Republican parties, the Populist Party platform, developed by farmers in the South and West, is publicly announced (1892).
- John Philip Sousa introduces a "new sound" for marching bands (1892).
- The World Columbian Exposition, commemorating the 400th anniversary of Christopher Columbus's voyage, opens in Chicago and showcases the latest technology (1893).
- William Jennings Bryan delivers his *Cross of Gold* speech, in which he promotes both gold and silver as legal tender in American monetary policy (1896).
- Based on the *New York Journal's* cartoon, The Yellow Kid, the phrase *yellow journalism* is coined to describe highly sensationalized journalism (1896).
- *New York Sun* Editor Francis Church responds to a letter from young Virginia O' Hanlon by affirming, "Yes, Virginia, there is a Santa Claus" (1897).
- The Spanish-American War commences, following the sinking of the battleship Maine in the harbor in Havana, Cuba (1898).
- Colonel Theodore Roosevelt leads his Rough Riders, including some African Americans troopers, to victory at San Juan Hill in Santiago, Cuba (1898)
- Scott Joplin publishes the *Maple Leaf Rag* and adds to the popularity of ragtime music (1899).

Sources:

Daniel, C. (1989). *Chronicle of America*. Mt. Kisco, NY: Chronicle Publications.
Events of the 1800s. Retrieved from https://en.wikipedia.org/wiki/19th_century
Mercer, D. (2000). *Millennium year by year*. New York: Dorling Kindersley Publications.

Questions for Further Research and Discussion

1. Read the entire text of *Plessy v. Ferguson*, then make a list of all the references, both direct and indirect, in the words used that might indicate the dominant attitudes and the value system regarding race and equality in mid-19th-century America.
2. Conduct further research on the Reconstruction era and on the origin of the words *carpetbagger* and *scalawag* during this period of history. Then summarize your thoughts on whether you agree that the Reconstruction efforts and the roles played by carpetbaggers and scalawags in Southern society may partially explain how *Plessy v. Ferguson* became the majority opinion of the United States Supreme Court.
3. Conduct further Internet research on the so-called Jim Crow legislation throughout the South during this period. Study specifically how those laws affect voting

rights, educational opportunities, and general social interactions between African Americans and their fellow white citizens. Then summarize your findings.
4. Based on the primary documentary material presented here, as well as other material you discover in the **Additional Selected References** at the end of this chapter, what additional federal policy or policies do you believe should have been developed or changed at that time? Describe those policies in detail. Recall that, in addition to a Supreme Court decision (i.e., *judicial*), a policy can be either *legislative* (i.e., a law), or *administrative* (i.e., an executive or organizational policy) in nature.
5. Select three events appearing under the **Linkage to Social Welfare** section (above), conduct further Internet research regarding them, then conclude whether you believe there exists any plausible relationship between the *Plessy v. Ferguson* decision and the events you have chosen. Use the analytical model presented in Appendix 1 of this book, or develop your own analytical model, to draw these conclusions.
6. Select one book from the **Additional Selected References** list at the end of this chapter. Briefly read through it, then summarize the main points contained in the book. Identify your own personal reaction to this book.

Additional Selected References

Aaseng, N. (2003). *Plessy v. Ferguson: Separate but equal*. San Diego, CA: Lucent Books.
Brook, T. (1997). *Plessy v. Ferguson: A brief history with documents*. Boston: Bedford Books.
Davis, T. J. (2012). *Plessy v. Ferguson*. Santa Barbara, CA: Greenwood.
Elliott, M. (2006). *Color-blind justice: Albion Tourgée and the quest for racial equality from the Civil War to Plessy v. Ferguson*. New York: Oxford University Press.
Goldstone, L. (2011). *Inherently unequal: The betrayal of equal rights by the Supreme Court, 1865–1903*. New York: Walker & Company.
Hoffer, W. (2012). *Plessy v. Ferguson: Race and inequality in Jim Crow America*. Lawrence, KS: University Press of Kansas.
Lofgren, C. A. (1987). *The Plessy case: A legal-historical interpretation*. New York: Oxford University Press.
Medley, K. W. (2003). *We as freemen: Plessy v. Ferguson*. Gretna, LA: Pelican Pub. Co.
Olsen, O. H., & American Institute for Marxist Studies. (1967). *The thin disguise: Turning point in Negro history: Plessy v. Ferguson: A documentary presentation, 1864–1896*. New York: Published for A.I.M.S. by Humanities Press.
Tischauser, L. V. (2012). *Jim Crow laws*. Santa Barbara, CA: Greenwood.
Tushnet, M. (2008). *I dissent: Great opposing opinions in landmark Supreme Court cases*. Boston: Beacon Press.

Credits

Fig. 12.1: Source: http://photos.nola.com/tpphotos/2011/09/175plessy_8.html.
Fig. 12.2: Source: https://commons.wikimedia.org/wiki/File:Albion_W._Tourgée.jpg.
Fig. 12.3: Source: https://commons.wikimedia.org/wiki/File:JudgeJMHarlan.jpg.

Chapter 13

Two Views of Racism

Booker T. Washington's *Up from Slavery* (1901)
and W.E.B. Du Bois's *The Souls of Black Folk* (1903)

Introduction

Born into slavery around 1856 on James and Elizabeth Burroughs's tobacco plantation in Franklin County, Virginia, before the outbreak of the Civil War, Booker Taliaferro Washington essentially taught himself to read and write with the encouragement of his mother, Jane. His father is unknown, as formal birth and marriage certificates were not kept for slaves during this period. Washington's surname came from his stepfather, whom his mother married sometime after his birth.

On the Burroughs's plantation, young Washington was assigned to carry the Burroughs's daughter's books to school for her, even though he could not attend the school himself. Following President Lincoln's *Emancipation Proclamation* and the end of hostilities, his family moved to West Virginia, where he worked in coal mines and eventually was able to enroll in the Hampton Normal and Agricultural Institute in Virginia, a historically black educational facility established in 1868 and funded by the Union Army to educate freed African American slaves after the Civil War. The curriculum at Hampton emphasized Christian values, hard work, and a broad industrial education with some classes in mathematics, grammar, and composition. Washington initially paid his tuition by working as a janitor. He excelled at Hampton (now Hampton University) and, after further formal education, eventually was hired as a teacher there. In 1881, Washington was asked to start the Tuskegee Normal and Industrial Institute in Alabama with generous funding from members of the white community. During his life, Washington advanced Tuskegee Institute

FIGURE 13.1 Portrait of Booker T. Washington.

(now Tuskegee University) into a major institution of higher education for the African American community.

Because Washington was committed solely to the industrial education of young African Americans in fields such as agriculture, tailoring, carpentry, cooking (for females), and other practical trades, he was not viewed as a threat to the white supremacy that existed throughout the South during the late-19th and early 20th centuries. Reflecting the era he lived in, Washington believed that African Americans should endure, temporarily at least, segregation and discrimination because only after African Americans proved their worth to society would the white community fully accept them.

In the broader context, Washington quietly accepted the social segregation of the freed African American community as long as they had full access to education and work opportunities and equal justice in the court system. He dismissed the value of agitation for change and any public confrontational activities to challenge racial segregation because he believed they would not be productive in the near or long term. Contrary to other reformers at the time, Washington urged African Americans to educate themselves first and not wish for some immediate change that provided them with full social, economic, and political rights.

Upon its publication in 1901, *Up From Slavery* became an immediate best seller. In this autobiography, Washington chronicles his life from his early days as a slave up through his own work experiences, personal relationships, and role as headmaster of an institution that championed vocational education for African Americans. In his book, Washington also emphasized the virtues of humility and industriousness during the turbulent era of the post-Reconstruction South dominated by a Jim Crow legislative culture. As his fame spread, Washington served as an advisor to Presidents Theodore Roosevelt and William Howard Taft. Controversy continued to follow Washington, however. Following an invitation to dinner at the White House by President Roosevelt in 1901, Washington was highly criticized by some in the white community for his presence there, which was viewed as an affront to the good manners expected of all African Americans. Washington is also noted for a quotation that has been referred to as the *Atlanta Compromise* in that it accepted outright the reality of racial segregation: "In all things that are purely social, we can be as separate as the finger, yet one as the hand in all things essential to human progress" (Chapter XIV: *The Atlanta Exposition Address*). This controversial compromise with Southern white leaders essentially agreed to not resist the segregation, discrimination, and disenfranchisement that they lived with in the South if the white majority state and local governments would allow African

Americans to receive basic educational services, a limited number of vocational prospects, and unopposed access to the legal remedies.

Seeing his role as a "neutral negotiator" between the races, Washington did indeed advocate for change, but he did so quietly and behind the scenes with the white power structure. This conciliatory tactic placed Washington in direct opposition to another African American reformer at the time, W.E.B. Du Bois, who promoted a broad liberal arts education for African Americans and a more active response to social problems.

William Edward Burghardt (W.E.B.) Du Bois was born in the North—Massachusetts—in 1868 and excelled early in formal education up through graduate school. In fact, he became the first African American to earn a PhD from Harvard University (his degree was in history), where his 1896 doctoral dissertation, *The Suppression of the African Slave Trade to the United States of America, 1638–1870*, developed into the first monograph published by Harvard University Press as part of its Historical Series. Although formally trained as a historian, Du Bois received rigorous training in the social sciences in Europe and the United States, and he received faculty appointments as a sociologist throughout his professional career. One of his seminal publications, *The Philadelphia Negro*, in 1899, was an extensive sociological study of the experiences of African Americans in one urban community.

FIGURE 13.2 Cover of the first edition of *Up from Slavery* by Booker T. Washington.

In 1905, Du Bois founded the Niagara Movement, a group of progressive African American professionals who advocated for vigorous social change in the area of race relations. Four years later, in 1909, Du Bois became one of the founding members of the National Association for the Advancement of Colored People (NAACP), where he served as director of publicity and research and also as editor of NAACP's monthly newsletter, *The Crisis*, until 1934.

Following the end of World War I, Du Bois and other African American leaders focused their activism on promoting the passage of anti-lynching legislation throughout the South. For most of his life, Du Bois identified as a socialist and pursued a black nationalist and racial separation agenda, rather than one that emphasized integration into the broader white-dominated society. He believed that meaningful change was possible only through protest and agitation against the white power structure and, unquestionably, not through attempts at peace, conciliation, and societal integration. On the international scene, Du Bois later in life supported pan-Africanism, an anticolonial movement that promoted the belief that all Africans and people of African descent faced similar problems

FIGURE 13.3   W.E.B. Du Bois.

from white-controlled governments and, thus, should cooperate together with the shared goal of overcoming their common oppression.

Du Bois is perhaps most celebrated for his collection of papers *The Souls of Black Folk: Essays and Sketches*, published in 1903. Encompassing 14 chapters, this work covered a wide-ranging series of topics, including, for example, his thoughts on the post-Civil War Reconstruction and both the failures and successes of the Freedmen's Bureau; his disagreements with Booker T. Washington; the influences of the old songs sung by slaves, which he called "sorrow songs;" and even some deeply personal reflections on the death of his infant son. Overall, *The Souls of Black Folk* proposes the notion that African Americans face a lifelong duality: what it means to be an American citizen coupled with what it means to be an African American in 19th-century America. Also running throughout the book was another aspect of that contrast, namely that there exists a need for all African Americans to possess a "double consciousness" that reminds them that how they view themselves must always be tempered by the opposite view of them held by white society.

Due undoubtedly to his international work for the cause of pan-Africanism, Du Bois was indicted in 1951 and charged with being an agent of a foreign government. He was eventually acquitted at trial for that contrived offense. After this incident, however, Du Bois felt abandoned by his country of birth and drifted further into his work with African nations, planning a series of pan-African congresses and serving as director of the *Encyclopedia Africana* project, a proposed compilation of stories about the African migration that was sponsored by the president of Ghana. Du Bois became a member of the Communist party in 1961, moved to Ghana to work full-time on the *Encyclopedia Africana* (which was never completed), and died there on August 27,1963, one day before the Civil Rights March in Washington, DC.

Although there were many illustrious civil rights leaders during this period, such as Du Bois, it can be stated unequivocally that Booker T. Washington holds a preeminent place among the most influential African Americans in the early decades of the 20th century.

- A national historical monument in honor of Booker T. Washington has been established and maintained by the National Parks Service in Hardy, Virginia (see https://www.nps.gov/bowa/a-birthplace-that-experienced-slavery-the-civil-war-and-emancipation.htm).
- Online resources maintained by the Booker T. Washington Society in Evansville, Indiana, are available at http://btwsociety.org/library/.

- For further resources on Du Bois, see the W.E.B. Du Bois Research Institute at the Hutchins Center, Harvard University, available at http://hutchinscenter.fas.harvard.edu/dubois/about-w-e-b-du-bois.
- Online resources (manuscripts, photographs, and books) for W.E.B. Du Bois, maintained by the Library of Congress, are available at https://www.loc.gov/rr/program/bib/dubois/.

Internet Sources for the Content of the Introduction Include:

https://www.pbs.org/wnet/jimcrow/stories_people_booker.html
https://www.theatlantic.com/entertainment/archive/2009/03/the-tragedy-and-betrayal-of-booker-t-washington/7092/
https://en.wikiquote.org/wiki/booker_t._washington
http://www.history.com/topics/black-history/booker-t-washington
https://www.biography.com/people/booker-t-washington-9524663
https://en.wikipedia.org/wiki/booker_t._washington
http://www.naacp.org/oldest-and-boldest/naacp-history-w-e-b-dubois/
https://www.britannica.com/biography/w-e-b-du-bois
http://www.blackpast.org/aah/dubois-william-edward-burghardt-1868-1963
https://en.wikipedia.org/wiki/w._e._b._du_bois
https://en.wikipedia.org/wiki/the_souls_of_black_folk

Linkage to Social Welfare History (1900–1925)

Social welfare historical events for this time period include the following:

- Approximately 3.5 million new immigrants arrive in the United States in the past 10 years, with an estimated 100 immigrants per hour being processed through Ellis Island in New York Harbor (1900).
- Army surgeon Dr. Walter Reed proves through a controlled experiment that yellow fever is transmitted through the bite of a mosquito. This discovery is a major influence on the successful completion of the Panama Canal between 1903 and 1914 (1900).
- Helen Keller, blinded as an infant and taught to read and write by her teacher, Anne Sullivan, publishes *The Story of My Life* (1903).
- Labor advocate Mother Jones leads a march of children from Philadelphia to the summer home of President Theodore Roosevelt in Oyster Bay, New York, to dramatize the evils of child labor. The president refuses to meet with her or the children (1903).
- Educator Graham Taylor helps create the Social Science Center for Practical Training in Philanthropic and Social Work, which in 1920 will evolve into a graduate department in Social Service Administration at the University of Chicago (1903).
- African American protesters demonstrate against *Jim Crow* laws by boycotting segregated streetcars in Atlanta, Georgia; Augusta, Georgia; Columbia, South Carolina; New Orleans, Louisiana; Mobile, Alabama; and, Houston, Texas (1904).

- Author Lincoln Steffens publishes his series of essays on the political corruption throughout urban America in his book *The Shame of Cities* (1904).
- University professor, and colleague of Jane Addams, Robert Hunter publishes *Poverty*, one of the early books on the topic of income distribution in America (1904).
- Following a meeting in Fort Erie, Canada, W.E.B. Du Bois announces the formation of the Niagara Movement, an organization committed to full equality for African Americans in all aspects of society (1905).
- Industrialist Andrew Carnegie establishes the Carnegie Foundation to distribute his wealth, with a special focus on funding public educational projects and a network of public libraries across the United States (1905).
- Author Upton Sinclair exposes the unsanitary health practices in the Chicago meat-packing industry in his book *The Jungle* (1906).
- President Roosevelt issues an *executive order* banning the admission into the United States of any Japanese or Korean laborer because of possible negative effects on American workers (1907).
- The United States Supreme Court rules that segregation of races is allowed on all trains traveling between states (1907).
- President Theodore Roosevelt orders the dishonorable discharge of 167 African American soldiers who were charged, without proof, of being involved in a murder and riot in Brownsville, Texas (1907).
- Author Clifford Beers publishes *A Mind That Found Itself*, an autobiographical study that describes his own confinement in a mental health institution (1908).
- Neurologist Dr. Sigmund Freud, accompanied by his student Dr. Carl Jung, arrives in the United States for a series of lectures on psychoanalysis at Clark University in Massachusetts (1909).
- President Theodore Roosevelt convenes the first White House Conference on Child Welfare in Washington, DC (1909).
- The National Association for the Advancement of Colored People (NAACP), an interracial union of African American and white reformers, is formally organized (1909).
- African American heavyweight boxer Jack Johnson defeats his white opponent Jim Jeffries in a stunning victory, leading to deadly race riots erupting across the nation in several cities (1910).
- Ruth Standish Baldwin and George Edmund Haynes formally establish the National Urban League (1910).
- Social reformer Jane Addams publishes her book on the settlement house movement, *Twenty Years at Hull House* (1910).
- In New York City, 146 immigrant women perish in a fire at the Triangle Shirtwaist Company factory due to blocked stairwells and the lack of a functional sprinkler system (1911).
- The International Workers of the World (IWW) labor union successfully settles a strike by textile workers against mill owners in Lawrence, Massachusetts, after weeks of deadly violence between strikers and local police forces (1912).

- Movie producer and director D. W. Phillips releases *Birth of a Nation*, a bitterly racist film that glorifies the Ku Klux Klan as valiant defenders of the white race during the post-Civil War Reconstruction era (1915).
- Birth control advocate Margaret Sanger opens the first public birth control clinic in Brooklyn, New York (1916).
- Because of the recruitment of men into the United States Armed Forces, government statistics indicate that 1.4 million women have replaced men in factories, government, and various business environments (1918).
- Socialist leader Eugene Debs is sentenced to prison for 10 years due to his support of the Bolshevik Revolution and pacifism (1918).
- The *Volstead Act*, prohibiting the production, use, or transport of liquor, becomes law (1919).
- Baseball manager Andrew "Rube" Foster organizes the National Negro Baseball League because African American players are excluded from all major league baseball teams (1920).
- Pan-Africanist advocate and leader of the Universal Negro Improvement Association (UNIA) Marcus Garvey proposes that any African American who wants to leave the United States should to return to Liberia, Africa, which he hoped to develop as an economic and social enterprise (1920).
- With the passage of the *19th Amendment* to the *Constitution of the United States*, women are granted the right to vote (1920).
- Despite widespread lynching of African Americans by white mobs across the South, the United States Congress fails to pass the *Dyer Anti-Lynching Bill* due to a filibuster by senators from Southern states (1922).
- The restructured Ku Klux Klan, driven by hatred of African Americans, Native Americans, Catholics, Jews, and immigrants, is reportedly gaining strength in many states across the nation (1923).
- Tennessee biology teacher John Scopes is found guilty of teaching evolution in what is known as the "Scopes Monkey Trial" that pitted defense lawyer Clarence Darrow against prosecuting attorney William Jennings Bryan (1925).

Note: For a more reflective and functional use of this list of contemporary social welfare historical events, see Question #4 under the **Questions for Further Research and Discussion** section (below).

Sources:

Daniel, C. (1989). *Chronicle of America*. Mt. Kisco, NY: Chronicle Publications.

Mercer, D. (2000). *Millennium year by year*. New York: Dorling Kindersley Publications.

Social welfare developments 1900–1950. (2011). Retrieved from https://socialwelfare.library.vcu.edu/events/1901-1950/

Primary Text Material

Up from Slavery: An Autobiography by Booker T. Washington (1901)

From Chapter 1

"I was born a slave on a plantation in Franklin County, Virginia. I am not quite sure of the exact place or exact date of my birth, but at any rate I suspect I must have been born somewhere and at some time. As nearly as I have been able to learn, I was born near a cross-roads post-office called Hale's Ford, and the year was 1858 or 1859. I do not know the month or the day. The earliest impressions I can now recall are of the plantation and the slave quarters—the latter being the part of the plantation where the slaves had their cabins.

My life had its beginning in the midst of the most miserable, desolate, and discouraging surroundings. This was so, however, not because my owners were especially cruel, for they were not, as compared with many others. I was born in a typical log cabin, about fourteen by sixteen feet square. In this cabin I lived with my mother and a brother and sister till after the Civil War, when we were all declared free.

Of my ancestry I know almost nothing. In the slave quarters, and even later, I heard whispered conversations among the colored people of the tortures which the slaves, including, no doubt, my ancestors on my mother's side, suffered in the middle passage of the slave ship while being conveyed from Africa to America. I have been unsuccessful in securing any information that would throw any accurate light upon the history of my family beyond my mother. She, I remember, had a half-brother and a half-sister. In the days of slavery not very much attention was given to family history and family records—that is, black family records. My mother, I suppose, attracted the attention of a purchaser who was afterward my owner and hers. Her addition to the slave family attracted about as much attention as the purchase of a new horse or cow. Of my father I know even less than of my mother. I do not even know his name. I have heard reports to the effect that he was a white man who lived on one of the near-by plantations. Whoever he was, I never heard of his taking the least interest in me or providing in any way for my rearing. But I do not find especial fault with him. He was simply another unfortunate victim of the institution which the Nation unhappily had engrafted upon it at that time . . .

". . . I cannot remember a single instance during my childhood or early boyhood when our entire family sat down to the table together, and God's blessing was asked, and the family ate a meal in a civilized manner. On the plantation in Virginia, and even later, meals were gotten by the children very much as dumb animals get theirs. It was a piece of bread here and a scrap of meat there. It was a cup of milk at one time and some potatoes at another. Sometimes a portion of our family would eat out of the skillet or pot, while some one else would eat from a tin plate held on the knees, and often using nothing but the hands with which to hold the food. When I had grown to sufficient size, I was required to go to the "big house" at meal-times to fan the flies from the table by means of a large set of paper fans operated by a pulley. Naturally much of the conversation of the white people turned upon the subject of freedom and the war, and I absorbed a good deal of it. I remember that at one time I saw two of my young mistresses and some lady visitors eating ginger-cakes, in the yard. At that time those cakes seemed to me to be absolutely the most tempting and desirable things that I had ever seen; and I then and there resolved that, if I ever got free, the height of my ambition would be reached if I could get to the point where I could secure and eat ginger-cakes in the way that I saw those ladies doing."

Source and full text available at https://www.gutenberg.org/files/2376/2376-h/2376-h.htm#link2HCH0005.

The Souls of Black Folk: Essays and Sketches by W.E.B. Du Bois (1903)

From The Forethought

"... I have sought here to sketch, in vague, uncertain outline, the spiritual world in which ten thousand, thousand Americans live and strive. First, in two chapters I have tried to show what Emancipation meant to them, and what was its aftermath. In a third chapter I have pointed out the slow rise of personal leadership, and criticized candidly the leader who bears the chief burden of his race to-day. Then, in two other chapters I have sketched in swift outline the two worlds within and without the Veil, and thus have come to the central problem of training men for life. Venturing now into deeper detail, I have in two chapters studied the struggles of the massed millions of the black peasantry, and in another have sought to make clear the present relations of the sons of master and man. Leaving, then, the white world, I have stepped within the Veil, raising it that you may view faintly its deeper recesses,—the meaning of its religion, the passion of its human sorrow, and the struggle of its greater souls. All this I have ended with a tale twice told but seldom written, and a chapter of song . . ."

From Chapter III. of Mr. Washington and Others

"... Mr. Washington represents in Negro thought the old attitude of adjustment and submission; but adjustment at such a peculiar time as to make his programme unique. This is an age of unusual economic development, and Mr. Washington's programme naturally takes an economic cast, becoming a gospel of Work and Money to such an extent as apparently almost completely to overshadow the higher aims of life. Moreover, this is an age when the more advanced races are coming in closer contact with the less developed races, and

Continued

the race-feeling is therefore intensified; and Mr. Washington's programme practically accepts the alleged inferiority of the Negro races. Again, in our own land, the reaction from the sentiment of war time has given impetus to race-prejudice against Negroes, and Mr. Washington withdraws many of the high demands of Negroes as men and American citizens. In other periods of intensified prejudice all the Negro's tendency to self-assertion has been called forth; at this period a policy of submission is advocated. In the history of nearly all other races and peoples the doctrine preached at such crises has been that manly self-respect is worth more than lands and houses, and that a people who voluntarily surrender such respect, or cease striving for it, are not worth civilizing.

In answer to this, it has been claimed that the Negro can survive only through submission. Mr. Washington distinctly asks that black people give up, at least for the present, three things,—

First, political power,

Second, insistence on civil rights,

Third, higher education of Negro youth,—and concentrate all their energies on industrial education, and accumulation of wealth, and the conciliation of the South. This policy has been courageously and insistently advocated for over fifteen years, and has been triumphant for perhaps ten years. As a result of this tender of the palm-branch, what has been the return? In these years there have occurred:

1. *The disfranchisement of the Negro.*
2. *The legal creation of a distinct status of civil inferiority for the Negro.*
3. *The steady withdrawal of aid from institutions for the higher training of the Negro.*

These movements are not, to be sure, direct results of Mr. Washington's teachings; but his propaganda has, without a shadow of doubt, helped their speedier accomplishment. The question then comes: Is it possible, and probable, that nine millions of men can make effective progress in economic lines if they are deprived of political rights, made a servile caste, and allowed only the most meagre chance for developing their exceptional men? If history and reason give any distinct answer to these questions, it is an emphatic NO . . .

. . . In failing thus to state plainly and unequivocally the legitimate demands of their people, even at the cost of opposing an honored leader, the thinking classes of American Negroes would shirk a heavy responsibility,—a responsibility to themselves, a responsibility to the struggling masses, a responsibility to the darker races of men whose future depends so largely on this American experiment, but especially a responsibility to this nation,—this common Fatherland. It is wrong to encourage a man or a people in evil-doing; it is wrong to aid and abet a national crime simply because it is unpopular not to do so. The growing spirit of kindliness and reconciliation between the North and South after the frightful difference of a generation ago ought to be a source of deep congratulation

> to all, and especially to those whose mistreatment caused the war; but if that reconciliation is to be marked by the industrial slavery and civic death of those same black men, with permanent legislation into a position of inferiority, then those black men, if they are really men, are called upon by every consideration of patriotism and loyalty to oppose such a course by all civilized methods, even though such opposition involves disagreement with Mr. Booker T. Washington. We have no right to sit silently by while the inevitable seeds are sown for a harvest of disaster to our children, black and white . . ."
>
> Source and full text available at https://www.gutenberg.org/files/408/408-h/408-h.htm.

Timeline of General Events in History, the Humanities, and Science During This Period (1900-1925)

These general historical events may help you understand more clearly the overall historical context during which the primary document was created.

- Eastman Kodak Company launches the Brownie box camera, which costs $1, thereby introducing use of photographic film to the mass market (1900).
- The first successful oil well in Texas, named Spindletop, gushes its treasure of "black gold," and the history of transportation is changed forever (1901).
- President Theodore Roosevelt warns against the power and negative influence of large interstate commercial trusts that are aligned against the consumer (1901).
- Henry Ford releases his first mass-produced car, the Model A, which sells for $385 (1903).
- Italian tenor Enrico Caruso debuts at the New York Metropolitan Opera and receives mixed reviews from music critics (1903).
- The Wright brothers successfully launch their motor-propelled flying machine, named the *Flyer*, at Kitty Hawk Beach in North Carolina (1903).
- The Saint Louis World's Fair introduces the country to two new food innovations: the ice cream cone and iced tea (1904).
- In New York City, restaurateur Gennaro Lombardi introduces a new menu item from Italy, which he calls pizza (1905).
- Noted engineer John F. Stevens oversees the beginning of the construction of the Panama Canal (1905).
- A destructive earthquake and resultant fire demolish much of San Francisco and cause the loss of approximately 3,000 lives (1906).
- U.S. Navy Commodore "Fighting Bob" Evans leads the "Great White Fleet" of 16 battleships on a global tour to impress all nations, especially Japan, of America's military power (1907).

- President Roosevelt establishes the National Conservation Commission with a mandate to preserve the nation's natural resources (1908).
- Henry Ford announces the arrival of a new Model T automobile with advanced features and a price tag of $850 (1908).
- Following a month's journey on the ice, Admiral Robert Peary arrives at the North Pole and plants the American flag (1908).
- The aspiring young architect Frank Lloyd Wright completes the building of the innovative Robie House on the South Side of Chicago, near the University of Chicago (1909).
- The United States Supreme Court orders the breakup of the massive Standard Oil Company, owned by John D. Rockefeller, into 37 distinct companies (1911).
- The White Star steamship *Titanic*, on its initial voyage from Southampton, England, to New York, scrapes an iceberg in the North Atlantic, then sinks with more than 850 people drowned and another 700 rescued by the nearby Cunard liner *Carpathia* (1912).
- The Irish Republican Army, seeking independence from British rule and the creation of the Irish Republic, fails to overcome the British army in the Easter Rising insurrection in Dublin (1916). This failure and the resulting punitive reaction by the British government, however, spur on the Irish to eventually win independence with the establishment of the Irish Free State, excluding the six counties of Northern Ireland, in 1922.
- The United States declares war against Germany after President Woodrow Wilson announces to the United States Congress that "the world must be made safe for democracy" (1917).
- Communist radicals, led by Vladimir Lenin and Leon Trotsky, seize control of the Russian government from President Alexander Kerensky, who took power after the forced abdication of Czar Nicholas II (1917).
- President Wilson proposes the *14 Points peace plan*, focusing on a new and positive world order (1918).
- Germany signs an armistice agreement ending World War I, the Great War, with an estimated toll of 8.5 million combatants killed, including 51,000 Americans, and more than 21 million wounded (1918).
- President Wilson proposes a *League of Nations* to the European allies as a way of maintaining world peace (1919).
- The *Treaty of Versailles* formally signals the collapse of the German Empire and the end of World War I (1919).
- In a Massachusetts criminal court decision that most believe reflect the current political climate against radical movements, admitted anarchists Nicola Sacco and Bartolomeo Vanzetti are found guilty of first-degree murder (1921).
- Russian engineer Vladimir Zworykin invents the iconoscope, which is an early television set that transmits pictures and moving images over the airwaves (1923).

- President-elect Calvin Coolidge is quoted as announcing "the business of America is business" (1925).
- Hitler publishes his autobiography, *Mein Kampf*, outlining his future political plans for Germany (1925).

Sources:

Daniel, C. (1989). *Chronicle of America*. Mt. Kisco, NY: Chronicle Publications.

Events of the 20th century. Retrieved from https://en.wikipedia.org/wiki/timeline_of_the_20th_century

Mercer, D. (2000). *Millennium year by year*. New York: Dorling Kindersley Publications.

Questions for Further Research and Discussion

1. Read further sections of Booker T. Washington's *Up From Slavery: An Autobiography*, then list the varied experiences he encountered and note his reactions to those events.
2. Read further sections of W.E.B. Du Bois's *The Souls of Black Folk: Essays and Sketches*, then list the varied experiences he encountered and note his reactions to those events.
3. Conduct further Internet research on the life and accomplishments of both Washington and Du Bois, then conclude which one you believe exerts greater influence today on civil rights issues. Justify your conclusion with specific examples.
4. Select three events appearing under the **Linkage to Social Welfare** section (above), conduct further Internet research regarding them, then conclude whether you believe there exists any plausible relationship between either *Up from Slavery: An Autobiography* or *The Souls of Black Folk* and the events you have chosen. Specify which book you have selected, then use the analytical model presented in Appendix 1 of this book, or develop your own analytical model, to draw these conclusions.
5. Select one book from the **Additional Selected References** list at the end of this chapter. Briefly read through it, then summarize the main points contained in the book. Identify your own personal reaction to this book.

Additional Selected References

Aldridge, D. P. (2008). *The educational thought of W.E.B. Du Bois: An intellectual history*. New York: Teachers College Press.

Bieze, M., & Gasman, M. (2012). *Booker T. Washington rediscovered*. Baltimore: Johns Hopkins University Press.

Boston, M. B. (2010). *The business strategy of Booker T. Washington: Its development and implementation*. Gainesville: University Press of Florida.

Calhoun, C. J. (2007). *Sociology in America: A history*. Chicago: University of Chicago Press.

Clarke, J. H. (1970). *Black titan: W.E.B. Du Bois*. Boston: Beacon Press.

Hamilton, K. M. (2017). *Booker T. Washington in American memory*. Urbana-Champaign, IL: University of Illinois Press.

Harlan, L. R. (1983). *Booker T. Washington: The wizard of Tuskegee, 1901–1915*. New York: Oxford University Press.

Harris, T. E. (1993). *Analysis of the clash over the issues between Booker T. Washington and W.E.B. Du Bois*. New York: Garland Pub.

Holt, T. C. (2010). *Children of fire: A history of African Americans*. New York: Hill and Wang.

Lewis, D. L. (2001). *W. E. B. Du Bois, 1919–1963: The fight for equality and the American century*. New York: Holt Paperbacks.

Marable, M. (1986). *W.E.B. Du Bois, Black radical democrat*. Boston: Twayne.

Moore, J. M. (2003). *Booker T. Washington, W.E.B. Du Bois, and the struggle for racial uplift*. Wilmington, DE: Scholarly Resources.

Norrell, R. J. (2009). *Up from history: The life of Booker T. Washington*. Boston: Belknap Press/Harvard University Press.

Smock, R. (2009). *Booker T. Washington: Black leadership in the age of Jim Crow*. Chicago: Ivan R. Dee.

West, M. R. (2006). *The education of Booker T. Washington: American democracy and the idea of race relations*. New York: Columbia University Press.

Wilson, F. R. (2006). *The segregated scholars: Black social scientists and the creation of Black labor studies, 1890–1950*. Charlottesville: University of Virginia Press.

Zimmerman, A. (2012). *Alabama in Africa: Booker T. Washington, the German empire, and the globalization of the New South*. Princeton, NJ: Princeton University Press.

Credits

Fig. 13.1: Source: https://commons.wikimedia.org/wiki/File:Booker_T._Washington_(large).jpg.

Fig. 13.2: Source: https://commons.wikimedia.org/wiki/File:UpFromSlavery_cover.jpg.

Fig. 13.3: Source: https://commons.wikimedia.org/wiki/File:WEB_DuBois_1918.jpg.

Chapter 14

Food Health and Safety

Upton Sinclair's *The Jungle* (1906)

Introduction

Upton Sinclair was born in Baltimore, Maryland, in 1878 into a family of two quite different generations of wealth. His father was an alcoholic and a salesman who had difficulty adequately supporting his family, whereas his mother's parents were wealthy. Thus, Sinclair lived between two economic worlds, knowing only near-poverty conditions in his own immediate family but exaggerated comfort when he visited his maternal grandparents.

By the time the family moved to New York City in 1888, Sinclair had become a voracious reader, especially of classic literature, and he eventually graduated from City College and Harvard University. Initially, he supported himself by writing low-priced novels that had popular appeal. During this period, he inevitably evolved toward a commitment to socialism, due undoubtedly to his contempt for the upper-class lifestyle that he had experienced as a youth.

In 1905, while working as a journalist for the socialist newspaper *Appeal to Reason*, Sinclair was sent to Chicago to examine the reported harsh working conditions of the laborers in the meat-packing industry and stockyards. He sought

FIGURE 14.1 Upton Sinclair early in his career.

employment and worked alongside the employees of a meat-packing plant, undercover, then, over a period of several weeks, mingled and interviewed others who labored in similar plants. The result of this investigative reporting was *The Jungle*, a novel that follows the plight of a young Lithuanian immigrant, Jurgis Rukus, who works in a slaughterhouse for low pay and under horrible and dangerous conditions. Sinclair recounted the incidents in which diseased, rotten, and vermin-ridden meats were daily processed and shipped to markets for sale to the general public. The book was an instant success. The general public reacted instinctively to the unsanitary food that was produced for their consumption, which led to the passage of the federal *Food and Drug Act* a few months after the book's release in 1906. This act prohibited the interstate commerce of all adulterated meat food products and empowered federal officials to seize the tainted products and prosecute the owner.

Reportedly, Sinclair was disappointed that the public received *The Jungle* as an indictment of the meat-packing industry because his primary goal was to call attention to the unhealthy working conditions of the mostly immigrant labor force. As Arthur (2006) noted, Sinclair announced to a group of reporters in Chicago when he first arrived to begin his research, "I've come here to write the *Uncle Tom's Cabin* of the Labor Movement!" (p. 43). Sinclair is also noted as having remarked after the public reaction to *The Jungle*, "I aimed at the public's heart and by accident I hit it in the stomach" (*Cosmopolitan*, 1906, https://en.wikiquote.org/wiki/Upton_Sinclair).

Before he completed *The Jungle*, Sinclair published *King Midas*, a novel about unrequited love, in 1901 and the *Journal of Arthur Stirling*, a novel about an unknown poet who commits suicide, in 1903. Both were recognized for their purely literary style, but neither ever gained the attention of the broader American public.

The causes that Sinclair championed were reflective of the Progressive Age and the muckraking movement in which he was a participant: free speech, workers' rights, consumer health and safety, and socialism. He was highly influenced by other noted muckraking journalists, including Ida Tarbell, who exposed the corrosive influences of big business in her 1904 book *The History of the Standard Oil Company*, and Lincoln Steffens, who revealed the corruption in municipal governments in his 1904 work *The Shame of Cities*. Continuing his lifelong commitment to socialism, Sinclair helped found the Intercollegiate Socialist Society in conjunction with novelist Jack London, social reformer Florence Kelley, and labor lawyer Clarence Darrow.

With financial resources gained from the success of *The Jungle*, Sinclair opened an experiential utopian community, *Helicon Hall*, based on socialist principles in Englewood, New Jersey, in 1906. It lasted only six months because it was destroyed by a devastating fire that was started, by some accounts, by a group of opponents of socialism. Sinclair followed the publication of *The Jungle* with a string of other muckraking works, including *King Coal* in 1917, *Oil!* in 1927, and *Boston*, a chronicle of the infamous Sacco and Vanzetti trial for treason, in 1928. None of these latter works received much public acclaim at the time, though *Oil!* did become the basis for the 2007 Academy Award-winning film *There Will Be Blood*, which starred Daniel Day-Lewis.

FIGURE 14.2 Cover of the 1st Edition of *The Jungle* by Upton Sinclair.

Over his lifetime, Sinclair published 90 books, 30 plays, and numerous newspaper and journal articles. He had some limited success when he turned to writing historical novels, most notably *Flivver King*, his 1937 account of the rise of Henry Ford, and *Dragon's Teeth*, his 1942 Pulitzer Prize-winning description of the rise of Adolph Hitler during the 1930s. During the Great Depression, Sinclair started the End Poverty in California (EPIC) movement, which called for a massive public works program and comprehensive tax reform and also served as his political platform for governor of California. He lost the 1934 election, but several of his ideas seem to have been adopted by President Franklin Roosevelt in some of the New Deal programs of his administration.

- For a short, visual overview of *The Jungle*, see the YouTube clips available at https://youtu.be/h2ppaJwQ9UM and https://www.youtube.com/watch?v=Xxe9nosWawM.

Internet Sources for the Content of the Introduction Include:

https://www.britannica.com/biography/upton-sinclair
http://www.encyclopedia.com/people/literature-and-arts/american-literature-biographies/upton-sinclair
https://www.amazon.com/jungle-uncensored-original-upton-sinclair/dp/1884365302
http://www.nytimes.com/ref/timestopics/topics_uptonsinclair.html
https://www.biography.com/people/upton-sinclair-9484897
https://en.wikipedia.org/wiki/upton_sinclair
http://www.motherjones.com/media/2006/01/jungle-100/

Linkage to Social Welfare History (1900–1925)

Social welfare historical events for this time period include the following:

- Approximately 3.5 million new immigrants arrive in the United States in the past 10 years, with an estimated 100 immigrants per hour being processed through Ellis Island in New York Harbor (1900).
- Army surgeon Dr. Walter Reed proves through a controlled experiment that yellow fever is transmitted through the bite of a mosquito. This discovery is a major influence on the successful completion of the Panama Canal between 1903 and 1914 (1900).
- Helen Keller, blinded as an infant and taught to read and write by her teacher, Anne Sullivan, publishes *The Story of My Life* (1903).
- Labor advocate Mother Jones leads a march of children from Philadelphia to the summer home of President Theodore Roosevelt in Oyster Bay, New York, to dramatize the evils of child labor. The president refuses to meet with her or the children (1903).
- Educator Graham Taylor helps create the Social Science Center for Practical Training in Philanthropic and Social Work, which in 1920 will evolve into a graduate department in Social Service Administration at the University of Chicago (1903).
- African American protesters demonstrate against *Jim Crow* laws by boycotting segregated streetcars in Atlanta, Georgia; Augusta, Georgia; Columbia, South Carolina; New Orleans, Louisiana; Mobile, Alabama; and, Houston, Texas (1904).
- Author Lincoln Steffens publishes his series of essays on the political corruption throughout urban America in his book *The Shame of Cities* (1904).
- University professor, and colleague of Jane Addams, Robert Hunter publishes *Poverty*, one of the early books on the topic of income distribution in America (1904).
- Following a meeting in Fort Erie, Canada, W.E.B Du Bois announces the formation of the Niagara Movement, an organization committed to full equality for African Americans in all aspects of society (1905).
- Industrialist Andrew Carnegie establishes the Carnegie Foundation to distribute his wealth, with a special focus on funding public educational projects and a network of public libraries across the United States (1905).

- President Theodore Roosevelt issues an *executive order* banning the admission into the United States of any Japanese or Korean laborer because of possible negative effects on American workers (1907).
- The United States Supreme Court rules that segregation of races is allowed on all trains traveling between states (1907).
- President Theodore Roosevelt orders the dishonorable discharge of 167 African American soldiers who were charged, without proof, of being involved in a murder and riot in Brownsville, Texas (1907).
- Author Clifford Beers publishes *A Mind That Found Itself*, an autobiographical study that describes his own confinement in a mental health institution (1908).
- Neurologist Dr. Sigmund Freud, accompanied by his student Dr. Carl Jung, arrives in the United States for a series of lectures on psychoanalysis at Clark University in Massachusetts (1909).
- President Theodore Roosevelt convenes the first White House Conference on Child Welfare in Washington, DC (1909).
- The National Association for the Advancement of Colored People (NAACP), an interracial union of African American and white reformers, is formally organized (1909).
- African American heavyweight boxer Jack Johnson defeats his white opponent Jim Jeffries in a stunning victory, leading to deadly race riots erupting across the nation in several cities (1910).
- Ruth Standish Baldwin and George Edmund Haynes formally establish the National Urban League (1910).
- Social reformer Jane Addams publishes her book on the settlement house movement, *Twenty Years at Hull House* (1910).
- In New York City, 146 immigrant women perish in a fire at the Triangle Shirtwaist Company factory due to blocked stairwells and the lack of a functional sprinkler system (1911).
- The International Workers of the World (IWW) labor union successfully settles a strike by textile workers against mill owners in Lawrence, Massachusetts, after weeks of deadly violence between strikers and local police forces (1912).
- Movie producer and director D. W. Phillips releases *Birth of a Nation*, a bitterly racist film that glorifies the Ku Klux Klan as valiant defenders of the white race during the post-Civil War Reconstruction era (1915).
- Birth control advocate Margaret Sanger opens the first public birth control clinic in Brooklyn, New York (1916).
- Because of the recruitment of men into the United States Armed Forces, government statistics indicate that 1.4 million women have replaced men in factories, government, and various business environments (1918).
- Socialist leader Eugene Debs is sentenced to prison for 10 years due to his support of the Bolshevik Revolution and pacifism (1918).

- The *Volstead Act*, prohibiting the production, use, or transport of liquor, becomes law (1919).
- Baseball manager Andrew "Rube" Foster organizes the National Negro Baseball League because African American players are excluded from all major league baseball teams (1920).
- Pan-Africanist advocate and leader of the Universal Negro Improvement Association (UNIA) Marcus Garvey proposes that any African American who wants to leave the United States should to return to Liberia, Africa, which he hoped to develop as an economic and social enterprise (1920).
- With the passage of the *19th Amendment* to the *Constitution of the United States*, women are granted the right to vote (1920).
- Despite widespread lynching of African Americans by white mobs across the South, the United States Congress fails to pass the *Dyer Anti-Lynching Bill* due to a filibuster by senators from Southern states (1922).
- The restructured Ku Klux Klan, driven by hatred of African Americans, Native Americans, Catholics, Jews, and immigrants, is reportedly gaining strength in many states across the nation (1923).
- Tennessee biology teacher John Scopes is found guilty of teaching evolution in what is known as the "Scopes Monkey Trial" that pitted defense lawyer Clarence Darrow against prosecuting attorney William Jennings Bryan (1925).

Note: For a more reflective and functional use of this list of contemporary social welfare historical events, see Question #5 under the **Questions for Further Research and Discussion** section (below).

Sources:

Daniel, C. (1989). *Chronicle of America*. Mt. Kisco, NY: Chronicle Publications.

Mercer, D. (2000). *Millennium year by year*. New York: Dorling Kindersley Publications.

Social welfare developments 1900–1950. (2011). Retrieved from https://socialwelfare.library.vcu.edu/events/1901-1950/

Primary Text Material

Upton Sinclair. (1906). *The Jungle*. New York: Doubleday, Page & Co.

"... Jurgis talked lightly about work, because he was young. They told him stories about the breaking down of men, there in the stockyards of Chicago, and of what had happened to them afterward—stories to make your flesh creep, but Jurgis would only laugh. He had only been there four months, and he was young, and a giant besides. There was too much health in him. He could not even imagine how it would feel to be beaten. "That is well enough for men like you," he would say, "silpnas, puny fellows—but my back is broad . . ." (Chapter 2)

". . . There was no heat upon the killing beds; the men might exactly as well have worked out of doors all winter. For that matter, there was very little heat anywhere in the building, except in the cooking rooms and such places—and it was the men who worked in these who ran the most risk of all, because whenever they had to pass to another room they had to go through ice-cold corridors, and sometimes with nothing on above the waist except a sleeveless undershirt. On the killing beds you were apt to be covered with blood, and it would freeze solid; if you leaned against a pillar, you would freeze to that, and if you put your hand upon the blade of your knife, you would run a chance of leaving your skin on it. The men would tie up their feet in newspapers and old sacks, and these would be soaked in blood and frozen, and then soaked again, and so on, until by nighttime a man would be walking on great lumps the size of the feet of an elephant. Now and then, when the bosses were not looking, you would see them plunging their feet and ankles into the steaming hot carcass of the steer, or darting across the room to the hot-water jets. The cruelest thing of all was that nearly all of them—all of those who used knives—were unable to wear gloves, and their arms would be white with frost and their hands would grow numb, and then of course there would be accidents. Also the air would be full of steam, from the hot water and the hot blood, so that you could not see five feet before you; and then, with men rushing about at the speed they kept up on the killing beds, and all with butcher knives, like razors, in their hands—well, it was to be counted as a wonder that there were not more men slaughtered than cattle . . ." (Chapter 7)

". . . Then one Sunday evening, Jurgis sat puffing his pipe by the kitchen stove, and talking with an old fellow whom Jonas had introduced, and who worked in the canning rooms at Durham's; and so Jurgis learned a few things about the great and only Durham canned goods, which had become a national institution. They were regular alchemists at Durham's; they advertised a mushroom-catsup, and the men who made it did not know what a mushroom looked like. They advertised "potted chicken,"—and it was like the boardinghouse soup of the comic papers, through which a chicken had walked with rubbers on. Perhaps they had a secret process for making chickens chemically—who knows? said Jurgis' friend; the things that went into the mixture were tripe, and the fat of pork, and beef suet, and hearts of beef, and finally the waste ends of veal, when they had any. They put these up in several grades, and sold them at several prices; but the contents of the cans all came out of the same hopper. And then there was "potted game" and "potted grouse," "potted ham," and "deviled ham"—de-vyled, as the men called it. "De-vyled" ham was made out of the waste ends of smoked beef that were too small to be sliced by the machines; and also tripe, dyed with chemicals so that it would not show white; and trimmings of hams and corned beef; and potatoes, skins and all; and finally the hard cartilaginous gullets of beef,

Continued

after the tongues had been cut out. All this ingenious mixture was ground up and flavored with spices to make it taste like something. Anybody who could invent a new imitation had been sure of a fortune from old Durham, said Jurgis' informant; but it was hard to think of anything new in a place where so many sharp wits had been at work for so long; where men welcomed tuberculosis in the cattle they were feeding, because it made them fatten more quickly; and where they bought up all the old rancid butter left over in the grocery stores of a continent, and "oxidized" it by a forced-air process, to take away the odor, rechurned it with skim milk, and sold it in bricks in the cities! Up to a year or two ago it had been the custom to kill horses in the yards—ostensibly for fertilizer; but after long agitation the newspapers had been able to make the public realize that the horses were being canned. Now it was against the law to kill horses in Packingtown, and the law was really complied with—for the present, at any rate. Any day, however, one might see sharp-horned and shaggy-haired creatures running with the sheep and yet what a job you would have to get the public to believe that a good part of what it buys for lamb and mutton is really goat's flesh! . . ." (Chapter 9)

Source and full text available at https://www.gutenberg.org/files/140/140-h/140-h.htm.

Timeline of General Events in History, the Humanities, and Science During This Period (1900–1925)

These general historical events may help you understand more clearly the overall historical context during which the primary document was created.

- Eastman Kodak Company launches the Brownie box camera, which costs $1, thereby introducing use of photographic film to the mass market (1900).
- The first successful oil well in Texas, named Spindletop, gushes its treasure of "black gold," and the history of transportation is changed forever (1901).
- President Theodore Roosevelt warns against the power and negative influence of large interstate commercial trusts that are aligned against the consumer (1901).
- Henry Ford releases his first mass-produced car, the Model A, which sells for $385 (1903).
- Italian tenor Enrico Caruso debuts at the New York Metropolitan Opera and receives mixed reviews from music critics (1903).
- The Wright brothers successfully launch their motor-propelled flying machine, named the *Flyer*, at Kitty Hawk Beach in North Carolina (1903).
- The Saint Louis World's Fair introduces the country to two new food innovations: the ice cream cone and iced tea (1904).
- In New York City, restaurateur Gennaro Lombardi introduces a new menu item from Italy, which he calls pizza (1905).

- Noted engineer John F. Stevens oversees the beginning of the construction of the Panama Canal (1905).
- A destructive earthquake and resultant fire demolish much of San Francisco and cause the loss of approximately 3,000 lives (1906).
- U.S. Navy Commodore "Fighting Bob" Evans leads the "Great White Fleet" of 16 battleships on a global tour to impress all nations, especially Japan, of America's military power (1907).
- President Roosevelt establishes the National Conservation Commission with a mandate to preserve the nation's natural resources (1908).
- Henry Ford announces the arrival of a new Model T automobile with advanced features and a price tag of $850 (1908).
- Following a month's journey on the ice, Admiral Robert Peary arrives at the North Pole and plants the American flag (1908).
- The aspiring young architect Frank Lloyd Wright completes the building of the innovative Robie House on the South Side of Chicago, near the University of Chicago (1909).
- The United States Supreme Court orders the breakup of the massive Standard Oil Company, owned by John D. Rockefeller, into 37 distinct companies (1911).
- The White Star steamship *Titanic*, on its initial voyage from Southampton, England, to New York, scrapes an iceberg in the North Atlantic, then sinks with more than 850 people drowned and another 700 rescued by the nearby Cunard liner *Carpathia* (1912).
- The Irish Republican Army, seeking independence from British rule and the creation of the Irish Republic, fails to confront the British Army in the Easter Rising insurrection in Dublin (1916). This failure and the resulting punitive reaction by the British government, however, spur on the Irish to eventually win independence with the establishment of the Irish Free State, excluding the six counties of Northern Ireland, in 1922.
- The United States declares war against Germany after President Woodrow Wilson announces to the United States Congress that "the world must be made safe for democracy" (1917).
- Communist radicals, led by Vladimir Lenin and Leon Trotsky, seize control of the Russian government from President Alexander Kerensky, who took power after the forced abdication of Czar Nicholas II (1917).
- President Wilson proposes the *14 Points peace plan*, focusing on a new and positive world order (1918).
- Germany signs an armistice agreement ending World War I, the Great War, with an estimated toll of 8.5 million combatants killed, including 51,000 Americans, and more than 21 million wounded (1918).
- President Wilson proposes a *League of Nations* to the European allies as a way of maintaining world peace (1919).

- The *Treaty of Versailles* formally signals the collapse of the German Empire and the end of World War I (1919).
- In a Massachusetts criminal court decision that most believe reflect the current political climate against radical movements, admitted anarchists Nicola Sacco and Bartolomeo Vanzetti are found guilty of first-degree murder (1921).
- Russian engineer Vladimir Zworykin invents the iconoscope, an early television set that transmits pictures and moving images over the airwaves (1923).
- President-elect Calvin Coolidge is quoted as announcing "the business of America is business" (1925).
- Adolph Hitler publishes his autobiography, *Mein Kampf*, outlining his future political plans for Germany (1925).

Sources:
Daniel, C. (1989). *Chronicle of America*. Mt. Kisco, NY: Chronicle Publications.
Events of the 20th century. https://en.wikipedia.org/wiki/timeline_of_the_20th_century
Mercer, D. (2000). *Millennium year by year*. New York: Dorling Kindersley Publications.

Questions for Further Research and Discussion

1. On the Internet, search the term *muckraking journalists*, and explore the writings of these authors, in addition to reading more sections of Upton Sinclair's *The Jungle*. Then list the various social issues that were exposed by these Progressive Era reformers.
2. View the C-SPAN film on Sinclair available at https://www.c-span.org/video/?165365-1/writings-upton-sinclair. Then compose a brief summary of your reactions to the dialogue and images portrayed of the Chicago immigrant community and the working conditions in the meat-packing industry both in the 1900s and the present day.
3. Assuming that Sinclair were alive today, make a list of current topics that you believe he would study as an investigative journalist and 21st-century muckraker. Provide a rationale for each item on your list, and theorize how he might approach each issue.
4. Based on the primary documentary material presented here, as well as other material you discover in the **Additional Selected References** at the end of this chapter, what additional federal policy or policies do you believe should have been developed or changed at that time? Describe those policies in detail. Recall that a policy could be either *legislative* (i.e., a law), *judicial* (i.e., a court decision), or *administrative* (i.e., an executive or organizational policy) in nature.
5. Select three events appearing under the **Linkage to Social Welfare** section (above), conduct further Internet research regarding them, then conclude whether you believe there exists any plausible relationship between *The Jungle* and the events

you have chosen. Use the analytical model presented in Appendix 1 of this book, or develop your own analytical model, to draw these conclusions.

6. Select one book from the **Additional Selected References** list at the end of this chapter. Briefly read through it, then summarize the main points contained in the book. Identify your own personal reaction to this book.

Additional Selected References

Arthur, A. (2006). *Radical innocent: Upton Sinclair*. New York: Random House.

Coodley, L. (Ed.). (2004). *The land of orange groves and jails: Upton Sinclair's California*. Berkeley, CA: Heyday Books.

Coodley, L. (2013). *Upton Sinclair: California socialist, celebrity intellectual*. Lincoln, NE: University of Nebraska Press.

Harris, L. (1975). *Upton Sinclair, American rebel*. New York: Thomas Y. Crowell Co.

Mattson, K. (2006). *Upton Sinclair and the other American century*. Hoboken, NJ: John Wiley & Sons.

Mitchell, G. (1991). *Campaign of the century: Upton Sinclair's E.P.I.C. race for governor of California*. New York: Random House.

Mitchell, G. (1991). *The campaign of the century: Upton Sinclair and the EPIC campaign in California*. New York: Atlantic Monthly Press.

Sinclair, U. (1962). *The autobiography of Upton Sinclair*. With Maeve Elizabeth Flynn III. New York: Harcourt, Brace & World.

Scott I. (1996). *Upton Sinclair: The forgotten socialist*. Lanham, MD: Univ. Press of America.

Yoder, J. A. (1975). *Upton Sinclair*. New York: Frederick Ungar.

Credits

Fig. 14.1: Source: https://www.biography.com/.image/t_share/MTM2ODMwNjg4NjYwODI1Njk3/upton_sinclair_1jpg.jpg.

Fig. 14.2: Source: https://pictures.abebooks.com/GLENNDAVIDBOOKS/17851368289.jpg.

Chapter 15

The Settlement House Movement

Jane Addams's *Twenty Years at Hull House* (1910)

Introduction

The youngest of eight children, Jane Addams was born in 1860 in Cedarville, Illinois, into a wealthy family. Her father, who was a strong supporter of Abraham Lincoln, was a successful banker and businessman involved in a variety of agricultural endeavors. Her father also exerted much influence on Addams's early life since her mother died when she was only 2 years old. After graduating from Rockford Female Seminary in Illinois in 1881, Addams, inspired by the works of Charles Dickens, attended medical school for one year but had to leave due to recurring medical problems. During this respite in 1887, Addams traveled to England with her friend, Ellen Starr. They visited the newly established Toynbee Hall, a settlement house located in the East End section of London in an impoverished working-class neighborhood. While there, they encountered students from Oxford and Cambridge universities actually residing in Toynbee Hall in order to learn about the social needs of the poor, collect data about their situations, help instruct the residents in basic skills, and directly improve the social and physical conditions in the community.

Addams and Starr returned to Chicago amazed and highly zealous to duplicate what they had experienced in Toynbee Hall. Using her own family's resources initially, Addams bought and refurbished a vacant building in Chicago's West Side in a poor African American neighborhood. It was named Hull House, in honor of its first owner, Charles Jerald Hull. Addams and Starr formally opened Hull House in 1889 with a commitment to live and work directly in the neighborhood and to teach not simply with words but also with actions. As Hull House progressed over the years, it was supported by donations from wealthy families and individuals and eventually evolved into

FIGURE 15.1 American social reformer Jane Addams (1860–1935).

13 buildings, a playground, and a summer camp situated near Lake Geneva in Wisconsin. Unfortunately, the majority of the original buildings were demolished in 1963 due to the expansion of the University of Illinois at Chicago. The original Hull House building, however, was preserved and serves as a monument to Addams's life and accomplishments. Further information about the existing Hull House Museum on the grounds of the University of Illinois at Chicago is available at http://www.hullhousemuseum.org/about-the-museum/.

Addams was able to attract many prominent educators and social reformers to live and contribute to the varied activities at Hull House for periods of time. Some of these noted activists include: Julia Lathrop, who eventually was appointed the first director of the Children's Bureau by President William Howard Taft in 1912; Florence Kelley, who championed factory inspection and child labor laws and would go on to positively influence federal and state labor legislation; Grace Abbott, a pioneer in immigrant rights who revealed the harsh conditions immigrants were exposed to at Ellis Island and who encouraged significant child labor legislation; Edith Abbott, who advocated for women's rights and helped found the School of Social Service Administration at the University of Chicago; Frances Perkins, who was later appointed as the Secretary of Labor by President Franklin Delano Roosevelt, thus becoming the first woman to serve in a presidential cabinet; and John Dewey, who emphasized that civic duty was essential for a democratic society and highlighted the importance of public education for all citizens.

Addams collaborated with other social reformers and contributed several ongoing developments in Chicago and the nation: the creation of the first juvenile court in Chicago; the passage of regulations for improving tenement buildings and neighborhoods; the law requiring eight-hour working days for women; rules requiring safety guidelines for workers in factories; the movement toward voting rights for women; and the promotion of total social equality for African Americans and immigrant groups. Because of her recognized accomplishments in these areas, Jane Addams served as the first female president of the National Conference on Charities and Corrections (later known as the National Conference on Social Welfare) in 1912. She also helped launch the Women's International League for Peace and Freedom in 1915, as well as the American Civil Liberties Union (ACLU) in 1920. In 1924, because of her leadership role in the Women's International League for Peace and Freedom, Addams was investigated for treason by the Federal Bureau of Investigation (FBI). For further information on this incident, see https://vault.fbi.gov/jane%20addams.

FIGURE 15.2 Hull House, Smith Hall, view north on South Halsted.

When fully operational, Hull House offered a wide array of concrete services for the community, including a day nursery; a gymnasium; an employment bureau; a community kitchen; a boarding home for young women; classes in art, music, theater, English, and mathematics; an art studio; training for young people interested in social work; a community center for varied immigrant groups; night school for working adults; ethnic cultural events; and public exhibitions. In addition to these community services, Hull House conducted research on the health needs and social problems of its neighborhood residents. As such, the Hull House model of service directly contrasts with the Charity Organization Society (COS) model, which encourages a personal "casework" approach to individuals and families experiencing problems. Addams, on the other hand, did not focus on the individual but intended instead to understand the underlying causes of social problems, like poverty, so that her organization could directly advocate for change by tactics such as lobbying for social legislation, exposing publicly the misdeeds of tenement owners, and openly challenging politicians who tolerated and defended institutional corruption.

Although deeply religious in her own life, Addams taught that secular humanism, not religion, should be the underlying motive to help people and form any functional community. Widely recognized as one of the most prominent American reformers during this nation's Progressive Era, Addams tried in vain to end World War I early by imploring President Woodrow Wilson to arrange peace terms between the warring nations. For her endeavors in this area, she was awarded a Nobel Peace Prize in 1931, along with Nicholas Murray Butler, a university president and presidential advisor. For human service workers, however, Addams's most prominent accomplishment is being universally recognized as the founder of the profession of social work in the United States

Internet Sources for the Content of the Introduction Include:
https://www.britannica.com/biography/jane-addams
http://www.naswfoundation.org/pioneers/a/addams.htm
http://ocp.hul.harvard.edu/ww/addams.html
https://www.nobelprize.org/nobel_prizes/peace/laureates/1931/addams-facts.html
https://en.wikipedia.org/wiki/jane_addams

Linkage to Social Welfare History (1900-1925)

Social welfare historical events for this time period include the following:

- Approximately 3.5 million new immigrants arrive in the United States in the past 10 years, with an estimated 100 immigrants per hour being processed through Ellis Island in New York Harbor (1900).
- Army surgeon Dr. Walter Reed proves through a controlled experiment that yellow fever is transmitted through the bite of a mosquito. This discovery is a major influence on the successful completion of the Panama Canal between 1903 and 1914 (1900).
- Helen Keller, blinded as an infant and taught to read and write by her teacher, Anne Sullivan, publishes *The Story of My Life* (1903).
- Labor advocate Mother Jones leads a march of children from Philadelphia to the summer home of President Theodore Roosevelt in Oyster Bay, New York, to dramatize the evils of child labor. The president refuses to meet with her or the children (1903).
- Educator Graham Taylor helps create the Social Science Center for Practical Training in Philanthropic and Social Work, which in 1920 will evolve into a graduate department in Social Service Administration at the University of Chicago (1903).
- African American protesters demonstrate against *Jim Crow* laws by boycotting segregated streetcars in Atlanta, Georgia; Augusta, Georgia; Columbia, South Carolina; New Orleans, Louisiana; Mobile, Alabama; and, Houston, Texas (1904).
- Author Lincoln Steffens publishes his series of essays on the political corruption throughout urban America in his book *The Shame of Cities* (1904).
- University professor, and colleague of Jane Addams, Robert Hunter publishes *Poverty*, one of the early books on the topic of income distribution in America (1904).
- Following a meeting in Fort Erie, Canada, W.E.B. Du Bois announces the formation of the Niagara Movement, an organization committed to full equality for African Americans in all aspects of society (1905).
- Industrialist Andrew Carnegie establishes the Carnegie Foundation to distribute his wealth, with a special focus on funding public educational projects and a network of public libraries across the United States (1905).

- Author Upton Sinclair exposes the unsanitary health practices in the Chicago meat-packing industry in his book *The Jungle* (1906).
- President Theodore Roosevelt issues an *executive order* banning the admission into the United States of any Japanese or Korean laborer because of possible negative effects on American workers (1907).
- The United States Supreme Court rules that segregation of races is allowed on all trains traveling between states (1907).
- President Theodore Roosevelt orders the dishonorable discharge of 167 African American soldiers who were charged, without proof, of being involved in a murder and riot in Brownsville, Texas (1907).
- Author Clifford Beers publishes *A Mind That Found Itself*, an autobiographical study that describes his own confinement in a mental health institution (1908).
- Neurologist Dr. Sigmund Freud, accompanied by his student Dr. Carl Jung, arrives in the United States for a series of lectures on psychoanalysis at Clark University in Massachusetts (1909).
- President Theodore Roosevelt convenes the first White House Conference on Child Welfare in Washington, DC (1909).
- The National Association for the Advancement of Colored People (NAACP), an interracial union of African American and white reformers, is formally organized (1909)
- African American heavyweight boxer Jack Johnson defeats his white opponent Jim Jeffries in a stunning victory, leading to deadly race riots erupting across the nation in several cities (1910).
- Ruth Standish Baldwin and George Edmund Haynes formally establish the Urban League (1910).
- In New York City, 146 immigrant women perish in a fire at the Triangle Shirtwaist Company factory due to blocked stairwells and the lack of a functional sprinkler system (1911).
- The International Workers of the World (IWW) labor union successfully settles a strike by textile workers against mill owners in Lawrence, Massachusetts, after weeks of deadly violence between strikers and local police forces (1912).
- Movie producer and director D. W. Phillips releases *Birth of a Nation*, a bitterly racist film that glorifies the Ku Klux Klan as valiant defenders of the white race during the post-Civil War Reconstruction era (1915).
- Birth control advocate Margaret Sanger opens the first public birth control clinic in Brooklyn, New York (1916).
- Because of the recruitment of men into the United States Armed Forces, government statistics indicate that 1.4 million women have replaced men in factories, government, and various business environments (1918).
- Socialist leader Eugene Debs is sentenced to prison for 10 years due to his support of the Bolshevik Revolution and pacifism (1918).
- The *Volstead Act*, prohibiting the production, use, or transport of liquor, becomes law (1919).

- Baseball manager Andrew "Rube" Foster organizes the National Negro Baseball League because African American players are excluded from all major league baseball teams (1920).
- Pan-Africanist advocate and leader of the Universal Negro Improvement Association (UNIA) Marcus Garvey proposes that any African American who wants to leave the United States should to return to Liberia, Africa, which he hoped to develop as an economic and social enterprise (1920).
- With the passage of the *19th Amendment* to the *Constitution of the United States*, women are granted the right to vote (1920).
- Despite widespread lynching of African Americans by white mobs across the South, the United States Congress fails to pass the *Dyer Anti-Lynching Bill* due to a filibuster by senators from Southern states (1922).
- The restructured Ku Klux Klan, driven by hatred of African Americans, Native Americans, Catholics, Jews, and immigrants, is reportedly gaining strength in many states across the nation (1923).
- Tennessee biology teacher John Scopes is found guilty of teaching evolution in what is known as the "Scopes Monkey Trial" that pitted defense lawyer Clarence Darrow against prosecuting attorney William Jennings Bryan (1925).

Note: For a more reflective and functional use of this list of contemporary social welfare historical events, see Question #5 under the **Questions for Further Research and Discussion** section (below).

Sources:

Daniel, C. (1989). *Chronicle of America*. Mt. Kisco, NY: Chronicle Publications.

Mercer, D. (2000). *Millennium year by year.* New York: Dorling Kindersley Publications.

Social welfare developments 1900–1950. (2011). Retrieved from https://socialwelfare.library.vcu.edu/events/1901-1950/

Primary Text Material

Twenty Years at Hull House with Autobiographical Notes by Jane Addams (1912)

From Chapter 7 The Problems of Poverty

"... *As social reformers gave themselves over to discussion of general principles, so the poor invariably accused poverty itself of their destruction. I recall a certain Mrs. Moran, who was returning one rainy day from the office of the county agent with her arms full of paper bags containing beans and flour which alone lay between her children and starvation. Although she had no money she boarded a street car in order to save her booty from complete destruction by the rain, and as the burst bags dropped "flour on the ladies' dresses" and ""beans all over the place," she was sharply reprimanded by the conductor, who was then further exasperated when he discovered she had no fare. He put her off, as she had hoped he would, almost in front of Hull House. She related to us her state of mind as she stepped off the car and saw the last of her wares disappearing; she admitted she forgot the proprieties and "cursed a little," but, curiously enough, she pronounced her malediction, not against the rain nor the conductor, nor yet against the worthless husband who had been set up to the city prison, but, true to the Chicago spirit of the moment, went to the root of the matter and roundly "cursed poverty . . ."*

. . . I recall a similar case of a woman who had supported her three children for five years, during which time her dissolute husband constantly demanded money for drink and kept her perpetually worried and intimidated. One Saturday, before the "blessed Easter," he came back from a long debauch, ragged and filthy, but in a state of lachrymose repentance. The poor wife received him as a returned prodigal, believed that his remorse would prove lasting, and felt sure that if she and the children went to church with him on Easter Sunday and he could be induced to take the pledge before the priest, all their troubles would be ended. After hours of vigorous effort and the expenditure of all her savings, he finally sat on the front doorstep the morning of Easter Sunday, bathed, shaved and arrayed in a fine new suit of clothes. She left him sitting there in the reluctant spring sunshine while she finished washing and dressing the children. When she finally opened the front door with the three shining children that they might all set forth together, the returned prodigal had disappeared, and was not seen again until midnight, when he came back in a glorious state of intoxication from the proceeds of his pawned clothes and clad once more in the dingiest attire. She took him in without comment, only to begin again the wretched cycle. There were of course instances of the criminal husband as well as of the merely vicious. I recall one woman who, during seven years, never missed a visiting day at the penitentiary when she might see her husband, and whose little children in the nursery proudly reported the messages from father with no notion that he was in disgrace, so absolutely did they reflect the gallant spirit of their mother . . ."

From Chapter 11 Immigrants and Their Children

". . . An evening similar in purpose to the one devoted to the Italians was organized for the Germans, in our first year. Owing to the superior education of our Teutonic guests and the clever leading of a cultivated German woman, these evenings reflected something of that cozy social intercourse which is found in its perfection in the fatherland. Our guests sang a great deal in the tender minor of the German folksong or in the rousing spirit of the Rhine, and they slowly but persistently pursued a course in German history and literature, recovering

Continued

> *something of that poetry and romance which they had long since resigned with other good things. We found strong family affection between them and their English-speaking children, but their pleasures were not in common, and they seldom went out together. Perhaps the greatest value of the Settlement to them was in placing large and pleasant rooms with musical facilities at their disposal, and in reviving their almost forgotten enthusiasms. I have seen sons and daughters stand in complete surprise as their mother's knitting needles softly beat time to the song she was singing, or her worn face turned rosy under the hand-clapping as she made an old-fashioned curtsy at the end of a German poem. It was easy to fancy a growing touch of respect in her children's manner to her, and a rising enthusiasm for German literature and reminiscence on the part of all the family, an effort to bring together the old life and the new, a respect for the older cultivation, and not quite so much assurance that the new was the best . . ."*
>
> Source and full text available at http://www.gutenberg.org/cache/epub/1325/pg1325-images.html.

Timeline of General Events in History, the Humanities, and Science During This Period (1900–1925)

These general historical events may help you understand more clearly the overall historical context during which the primary document was created.

- Eastman Kodak Company launches the Brownie box camera, which costs $1, thereby introducing use of photographic film to the mass market (1900).
- The first successful oil well in Texas, named Spindletop, gushes its treasure of "black gold," and the history of transportation is changed forever (1901).
- President Theodore Roosevelt warns against the power and negative influence of large interstate commercial trusts that are aligned against the consumer (1901).
- Henry Ford releases his first mass-produced car, the Model A, which sells for $385 (1903).
- Italian tenor Enrico Caruso debuts at the New York Metropolitan Opera and receives mixed reviews from music critics (1903).
- The Wright brothers successfully launch their motor-propelled flying machine, named the *Flyer*, at Kitty Hawk Beach in North Carolina (1903).
- The Saint Louis World's Fair introduces the country to two new food innovations: the ice cream cone and iced tea (1904).
- In New York City, restaurateur Gennaro Lombardi introduces a new menu item from Italy, which he calls pizza (1905).
- Noted engineer John F. Stevens oversees the beginning of the construction of the Panama Canal (1905).

- A destructive earthquake and resultant fire demolish much of San Francisco and cause the loss of approximately 3,000 lives (1906).
- U.S. Navy Commodore "Fighting Bob" Evans leads the "Great White Fleet" of 16 battleships on a global tour to impress all nations, especially Japan, of America's military power (1907).
- President Theodore Roosevelt establishes the National Conservation Commission with a mandate to preserve the nation's natural resources (1908).
- Henry Ford announces the arrival of a new Model T automobile with advanced features and a price tag of $850 (1908).
- Following a month's journey on the ice, Admiral Robert Peary arrives at the North Pole and plants the American flag (1908).
- The aspiring young architect Frank Lloyd Wright completes the building of the innovative Robie House on the South Side of Chicago, near the University of Chicago (1909).
- The United States Supreme Court orders the breakup of the massive Standard Oil Company, owned by John D. Rockefeller, into 37 distinct companies (1911).
- The White Star steamship *Titanic*, on its initial voyage from Southampton, England, to New York, scrapes an iceberg in the North Atlantic, then sinks with more than 850 people drowned and another 700 rescued by the nearby Cunard liner *Carpathia* (1912).
- The Irish Republican Army, seeking independence from British rule and the creation of the Irish Republic, fails to confront the British Army in the Easter Rising insurrection in Dublin (1916). This failure and the resulting punitive reaction by the British government, however, spur on the Irish to eventually win independence with the establishment of the Irish Free State, excluding the six counties of Northern Ireland, in 1922.
- The United States declares war against Germany after President Woodrow Wilson announces to the United States Congress that "the world must be made safe for democracy" (1917).
- Communist radicals, led by Vladimir Lenin and Leon Trotsky, seize control of the Russian government from President Alexander Kerensky, who took power after the forced abdication of Czar Nicholas II (1917).
- President Wilson proposes the *14 Points peace plan*, focusing on a new and positive world order (1918).
- Germany signs an armistice agreement ending World War I, the Great War, with an estimated toll of 8.5 million combatants killed, including 51,000 Americans, and more than 21 million wounded (1918).
- President Wilson proposes a *League of Nations* to the European allies as a way of maintaining world peace (1919).
- The *Treaty of Versailles* formally signals the collapse of the German Empire and the end of World War I (1919).

- In a Massachusetts criminal court decision that most believe reflect the current political climate against radical movements, admitted anarchists Nicola Sacco and Bartolomeo Vanzetti are found guilty of first-degree murder (1921).
- Russian engineer Vladimir Zworykin invents the iconoscope, an early television set that transmits pictures and moving images over the airwaves (1923).
- President-elect Calvin Coolidge is quoted as announcing "the business of America is business" (1925).
- Hitler publishes his autobiography, *Mein Kampf*, outlining his future political plans for Germany (1925).

Questions for Further Research and Discussion

1. Read further excerpts from Jane Addams's *Twenty Years at Hull House with Autobiographical Notes*, and list what specific social problems she was facing at Hull House and what concrete services she used to confront those problems.
2. Hull House served many recently arrived immigrant groups including Germans, Greeks, Irish, French Canadians, Italians, Russian Jews, and German Jews. After reading further sections of Addams's *Twenty Years at Hull House with Autobiographical Notes*, list any particular issues that arose among the different ethnic and religious groups, and report on how the Hull House staff handled those issues. In other words, for example, did the German immigrants (or any other group) experience any unique problems adapting to American society, and how was that addressed?
3. Conduct an Internet search of the Charity Organization Society model of social services delivery, then contrast its strategy and tactics with what you have learned about the strategy and tactics used in the settlement house model.
4. Based on the primary documentary material presented here, as well as other material you discover in the **Additional Selected References** at the end of this chapter, what additional federal policy or policies do you believe should have been developed or changed at that time? Describe those policies in detail. Recall that a policy could be either *legislative* (i.e., a law), *judicial* (i.e., a court decision), or *administrative* (i.e., an executive or organizational policy) in nature.
5. Select three events appearing under the **Linkage to Social Welfare** section (above), conduct further Internet research regarding them, then conclude whether you believe there exists any plausible relationship between the settlement house movement or Hull House and the events you have chosen. Use the analytical model presented in Appendix 1 of this book, or develop your own analytical model, to draw these conclusions.
6. Select one book from the **Additional Selected References** list at the end of this chapter. Briefly read through it, then summarize the main points contained in the book. Identify your own personal reaction to this book.

Additional Selected References

Berson, R. K. (2004). *Jane Addams: A biography*. Westport, CT: Greenwood Press.

Briggs, A., & Macartney, A. (1984). *Toynbee Hall. The first hundred years*. London: Routledge and Kegan Paul.

Brown, V. (2004). *The education of Jane Addams*. Philadelphia: University of Pennsylvania Press.

Davis, A. F. (1973). *American heroine: The life and legend of Jane Addams*. New York: Oxford University Press.

Elshtain, J. B. (2002). *Jane Addams and the dream of American democracy: A life*. New York: Basic Books.

Hamington, M. (2009). *The social philosophy of Jane Addams*. Urbana-Champaign, IL: University of Illinois Press.

Harvey, B. C. (1999). *Jane Addams: Nobel Prize winner and founder of Hull House*. Berkeley Heights, NJ: Enslow Publishers.

Josyln, C. (2004). *Jane Addams: A writer's life*. Urbana-Champaign, IL: University of Illinois Press.

Knight, L. W. (2010). *Jane Addams: Spirit in action*. New York: W.W. Norton.

Opdycke, S. (2012). *Jane Addams and her vision for America*. Boston: Prentice Hall.

Polacheck, H. S. (1989). *I came a stranger: The story of a Hull House girl*. Urbana-Champaign, IL: University of Illinois Press.

Shields, P. M. (2017). *Jane Addams: Progressive pioneer of peace, philosophy, sociology, social work, and public administration*. New York: Springer.

Credits

Fig. 15.1: Source: https://commons.wikimedia.org/wiki/File:Jane_Addams_profile.jpg.

Fig. 15.2: Source: https://commons.wikimedia.org/wiki/File:The_Hull_House,_Chicago_(front).tif.

Chapter 16

Voting Equality for Women

The *19th Amendment* to the *Constitution of the United States* (1920)

Introduction

The year 1848 is typically identified as the formal organizational launch of the movement for women's suffrage because that is the year of the Seneca Falls Convention in northern New York State. Although the issue of women's suffrage was not the only focus of the convention, it did emerge as one of the final action principles that emanated from the gathering. At the Convention, several progressive leaders, notably Elizabeth Cady Stanton and Lucretia Mott, heralded the mission of attaining full equality with men in the voting booth as well as achieving a long list of other gender-specific needs. The Seneca Falls Convention produced a formal *Declaration of Sentiments and Resolutions*, which was modeled after the *United States Declaration of Independence* following the Revolutionary War, and argued, in one of its statements, for full equality for women as well as men in all aspects of economic and social interactions.

In addition to Stanton and Mott, the cause of universal suffrage was championed by many other enlightened women and men, including Susan B. Anthony, Henry Blackwell, Frederick Douglass, Lucy Stone, and Sojourner Truth. Anthony was actually arrested in 1872 for illegally voting in a presidential election and fined $100, but she never paid it and was never pursued for any further legal action.

Certainly, there were different approaches among these early reformers, and they did not always agree on action tactics, but their overall strategy was the same: to equalize the right to vote for all American citizens. Most of these early champions for universal suffrage were also active in the abolitionist movement, thereby expressing a consistent commitment to full equality for all men and women without regard to race or gender.

Despite the view that the principle of equality for all, as expressed in the *14th Amendment* to the *United States Constitution*, did indeed include voting rights, this amendment was widely interpreted at the time as applying to women regarding only aspects of their typical day-to-day social activities—such as going to school or church, shopping, holding a conversation, getting married or divorced, joining an organization, and so on—but not voting. To further complicate the issue, the United States Supreme Court in 1875 decreed in *Minor v. Happersett* that the *14th Amendment* did not give women the right to vote.

After the Civil War, the country experienced a massive westward expansion of people and institutions as new states and new territories were formed. In these new areas, the issue of women's suffrage became dominant, so much so that Utah, the Washington territory, and the Wyoming territory granted women the right to vote in state and local elections.

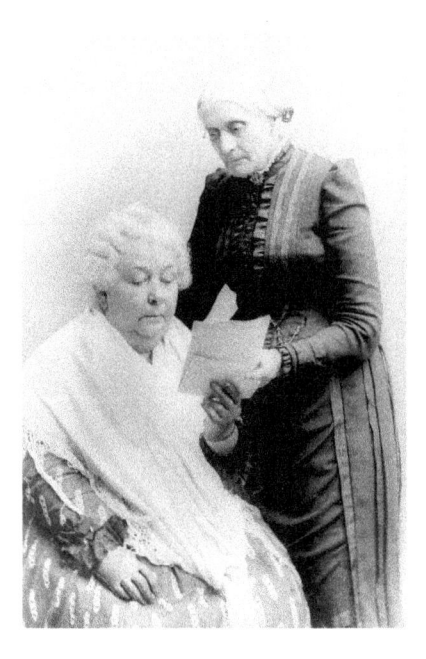

FIGURE 16.1   Elizabeth Cady Stanton (seated) with Susan B. Anthony (standing).

Still, most states did not allow women to vote in local and state elections, and not one of them allowed women to vote in national elections. A further complicating dynamic on this issue that many men exploited was the fact that the *15th Amendment* to the *Constitution of the United States* in 1870 declared that African American men—not women—whether born free or as former slaves, had the right to vote.

FIGURE 16.2   Members of the National American Woman Suffrage Association, seeking the right to vote in elections, march down Pennsylvania Avenue in Washington, DC.

During the 19th century, one societal factor that contributed to the denial of voting rights to women was a communal value system in what has been termed the "cult of true womanhood." In this mindset, women must be protected from the dangers inherent in realities such as war, employment, and politics. Some states even prevented women from owning property or testifying in a court of law. Women were relegated to "safe professions" such as nursing or teaching. There were even beliefs by some that women were unqualified to vote because they lacked the practical knowledge relating to political issues. This sexist attitude concluded that the ideal woman should passively obey her husband and bestow her full attention to maintaining household affairs and nurturing children. She should completely shun the world of politics, which, in addition to being intellectually challenging and conflictual, would inevitably sully her good reputation.

Despite its genesis in the mid-19th century, the concept of full voting equality was not seriously considered until 1918. That year, President Woodrow Wilson linked the cause of women's suffrage with the nation's struggle for freedom and democracy, which was the motivating element in our nation's entrance into World War I. In fact, during the war, the major contributions that women provided toward the general war effort helped to strengthen their call for universal suffrage and diminish the resistance of many men.

In 1919, the United States Congress passed the *19th Amendment* to the *Constitution of the United States*, which affirmed women's right to vote in local, state, and federal elections, therein overruling *Minor v. Happersett* (1875). Most of the Southern states, except Tennessee, refused to ratify the *19th Amendment*, but it eventually was ratified by the required two-thirds majority of all states on August 18, 1920. Yet initially upon ratification, the number of women voting in national elections was surprisingly low, probably due to the continued presence of barriers such as literacy tests, poll taxes, and long residency requirements.

It would take an additional 64 years for all of the states to ratify the *19th Amendment*. The last challenger was the State of Mississippi, which finally ratified the amendment in 1984. As history has revealed, complete gender fairness was not fully achieved in the *19th Amendment*, and the struggle for comprehensive gender equality in all aspects of life, whether economic, political, or social in nature, remains an ongoing and unfulfilled goal even today.

- A large and comprehensive collection of additional photographs of activities of the women's suffrage movement in the United States are available, starting at http://www.old-picture.com/womens-suffrage-index-001.htm.
- For a short, somewhat lighthearted, but informative overview of the women's suffrage movement from Josh Green's *Crash Course in US History*, see https://www.youtube.com/watch?v=HGEMscZE5dY&feature=youtu.be.
- There is also a PBS film by Ken Burns, *Not For Ourselves Alone: The Story of Elizabeth Cady Stanton and Susan B. Anthony*, which may be available in your university media library collection.

Internet Sources for the Content of This Introduction Include:

http://www.history.com/topics/womens-history/19th-amendment
https://www.biography.com/news/19th-amendment-famous-suffragists
http://www.ajc.com/news/national/things-you-never-knew-about-the-19th-amendment-and-women-suffrage/GgGfKwBeauIkiKwkZW4SnK/
https://en.wikipedia.org/wiki/nineteenth_amendment_to_the_united_states_constitution
https://constitutioncenter.org/interactive-constitution/amendments/amendment-xix
http://www.pbs.org/stantonanthony/resources/index.html?body=biography.html

Linkage to Social Welfare History (1900–1925)

Social welfare historical events for this time period include the following:

- Approximately 3.5 million new immigrants arrive in the United States in the past 10 years, with an estimated 100 immigrants per hour currently being processed through Ellis Island in New York Harbor (1900).
- Army surgeon Dr. Walter Reed proves through a controlled experiment that yellow fever is transmitted through the bite of a mosquito. This discovery is a major influence on the successful completion of the Panama Canal between 1903 and 1914 (1900).
- Helen Keller, blinded as an infant and taught to read and write by her teacher, Anne Sullivan, publishes *The Story of My Life* (1903).
- Labor advocate Mother Jones leads a march of children from Philadelphia to the summer home of President Theodore Roosevelt in Oyster Bay, New York, to dramatize the evils of child labor. The president refuses to meet with her or the children (1903).
- Educator Graham Taylor helps create the Social Science Center for Practical Training in Philanthropic and Social Work, which in 1920 will evolve into a graduate department in Social Service Administration at the University of Chicago (1903).
- African American protesters demonstrate against *Jim Crow* laws by boycotting segregated streetcars in Atlanta, Georgia; Augusta, Georgia; Columbia, South Carolina; New Orleans, Louisiana; Mobile, Alabama; and, Houston, Texas (1904).
- Author Lincoln Steffens publishes his series of essays on the political corruption throughout urban America in his book *The Shame of Cities* (1904).
- University professor, and colleague of Jane Addams, Robert Hunter publishes *Poverty*, one of the early books on the topic of income distribution in America (1904).
- Following a meeting in Fort Erie, Canada, W.E.B. Du Bois announces the formation of the Niagara Movement, an organization committed to full equality for African Americans in all aspects of society (1905).
- Industrialist Andrew Carnegie establishes the Carnegie Foundation to distribute his wealth, with a special focus on funding public educational projects and a network of public libraries across the United States (1905).

- Author Upton Sinclair exposes the unsanitary health practices in the Chicago meat-packing industry in his book *The Jungle* (1906).
- President Theodore Roosevelt issues an *executive order* banning the admission into the United States of any Japanese or Korean laborer because of possible negative effects on American workers (1907).
- The United States Supreme Court rules that segregation of races is allowed on all trains traveling between states (1907).
- President Theodore Roosevelt orders the dishonorable discharge of 167 African American soldiers who were charged, without proof, of being involved in a murder and riot in Brownsville, Texas (1907).
- Author Clifford Beers publishes *A Mind That Found Itself*, an autobiographical study that describes his own confinement in a mental health institution (1908).
- Neurologist Dr. Sigmund Freud, accompanied by his student Dr. Carl Jung, arrives in the United States for a series of lectures on psychoanalysis at Clark University in Massachusetts (1909).
- President Theodore Roosevelt convenes the first White House Conference on Child Welfare in Washington, DC (1909).
- The National Association for the Advancement of Colored People (NAACP), an interracial union of African American and white reformers, is formally organized (1909).
- African American heavyweight boxer Jack Johnson defeats his white opponent Jim Jeffries in a stunning victory, leading to deadly race riots erupting across the nation in several cities (1910).
- Ruth Standish Baldwin and George Edmund Haynes formally establish the National Urban League (1910).
- Social reformer Jane Addams publishes her book on the settlement house movement, *Twenty Years at Hull House* (1910).
- In New York City, 146 immigrant women perish in a fire at the Triangle Shirtwaist Company factory due to blocked stairwells and the lack of a functional sprinkler system (1911).
- The International Workers of the World (IWW) labor union successfully settles a strike by textile workers against mill owners in Lawrence, Massachusetts, after weeks of deadly violence between strikers and local police forces (1912).
- Movie producer and director D. W. Phillips releases *Birth of a Nation*, a bitterly racist film that glorifies the Ku Klux Klan as valiant defenders of the white race during the post-Civil War Reconstruction era (1915).
- Birth control advocate Margaret Sanger opens the first public birth control clinic in Brooklyn, New York (1916).
- Because of the recruitment of men into the United States Armed Forces, government statistics indicate that 1.4 million women have replaced men in factories, government, and various business environments (1918).
- Socialist leader Eugene Debs is sentenced to prison for 10 years due to his support of the Bolshevik Revolution and pacifism (1918).

- The *Volstead Act*, prohibiting the production, use, or transport of liquor, becomes law (1919).
- Baseball manager Andrew "Rube" Foster organizes the National Negro Baseball League because African American players are excluded from all major league baseball teams (1920).
- Pan-Africanist advocate and leader of the Universal Negro Improvement Association (UNIA) Marcus Garvey proposes that any African American who wants to leave the United States should to return to Liberia, Africa, which he hoped to develop as an economic and social enterprise (1920).
- Despite widespread lynching of African Americans by white mobs across the South, the United States Congress fails to pass the *Dyer Anti-Lynching Bill* due to a filibuster by senators from Southern states (1922).
- The restructured Ku Klux Klan, driven by hatred of African Americans, Native Americans, Catholics, Jews, and immigrants, is reportedly gaining strength in many states across the nation (1923).
- Tennessee biology teacher John Scopes is found guilty of teaching evolution in what is known as the "Scopes Monkey Trial" that pitted defense lawyer Clarence Darrow against prosecuting attorney William Jennings Bryan (1925).

Note: For a more reflective and functional use of this list of contemporary social welfare historical events, see Question #6 under the **Questions for Further Research and Discussion** section (below).

Sources:

Daniel, C. (1989). *Chronicle of America*. Mt. Kisco, NY: Chronicle Publications.
Mercer, D. (2000). *Millennium year by year*. New York: Dorling Kindersley Publications.
Social welfare developments 1900–1950. (2011). Retrieved from https://socialwelfare.library.vcu.edu/events/1901-1950/

Primary Text Material

Declaration of Sentiments and Resolutions, Seneca Falls, New York (July 1848)

"... Resolved, *That woman is man's equal—was intended to be so by the Creator, and the highest good of the race demands that she should be recognized as such.*

Resolved, *That the women of this country ought to be enlightened in regard to the laws under which they live, that they may no longer publish their degradation, by declaring themselves satisfied with their present position, nor their ignorance, by asserting that they have all the rights they want.*

Resolved, *That inasmuch as man, while claiming for himself intellectual superiority, does accord to woman moral superiority, it is pre-eminently his duty to encourage her to speak, and teach, as she has an opportunity, in all religious assemblies.*

Resolved, *That the same amount of virtue, delicacy, and refinement of behavior, that is required of woman in the social state, should also be required of man, and the same transgressions should be visited with equal severity on both man and woman. . . ."*

Source and full text available at http://ecssba.rutgers.edu/docs/seneca.html.

Transcript of *19th Amendment* to the U.S. *Constitution*: Women's Right to Vote (1920)

"Sixty-sixth Congress of the United States of America; At the First Session,
Begun and held at the City of Washington on Monday, the nineteenth day of May one thousand nine hundred and nineteen.
JOINT RESOLUTION
Proposing an amendment to the Constitution extending the right of suffrage to women.
Resolved by the Senate and House of Representatives of the United States of America in Congress assembled (two-thirds of each House concurring therein), That the following article is proposed as an amendment to the Constitution, which shall be valid to all intents and purposes as part of the Constitution when ratified by the legislature of three-fourths of the several States.
ARTICLE ———.
The right of citizens of the United States to vote shall not be denied or abridged by the United States or by any State on account of sex.
Congress shall have power to enforce this article by appropriate legislation."

Source and full text available at: https://www.ourdocuments.gov/print_friendly.php?flash=false&page=transcript&doc=63&title=Transcript+of+19th+Amendment+to+the+U.S.+Constitution%3A+Womens+Right+to+Vote+%281920%29

Timeline of General Events in History, the Humanities, and Science During This Period (1900–1925)

These general historical events may help you understand more clearly the overall historical context during which the primary document was created.

- Eastman Kodak Company launches the Brownie box camera, which costs $1, thereby introducing use of photographic film to the mass market (1900).
- The first successful oil well in Texas, named Spindletop, gushes its treasure of "black gold," and the history of transportation is changed forever (1901).

- President Theodore Roosevelt warns against the power and negative influence of large interstate commercial trusts that are aligned against the consumer (1901).
- Henry Ford releases his first mass-produced car, the Model A, which sells for $385 (1903).
- Italian tenor Enrico Caruso debuts at the New York Metropolitan Opera and receives mixed reviews from music critics (1903).
- The Wright brothers successfully launch their motor-propelled flying machine, named the *Flyer*, at Kitty Hawk Beach in North Carolina (1903).
- The Saint Louis World's Fair introduces the country to two new food innovations: the ice cream cone and iced tea (1904).
- In New York City, restaurateur Gennaro Lombardi introduces a new menu item from Italy, which he calls pizza (1905).
- Noted engineer John F. Stevens oversees the beginning of the construction of the Panama Canal (1905).
- A destructive earthquake and resultant fire demolish much of San Francisco and cause the loss of approximately 3,000 lives (1906).
- U.S. Navy Commodore "Fighting Bob" Evans leads the "Great White Fleet" of 16 battleships on a global tour to impress all nations, especially Japan, of America's military power (1907).
- President Roosevelt establishes the National Conservation Commission with a mandate to preserve the nation's natural resources (1908).
- Henry Ford announces the arrival of a new Model T automobile with advanced features and a price tag of $850 (1908).
- Following a month's journey on the ice, Admiral Robert Peary arrives at the North Pole and plants the American flag (1908).
- The aspiring young architect Frank Lloyd Wright completes the building of the innovative Robie House on the South Side of Chicago, near the University of Chicago (1909).
- The United States Supreme Court orders the breakup of the massive Standard Oil Company, owned by John D. Rockefeller, into 37 distinct companies (1911).
- The White Star steamship *Titanic*, on its initial voyage from Southampton, England, to New York, scrapes an iceberg in the North Atlantic then sinks with more than 850 people drowned and another 700 rescued by the nearby Cunard liner *Carpathia* (1912).
- The Irish Republican Army, seeking independence from British rule and the creation of the Irish Republic, fails to confront the British Army in the Easter Rising insurrection in Dublin (1916). This failure and the resulting punitive reaction by the British government, however, spur on the Irish to eventually win independence with the establishment of the Irish Free State, excluding the six counties of Northern Ireland, in 1922.
- The United States declares war against Germany after President Woodrow Wilson announces to the United States Congress that "the world must be made safe for democracy" (1917).
- Communist radicals, led by Vladimir Lenin and Leon Trotsky, seize control of the Russian government from President Alexander Kerensky, who took power after the forced abdication of Czar Nicholas II (1917).

- President Wilson proposes the *14 Points peace plan*, focusing on a new and positive world order (1918).
- Germany signs an armistice agreement ending World War I, the Great War, with an estimated toll of 8.5 million combatants killed, including 51,000 Americans, and more than 21 million wounded (1918).
- President Wilson proposes a League of Nations to the European allies as a way of maintaining world peace (1919).
- The *Treaty of Versailles* formally signals the collapse of the German Empire and the end of World War I (1919).
- In a Massachusetts criminal court decision that most believe reflect the current political climate against radical movements, admitted anarchists Nicola Sacco and Bartolomeo Vanzetti are found guilty of first-degree murder (1921).
- Russian engineer Vladimir Zworykin invents the iconoscope, an early television set that transmits pictures and moving images over the airwaves (1923).
- President-elect Calvin Coolidge is quoted as announcing "the business of America is business" (1925).
- Hitler publishes his autobiography, *Mein Kampf*, outlining his future political plans for Germany (1925).

Sources:

Daniel, C. (1989). *Chronicle of America*. Mt. Kisco, NY: Chronicle Publications.
Events of the 20th century. https://en.wikipedia.org/wiki/timeline_of_the_20th_century
Mercer, D. (2000). *Millennium year by year*. New York: Dorling Kindersley Publications.

Questions for Further Research and Discussion

1. Choose one or more of the early reformers in the issue of women's suffrage (noted above) and, following further library and Internet research, summarize her or his life with an emphasis on her or his contributions to voting equality.
2. Conduct further research on the value system noted as the "cult of true womanhood," and discuss its original effect on society as well as whether, in your opinion, any elements of it linger in today's society. Justify your opinions with factual data.
3. Search on the Internet for further information on the process that went on for many years before all 50 states ratified the *19th Amendment*. Then report what your research reveals about the culture of different states regarding equality for women, as well as any historical data that may explain why there was resistance to full ratification at the time.
4. Read the full text of the *Declaration of Sentiments and Resolutions* developed at Seneca Falls in 1848, referenced above, then summarize all the significant ideas put forth in this revolutionary document.
5. Based on the primary documentary material presented here, as well as other material you discover in the **Additional Selected References** at the end of this chapter, what additional federal policy or policies do you believe should have been

developed or changed at that time? Describe those policies in detail. Recall that a policy could be either *legislative* (i.e., a law), *judicial* (i.e., a court decision), or *administrative* (i.e., an executive or organizational policy) in nature.

6. Select three events appearing under the **Linkage to Social Welfare** section (above), conduct further Internet research regarding them, then conclude whether you believe there exists any plausible relationship between the struggle for voting equality of women and men and the events you have chosen. Use the analytical model presented in Appendix 1 of this book, or develop your own analytical model, to draw these conclusions.

7. Select one book from the **Additional Selected References** list at the end of this chapter. Briefly read through it, then summarize the main points contained in the book. Identify your own personal reaction to this book.

Additional Selected References

Baker, J. H. (Ed.). (2002). *Votes for women: The struggle for suffrage revisited*. New York: Oxford University Press.

Banaszak, L. A. (1996). *Why movements succeed or fail: Opportunity, culture, and the struggle for women's suffrage*. Princeton, NJ: Princeton University Press.

DuBois, E. C. (1998). *Woman suffrage and women's rights*. New York: New York University Press.

Flexner, E. (1959). *Century of struggle*. Cambridge, MA: Belknap Press of Harvard University.

Fredericks, C. (2009). *Amendment XIX: Granting women the right to vote*. Detroit: Greenhaven Press.

Free, L. E. (2015). *Suffrage reconstructed: Gender, race, and voting rights in the Civil War era*. Ithaca, NY: Cornell University Press.

Goldstone, L. (2011). *Inherently unequal: The betrayal of equal rights by the Supreme Court, 1865–1903*. New York: Walker & Company.

Hakim, J. (1995). *Book 9: War, peace, and all that jazz. A history of the United States*. New York: Oxford University Press.

Joannou, M., & Purvis, J. (1998). *The women's suffrage movement: New feminist perspectives*. Manchester, UK: Manchester University Press.

Moses, C. G., & Hartmann, H. I. (1995). *U.S. women's struggle: A feminist studies anthology*. Champaign, IL: University of Illinois Press.

Salsini, B. (1973). *Elizabeth Stanton, a leader of the women's suffrage movement*. Charlotteville, NY: SamHar Press.

Stalcup, B. (2000). *Women's suffrage*. San Diego, CA: Greenhaven Press.

Wheeler, M. S. (1993). *New women of the new South: The leaders of the woman suffrage movement in the Southern states*. New York: Oxford University Press.

Credits

Fig. 16.1: Source: https://commons.wikimedia.org/wiki/File:Elizabeth_Cady_Stanton_and_Susan_B._Anthony.jpg.

Fig. 16.2: Source: https://cdn.theculturetrip.com/wp-content/uploads/2017/01/heralds-leading-parade-with-mrs—richard-coke-burleson.jpg.

Chapter 17

The Era of Forced Sterilizations

Buck v. Bell, 274 U.S. 200 (1927)

Introduction

To fully understand the culture and values that led to court decisions such as *Buck v. Bell* in 1927, it is necessary to explore the phenomenon of the field of eugenics that was current during the early decades of the 20th century. Originating in Great Britain, *eugenics* (meaning "well born") was a philosophy that emphasized biological determinism and promoted the improvement of hereditary traits in people through the encouragement of "good breeding" among healthy individuals. Its early pioneer, Sir Francis Galton, was a cousin of Charles Darwin and the first to try to apply Darwin's theories to humankind. A number of early social science researchers collected data that they concluded would prove that some societal problems, such as crime, prostitution, or feeble-mindedness, were inherited over generations and needed to be obliterated from society as soon as possible. Furthermore, many also concluded that several ethnic and racial groups, such as African Americans and Native Americans, and poor people in general had inherited "weak genes" and, thus, were unable to compete successfully in modern society. The "data" that these social scientists relied upon proved to be drawn from either very limited and biased samples or from subjective and purely anecdotal incidents.

Closely related to the Darwinian theory of natural selection, eugenics also cruelly advocated for the forced sterilization of anyone judged to be mentally ill or a likely burden on society. Eugenics theory was even somewhat supported by some members of the progressive movement for a time in the 1920s. Emphasizing birth control rather than sterilization, these early reformers believed that society could positively transform itself into a more productive place for all people. Eugenics, in their mind, offered a relatively simple way to strengthen families over time to achieve a more future-focused society that would experience only minimal social problems. By the 1930s, the eugenics movement was fully adopted by Adolph Hitler and the Nazi Party in Germany in their drive to

FIGURE 17.1 Sir Francis Galton.

produce a "master race." This approbation of eugenics theory by the Nazis during the 1930s and 1940s led to the eugenics movement's eventual condemnation and downfall.

Carrie Buck was born in 1906. Her mother had been committed to the Virginia Colony for Epileptics and the Feeble-Minded in Lynchburg, Virginia, so her foster parents, John and Alice Dobbs, raised her from the time she was 3 years old. When Buck was 16, she became pregnant and alleged that it was a result of being raped by the Dobbs' nephew. Her foster parents changed their attitude toward her after this accusation and petitioned the local court to have her committed to the Virginia Colony for Epileptics and the Feeble-Minded. After the birth of the child in March 1924, Buck was committed, joining her mother at the Colony. A short time before Buck's arrival at the Colony, the State of Virginia had passed the *Virginia Eugenical Sterilization Act*, a law that legitimized the forced sterilization of anyone, male or female, considered to be "unfit" due to her or his genetic makeup. This included people who embodied certain social problems such as poverty, prostitution, and something simply called "shiftlessness." In order to test the constitutionality of the Virginia statute, Colony Superintendent Albert Priddy successfully argued the case against Buck in a local Virginia court. Following Priddy's death in 1925, his successor at the Colony, John Bell, managed the case through the Virginia Court of Appeals and up to the United States Supreme Court.

The May 2, 1927, outcome of *Buck vs. Bell* upheld the Virginia law by an 8–1 vote, with the Supreme Court Justices essentially ruling that this law did not violate the *due process clause* of the 14th Amendment to the *United States Constitution*. This momentous Supreme Court decision immediately rippled through the nation and was used in several states over time to justify the nationwide sterilization of approximately 65,000 to 70,000 individuals without their knowledge or consent during the 1920s and 1930s. Buck was unexpectedly sterilized in October 1927, released from the Colony one month later, and sent to work as a domestic helper to a family in Virginia.

Tragically, later research revealed it is probable that neither Buck nor her daughter were mentally ill or developmentally disabled. Buck, it is now believed, was institutionalized by her foster parents as retaliation for accusing their nephew of rape and not due to any intellectual or mental disability. She lived until 1983, married twice, and is reported to have been an avid reader all of her adult life. Furthermore, her child, Vivian, died young, at the age of 8, from complications following measles, but historians record that she made the honor role during the two years she attended elementary school before her death.

FIGURE 17.2 Justices of the Supreme Court and presumably others. Chief Justice Taft carries a cane and is front and center. Discernible by his spectacular mustache is Justice Oliver Wendell Holmes.

Buck v. Bell has been uniquely immortalized in legal history primarily due to one insensitive comment delivered by Justice Oliver Wendell Holmes in his majority opinion. Citing the lower court descriptions of Buck and her mother as "feeble-minded" and "promiscuous" and hypothesizing about the physical and psychological health of Buck's young baby, Holmes wrote: "Three generations of imbeciles are enough." There was one dissenting voice Justice Pierce Butler, but he did not put forward to the court a written dissent. Reflective of the era in which this decision was handed down, the outcome of the *Buck v. Bell* case was widely praised in published newspaper accounts and editorials at the time.

In an ironic twist of fate, several of the Nazi military doctors at the Nuremberg War Criminal Trials following World War II referred to the *Buck v. Bell* case in a vain attempt to vindicate their wartime actions. Their defense attorneys even quoted Oliver Wendell Holmes's majority opinion and argued that the United States government was complicit in authorizing some medical interventions on institutionalized individuals similar to what Nazi doctors did to prisoners of war during their scientific experiments.

The Virginia law allowing forced sterilizations remained in effect until its repeal in 1974. A few years later, in 1981, following actions by the Virginia Chapter of the American Civil Liberties Union (ACLU), the state settled out of court with one Virginia citizen who had been forcibly sterilized during this period. It took until May 2, 2002, however, for the Virginia State's governor at the time, Mark Warner, to formally apologize to the individuals and families who had been affected by this tragic mistake in human reasoning, a mistake that had such frightful and shocking consequences.

Buck v. Bell is another example of how society rejects "the other" simply because they do not fit into some predetermined set of expectations. It is also an indictment of the state of social science knowledge and activity at the time that sanctioned quietly such intrusions into vulnerable people's lives and allowed such false belief systems to creep into social welfare policy.

- For a brutal and chilling piece of poetry on people with disabilities, see *Mendel's Law: A Plea for a Better Race of Men*, composed by Joseph Spencer DeJarnette, a noted eugenicist and prosecution witness at the Buck v. Bell trial, available at https://www.encyclopediavirginia.org/_mendel_s_law_a_plea_for_a_better_race_of_men.
- Note the detailed timeline of events involving Carrie Buck and pictures of significant individuals at https://www.encyclopediavirginia.org/buck_v_bell_1927#start_entry.
- There was a reference to *Buck v. Bell* in the 1961 Stanley Kramer film *Judgment at Nuremberg*, starring Spencer Tracy as the chief judge. There was also produced in 1994 a less-well known television movie about this series of events, *Against Her Will: The Carrie Buck Story*.

Internet Sources for the Content of This Introduction Include:

http://www.eugenicsarchive.org/html/eugenics/static/themes/39.html

https://www.encyclopediavirginia.org/buck_v_bell_1927

https://www.npr.org/sections/health-shots/2016/03/07/469478098/the-supreme-court-ruling-that-led-to-70-000-forced-sterilizations

http://embryo.asu.edu/pages/buck-v-bell-1927

https://en.wikipedia.org/wiki/buck_v._bell

https://www.npr.org/sections/health-shots/2016/03/07/469478098/the-supreme-court-ruling-that-led-to-70-000-forced-sterilizations

Linkage to Social Welfare History (1925-1950)

Social welfare historical events for this time period include the following:

- Following the legal battle between noted lawyers William Jennings Bryan for the prosecution and Clarence Darrow for the defense, a Tennessee court convicts biology teacher John Scopes for teaching evolution in the legendary "Scopes Monkey Trial" (1925).
- Resistance to the Prohibition Law around the nation surfaces in a series of speakeasies, surreptitious places where introductions are needed and alcohol can be purchased and consumed (1925).
- Watched by more than an estimated 200,000 bystanders, 400,00 members of the Ku Klux Klan march, waving American flags, toward the Washington Monument in Washington, DC (1925).
- Appearing in blackface, which was embarrassingly common at the time, Al Jolson stars in the film *The Jazz Singer* (1927).

- The *Harlem Renaissance*, a major cultural movement featuring African American authors, musicians, and visual artists, flourishes in New York City and beyond (1928).
- A frenzied selling off of stocks on Wall Street culminates on Black Tuesday, a day memorialized in American history as the day that signaled the beginning of the Great Depression (1929).
- The 1930 census reveals that America has reached a population growth of 122 million, the life expectancy of the typical American is 61 years, and there are more than 26 million cars in use (1930).
- President Herbert Hoover establishes the Veterans Administration by executive order (1930).
- Census officials report that the number of unemployed is between 4 million and 5 million Americans and, furthermore, that they have removed from the unemployed lists those unemployed who sell apples on street corners across the nation (1931).
- Social reformer Jane Addams is awarded the Nobel Peace Prize (1931).
- In the annual State of the Union address, President Herbert Hoover announces a major construction plan that will aid the business community but rejects any direct or indirect resources for the unemployed (1931).
- President Hoover orders the military, under the command of Army General Douglas MacArthur, to disperse from Washington, DC members of the "Bonus Army," a group of World War I army veterans who rallied there to collect a bonus that was promised to them for their loyal army service (1932).
- Former New York Governor Franklin Delano Roosevelt is elected president of the United States with a pledge for a "New Deal" for the American people, who are struggling through the effects of the Great Depression (1932).
- During the first 100 days of his presidency, President Franklin Delano Roosevelt passes significant social legislation and launches the first of his many "alphabet soup" programs, namely the Civilian Conservation Corps (CCC), the Federal Emergency Relief Act (FERA), the Agricultural Adjustment Act (AAA), the Emergency Farm Mortgage Act, the Truth in Lending Act (TILA), and the Glass-Steagall Act (1933).
- The *21st Amendment* to the *United States Constitution*, rescinding the prohibition of alcohol, receives the required two-thirds majority approval, thus legitimizing the social benefits of alcohol when used in moderation (1933).
- President Franklin Delano Roosevelt appoints Frances Perkins as Secretary of Labor, thereby making her the first woman ever appointed to a federal cabinet post (1933).
- In California, reformer Dr. Francis Townsend reveals his proposal for a pension plan for senior citizens that would provide the aged poor with a monthly allowance and help stabilize the nation's economy (1934).
- President Franklin Delano Roosevelt authorizes the Works Progress Administration (WPA), a major employment program that focuses on large industrial projects

using a highly skilled workforce. The United States Congress also passes the *National Labor Relations Act (Wagner Act)*, which strengthens labor unions (1935).
- President Franklin Delano Roosevelt signs the *Social Security Act*, which dramatically transforms the modern social welfare system structure (1935).
- The United Automobile Workers union wins its strike against General Motors, the United Steelworkers union is similarly victorious against United States Steel Corporation, and several longshoremen's unions along the East and West coasts triumph in their struggles against the shipping industry, thus confirming the increasing influence of the labor union movement for workers' rights (1936).
- President Franklin Delano Roosevelt signs the *Fair Labor Standards Act*, which sets a minimum wage and places a specified limit on the number of hours worked per week (1938).
- President Franklin Delano Roosevelt also authorizes the *Emergency Relief Appropriations Act*, which allocates $3 million to expand existing and new public works programs (1935).
- Drs. Alton Ochsner and Michael DeBakey first note the spread of lung cancer in Louisiana and conclude that the cause might be linked to cigarette smoking (1938).
- Concert singer Marian Anderson is denied access to sing in Constitution Hall in Washington, DC by the Daughters of the American Revolution (DAR) simply because she is African American. She sings instead in front of the Lincoln Memorial through the intercession of Eleanor Roosevelt, the president's wife (1939).
- John Steinbeck publishes *The Grapes of Wrath*, a novel that describes rural poverty and displacement during the time of the Midwest *Dust Bowl* (1939).
- Seeking to calm the rising anger of African Americans, President Roosevelt signs an executive order creating the Fair Employment Practices Commission to investigate charges of discrimination based on race, creed, or national origin in any corporation that is part of the defense industry (1941).
- President Franklin Delano Roosevelt signs *Executive Order 9066*, which empowers the War Department to forcibly intern 110,000 Japanese nationals and Japanese American citizens in Hawaii and along the West Coast of the United States (1942).
- The notorious radical "radio priest" Reverend Charles Coughlin is silenced, and his anti-Semitic weekly newspaper, *Social Justice*, is banned under the principles of the 1917 *Espionage Act* (1942).
- The United States Foreign Affairs Committee reports that, since 1933, more than 600,000 immigrants fleeing Nazi Germany persecution, many of them Jews, have been granted admittance to the United States (1943).
- The United States Congress passes the *Servicemen's Readjustment Act*, more commonly referred to as the *G.I. Bill of Rights*, which provides a variety of resources to veterans, including education and training, low-interest home mortgage loans, job counselling, and employment placement (1944).
- American soldiers liberate the concentration camps at Dachau and Buchenwald and assist the survivors with medical help (1945).

- President Harry Truman signs the *National Mental Health Act*, which provides substantial resources for mental health education and research and leads to the creation, in 1949, of the National Institute on Mental Health (NIMH) (1946).
- The *Taft-Hartley Act* diminishes many of the advantages gained by labor unions during the New Deal (1947).
- In the face of resistance from several Southern baseball teams and bigoted baseball fans, African American baseball player Jackie Robinson breaks the "color line" when he signs on to play in the major leagues with the Brooklyn Dodgers (1947).
- President Truman orders the full integration of the Armed Services by issuing *Executive Order 9981* (1948).
- Dr. Alfred Kinsey publishes *Sexual Behavior in the Human Male*, based on a survey of the sexual activities of 5,000 men (1948).
- Diplomat Ralph Bunche receives the Nobel Peace Prize for his work trying to resolve the conflict between Arabs and Jews in Israel, thus becoming the first African American to earn that honor (1950).
- The latest census tally reveals the presence of 151 million Americans, 64% of whom reside in urban areas (1950).

Note: For a more reflective and functional use of this list of contemporary social welfare historical events, see Question #5 under the **Questions for Further Research and Discussion** section (below).

Sources:

Daniel, C. (1989). *Chronicle of America*. Mt. Kisco, NY: Chronicle Publications.

Mercer, D. (2000). *Millennium year by year*. New York: Dorling Kindersley Publications.

Social welfare developments 1900–1950. (2011). Retrieved from https://socialwelfare.library.vcu.edu/events/1901-1950/

Primary Text Material

Buck v. Bell (1927)

"... Mr. JUSTICE HOLMES delivered the opinion of the Court.

This is a writ of error to review a judgment of the Supreme Court of Appeals of the State of Virginia, affirming a judgment of the Circuit Court of Amherst County, by which the defendant in error, the superintendent of the State Colony for Epileptics and Feeble Minded, was ordered to perform the operation of salpingectomy upon Carrie Buck, the plaintiff in error, for the purpose of making her sterile. 143 Va. 310. The case comes here upon the contention that the statute

Continued

> *authorizing the judgment is void under the Fourteenth Amendment as denying to the plaintiff in error due process of law and the equal protection of the laws.*
>
> *Carrie Buck is a feeble-minded white woman who was committed to the State Colony above mentioned in due form. She is the daughter of a feeble-minded mother in the same institution, and the mother of an illegitimate feeble-minded child. . . .*
>
> *The judgment finds the facts that have been recited and that Carrie Buck "is the probable potential parent of socially inadequate offspring, likewise afflicted, that she may be sexually sterilized without detriment to her general health and that her welfare and that of society will be promoted by her sterilization," and thereupon makes the order. In view of the general declarations of the legislature and the specific findings of the Court, obviously we cannot say as matter of law that the grounds do not exist, and if they exist they justify the result. We have seen more than once that the public welfare may call upon the best citizens for their lives. It would be strange if it could not call upon those who already sap the strength of the State for these lesser sacrifices, often not felt to be such by those concerned, in order to prevent our being swamped with incompetence. It is better for all the world, if instead of waiting to execute degenerate offspring for crime, or to let them starve for their imbecility, society can prevent those who are manifestly unfit from continuing their kind. The principle that sustains compulsory vaccination is broad enough to cover cutting the Fallopian tubes. Jacobson v. Massachusetts, 197 U.S. 11. Three generations of imbeciles are enough . . ."*
>
> Source and full text available at https://scholar.google.com/scholar_case?case=1700304772805702914.

Timeline of General Events in History, the Humanities, and Science During This Period (1925–1950)

These general historical events may help you understand more clearly the overall historical context during which the primary document was created.

- Referencing the economic growth of the nation during this period, President-elect Calvin Coolidge announces, "The business of America is business" (1925).
- Industrialist Henry Ford introduces the practice of a 40-hour, five-day workweek in his automobile factories (1926).
- Physics professor Robert Goddard demonstrates his invention, a liquid-fueled rocket capable of climbing into the atmosphere (1926).
- Aspiring author Earnest Hemingway publishes his first novel, *The Sun Also Rises* (1926).
- Aviator Charles Lindbergh pilots his plane, *The Spirit of St. Louis*, 3,600 miles nonstop from New York to Paris in 33.5 hours (1927).

- Filmmaker Walt Disney screens the first cartoon with sound, *Steamboat Willie*, and introduces Mickey Mouse to the American public (1928).
- Cartoonist Chester Gould introduces a new newspaper comic strip that features the character of Dick Tracy, a police officer who tracks and arrests criminals relentlessly (1931).
- Aviator Amelia Earhart completes her solo transatlantic flight, originating in Newfoundland and a landing in Northern Ireland, thus becoming the first woman to do so (1932).
- The Hindenburg, a dirigible offering transatlantic air service and sent by Nazi Germany, partly as a propaganda gesture, explodes in flames in Lakewood, NJ, killing 35 passengers and one crew member (1937).
- Radio announcer Orson Wells and his Mercury Theatre players, dramatically reading sections of H. G. Wells's novel *War of the Worlds*, frighten more than 1 million radio listeners into believing that the earth was actually being invaded by Martians (1938).
- The New York World's Fair, representing 60 nations, opens in New York City with the theme of "The World of Tomorrow" and features color film by Kodak, an experimental television set by NBC, a preview of future autos by General Motors, long-distance telephone calling by AT&T, and a prototype of a futuristic 2036 urban area (1939).
- Following Adolph Hitler's vicious invasion of Poland, Great Britain and France declare war on Germany, with the United States opting to remain neutral (1939).
- Reflective of the nation's increasingly positive view on the economy, Hollywood explodes with new films, some of them classics even today, including *Gone With the Wind*, starring Vivien Leigh and Clark Gable; *The Wizard of Oz*, featuring Judy Garland; John Ford's *Stagecoach*, Disney's *Pinocchio*; *Beau Geste*; and *The Roaring Twenties*, starring James Cagney and Humphrey Bogart; among others (1939–1940).
- President Franklin Delano Roosevelt transforms the nation's industrial base to aid the war effort, then proclaims that the United States must be an "arsenal of democracy" and pledges to assist the Allied forces with military supplies and machinery (1940).
- President Franklin Delano Roosevelt inches closer to war as he announces a plan to provide a billion-dollar "lend-lease" program of war material and aid to the Allies fighting Nazi Germany based on his international Four Freedoms: freedom of speech, freedom to worship God, freedom from want, and freedom from fear (1941).
- Following rising tensions between the United States and Japan over Japan's military actions throughout the Pacific, the United States initiates an embargo on all oil and rice imports to Japan (1941).
- Japan initiates a surprise attack on the American naval base and airfields on Pearl Harbor, Hawaii, prompting the United States to declare war on Japan (1941).
- Following the dictates of their Tripartite Pact with Japan, Germany and Italy declare war on the United States (1941).

- More than 10,000 American-born sons of Japanese immigrants, identified as *nisei*, volunteer to join the American military forces (1942).
- Italian physicist Enrico Fermi, working outdoors at the University of Chicago, creates the first controlled atomic chain reaction of fissionable uranium, thereby launching the United States into the nuclear age (1942).
- In order to support the war effort, the federal government introduces the rationing of some food items while President Roosevelt directs the freezing of wages and prices and mandates a 48-hour week at all defense industry factories (1943).
- Victory in Europe over Nazi Germany is declared (1945).
- The United States unleashes atomic bombs over Hiroshima and Nagasaki, leading Japan to surrender and triggering the end of World War II (1945).
- The United Nations is formed to maintain world peace and security, with five nations—China, France, Great Britain, the Soviet Union, and the United States—assigned a leadership role as permanent members of the Security Council (1945).
- The war-crimes trial for German Nazi officers begins in Nuremberg, Germany (1946).
- The Congressional *House Un-American Activities Committee* investigates suspected Communist infiltration of the Hollywood film industry, resulting in the blacklisting of 10 noted film professionals, mostly screenwriters, by the film industry itself (1947).
- In order to assist Western Europe in its recovery from World War II, the United States launches a massive foreign aid program, the Marshall Plan (1948).
- Despite the United Nations plan to divide Palestine into an Arab and Jewish state with Jerusalem as an international city following the cessation of British control over Palestine, the United States recognizes the independent state of Israel, and war breaks out between Israel and several Arab nations (1948).
- The United States provides economic and military aid to the Republic of South Korea after it is invaded by the Communist North Korean Army (1950).
- A United States senator from Wisconsin, Joe McCarthy, releases his alleged list of Communists who are working in the United States Department of State (1950).

Sources:

Daniel, C. (1989). *Chronicle of America*. Mt. Kisco, NY: Chronicle Publications.

Events of the 20th century. Retrieved from https://en.wikipedia.org/wiki/timeline_of_the_20th_century

Mercer, D. (2000). *Millennium year by year*. New York: Dorling Kindersley Publications.

Questions for Further Research and Discussion

1. Explore further the history of the eugenics movement in the United States, and summarize what social policies and/or programs were initiated based on its underlying

philosophy. Were there certain areas in the country or individual organizations that enthusiastically adopted the eugenics value system? What were the reactions to the eugenics movement by the leaders of organized religion at the time?

2. Using the Internet, search for editorial material in Virginia newspapers as well as in national publications following the *Buck v. Bell* decision in early May 1927. Summarize what the general reactions were, and note the rationale provided by various editorial writers.
3. Conduct further Internet research on the subject of the progressive movement's involvement with the eugenics movement during this period. Summarize your findings highlighting whether you found any dissent or contrary opinions among progressive leaders on this subject.
4. Based on the primary documentary material presented here, as well as other material you discover in the **Additional Selected References** at the end of this chapter, what additional federal policy or policies do you believe should have been developed or changed at that time regarding the rights of institutionalized developmentally disabled individuals? Describe those policies in detail. Recall that a policy could be either *legislative* (i.e., a law), *judicial* (i.e., a court decision), or *administrative* (i.e., an executive or organizational policy) in nature.
5. Select three events appearing under the **Linkage to Social Welfare** section (above), conduct further Internet research regarding them, then conclude whether you believe there exists any plausible relationship between the *Buck v. Bell* decision in 1927 and the events you have chosen. Use the analytical model presented in Appendix 1 of this book, or develop your own analytical model, to draw these conclusions.
6. Select one book from the **Additional Selected References** list at the end of this chapter. Briefly read through it, then summarize the main points contained in the book. Identify your own personal reaction to this book.

Additional Selected References

Bruinius, H. (2007). *Better for all the world: The secret history of forced sterilization and America's quest for racial purity.* New York: Vintage Books.

Cohen, A. (2016). *Imbeciles: The Supreme Court, American eugenics, and the sterilization of Carrie Buck.* New York: Penguin.

Dyck, E. (2013). *Facing eugenics: Reproduction, sterilization, and the politics of choice.* Toronto: University of Toronto Press.

Hansen, R., & King, D. S. (2013). *Sterilized by the state: Eugenics, race, and the population scare in twentieth-century North America.* New York: Cambridge University Press.

Harrison, M., Gilbert, S., & United States. (1991). *Landmark decisions of the United States Supreme Court.* Beverly Hills, CA: Excellent Books.

Largent, M. A. (2008). *Breeding contempt: The history of coerced sterilization in the United States.* New Brunswick, NJ: Rutgers University Press.

Lombardo, P. (2008). *Three generations, no imbeciles: Eugenics, the Supreme Court, and Buck v. Bell*. Baltimore: Johns Hopkins University Press.

Lombardo, P. A. (Ed.). (2011). *A century of eugenics in America: From the Indiana experiment to the human genome era*. Bloomington, ID: Indiana University Press.

Laughlin, H. H. (1922). *Eugenical sterilization in the United States*. Chicago: Psychopathic Laboratory of the Municipal Court of Chicago.

Smith, J. D. (1989). *The sterilization of Carrie Buck*. Liberty Corner, NJ: New Horizon Press.

Credits

Fig. 17.1: Source: https://www.obekti.bg/sites/default/files/styles/article_large/public/images/5_395.jpg?itok=MN55EExw.

Fig. 17.2: Source: https://commons.wikimedia.org/wiki/File:Supreme_Court_justices_1923.jpeg.

Chapter 18

Confronting the Great Depression

The New Deal and *The Social Security Act* (1935)

Introduction

The Stock Market Crash of 1929 and the Great Depression that followed engulfed the nation through most of the 1930s and forced the United States government to introduce a major reconstruction of the role of government in people's lives. This dramatic change gave rise to an "alphabet soup" of new programs during the era of the New Deal and ultimately led to the passage of the *Social Security Act* in August 1935. More than any other piece of legislation, the *Social Security Act,* and its many amendments, serves as a solid foundation for the entire structure of the modern social welfare system in the United States.

By the time President Franklin Delano Roosevelt assumed the presidency in March 1933, it was clear that the effects of the prior Hoover administration's approach to directly aiding businesses and not individuals had failed to alleviate the economic problems facing the nation. The underlying cause of the Great Depression was subject to disagreement among economists then and even today. However, with the election of President Roosevelt, who was a Democrat, the decision was made that inadequate consumer demand was the underlying cause, which led to a Keynesian approach of robust governmental intervention in order to stabilize consumer demand. Keynesian economics argues for a "managed market economy," one that requires a strong private sector and immediate government intervention in times of recessions and depressions. Thus, a goal of the new administration during 1933 and 1934 was to get as much money flowing through the nation by direct grants to individuals, new public service jobs, and short-term infrastructure projects that could be started with minimal planning.

Globally, the Great Depression was a worldwide phenomenon of the late 1920s and early 1930s that affected, in addition to the United States,

FIGURE 18.1 Works Progress Administration: The unemployed at a Volunteers for America soup kitchen in Washington, DC.

countries such as Argentina, Brazil, Canada, France, Great Britain, Germany, and Poland, as well as nations across Southeast Asia.

The entire gross domestic product (GDP), which is the total value of all goods and services produced in one year, of all these nations fell 15% across the world during this time. In the United States, 37% of non-farm workers had lost their jobs by 1933.

A thorough description of all of the New Deal programs initiated through the 1930s is beyond the scope of this chapter. Further independent research is advised, however, to fully understand the details of notable federal interventions during this period, such as the *Emergency Banking Act*, the *Federal Emergency Relief Administration (FERA)*, the *Civil Works Administration (CWA)*, the *Securities Act of 1933*, the *National Recovery Administration (NRA)*, the *Wagner Act*, the *Works Progress Administration (WPA)*, the *United States Housing Authority*, and the *Farm Security Administration*, among others. In some respects, the *Social Security Act* was a culmination of all these new federal efforts to confront the terrible economic condition of the nation. The ultimate, overarching goal of the *Social Security Act* was simple: to get people back to work.

The original *Social Security Act*, passed in 1935, focused on three specific groups of individuals: senior citizens who needed some type of insurance against poverty; the unemployed while they sought to regain employment; and poor, dependent children who needed direct, basic financial support. At its initiation, the *Social Security Act* had 11 sections, technically named "Titles," in numeric order listed in Roman numerals (e.g., Title I, Title II, Title III, Title IX, etc.) Over the years, these Titles have been amended several times, and new Titles have been added (e.g., Title XVIII—Medicare and Title XIX—Medicaid were both added in 1965 by the Lyndon Johnson administration).

For senior citizens, the *Social Security Act* instituted a permanent pension system paid through both employee and employer contributions into a specialized insurance-based trust fund. This component was later expanded to include disabled individuals and dependents of wage earners. Railroad workers, apparently for political reasons at the time, had a different, but similar, pension system authorized by the *Railroad Retirement Act* and funded through a separate insurance trust fund. An essential aspect of these pension funds is that they are not financed from general governmental revenues and, therefore, are considered contributory *social insurance* programs, which should exist without stigma, require no financial means test for eligibility, and operate similar to how home insurance, auto insurance, or life insurance functions.

FIGURE 18.2   President Roosevelt signs the Social Security Act at approximately 3:30 p.m. ET on August 14, 1935. Standing with Roosevelt are Representative Robert Doughton (D-NC), unknown person in shadow, Senator Robert Wagner (D-NY), Representative John Dingell (D-MI), Representative Joshua Twing Brooks (D-PA), Secretary of Labor Frances Perkins, Senator Pat Harrison (D-MS), and Representative David Lewis (D-MD).

In general, the *Social Security Act* fashioned the infrastructure of the modern social welfare system in the America—a combination of federal leadership actively engaged in a partnership with individual states in the administration of distinct social welfare programs. This federal/state arrangement can sometimes create an inherent dynamic tension between federal and state governments, especially when some social problems, such as poverty, family violence, and prejudice, are defined as national in scope, thereby, perhaps, differing from some state definitions. The fact that these programs are administered at a local state level, however, reflects the federal government's recognition of the state's intimate knowledge and ultimate responsibility for the welfare of its own citizens.

Rather than going into great detail the sections of the original *Social Security Act*, it is more important to understand how this pivotal piece of federal legislation still operates today, including all of the changes that have been added over the decades. All of current major social programs that are considered as "Social Security" are:

- *Social Security* itself provides cash retirement benefits (i.e., a pension) for those who are retired, disabled, or a dependent of a deceased worker.

- *Social Security disability insurance* is for those workers unable to continue working due to long-term disability.
- *Unemployment insurance* is for those workers forced out of the job market through no fault of their own.
- *Temporary Assistance to Needy Families* (TANF), formally known as Aid to Dependent Children (ADC), then Aid to Families with Dependent Children (AFDC). This is the primary needs-based social program designed to protect children and families by providing direct financial resources and other social services.
- *Supplemental Security Income* (SSI) is a needs-based program for retired or disabled individuals whose income is insufficient (even with Social Security benefits) to meet normal daily expenses for food, clothing, and housing.
- *Medicare* is a health insurance for anyone older than 65 years of age, funded by contributions of employees and employers and managed through the Medicare trust fund.
- *Medicaid* is a means-tested health insurance program for individuals who lack sufficient financial resources to pay directly for health care.
- The *Social Security Administration* is the current name for the federal agency that has comprehensive authority for the management of all current social welfare programs authorized by the *Social Security Act*, as amended.

In addition, there currently exist several *New Deal* programs, independent of the *Social Security Act*, that are still operational today. Some of these major programs are:

- The *Securities and Exchange Commission* (SEC) is charged with protecting the economy by monitoring and regulating the financial securities markets.
- The *Federal Housing Administration* (FHA) provides federal insurance coverage of mortgages to encourage the purchase of individual homes.
- The *Federal Deposit Insurance Commission* (FDIC) safeguards the stability of the private banking system by insuring all individual deposits up to specified monetary limits.
- The *Farm Credit Administration* (FCA) subsidizes mortgage loans for farmers at below-market rates in order to stabilize families in rural America.
- The *Tennessee Valley Authority* (TVA) was originally established to control flooding across several southeastern states, but its mandate evolved into expanding the electrical grid into that area and generally improving the standard of living in a region that had been severely underdeveloped.

After reviewing all of these currently functioning aspects of the *Social Security Act*, as well as some associated *New Deal* programs that are still operational, it should be clear that these are not simply interesting historical phenomena. In fact, this monumental federal law and several "alphabet soup" agencies continue to constructively impact virtually all of American society. In that sense, then, the *Social Security Act* stands as one of the foundational social welfare policies in the nation and one that must be protected from those who would seek to limit or drastically alter the role of the federal government in ensuring equality as well as social and economic justice for all Americans.

- For a clear history of pension programs that existed before the *Social Security Act*, see https://www.ssa.gov/history/briefhistory3.html.
- For a recent PBS film on the Great Depression, specifically how it affected the city of Detroit, Michigan, see https://www.youtube.com/watch?v=IQ_lizW5zSI.
- For more extensive coverage of the Great Depression in seven parts, see the following:
  Part 1: https://www.youtube.com/watch?v=bCEJ65H_1XE
  Part 2: https://www.youtube.com/watch?v=a5n4u4cF4Pg
  Part 3: https://www.youtube.com/watch?v=a5n4u4cF4Pg&t=2s
  Part 4: https://www.youtube.com/watch?v=6BcShxauDgk
  Part 5: https://www.youtube.com/watch?v=A4RRf5T-bMM
  Part 6: https://www.youtube.com/watch?v=MI6Y5vNxCag&t=1512s
  Part 7: https://www.youtube.com/watch?v=nl6lESiR3Os&t=1535s
- For some noteworthy photos from the Franklin D. Roosevelt Presidential Library and Museum that chronicle several New Deal programs, such as the *Works Progress Administration*, the *Civilian Conservation Corps* and the *National Youth Administration*, see http://docs.fdrlibrary.marist.edu:8000/browse.cgi?db=1&pos=1.
- For an extensive array of color photos of the Great Depression produced by the Farm Credit Administration, see http://www.loc.gov/pictures/search/?st=grid&co=fsac.
- For an interesting photo essay on the Great Depression, see http://www.english.illinois.edu/maps/depression/photoessay.htm.
- For a *New York Times* review of the book *A Square Meal* regarding the poor quality of the food consumed by many during the Great Depression, see https://www.nytimes.com/2016/08/17/dining/great-depression-food-square-meal-book.html?rref=collection%2Ftimestopic%2fgreat%20depression%20(1930%27s)&action=click&contentcollection=timestopics&region=stream&module=stream_unit&version=latest&contentplacement=4&pgtype=collection.

Internet Sources for the Content of This Introduction Include:
https://www.britannica.com/topic/social-security-act-united-states-1935
https://www.britannica.com/list/7-alphabet-soup-agencies-that-stuck-around
https://www.britannica.com/event/great-depression
http://socialsecurity.findlaw.com/social-security-basics/the-social-security-act-overview.html
http://www.history.com/this-day-in-history/fdr-signs-social-security-act
http://rooseveltinstitute.org/social-security-act/
https://en.wikipedia.org/wiki/social_security_act
https://en.wikipedia.org/wiki/new_deal
http://www.econlib.org/library/enc/greatdepression.html
https://en.wikipedia.org/wiki/great_depression

Linkage to Social Welfare History (1925-1950)

Social welfare historical events for this time period include the following:

- Following the legal battle between noted lawyers William Jennings Bryan for the prosecution and Clarence Darrow for the defense, a Tennessee court convicts biology teacher John Scopes for teaching evolution in the legendary "Scopes Monkey Trial" (1925).
- Watched by more than an estimated 200,000 bystanders, 400,00 members of the Ku Klux Klan march, waving American flags, toward the Washington Monument in Washington, DC (1925).
- Resistance to the Prohibition Law around the nation surfaces in a series of speakeasies, surreptitious places where introductions are needed, and alcohol can be purchased and consumed (1925).
- Appearing in blackface, which was embarrassingly common at the time, Al Jolson stars in the film *The Jazz Singer* (1927).
- The Unites States Supreme Court, in *Buck v. Bell*, decreed that it is constitutional to forcibly sterilize men and women who were deemed to be feeble-minded, and, thus, a future burden on society (1927).
- The *Harlem Renaissance*, a major cultural movement featuring African American authors, musicians, and visual artists, flourishes in New York City and beyond (1928).
- A frenzied selling off of stocks on Wall Street culminates on Black Tuesday, a day memorialized in American history as the day that signaled the beginning of the Great Depression (1929).
- The 1930 census reveals that America has reached a population growth of 122 million, the life expectancy of the typical American is 61 years, and there are more than 26 million cars in use (1930).
- President Herbert Hoover establishes the Veterans Administration by executive order (1930).
- Census officials report that the number of unemployed is between 4 million and 5 million Americans and, furthermore, that they have removed from the unemployed lists those unemployed who sell apples on street corners across the nation (1931).
- Social reformer Jane Addams is awarded the Nobel Peace Prize (1931).
- In the annual State of the Union address, President Herbert Hoover announces a major construction plan that will aid the business community but rejects any direct or indirect resources for the unemployed (1931).
- President Hoover orders the military, under the command of Army General Douglas MacArthur, to disperse from Washington, DC members of the "Bonus Army," a group of World War I army veterans who rallied there to collect a bonus that was promised to them for their loyal army service (1932).
- Former New York Governor Franklin Delano Roosevelt is elected president of the United States with a pledge for a "New Deal" for the American people, who are struggling through the effects of the Great Depression (1932).

- During the first 100 days of his presidency, President Roosevelt passes significant social legislation and launches the first of his many "alphabet soup" programs, namely the Civilian Conservation Corps (CCC), the Federal Emergency Relief Act (FERA), the Agricultural Adjustment Act (AAA), the Emergency Farm Mortgage Act, the Truth in Lending Act (TILA), and the Glass-Steagall Act (1933).
- The *21st Amendment* to the *United States Constitution*, rescinding the prohibition of alcohol, receives the required two-thirds majority approval, thus legitimizing the social benefits of alcohol when used in moderation (1933).
- President Franklin Delano Roosevelt appoints Frances Perkins as Secretary of Labor, thereby making her the first woman ever appointed to a federal cabinet post (1933).
- In California, reformer Dr. Francis Townsend reveals his proposal for a pension plan for senior citizens that would provide the aged poor with a monthly allowance and help stabilize the nation's economy (1934).
- President Franklin Delano Roosevelt authorizes the Works Progress Administration (WPA), a major employment program that focuses on large industrial projects using a highly skilled workforce. The United States Congress also passes the *National Labor Relations Act (Wagner Act)*, which strengthens labor unions (1935).
- The United Automobile Workers Union wins its strike against General Motors, the United Steelworkers union is similarly victorious against United States Steel Corporation, and several longshoremen's unions along the East and West coasts triumph in their struggles against the shipping industry, thus confirming the increasing influence of the labor union movement for workers' rights (1936).
- President Franklin Delano Roosevelt signs the *Fair Labor Standards Act*, which sets a minimum wage and places a specified limit on the number of hours worked per week (1938).
- President Franklin Delano Roosevelt also authorizes the *Emergency Relief Appropriations Act*, which allocates $3 million to expand the existing and new public works programs (1935).
- Drs. Alton Ochsner and Michael DeBakey first note the spread of lung cancer in Louisiana and conclude that the cause might be linked to cigarette smoking (1938).
- Concert singer Marian Anderson is denied access to sing in Constitution Hall in Washington, DC by the Daughters of the American Revolution (DAR) simply because she is African American. She sings instead in front of the Lincoln Memorial through the intercession of Eleanor Roosevelt, the president's wife (1939).
- John Steinbeck publishes *The Grapes of Wrath*, a novel that describes rural poverty and displacement during the time of the Midwest *Dust Bowl* (1939).
- Seeking to calm the rising anger of African Americans, President Franklin Delano Roosevelt signs an executive order creating the Fair Employment Practices Commission to investigate charges of discrimination based on race, creed, or national origin in any corporation that is part of the defense industry (1941).

- President Roosevelt signs *Executive Order 9066*, which empowers the War Department to forcibly intern 110,000 Japanese nationals and Japanese American citizens in Hawaii and along the West Coast of the United States (1942).
- The notorious radical "radio priest" Reverend Charles Coughlin is silenced, and his anti-Semitic weekly newspaper, *Social Justice*, is banned under the principles of the 1917 *Espionage Act* (1942).
- The United States Foreign Affairs Committee reports that, since 1933, more than 600,000 immigrants fleeing Nazi Germany persecution, many of them Jews, have been granted admittance to the United States (1943).
- The United States Congress passes the *Servicemen's Readjustment Act*, more commonly referred to as the *G.I. Bill of Rights*, which provides a variety of resources to veterans, including education and training, low-interest home mortgage loans, job counselling and employment placement (1944).
- American soldiers liberate the concentration camps at Dachau and Buchenwald and assist the survivors with medical help (1945).
- President Harry Truman signs the *National Mental Health Act*, which provides substantial resources for mental health education and research and leads to the creation, in 1949, of the National Institute on Mental Health (NIMH) (1946).
- The *Taft-Hartley Act* diminishes many of the advantages gained by labor unions during the New Deal (1947).
- In the face of resistance from several Southern baseball teams and bigoted baseball fans, African American baseball player Jackie Robinson breaks the "color line" when he signs on to play in the major leagues with the Brooklyn Dodgers (1947).
- President Harry Truman orders the full integration of the Armed Services by issuing *Executive Order 9981* (1948).
- Dr. Alfred Kinsey publishes *Sexual Behavior in the Human Male*, based on a survey of the sexual activities of 5,000 men (1948).
- Diplomat Ralph Bunche receives the Nobel Peace Prize for his work trying to resolve the conflict between Arabs and Jews in Israel, thus becoming the first African American to earn that honor (1950).
- The latest census tally reveals the presence of 151 million Americans, 64% of whom reside in urban areas (1950).

Note: For a more reflective and functional use of this list of contemporary social welfare historical events, see Question #6 under the **Questions for Further Research and Discussion** section (below).

Sources:
Daniel, C. (1989). *Chronicle of America*. Mt. Kisco, NY: Chronicle Publications.

Mercer, D. (2000). *Millennium year by year*. New York: Dorling Kindersley Publications.

Social welfare developments 1900–1950. (2011). Retrieved from https://socialwelfare.library.vcu.edu/events/1901-1950/

Primary Text Material

There are 11 Titles in the original 1935 *Social Security Act*, and several more were added over the years. Of most significance to the study of social welfare policy are the following:

Title I—Grants to the States for Old-Age Assistance
Title II—Federal Old-Age Benefits
Title III—Grants to the States for Unemployment Compensation Administration
Title IV—Grants to the States for Aid to Dependent Children
Title V—Grants to the States for Maternal and Child Welfare
Title VI—Public Health Work
Title VII—Social Security Board
Title X—Grants to the States for Aid to the Blind
Title XVIII—Medicare
Title XIX—Medicaid

What follows are the Preamble and brief selections from Title I and Title V of the 1935 *Social Security Act*:

The Social Security Act (1935)

"AN ACT to provide for the general welfare by establishing a system of Federal old-age benefits, and by enabling the several States to make more adequate provision for aged persons, blind persons, dependent and crippled children, maternal and child welfare, public health, and the administration of their unemployment compensation laws; to establish a Social Security Board; to raise revenue; and for other purposes.

Be it enacted by the Senate and House of Representatives of the United States of America in Congress assembled,
TITLE I—GRANTS TO STATES FOR OLD-AGE ASSISTANCE
APPROPRIATION
SECTION 1. For the purpose of enabling each State to furnish financial assistance, as far as practicable under the conditions in such State, to aged needy individuals, there is hereby authorized to be appropriated for the fiscal year ended June 30, 1936, the sum of $49,750,000, and there is hereby authorized to be appropriated for each fiscal year thereafter a sum sufficient to carry out the purposes of this title. The sums made available under this section shall be used for making payments to States which have submitted, and had approved by the Social Security Board established by Title VII (hereinafter referred to as the Board), State plans for old-age assistance . . .

Continued

> ... TITLE V—GRANTS TO STATES FOR MATERNAL AND CHILD WELFARE
> ... PART 3—CHILD WELFARE SERVICES
>
> SEC. 521. (a) For the purpose of enabling the United States, through the Children's Bureau, to cooperate with State public-welfare agencies establishing, extending, and strengthening, especially in predominantly rural areas, public-welfare services (hereinafter in this section referred to as child-welfare services) for the protection and care of homeless, dependent, and neglected children, and children in danger of becoming delinquent, there is hereby authorized to be appropriated for each fiscal year, beginning with the year ending June 30, 1936, the sum of $1,500,000. Such amount shall be allotted by the Secretary of Labor for use by cooperating State public-welfare agencies on the basis of plans developed jointly by the State agency and the Children's Bureau, to each State, $10,000, and the remainder to each State on the basis of such plans, not to exceed such part of the remainder as the rural population of such State bears to the total rural population of the United States. The amount so allotted shall be expended for payment of part of the cost of district, county or other local child- welfare services in areas predominantly rural, and for developing State services for the encouragement and assistance of adequate methods of community child-welfare organization in areas predominantly rural and other areas of special need. The amount of any allotment to a State under this section for any fiscal year remaining unpaid to such State at the end of such fiscal year shall be available for payment to such State under this section until the end of the second succeeding fiscal year. No payment to a State under this section shall be made out of its allotment for any fiscal year until its allotment for the preceding fiscal year has been exhausted or has ceased to be available.
>
> (b) From the sums appropriated therefor and the allotments available under subsection (a) the Secretary of Labor shall from time to time certify to the Secretary of the Treasury the amounts to be paid to the States, and the Secretary of the Treasury shall, through the Division of Disbursement of the Treasury Department and prior to audit or settlement by the General Accounting Office, make payments of such amounts from such allotments at the time or times specified by the Secretary of Labor . . ."
>
> Source and full text available at https://www.ourdocuments.gov/doc.php?flash=false&doc=68.
>
> Also available at https://www.ssa.gov/history/35act.html.

Timeline of General Events in History, the Humanities, and Science During This Period (1925–1950)

These general historical events may help you understand more clearly the overall historical context during which the primary document was created.

- Referencing the economic growth of the nation during this period, President-elect Calvin Coolidge announces, "The business of America is business" (1925).

- Industrialist Henry Ford introduces the practice of a 40-hour, five-day workweek in his automobile factories (1926).
- Physics professor Robert Goddard demonstrates his invention, a liquid-fueled rocket capable of climbing into the atmosphere (1926).
- Aspiring author Earnest Hemingway publishes his first novel, *The Sun Also Rises* (1926).
- Aviator Charles Lindbergh pilots his plane, *The Spirit of St. Louis*, 3,600 miles nonstop from New York to Paris in 33.5 hours (1927).
- Filmmaker Walt Disney screens the first cartoon with sound, *Steamboat Willie*, and introduces Mickey Mouse to the American public (1928).
- Cartoonist Chester Gould introduces a new newspaper comic strip that features the character of Dick Tracy, a police officer who tracks and arrests criminals relentlessly (1931).
- Aviator Amelia Earhart completes her solo transatlantic flight, originating in Newfoundland and a landing in Northern Ireland, thus becoming the first woman to do so (1932).
- The Hindenburg, a dirigible offering transatlantic air service and sent by Nazi Germany, partly as a propaganda gesture, explodes in flames in Lakewood, NJ, killing 35 passengers and one crew member (1937).
- Radio announcer Orson Wells and his Mercury Theatre players, dramatically reading sections of H. G. Wells's novel *War of the Worlds*, frighten more than 1 million radio listeners into believing that the earth was actually being invaded by Martians (1938).
- The New York World's Fair, representing 60 nations, opens in New York City with the theme of "The World of Tomorrow" and features color film by Kodak, an experimental television set by NBC, a preview of future autos by General Motors, long-distance telephone calling by AT&T, and a prototype of a futuristic 2036 urban area (1939).
- Following Adolph Hitler's vicious invasion of Poland, Great Britain and France declare war on Germany, with the United States opting to remain neutral (1939).
- Reflective of the nation's increasingly positive view on the economy, Hollywood explodes with new films, some of them classics even today, including *Gone With the Wind*, starring Vivien Leigh and Clark Gable; *The Wizard of Oz*, featuring Judy Garland; John Ford's *Stagecoach*; Disney's *Pinocchio*; *Beau Geste*; and *The Roaring Twenties*, starring James Cagney and Humphrey Bogart; among others (1939–1940).
- President Franklin Delano Roosevelt transforms the nation's industrial base to aid the war effort, then proclaims that the United States must be an "arsenal of democracy" and pledges to assist the Allied forces with military supplies and machinery (1940).
- President Franklin Delano Roosevelt inches closer to war as he announces a plan to provide a billion-dollar "lend-lease" program of war material and aid to

the Allies fighting Nazi Germany based on his international Four Freedoms: freedom of speech, freedom to worship God, freedom from want, and freedom from fear (1941).
- Following rising tensions between the United States and Japan over Japan's military actions throughout the Pacific, the United States initiates an embargo on all oil and rice imports to Japan (1941).
- Japan initiates a surprise attack on the American naval base and airfields on Pearl Harbor, Hawaii, prompting the United States to declare war on Japan (1941).
- Following the dictates of their Tripartite Pact with Japan, Germany and Italy declare war on the United States (1941).
- More than 10,000 American-born sons of Japanese immigrants, identified as *nisei*, volunteer to join the American military forces (1942).
- Italian physicist Enrico Fermi, working outdoors at the University of Chicago, creates the first controlled atomic chain reaction of fissionable uranium, thereby launching the United States into the nuclear age (1942).
- In order to support the war effort, the federal government introduces the rationing of some food items while President Roosevelt directs the freezing of wages and prices and mandates a 48-hour week at all defense industry factories (1943).
- Victory in Europe over Nazi Germany is declared (1945).
- The United States unleashes atomic bombs over Hiroshima and Nagasaki, leading Japan to surrender and triggering the end of World War II (1945).
- The United Nations is formed to maintain world peace and security, with five nations—China, France, Great Britain, the Soviet Union, and the United States—assigned a leadership role as permanent members of the Security Council (1945).
- The war-crimes trial for German Nazi officers begins in Nuremberg, Germany (1946).
- The Congressional *House Un-American Activities Committee* investigates suspected Communist infiltration of the Hollywood film industry, resulting in the blacklisting of 10 noted film professionals, mostly screenwriters, by the film industry itself (1947).
- In order to assist Western Europe in its recovery from World War II, the United States launches a massive foreign aid program, the Marshall Plan (1948).
- Despite the United Nations plan to divide Palestine into an Arab and Jewish state with Jerusalem as an international city following the cessation of British control over Palestine, the United States recognizes the independent state of Israel, and war breaks out between Israel and several Arab nations (1948).
- The United States provides economic and military aid to the Republic of South Korea after it is invaded by the Communist North Korean Army (1950).
- A United States senator from Wisconsin, Joe McCarthy, releases his alleged list of Communists who are working in the United States Department of State (1950).

Sources:

Daniel, C. (1989). *Chronicle of America*. Mt. Kisco, NY: Chronicle Publications.

Events of the 20th century. Retrieved from https://en.wikipedia.org/wiki/timeline_of_the_20th_century

Mercer, D. (2000). *Millennium year by year*. New York: Dorling Kindersley Publications.

Questions for Further Research and Discussion

1. Select three or four programs formed under the *New Deal* initiative of the Roosevelt administration, then study them further and summarize each program's purpose and how successful the program was in achieving its stated objectives.
2. Select one other Title of the *Social Security Act*, then skim through it, noting its major points, and summarize what you have learned from your study.
3. Explore further the substantial differences between *social insurance* programs and *means-tested* economic benefit programs, then discuss specific program examples of each type and the implications those differences have today in terms of program stability and public acceptance throughout society.
4. Determine through further Internet research whether there existed any overt or covert examples of racism and/or sexism in the various *New Deal* programs. Then summarize your findings with specific examples of either racism and/or sexism, if present.
5. Conduct further research on current strategies for improving the financial stability of *Social Security* retirement benefits and the *Medicare* program. Summarize the major approaches, and note any trends you may notice in the various options.
6. Select three events appearing under the **Linkage to Social Welfare** section (above), conduct further Internet research regarding them, then conclude whether you believe there exists any plausible relationship between the *Social Security Act* and the events you have chosen. Use the analytical model presented in Appendix 1 of this book, or develop your own analytical model, to draw these conclusions.
7. Select one book from the **Additional Selected References** list at the end of this chapter. Briefly read through it, then summarize the main points contained in the book. Identify your own personal reaction to this book.

Additional Selected References

Bernan Press. (2015). *Social Security handbook: Overview of Social Security programs*. Lanham, MD: Bernam Press.

Davies, P., & Morgan, I. W. (Eds.). (2016). *Hollywood and the Great Depression: American film, politics, and society in the 1930s*. Edinburgh: Edinburgh University Press.

Folsom, B. W. (2008). *New Deal or raw deal? How FDR's economic legacy has damaged America*. New York: Threshold Editions.

Haytock, J. A. (2013). *The middle class in the Great Depression: Popular women's novels of the 1930s.* New York: Palgrave Macmillan.

Himmelberg, Robert F. (Ed.). (2001). *The Great Depression and the New Deal.* Westport, CT: Greenwood Press.

Kasson, J. F. (2014). *The little girl who fought the Great Depression: Shirley Temple and 1930s America.* New York: W.W. Norton & Company.

McElvaine, R. S. (Ed.). (2008). *Down and out in the Great Depression: Letters from the forgotten man.* Chapel Hill: University of North Carolina Press.

Mitchell, B. (1975). *Depression decade: From new era through New Deal, 1929–1941. Volume IX, The economic history of the United States.* New York: Routledge.

Rogne, L. (2009). *Social insurance and social justice: Social security, Medicare, and the campaign against entitlements.* New York: Springer.

Schieber, S. J., & Shoven, J. B. (1999). *The real deal: The history and future of Social Security.* New Haven: Yale University Press.

United States. (1995). *A brief history of the Social Security Administration.* Baltimore, MD: Social Security Administration.

Young, W. H., & Young, N. K. (2007). *The Great Depression in America: A cultural encyclopedia.* Westport, CT: Greenwood Press.

Credits

Fig. 18.1: Source: http://www.fdrlibrary.marist.edu/archives/collections/franklin/?p=digitallibrary/digitalcontent&id=3296.

Fig. 18.2: Source: https://commons.wikimedia.org/wiki/File:Signing_Of_The_Social_Security_Act.jpg.

Chapter 19

Rural Poverty and Displacement

John Steinbeck's *The Grapes of Wrath* (1939)

Introduction

John Steinbeck was born in 1902 and raised in Salinas, California, a fertile agricultural area in the Central Valley known colloquially as the "nation's salad bowl." His father was a manager at a local flour mill, and his mother was a teacher who instilled in her children a sense of academic rigor and a love of literature. Steinbeck often used the Central Valley as the setting for his novels and portrayed wealthy landowners in less than sympathetic terms.

Showing an early interest in writing by composing stories for friends and contributing to his high school newspaper, Steinbeck attended Sanford University sporadically over several years, taking creative writing and science courses. He worked at manual labor jobs in New York City in the late 1920s, then returned to California doing the same kind of work but always managed to keep writing in his spare time. During these early years, Steinbeck published *Cup of Gold* (1929), *The Pastures of Heaven* (1932), *To a God Unknown* (1933), four *Red Pony* books (1933–1937), and *The Long Valley* (1938), none of which produced any financial success.

Tortilla Flat (1935), however, did produce some measure of financial reward as well as positive notoriety. During this period, Steinbeck also published *In Dubious Battle* (1936), a story devoted to an agricultural strike by workers against management. Another of his novels, *Of Mice and Men* (1937), a poignant story about two agricultural workers struggling together in a migrant labor camp during the Great Depression, was highly successful and eventually made into a Hollywood movie in 1939 and again as a remake in 1992.

The basic plot for Steinbeck's 1939 signature novel, *The Grapes of Wrath*, was generated from a newspaper writing assignment he received to research the daily living and working conditions of migrant worker camps in Bakersfield,

FIGURE 19.1 John Steinbeck (center) during a visit with President B. Lyndon Johnson at the Oval Office in the White House.

California. What he visually and emotionally experienced during this assignment spurred Steinbeck to write a novel that personalized what it means to be caught in the unending cycle of rural poverty.

The Grapes of Wrath portrays a destitute Oklahoma family, the Joads, forced to flee their family farm from the destruction caused throughout the Dust Bowl and drive through Texas, New Mexico, and Arizona to Southern California in a dilapidated car filled with relatives and all of their worldly possessions. What the family finds is a few temporary jobs, low wages, substandard housing conditions, greedy owners, desperate migrant co-workers, and a bleak scenario for their future. In this widely read novel, Steinbeck creatively tackles the theme of the social and economic dichotomy in America during the 1930s and 1940s. He posits that wealthy California property owners and businessmen typically disparage the poor, landless, and homeless migrant workers and treat them as subhuman creatures whose only purpose is to provide the hard labor from which the upper classes profit. The inherent strength and mutual support within the Joad family, however, stands in firm opposition to the planned dehumanization of the poor in ways so ingeniously created by Steinbeck's language and images. Though a fictional family—or, rather, a composite of families interviewed by Steinbeck—the Joads became a symbol of the plight of the rural poor during the Great Depression and a call for the federal government to regulate the private sector and offer financial assistance to those in need.

The reaction to *The Grapes of Wrath* was swift and varied. The general public was enthralled by the plot and applauded Steinbeck's literary skills; rural poverty became the subject of interest and open discussion, especially among progressives; Oklahoma state officials were publicly embarrassed by the portrayal of human hardship in their state and reacted negatively to the novel; California farmers and fruit growers were outraged by the depiction of themselves as greedy and insensitive to the needs of poor migrant workers; and several California public officials were similarly infuriated by how the county was portrayed. The Board of Supervisors in Kern County even banned the sale of *The Grapes of Wrath* in the area for two years following its publication. The Federal Bureau of Investigation (FBI) is reported to have investigated Steinbeck on suspicion of being a member of the Communist Party or having pro-Communist leanings. On a more positive note, Eleanor Roosevelt, the president's wife, is described as being deeply influenced by *The Grapes of Wrath*, so much so that she engineered congressional hearings on migrant work camps that resulted in revised labor laws affecting migrant workers living in work camps throughout California and other Western states.

During World War II, Steinbeck served as a war correspondent for the *New York Herald Tribune*. After the war, he continued to write novels, most notably *East of Eden* (1952), a work about a complex and conflicted family and one that literary critics believe contains many autobiographical elements. During this period, Steinbeck also wrote *The Winter of Our Discontent* (1961), for which he received a Nobel prize in literature, and *Travels with Charley in Search of America* (1962), a travelogue he completed on a road trip with his loyal dog, Charley. In 1964, President Lyndon Johnson presented Steinbeck with the Presidential Medal of Freedom in Washington, DC. His final work, *America and Americans* (1966), is a compilation of more than 50 essays and newspaper articles.

In 1940, *The Grapes of Wrath* was made into a Hollywood movie, produced by Darryl Zanuck, directed by the renowned John Ford, and starring Henry Fonda in a role that won him an Academy Award. Other cast

FIGURE 19.2   Actor Henry Fonda as Tom Joad.

members, as well as the film itself, have received numerous awards from several film industry societies, and it is consistently ranked by rating organizations as one of the 25 top American films of all time.

- For a very brief video introduction of Ken Burns's PBS film, *The Dust Bowl*, see http://www.pbs.org/kenburns/dustbowl/.
- For a longer discussion with Ken Burns on his film, as well as additional video segments, see https://www.youtube.com/watch?v=g9GkNQa5of8.
- For a short description of the causes and effects surrounding the Dust Bowl, produced in 1950 and including newsreel interviews with eyewitnesses, see https://www.youtube.com/watch?v=CM3ZHMBhP2k.
- To view the trailer to *The Grapes of Wrath* film, see https://www.youtube.com/watch?v=fOuAZLA_jWQ.
- For an extensive summary of the film *The Grapes of Wrath*, with selected quotations, see http://www.filmsite.org/grap.html.

Internet Sources for the Content of This Introduction Include:

http://www.steinbeck.org
http://www.roosevelthouse.hunter.cuny.edu/roosevelts-john-steinbeck-75th-anniversary-grapes-wrath/
https://www.nationalgeographic.org/news/grapes-wrath/
https://www.biography.com/people/john-steinbeck-9493358
http://www.sparknotes.com/lit/grapesofwrath/
https://www.theguardian.com/books/2011/nov/21/melvyn-bragg-on-john-steinbeck
https://www.britannica.com/biography/john-steinbeck
https://en.wikipedia.org/wiki/john_steinbeck
https://en.wikipedia.org/wiki/the_grapes_of_frath
https://www.britannica.com/topic/the-grapes-of-wrath
https://www.theguardian.com/books/2014/dec/15/robert-mcrum-100-best-novels-observer-steinbeck-grapes-wrath

Linkage to Social Welfare History (1925–1950)

Social welfare historical events for this time period include the following:

- Following the legal battle between noted lawyers William Jennings Bryan for the prosecution and Clarence Darrow for the defense, a Tennessee court convicts biology teacher John Scopes for teaching evolution in the legendary "Scopes Monkey Trial" (1925).
- Watched by more than an estimated 200,000 bystanders, 400,00 members of the Ku Klux Klan march, waving American flags, toward the Washington Monument in Washington, DC (1925).

- Resistance to the Prohibition Law around the nation surfaces in a series of speakeasies, surreptitious places where introductions are needed and alcohol can be purchased and consumed (1925).
- Appearing in blackface, which was embarrassingly common at the time, Al Jolson stars in the film *The Jazz Singer* (1927).
- The Unites States Supreme Court, in *Buck v. Bell*, decreed that it is constitutional to forcibly sterilize men and women who were deemed to be feeble-minded, and, thus, a future burden on society (1927)
- The *Harlem Renaissance*, a major cultural movement featuring African American authors, musicians, and visual artists, flourishes in New York City and beyond (1928).
- A frenzied selling off of stocks on Wall Street culminates on Black Tuesday, a day memorialized in American history as the day that signaled the beginning of the Great Depression (1929).
- The 1930 census reveals that America has reached a population growth of 122 million, the life expectancy of the typical American is 61 years, and there are more than 26 million cars in use (1930).
- President Herbert Hoover establishes the Veterans Administration by executive order (1930).
- Census officials report that the number of unemployed is between 4 million and 5 million Americans and, furthermore, that they have removed from the unemployed lists those unemployed who sell apples on street corners across the nation (1931).
- Social reformer Jane Addams is awarded the Nobel Peace Prize (1931).
- In the annual State of the Union address, President Herbert Hoover announces a major construction plan that will aid the business community but rejects any direct or indirect resources for the unemployed (1931).
- President Herbert Hoover orders the military, under the command of Army General Douglas MacArthur, to disperse from Washington, DC members of the "Bonus Army," a group of World War I army veterans who rallied there to collect a bonus that was promised to them for their loyal army service (1932).
- Former New York Governor Franklin Delano Roosevelt is elected president of the United States with a pledge for a "New Deal" for the American people, who are struggling through the effects of the Great Depression (1932).
- During the first 100 days of his presidency, President Roosevelt passes significant social legislation and launches the first of his many "alphabet soup" programs, namely the Civilian Conservation Corps (CCC), the Federal Emergency Relief Act (FERA), the Agricultural Adjustment Act (AAA), the Emergency Farm Mortgage Act, the Truth in Lending Act (TILA), and the Glass-Steagall Act (1933).
- The *21st Amendment* to the *United States Constitution*, rescinding the prohibition of alcohol, receives the required two-thirds majority approval, thus legitimizing the social benefits of alcohol when used in moderation (1933).
- President Franklin Delano Roosevelt appoints Frances Perkins as Secretary of Labor, thereby making her the first woman ever appointed to a federal cabinet post (1933).

- In California, reformer Dr. Francis Townsend reveals his proposal for a pension plan for senior citizens that would provide the aged poor with a monthly allowance and help stabilize the nation's economy (1934).
- President Franklin Delano Roosevelt authorizes the Works Progress Administration (WPA), a major employment program that focuses on large industrial projects using a highly skilled workforce. The United States Congress also passes the *National Labor Relations Act (Wagner Act)*, which strengthens labor unions (1935).
- President Franklin Delano Roosevelt also authorizes the *Emergency Relief Appropriations Act*, which allocates $3 million to expand the existing and new public works programs (1935).
- President Franklin Delano Roosevelt signs the *Social Security Act*, which dramatically transforms the modern social welfare system structure (1935).
- The United Automobile Workers Union wins its strike against General Motors, the United Steelworkers union is similarly victorious against United States Steel Corporation, and several longshoremen's unions along the East and West coasts triumph in their struggles against the shipping industry, thus confirming the increasing influence of the labor union movement for workers' rights (1936).
- President Franklin Delano Roosevelt signs the *Fair Labor Standards Act*, which sets a minimum wage and places a specified limit on the number of hours worked per week (1938).
- Drs. Alton Ochsner and Michael DeBakey first note the spread of lung cancer in Louisiana and conclude that the cause might be linked to cigarette smoking (1938).
- Concert singer Marian Anderson is denied access to sing in Constitution Hall in Washington, DC by the Daughters of the American Revolution (DAR) simply because she is African American. She sings instead in front of the Lincoln Memorial through the intercession of Eleanor Roosevelt, the president's wife (1939).
- Seeking to calm the rising anger of African Americans, President Franklin Delano Roosevelt signs an executive order creating the Fair Employment Practices Commission to investigate charges of discrimination based on race, creed, or national origin in any corporation that is part of the defense industry (1941).
- President Franklin Delano Roosevelt signs *Executive Order 9066*, which empowers the War Department to forcibly intern 110,000 Japanese nationals and Japanese American citizens in Hawaii and along the West Coast of the United States (1942).
- The notorious radical "radio priest" Reverend Charles Coughlin is silenced, and his anti-Semitic weekly newspaper, *Social Justice*, is banned under the principles of the 1917 *Espionage Act* (1942).
- The United States Foreign Affairs Committee reports that, since 1933, more than 600,000 immigrants fleeing Nazi Germany persecution, many of them Jews, have been granted admittance to the United States (1943).
- The United States Congress passes the *Servicemen's Readjustment Act*, more commonly referred to as the *G.I. Bill of Rights*, which provides a variety of resources

to veterans, including education and training, low-interest home mortgage loans, job counselling and employment placement (1944).
- American soldiers liberate the concentration camps at Dachau and Buchenwald and assist the survivors with medical help (1945).
- President Harry Truman signs the *National Mental Health Act*, which provides substantial resources for mental health education and research and leads to the creation, in 1949, of the National Institute on Mental Health (NIMH) (1946).
- The *Taft-Hartley Act* diminishes many of the advantages gained by labor unions during the New Deal (1947).
- In the face of resistance from several Southern baseball teams and bigoted baseball fans, African American baseball player Jackie Robinson breaks the "color line" when he signs on to play in the major leagues with the Brooklyn Dodgers (1947).
- President Truman orders the full integration of the Armed Service by issuing *Executive Order 9981* (1948)
- Dr. Alfred Kinsey publishes *Sexual Behavior in the Human Male*, based on a survey of the sexual activities of 5,000 men (1948).
- Diplomat Ralph Bunche receives the Nobel Peace Prize for his work trying to resolve the conflict between Arabs and Jews in Israel, thus becoming the first African American to earn that honor (1950).
- The latest census tally reveals the presence of 151 million Americans, 64% of whom reside in urban areas (1950).

Note: For a more reflective and functional use of this list of contemporary social welfare historical events, see Question #5 under the **Questions for Further Research and Discussion** section (below).

Sources:

Daniel, C. (1989). *Chronicle of America*. Mt. Kisco, NY: Chronicle Publications.
Mercer, D. (2000). *Millennium year by year*. New York: Dorling Kindersley Publications.
Social welfare developments 1900–1950. (2011). Retrieved from https://socialwelfare.library.vcu.edu/events/1901-1950/

Primary Text Material

The Grapes of Wrath

Chapter 21

". . . THE MOVING, QUESTING people were migrants now. Those families who had lived on a little piece of land, who had lived and died on forty acres, had

Continued

eaten or starved on the produce of forty acres, had now the whole West to rove in. And they scampered about, looking for work; and the highways were streams of people, and the ditch banks were lines of people. Behind them more were coming. The great highways streamed with moving people. There in the Middle—and Southwest had lived a simple agrarian folk who had not changed with industry, who had not farmed with machines or known the power and danger of machines in private hands. They had not grown up in the paradoxes of industry. Their senses were still sharp to the ridiculousness of the industrial life.

And then suddenly the machines pushed them out and they swarmed on the highways. The movement changed them; the highways, the camps along the road, the fear of hunger and the hunger itself, changed them. The children without dinner changed them, the endless moving changed them. They were migrants. And the hostility changed them, welded them, united them—hostility that made the little towns group and arm as though to repel an invader, squads with pick handles, clerks and storekeepers with shotguns, guarding the world against their own people.

In the West there was panic when the migrants multiplied on the highways. Men of property were terrified for their property. Men who had never been hungry saw the eyes of the hungry. Men who had never wanted anything very much saw the flare of want in the eyes of the migrants. And the men of the towns and of the soft suburban country gathered to defend themselves; and they reassured themselves that they were good and the invaders bad, as a man must do before he fights. They said, These goddamned Okies are dirty and ignorant. They're degenerate, sexual maniacs. Those goddamned Okies are thieves. They'll steal anything. They've got no sense of property rights.

And the latter was true, for how can a man without property know the ache of ownership? And the defending people said, They bring disease, they're filthy. We can't have them in the schools. They're strangers. How'd you like to have your sister go out with one of 'em?

The local people whipped themselves into a mold of cruelty. Then they formed units, squads, and armed them—armed them with clubs, with gas, with guns. We own the country. We can't let these Okies get out of hand. And the men who were armed did not own the land, but they thought they did. And the clerks who drilled at night owned nothing, and the little storekeepers possessed only a drawerful of debts. But even a debt is something, even a job is something. The clerk thought, I get fifteen dollars a week. S'pose a goddamn Okie would work for twelve? And the little storekeeper thought, How could I compete with a debtless man?

And the migrants streamed in on the highways and their hunger was in their eyes, and their need was in their eyes. They had no argument, no system, nothing but their numbers and their needs. When there was work for a man, ten men fought for it—fought with a low wage. If that fella'll work for thirty cents, I'll work for twenty-five. If he'll take twenty-five, I'll do it for twenty. No, me, I'm hungry. I'll work for fifteen. I'll work for food. The kids. You ought to see them.

Little boils, like, comin' out, an' they can't run aroun'. Give 'em some windfall fruit, an' they bloated up. Me, I'll work for a little piece of meat.

And this was good, for wages went down and prices stayed up. The great owners were glad and they sent out more handbills to bring more people in. And wages went down and prices stayed up. And pretty soon now we'll have serfs again.

And now the great owners and the companies invented a new method. A great owner bought a cannery. And when the peaches and the pears were ripe he cut the price of fruit below the cost of raising it. And as cannery owner he paid himself a low price for the fruit and kept the price of canned goods up and took his profit. And the little farmers who owned no canneries lost their farms, and they were taken by the great owners, the banks, and the companies who also owned the canneries. As time went on, there were fewer farms. The little farmers moved into town for a while and exhausted their credit, exhausted their friends, their relatives. And then they too went on the highways. And the roads were crowded with men ravenous for work, murderous for work.

And the companies, the banks worked at their own doom and they did not know it. The fields were fruitful, and starving men moved on the roads. The granaries were full and the children of the poor grew up rachitic, and the pustules of pellagra swelled on their sides. The great companies did not know that the line between hunger and anger is a thin line. And money that might have gone to wages went for gas, for guns, for agents and spies, for blacklists, for drilling. On the highways the people moved like ants and searched for work, for food. And the anger began to ferment . . ."

Source: Steinbeck, J. (2002). *The Grapes of Wrath*. New York: Penguin Books.

Timeline of General Events in History, the Humanities, and Science During This Period (1925–1950)

These general historical events may help you understand more clearly the overall historical context during which the primary document was created.

- Referencing the economic growth of the nation during this period, President-elect Calvin Coolidge announces, "The business of America is business" (1925).
- Industrialist Henry Ford introduces the practice of a 40-hour, five-day workweek in his automobile factories (1926).
- Physics professor Robert Goddard demonstrates his invention, a liquid-fueled rocket capable of climbing into the atmosphere (1926).
- Aspiring author Earnest Hemingway publishes his first novel, *The Sun Also Rises* (1926).
- Aviator Charles Lindbergh pilots his plane, *The Spirit of St. Louis*, 3,600 miles nonstop from New York to Paris in 33.5 hours (1927).

- Filmmaker Walt Disney screens the first cartoon with sound, *Steamboat Willie*, and introduces Mickey Mouse to the American public (1928).
- Cartoonist Chester Gould introduces a new newspaper comic strip that features the character of Dick Tracy, a police officer who tracks and arrests criminals relentlessly (1931).
- Aviator Amelia Earhart completes her solo transatlantic flight, originating in Newfoundland and a landing in Northern Ireland, thus becoming the first woman to do so (1932).
- The Hindenburg, a dirigible offering transatlantic air service and sent by Nazi Germany, partly as a propaganda gesture, explodes in flames in Lakewood, NJ, killing 35 passengers and one crew member (1937).
- Radio announcer Orson Wells and his Mercury Theatre players, dramatically reading sections of H. G. Wells's novel *War of the Worlds*, frighten more than 1 million radio listeners into believing that the earth was actually being invaded by Martians (1938).
- The New York World's Fair, representing 60 nations, opens in New York City with the theme of "The World of Tomorrow" and features color film by Kodak, an experimental television set by NBC, a preview of future autos by General Motors, long-distance telephone calling by AT&T, and a prototype of a futuristic 2036 urban area (1939).
- Following Adolph Hitler's vicious invasion of Poland, Great Britain and France declare war on Germany, with the United States opting to remain neutral (1939).
- Reflective of the nation's increasingly positive view on the economy, Hollywood explodes with new films, some of them classics even today, including *Gone With the Wind*, starring Vivien Leigh and Clark Gable; *The Wizard of Oz*, featuring Judy Garland; John Ford's *Stagecoach*; Disney's *Pinocchio*; *Beau Geste*; and *The Roaring Twenties*, starring James Cagney and Humphrey Bogart; among others (1939–1940).
- President Franklin Delano Roosevelt transforms the nation's industrial base to aid the war effort, then proclaims that the United States must be an "arsenal of democracy" and pledges to assist the Allied forces with military supplies and machinery (1940).
- President Roosevelt inches closer to war as he announces a plan to provide a billion-dollar "lend-lease" program of war material and aid to the Allies fighting Nazi Germany based on his international Four Freedoms: freedom of speech, freedom to worship God, freedom from want, and freedom from fear (1941).
- Following rising tensions between the United States and Japan over Japan's military actions throughout the Pacific, the United States initiates an embargo on all oil and rice imports to Japan (1941).
- Japan initiates a surprise attack on the American naval base and airfields on Pearl Harbor, Hawaii, prompting the United States to declare war on Japan (1941).
- Following the dictates of their Tripartite Pact with Japan, Germany and Italy declare war on the United States (1941).
- More than 10,000 American-born sons of Japanese immigrants, identified as *nisei*, volunteer to join the American military forces (1942).
- Italian physicist Enrico Fermi, working outdoors at the University of Chicago, creates the first controlled atomic chain reaction of fissionable uranium, thereby launching the United States into the nuclear age (1942).

- In order to support the war effort, the federal government introduces the rationing of some food items while President Roosevelt directs the freezing of wages and prices and mandates a 48-hour week at all defense industry factories (1943).
- Victory in Europe over Nazi Germany is declared (1945).
- The United States unleashes atomic bombs over Hiroshima and Nagasaki, leading Japan to surrender and triggering the end of World War II (1945).
- The United Nations is formed to maintain world peace and security, with five nations—China, France, Great Britain, the Soviet Union, and the United States—assigned a leadership role as permanent members of the Security Council (1945).
- The war-crimes trial for German Nazi officers begins in Nuremberg, Germany (1946).
- The Congressional *House Un-American Activities Committee* investigates suspected Communist infiltration of the Hollywood film industry, resulting in the blacklisting of 10 noted film professionals, mostly screenwriters, by the film industry itself (1947).
- In order to assist Western Europe in its recovery from World War II, the United States launches a massive foreign aid program, the Marshall Plan (1948).
- Despite the United Nations plan to divide Palestine into an Arab and Jewish state with Jerusalem as an international city following the cessation of British control over Palestine, the United States recognizes the independent state of Israel, and war breaks out between Israel and several Arab nations (1948).
- The United States provides economic and military aid to the Republic of South Korea after it is invaded by the Communist North Korean Army (1950).
- A United States senator from Wisconsin, Joe McCarthy, releases his alleged list of Communists who are working in the United States Department of State (1950).

Sources:

Daniel, C. (1989). *Chronicle of America*. Mt. Kisco, NY: Chronicle Publications.

Events of the 20th century. Retrieved from https://en.wikipedia.org/wiki/timeline_of_the_20th_century

Mercer, D. (2000). *Millennium year by year*. New York: Dorling Kindersley Publications.

Questions for Further Research and Discussion

1. Conduct further Internet research on Eleanor Roosevelt, President Roosevelt's wife, then list the notable accomplishments she achieved in the general area of social welfare during her life.
2. Read further sections of *The Grapes of Wrath*, and list the specific elements in the Joad family that allow them to overcome, or not, the debilitating conditions that were thrust upon them.
3. Chose one of John Steinbeck's other novels, read through it purposively to discover any social and/or economic themes that are present, then compose a brief summary of your findings
4. Based on the primary documentary material presented here, as well as other material you discover in the **Additional Selected References** at the end of this chapter,

what new federal policy or policies do you believe should have been developed or changed at that time especially regarding rural poverty? Describe those policies in detail. Recall that a policy could be either *legislative* (i.e., a law), *judicial* (i.e., a court decision), or *administrative* (i.e., an executive or organizational policy) in nature.
5. Select three events appearing under the **Linkage to Social Welfare** section (above), conduct further Internet research regarding them, then conclude whether you believe there exists any plausible relationship between *The Grapes of Wrath* and the events you have chosen. Use the analytical model presented in Appendix 1 of this book, or develop your own analytical model, to draw these conclusions.
6. Select one book from the **Additional Selected References** list at the end of this chapter. Briefly read through it, then summarize the main points contained in the book. Identify your own personal reaction to this book.

Additional Selected References

Brown, D. (2013). *The great American Dust Bowl*. New York: Houghton, Mifflin Harcourt.
Davis, R. C. (1982). *The grapes of wrath: A collection of critical essays*. Englewood Cliffs: Prentice-Hall.
DeAngelis, T., & DeAngelis, G. (2002). *The Dust Bowl*. Philadelphia: Chelsea House Publishers.
Ditsky, J. (Ed.). (1989). *Critical essays on Steinbeck's The grapes of wrath*. Boston, MA: G.K. Hall.
Donohue, A. M. N. (1968). *A casebook on The grapes of wrath*. New York: Crowell.
Duncan, D. (2012). *The Dust Bowl: An illustrated history*. San Francisco: Chronicle Books.
French, W. G. (1963). *A companion to The grapes of wrath*. New York: Viking Press.
Heavilin, B. A. (2000). *The critical response to John Steinbeck's The grapes of wrath*. Westport, CT: Greenwood Press.
Lookingbill, B. D. (2001). *Dust Bowl, USA: Depression America and the ecological imagination, 1929–1941*. Athens: Ohio University Press.
Owens, L. (1989). *The grapes of wrath: Trouble in the promised land*. Boston: Twayne.
Shillinglaw, S. (2014). *On reading the Grapes of Wrath*. New York: Penguin Books.
Shindo, C. J. (1997). *Dust bowl migrants in the American imagination*. Lawrence, KS: University Press of Kansas.
Wartzman, R. (2008). *Obscene in the extreme: The burning and banning of John Steinbeck's The grapes of wrath*. New York: PublicAffairs.
Wyatt, D. (Ed.). (1990). *New essays on The grapes of wrath*. New York: Cambridge University Press.
Yancey, D. (2004). *Life during the Dust Bowl*. San Diego, CA: Lucent Books.

Credits

Fig. 19.1: Source: https://commons.wikimedia.org/wiki/File:JohnSteinbeck.JPG.
Fig. 19.2: Source: https://i.pinimg.com/736x/9e/5b/d1/9e5bd1bbe866c11e91fee31719b95886—the-grapes-classic-films.jpg.
John Steinbeck, The Grapes of Wrath. Copyright © 2002 by Penguin Random House LLC. Reprinted with permission.

Chapter 20

The Japanese Relocation Order

Executive Order 9066 (1942)

Introduction

Barely two months after the Pearl Harbor attack on Unites States Naval forces, President Franklin Delano Roosevelt issued the now infamous *Executive Order 9066*, which forced the relocation of approximately 110,000 Japanese nationals and Japanese American citizens to what were essentially prison camps throughout several western states in America. Approximately one-third were aliens of Japanese descent, and two-thirds were Japanese American citizens. One month later, *Public Law 506* empowered all federal courts to decide on any case or legal issue arising from *Executive Order 9066*.

Japanese businesses and private homes had to be sold quickly or simply closed and left vacant. The internees were instructed to take with them only what they could carry or easily transport on assigned busses. According to the United States Census, approximately 127,000 people with Japanese ancestry lived in the United States at the time, the vast majority of whom lived in Washington, Oregon, and California.

Although the executive order did not specifically mention Japanese ancestry as its focus, the results reveal, rather blatantly, that being Japanese was the dominant factor for removal. Technically, *Executive Order 9066* only authorized the Secretary of War, or his designee, to remove specified individuals from selected geographic areas in the United States that were loosely defined as military zones. The military authorities designated virtually the entire West Coast as military zones, which then provided the excuse for the mass relocation of anyone of Japanese ancestry, whether they were citizens or not. Also during this period, the United States Treasury Department froze all assets, including bank accounts, pension funds, and real estate properties, of all Japanese aliens and Japanese American citizens living in these zones. Remarkably, there was no forced relocation or assets seizure of Japanese nationals or Japanese American citizens in Hawaii, which, at the time, included approximately 40% of its residents.

FIGURE 20.1 Sign placed in a store in Oakland, California, shortly after the Pearl Harbor attack. The store was closed following orders that persons of Japanese descent had to evacuate from certain West Coast areas.

Internment lasted, in most cases, for two and a half years in one of 10 internment camps maintained by the United States Army across Washington State, Oregon, California, Wyoming, Utah, and Arizona. The daily living conditions for the confined men, women, and children are reported to have been severe and even ruthless at times. Some military guards, as an example, took out their frustrations over the Pearl Harbor attack by delivering brutal physical punishments for any rule infraction at the camps.

Although not generally known, approximately 5,000 aliens of German descent and 300 aliens of Italian descent, suspected of espionage, were also detained in internment camps during World War II. It is clear, however, that Japanese people, whether aliens or United States citizens, were specifically targeted, most probably because of a lingering prejudice against all Asian people as witnessed by the earlier passage of the *Chinese Exclusion Act* in 1882.

Any resistance to the internment process was dispatched with swiftly. Fred Korematsu, the son of Japanese immigrants, was an American citizen born in Oakland, California. At 23 years old, he refused to report to his designated internment center and was arrested, convicted of violating valid United States military orders, and sentenced to five years of probation. Korematsu was subsequently removed to the Topaz Internment Camp in Utah. After losing several levels of appeal, he, with the American Civil Liberties Union's assistance, appealed to the United States Supreme Court (*Korematsu v. United States*,

323 U.S. 214). By a vote of 6–3, the United States Supreme Court on December 18, 1944, upheld Korematsu's conviction on constitutional grounds that it was a military necessity. One of the dissenting justices, Justice Robert Jackson, argued unsuccessfully that Korematsu was a native-born American citizen who gave no indication that he might be a threat to our nation's security. In fact, Jackson maintained that Korematsu's only "crime" was to have parents of Japanese descent and to be living in one of the designated military zones in California during World War II. As a postscript, in 2011, the acting Solicitor General, Neal Katyal, revealed that during the *Korematsu v. United States* trial, the prosecution withheld evidence from the court regarding a report from Naval Intelligence at the time that stated Japanese American citizens in general were not to be considered as dangerous or a threat to our nation's security.

All Japanese and Japanese Americans were released from the internment camps and allowed to return home on January 2, 1945, following the issuance by the Army of *Public Proclamation No. 21*. Three years later, in 1948, President Harry Truman signed the *Evacuation Claims Act*, which allowed all those relocated to file claims for property lost during their internment. It has been estimated that the funds allocated under this act, $38 million, computes out to approximately 10 cents for every dollar of property lost. Years later, in 1988, the United States Congress admitted that a "grave injustice" had been committed and thus provided an additional $1.6 billion into a fund for individuals forcibly removed from their homes or businesses or to their heirs.

FIGURE 20.2   The loading of families of Japanese descent onto a bus on the way to a relocation camp.

Today, the 10 internment camps are designated as National Historic Landmark sites and maintained by either the National Park Service or by state historical societies. The names and locations of these 10 internment camps are:

- Arizona: Poston and Gila River
- Arkansas: Rohwer and Jerome
- California: Tule Lake and Manzanar
- Colorado: Granada
- Idaho: Minidoka
- Utah: Topaz
- Wyoming: Heart Mountain

Each of these internment camps has its own story to tell, as revealed by photographs, letters, diaries, and personal effects left by former internees.

The stated purpose for such mass relocation of thousands of individuals and families was because of a "military necessity" to protect the nation from possibly hostile forces who might work to undermine the war effort against Japan. As a point of fact, 10 Americans were indeed arrested and convicted of espionage during World War II, but not one of them was of Japanese ancestry.

Tragically, similar forced internment of a class of individuals could happen again because the United States Supreme Court decision in *Korematsu v. United States* has never been rescinded. In some dystopian future in the United States, sources such as blind prejudice, war hysteria, or some fabricated illogical reasoning could arise again and pressure our government to lose our nation's historic commitment to fairness and equal justice for all regardless of race, creed, or national origin.

- See also materials collected by the Japanese American National Museum on the relocation centers available at http://www.janm.org.
- For a clearly biased propaganda film offering an indefensible rationale for the internment of Japanese aliens and Japanese Americans, which was produced by the United States Office of War Information in 1942, see https://www.youtube.com/watch?v=esVege1S0OE.
- For some photos by noted photographer Ansel Adams of what life was like for the internees at one relocation center—Manzanar in California—see: https://www.loc.gov/teachers/classroommaterials/connections/manzanar/history3.html.
- See also a short clip produced by NBC News entitled *The "Two Faces" of Japanese American Internment Camps* at https://www.nbcnews.com/news/asian-america/remembering-executive-order-9066-single-act-began-internment-n706371.

Internet Sources for the Content of This Introduction Include:

http://historymatters.gmu.edu/d/5154

http://www.history.com/this-day-in-history/roosevelt-signs-executive-order-9066

https://www.britannica.com/topic/executive-order-9066

http://encyclopedia.densho.org/executive_order_9066/
https://www.nps.gov/articles/historyinternment.htm
https://en.wikipedia.org/wiki/korematsu_v._united_states
http://www.uscourts.gov/educational-resources/educational-activities/facts-and-case-summary-korematsu-v-us

Linkage to Social Welfare History (1925-1950)

Social welfare historical events for this time period include the following:

- Following the legal battle between noted lawyers William Jennings Bryan for the prosecution and Clarence Darrow for the defense, a Tennessee court convicts biology teacher John Scopes for teaching evolution in the legendary "Scopes Monkey Trial" (1925).
- Watched by more than an estimated 200,000 bystanders, 400,00 members of the Ku Klux Klan march, waving American flags, toward the Washington Monument in Washington, DC (1925).
- Resistance to the Prohibition Law around the nation surfaces in a series of speakeasies, surreptitious places where introductions are needed and alcohol can be purchased and consumed (1925).
- Appearing in blackface, which was embarrassingly common at the time, Al Jolson stars in the film *The Jazz Singer* (1927).
- The Unites States Supreme Court, in *Buck v. Bell*, decreed that it is constitutional to forcibly sterilize men and women who were deemed to be feeble-minded, and, thus, a future burden on society (1927).
- The *Harlem Renaissance*, a major cultural movement featuring African American authors, musicians, and visual artists, flourishes in New York City and beyond (1928).
- A frenzied selling off of stocks on Wall Street culminates on Black Tuesday, a day memorialized in American history as the day that signaled the beginning of the Great Depression (1929).
- The 1930 census reveals that America has reached a population growth of 122 million, the life expectancy of the typical American is 61 years, and there are more than 26 million cars in use (1930).
- President Herbert Hoover establishes the Veterans Administration by executive order (1930).
- Census officials report that the number of unemployed is between 4 million and 5 million Americans and, furthermore, that they have removed from the unemployed lists those unemployed who sell apples on street corners across the nation (1931).
- Social reformer Jane Addams is awarded the Nobel Peace Prize (1931).
- In the annual State of the Union address, President Herbert Hoover announces a major construction plan that will aid the business community but rejects any direct or indirect resources for the unemployed (1931).

- President Hoover orders the military, under the command of Army General Douglas MacArthur, to disperse from Washington, D.C. members of the "Bonus Army," a group of World War I army veterans who rallied there to collect a bonus that was promised to them for their loyal army service (1932).
- Former New York Governor Franklin Delano Roosevelt is elected president of the United States with a pledge for a "New Deal" for the American people, who are struggling through the effects of the Great Depression (1932).
- During the first 100 days of his presidency, President Roosevelt passes significant social legislation and launches the first of his many "alphabet soup" programs, namely the Civilian Conservation Corps (CCC), the Federal Emergency Relief Act (FERA), the Agricultural Adjustment Act (AAA), the Emergency Farm Mortgage Act, the Truth in Lending Act (TILA), and the Glass-Steagall Act (1933).
- The *21st Amendment* to the *United States Constitution*, rescinding the prohibition of alcohol, receives the required two-thirds majority approval, thus legitimizing the social benefits of alcohol when used in moderation (1933).
- President Roosevelt appoints Frances Perkins as Secretary of Labor, thereby making her the first woman ever appointed to a federal cabinet post (1933).
- In California, reformer Dr. Francis Townsend reveals his proposal for a pension plan for senior citizens that would provide the aged poor with a monthly allowance and help stabilize the nation's economy (1934).
- President Roosevelt authorizes the Works Progress Administration (WPA), a major employment program that focuses on large industrial projects using a highly skilled workforce. The United States Congress also passes the *National Labor Relations Act (Wagner Act)*, which strengthens labor unions (1935).
- President Roosevelt signs the *Social Security Act*, which dramatically transforms the modern social welfare system structure (1935).
- The United Automobile Workers Union wins its strike against General Motors, the United Steelworkers union is similarly victorious against United States Steel Corporation, and several longshoremen's unions along the East and West coasts triumph in their struggles against the shipping industry, thus confirming the increasing influence of the labor union movement for workers' rights (1936).
- President Franklin Delano Roosevelt signs the *Fair Labor Standards Act*, which sets a minimum wage and places a specified limit on the number of hours worked per week (1938).
- President Franklin Delano Roosevelt also authorizes the *Emergency Relief Appropriations Act*, which allocates $3 million to expand the existing and new public works programs (1935).
- Drs. Alton Ochsner and Michael DeBakey first note the spread of lung cancer in Louisiana and conclude that the cause might be linked to cigarette smoking (1938).
- Concert singer Marian Anderson is denied access to sing in Constitution Hall in Washington, DC by the Daughters of the American Revolution (DAR) simply

because she is African American. She sings instead in front of the Lincoln Memorial through the intercession of Eleanor Roosevelt, the president's wife (1939).
- John Steinbeck publishes *The Grapes of Wrath*, a novel that describes rural poverty and displacement during the time of the Midwest *Dust Bowl* (1939).
- Seeking to calm the rising anger of African Americans, President Roosevelt signs an executive order creating the Fair Employment Practices Commission to investigate charges of discrimination based on race, creed, or national origin in any corporation that is part of the defense industry (1941).
- The notorious radical "radio priest" Reverend Charles Coughlin is silenced, and his anti-Semitic weekly newspaper, *Social Justice*, is banned under the principles of the 1917 *Espionage Act* (1942).
- The United States Foreign Affairs Committee reports that, since 1933, more than 600,000 immigrants fleeing Nazi Germany persecution, many of them Jews, have been granted admittance to the United States (1943).
- The United States Congress passes the *Servicemen's Readjustment Act*, more commonly referred to as the *G.I. Bill of Rights*, which provides a variety of resources to veterans, including education and training, low-interest home mortgage loans, job counselling, and employment placement (1944).
- American soldiers liberate the concentration camps at Dachau and Buchenwald and assist the survivors with medical help (1945).
- President Harry Truman signs the *National Mental Health Act*, which provides substantial resources for mental health education and research and leads to the creation, in 1949, of the National Institute on Mental Health (NIMH) (1946).
- The *Taft-Hartley Act* diminishes many of the advantages gained by labor unions during the New Deal (1947).
- In the face of resistance from several Southern baseball teams and bigoted baseball fans, African American baseball player Jackie Robinson breaks the "color line" when he signs on to play in the major leagues with the Brooklyn Dodgers (1947).
- President Harry Truman orders the full integration of the Armed Services by issuing *Executive Order 9981* (1948).
- Dr. Alfred Kinsey publishes *Sexual Behavior in the Human Male*, based on a survey of the sexual activities of 5,000 men (1948).
- Diplomat Ralph Bunche receives the Nobel Peace Prize for his work trying to resolve the conflict between Arabs and Jews in Israel, thus becoming the first African American to earn that honor (1950).
- The latest census tally reveals the presence of 151 million Americans, 64% of whom reside in urban areas (1950).

Note: For a more reflective and functional use of this list of contemporary social welfare historical events, see Question #5 under the **Questions for Further Research and Discussion** section (below).

Sources:
Daniel, C. (1989). *Chronicle of America*. Mt. Kisco, NY: Chronicle Publications.
Mercer, D. (2000). *Millennium year by year*. New York: Dorling Kindersley Publications.
Social welfare developments 1900–1950. (2011). Retrieved from https://socialwelfare.library.vcu.edu/events/1901-1950/

Primary Text Material

What follows are significant portions of *Executive Order 9066*.

Portions of the Transcript of *Executive Order 9066*: Resulting in the Relocation of Japanese (1942)

"The President
   Executive Order
   Authorizing the Secretary of War to Prescribe Military Areas
   Whereas the successful prosecution of the war requires every possible protection against espionage and against sabotage to national-defense material, national-defense premises, and national-defense utilities . . .
   . . . Now, therefore, by virtue of the authority vested in me as President of the United States, and Commander in Chief of the Army and Navy, I hereby authorize and direct the Secretary of War, and the Military Commanders whom he may from time to time designate, whenever he or any designated Commander deems such action necessary or desirable, to prescribe military areas in such places and of such extent as he or the appropriate Military Commander may determine, from which any or all persons may be excluded, and with respect to which, the right of any person to enter, remain in, or leave shall be subject to whatever restrictions the Secretary of War or the appropriate Military Commander may impose in his discretion. The Secretary of War is hereby authorized to provide for residents of any such area who are excluded therefrom, such transportation, food, shelter, and other accommodations as may be necessary, in the judgment of the Secretary of War or the said Military Commander, and until other arrangements are made, to accomplish the purpose of this order. . . .
   . . . I hereby further authorize and direct the Secretary of War and the said Military Commanders to take such other steps as he or the appropriate Military Commander may deem advisable to enforce compliance with the restrictions applicable to each Military area hereinabove authorized to be designated, including the use of Federal troops and other Federal Agencies, with authority to accept assistance of state and local agencies.
   I hereby further authorize and direct all Executive Departments, independent establishments and other Federal Agencies, to assist the Secretary of War or the said Military Commanders in carrying out this Executive Order, including

> *the furnishing of medical aid, hospitalization, food, clothing, transportation, use of land, shelter, and other supplies, equipment, utilities, facilities, and services.*
>
> *This order shall not be construed as modifying or limiting in any way the authority heretofore granted under Executive Order No. 8972, dated December 12, 1941, nor shall it be construed as limiting or modifying the duty and responsibility of the Federal Bureau of Investigation, with respect to the investigation of alleged acts of sabotage or the duty and responsibility of the Attorney General and the Department of Justice under the Proclamations of December 7 and 8, 1941, prescribing regulations for the conduct and control of alien enemies, except as such duty and responsibility is superseded by the designation of military areas hereunder.*
>
> *Franklin D. Roosevelt*
> *The White House,*
> *February 19, 1942"*
>
> Source and full text available at https://www.ourdocuments.gov/doc.php?flash=false&doc=74&page=transcript.

Timeline of General Events in History, the Humanities, and Science During This Period (1925–1950)

These general historical events may help you understand more clearly the overall historical context during which the primary document was created.

- Referencing the economic growth of the nation during this period, President-elect Calvin Coolidge announces, "The business of America is business" (1925).
- Industrialist Henry Ford introduces the practice of a 40-hour, five-day workweek in his automobile factories (1926).
- Physics professor Robert Goddard demonstrates his invention, a liquid-fueled rocket capable of climbing into the atmosphere (1926).
- Aspiring author Earnest Hemingway publishes his first novel, *The Sun Also Rises* (1926).
- Aviator Charles Lindbergh pilots his plane, *The Spirit of St. Louis*, 3,600 miles nonstop from New York to Paris in 33.5 hours (1927).
- Filmmaker Walt Disney screens the first cartoon with sound, *Steamboat Willie*, and introduces Mickey Mouse to the American public (1928).
- Cartoonist Chester Gould introduces a new newspaper comic strip that features the character of Dick Tracy, a police officer who tracks and arrests criminals relentlessly (1931).
- Aviator Amelia Earhart completes her solo transatlantic flight, originating in Newfoundland and a landing in Northern Ireland, thus becoming the first woman to do so (1932).

- The Hindenburg, a dirigible offering transatlantic air service and sent by Nazi Germany, partly as a propaganda gesture, explodes in flames in Lakewood, NJ, killing 35 passengers and one crew member (1937).
- Radio announcer Orson Wells and his Mercury Theatre players, dramatically reading sections of H. G. Wells's novel *War of the Worlds*, frighten more than 1 million radio listeners into believing that the earth was actually being invaded by Martians (1938).
- The New York World's Fair, representing 60 nations, opens in New York City with the theme of "The World of Tomorrow" and features color film by Kodak, an experimental television set by NBC, a preview of future autos by General Motors, long-distance telephone calling by AT&T, and a prototype of a futuristic 2036 urban area (1939).
- Following Adolph Hitler's vicious invasion of Poland, Great Britain and France declare war on Germany, with the United States opting to remain neutral (1939).
- Reflective of the nation's increasingly positive view on the economy, Hollywood explodes with new films, some of them classics even today, including *Gone With the Wind*, starring Vivien Leigh and Clark Gable; *The Wizard of Oz*, featuring Judy Garland; John Ford's *Stagecoach*; Disney's *Pinocchio*; *Beau Geste*; and *The Roaring Twenties*, starring James Cagney and Humphrey Bogart; among others (1939–1940).
- President Franklin Delano Roosevelt transforms the nation's industrial base to aid the war effort, then proclaims that the United States must be an "arsenal of democracy" and pledges to assist the Allied forces with military supplies and machinery (1940).
- President Roosevelt inches closer to war as he announces a plan to provide a billion-dollar "lend-lease" program of war material and aid to the Allies fighting Nazi Germany based on his international Four Freedoms: freedom of speech, freedom to worship God, freedom from want, and freedom from fear (1941).
- Following rising tensions between the United States and Japan over Japan's military actions throughout the Pacific, the United States initiates an embargo on all oil and rice imports to Japan (1941).
- Japan initiates a surprise attack on the American naval base and airfields on Pearl Harbor, Hawaii, prompting the United States to declare war on Japan (1941).
- Following the dictates of their Tripartite Pact with Japan, Germany and Italy declare war on the United States (1941).
- More than 10,000 American-born sons of Japanese immigrants, identified as *nisei*, volunteer to join the American military forces (1942).
- Italian physicist Enrico Fermi, working outdoors at the University of Chicago, creates the first controlled atomic chain reaction of fissionable uranium, thereby launching the United States into the nuclear age (1942).
- In order to support the war effort, the federal government introduces the rationing of some food items while President Franklin Delano Roosevelt directs the freezing of wages and prices and mandates a 48-hour week at all defense industry factories (1943).
- Victory in Europe over Nazi Germany is declared (1945).
- The United States unleashes atomic bombs over Hiroshima and Nagasaki, leading Japan to surrender and triggering the end of World War II (1945).

- The United Nations is formed to maintain world peace and security, with five nations—China, France, Great Britain, the Soviet Union, and the United States—assigned a leadership role as permanent members of the Security Council (1945).
- The war-crimes trial for German Nazi officers begins in Nuremberg, Germany (1946).
- The Congressional *House Un-American Activities Committee* investigates suspected Communist infiltration of the Hollywood film industry, resulting in the blacklisting of 10 noted film professionals, mostly screenwriters, by the film industry itself (1947).
- In order to assist Western Europe in its recovery from World War II, the United States launches a massive foreign aid program, the Marshall Plan (1948).
- Despite the United Nations plan to divide Palestine into an Arab and Jewish state with Jerusalem as an international city following the cessation of British control over Palestine, the United States recognizes the independent state of Israel, and war breaks out between Israel and several Arab nations (1948).
- The United States provides economic and military aid to the Republic of South Korea after it is invaded by the Communist North Korean Army (1950).
- A United States senator from Wisconsin, Joe McCarthy, releases his alleged list of Communists who are working in the United States Department of State (1950).

Sources:

Daniel, C. (1989). *Chronicle of America*. Mt. Kisco, NY: Chronicle Publications.

Events of the 20th century. Retrieved from https://en.wikipedia.org/wiki/timeline_of_the_20th_century

Mercer, D. (2000). *Millennium year by year*. New York: Dorling Kindersley Publications.

Questions for Further Research and Discussion

1. Study the immediate historical context (i.e., politically, economically, and socially) during which *Executive Order 9066* was promulgated. Beyond the obvious trigger of the Pearl Harbor attack, what else was occurring nationally and internationally that might help explain such a drastic reaction on the part of President Roosevelt and the nation?
2. Using the Internet, research three or four major newspapers published after the issuance of *Executive Order 9066*, then summarize any themes or patterns of belief that emerge from the editorials and/or letters to the editor appearing in them.
3. Choose one of the 10 sites of the internment camps mentioned above. Then conduct further Internet research on that camp and summarize your findings, noting especially any photos, letters, diaries, or personal effects of the former internees that you uncover.
4. Based on the primary documentary material presented here, as well as other material you discover in the **Additional Selected References** at the end of this chapter, what additional federal policy or policies do you believe should have been developed or changed at that time? Describe those policies in detail. Recall that

a policy could be either *legislative* (i.e., a law), *judicial* (i.e., a court decision), or *administrative* (i.e., an executive or organizational policy) in nature.
5. Select three events appearing under the **Linkage to Social Welfare** section (above), conduct further Internet research regarding them, then conclude whether you believe there exists any plausible relationship between *Executive Order 9066* and the events you have chosen. Use the analytical model presented in Appendix 1 of this book, or develop your own analytical model, to draw these conclusions.
6. Select one book from the **Additional Selected References** list at the end of this chapter. Briefly read through it, then summarize the main points contained in the book. Identify your own personal reaction to this book.

Additional Selected References

Alonso, K. (1998). *Korematsu v. United States: Japanese American internment camps.* Springfield, NJ: Enslow.

Blankenship, A. M. (2016). *Christianity, social justice, and the Japanese American incarceration during World War II.* Chapel Hill: University of North Carolina Press.

Collins, D.E. (1985). *Native American aliens: Disloyalty and the renunciation of citizenship by Japanese Americans during World War II.* Westport, CT: Greenwood Press.

Conrat, M., Conrat, R., Lange, D., & California Historical Society. (1972). *Executive Order 9066: The internment of 110,000 Japanese Americans.* Cambridge, MA: MIT Press for the California Historical Society.

Dickerson, J. (2010). *Inside America's concentration camps: Two centuries of internment and torture.* Chicago, IL: Lawrence Hill Books.

Dudley, W. (2002). *Japanese American internment camps.* San Diego: Greenhaven Press.

Kikuchi, C. (1973). *The Kikuchi diary: Chronicle from an American concentration camp.* Urbana, IL: University of Illinois Press.

Nelson, D. W. (1976). *Heart Mountain: The history of an American concentration camp.* Madison, WI: The State Historical Society of Wisconsin.

Reeves, R. (2015). *Infamy: The shocking story of the Japanese American internment in World War II.* New York: Henry Holt and Company.

Robinson, G. (2001). *By order of the president: FDR and the internment of Japanese Americans.* Cambridge, MA: Harvard University Press.

Shimabukuro, M. (2015). *Relocating authority: Japanese Americans writing to redress mass incarceration.* Boulder, CO: University of Colorado Press.

Stanley, J. (1994). *I am an American: A true story of Japanese internment.* New York: Crown Publishers.

Credits

Fig. 20.1: Source: https://commons.wikimedia.org/wiki/File:JapaneseAmericanGrocer1942.jpg.

Fig. 20.2: Source: https://commons.wikimedia.org/wiki/File:Japanese_war_relocation.tif.

Chapter 21

Small Steps for Racial Equality

Integration of the Armed Services, *Executive Order 9981* (1948)

Introduction

After the end of World War II, A. Philip Randolph, the influential African American leader of the Brotherhood of Sleeping Car Porters, as well as leaders of organizations such as the National Association for the Advancement of Colored People (NAACP) and the National Urban League pressured President Harry Truman to nullify the segregationist policies that affected African American military personnel. At that time, the only truly integrated military organization was the Veterans Administration (VA) hospital network in its inpatient and outpatient care for veterans. This was not a moral decision on the part of the VA at the time but a purely practical one: The cost of maintaining separate, segregated hospitals would be prohibitive.

Reacting to this outside advocacy for change, as well as his own concern over racial discrimination in the broader American society, in 1946 President Truman formed and charged the President's Committee on Civil Rights to investigate the condition of African Americans in all the branches of the United States military forces. The conclusion of that study, *To Secure Their Rights*, revealed that racial segregation was rampant among all the branches of the military. Predicting some opposition, President Truman waited until after the 1948 Democratic National Convention, which offered a progressive platform for civil rights, to activate his plan for an executive order that would end all forms of segregation based on race, color, creed, or national origin within the Armed Services. President Truman opted for an executive order rather than a piece of federal legislation apparently because he knew many Southern senators and representatives could have successfully resisted any new law that fostered integration in any context.

FIGURE 21.1 Photograph of several racially segregated Tuskegee airmen during World War II.

Issued July 26, 1948, *Executive Order 9981* effectively abolished racial segregation and discrimination throughout the United States military. The destructive force of the Jim Crow laws on American society were eradicated across the military establishment with the literal stroke of the president's pen. *Executive Order 9981* also established a new federal committee: the President's Committee on Equality of Treatment and Opportunity in the Armed Services, whose mandate was to monitor the implementation of the executive order and suggest future policy and/or program changes.

The actual integration of all military units, however, did not start immediately. Some limited integration of several military combat units did indeed materialize for a time with the outbreak of the Korean War (technically, a "police action" authorized by the United Nations) in 1950. As that police action progressed, it was necessary for pragmatic reasons to abandon segregated army units on the frontlines as soldiers of all races needed to work together for their own survival against the armies of North Korea and China. Overall, however, there existed broad initial resistance to racial integration by both officers and enlisted personnel in the Army, Air Force, Navy, and Marines.

Historically, there is some evidence that both free-born African Americans and former slaves served valiantly alongside their white counterparts in the Continental Army during the American Revolution and the War of 1812 against Great Britain. Segregated military units were introduced during the Civil War, and that unjust situation lingered well into the 1950s. The stage was set for eventual integration of the military, however, when President Franklin Delano Roosevelt, as the country prepared for war in 1941, issued *Executive Order 8802*, which prohibited any discrimination based on race, color, or national origin in the defense industry and in the federal government. Segregation in the Armed Services, however, continued unabated until President Truman's *Executive Order 9981*.

As mentioned above, the reaction to President Truman's action was mixed, at least initially, among the military services. The Navy reacted the most positively to the executive order because there already existed some level of integration of Navy personnel aboard ships. This integration on ships, however, was in the context of a rigid "caste system" in which African American sailors were typically placed in low-level service positions in the kitchen and in officers' dining rooms. The Air Force and Marines also responded constructively because they viewed this development as helpful in attracting new voluntary recruits into their ranks. The Army, despite its brief experience with integrated combat units during the Korean War, was most resistant to change because of a belief that permanently integrated units would not meet the standard of "combat effectiveness" in a dangerous world. By 1953, however, the Army reported that more than 90% of its African American troops had been placed in integrated units. In general, African American recruits comprised 10% of all military personnel, and they were eventually seen as a force that could no longer be ignored or placed in subservient positions, especially as the Cold War intensified and the Soviet Union emerged as a serious international threat. The Army's last segregated military unit was finally dissolved in 1955.

Essentially, *Executive Order 9981* was a common-sense solution to a dilemma facing President Truman: how to balance the fact that military history has chronicled the patriotism, bravery, and accomplishments of segregated military units and individuals since the Revolutionary War with the reality that American society's discriminatory attitudes in the 1940s that denied African American soldiers and sailors equal access to assignments, promotions, and quality of life in military service. President Truman answered that dilemma progressively and, in so doing, advanced the nation one step further toward the goal of full and unequivocal justice for all without regard to race, color, creed, or national origin.

FIGURE 21.2   President Harry Truman.

Internet Sources for the Content of This Introduction Include:

https://armyhistory.org/executive-order-9981-integration-of-the-armed-forces/
https://newrepublic.com/article/78402/military-integration-civil-rights-report
https://thegrio.com/2012/05/28/harry-truman-and-the-desegregation-of-the-military-a-timeline/
https://www.britannica.com/topic/executive-order-9981#ref1081334
https://en.wikipedia.org/wiki/executive_order_9981
http://www.pbs.org/black-culture/connect/talk-back/executive-order-9981/
https://blog.history.in.gov/?p=3261

Linkage to Social Welfare History (1925–1950)

Social welfare historical events for this time period include the following:

- Following the legal battle between noted lawyers William Jennings Bryan for the prosecution and Clarence Darrow for the defense, a Tennessee court convicts biology teacher John Scopes for teaching evolution in the legendary "Scopes Monkey Trial" (1925).
- Watched by more than an estimated 200,000 bystanders, 400,00 members of the Ku Klux Klan march, waving American flags, toward the Washington Monument in Washington, DC (1925).
- Resistance to the Prohibition Law around the nation surfaces in a series of speakeasies, surreptitious places where introductions are needed and alcohol can be purchased and consumed (1925).
- Appearing in blackface, which was embarrassingly common at the time, Al Jolson stars in the film *The Jazz Singer* (1927).
- The Unites States Supreme Court, in *Buck v. Bell*, decreed that it is constitutional to forcibly sterilize men and women who were deemed to be feeble-minded, and, thus, a future burden on society (1927)
- The *Harlem Renaissance*, a major cultural movement featuring African American authors, musicians, and visual artists, flourishes in New York City and beyond (1928).
- A frenzied selling off of stocks on Wall Street culminates on Black Tuesday, a day memorialized in American history as the day that signaled the beginning of the Great Depression (1929).
- The 1930 census reveals that America has reached a population growth of 122 million, the life expectancy of the typical American is 61 years, and there are more than 26 million cars in use (1930).
- President Herbert Hoover establishes the Veterans Administration by executive order (1930).
- Census officials report that the number of unemployed is between 4 million and 5 million Americans and, furthermore, that they have removed from the unemployed lists those unemployed who sell apples on street corners across the nation (1931).

- Social reformer Jane Addams is awarded the Nobel Peace Prize (1931).
- In the annual State of the Union address, President Herbert Hoover announces a major construction plan that will aid the business community but rejects any direct or indirect resources for the unemployed (1931).
- President Herbert Hoover orders the military, under the command of Army General Douglas MacArthur, to disperse from Washington, DC members of the "Bonus Army," a group of World War I army veterans who rallied there to collect a bonus that was promised to them for their loyal army service (1932).
- Former New York Governor Franklin Delano Roosevelt is elected president of the United States with a pledge for a "New Deal" for the American people, who are struggling through the effects of the Great Depression (1932).
- During the first 100 days of his presidency, President Roosevelt passes significant social legislation and launches the first of his many "alphabet soup" programs, namely the Civilian Conservation Corps (CCC), the Federal Emergency Relief Act (FERA), the Agricultural Adjustment Act (AAA), the Emergency Farm Mortgage Act, the Truth in Lending Act (TILA), and the Glass-Steagall Act (1933).
- The *21st Amendment* to the *United States Constitution*, rescinding the prohibition of alcohol, receives the required two-thirds majority approval, thus legitimizing the social benefits of alcohol when used in moderation (1933).
- President Franklin Delano Roosevelt appoints Frances Perkins as Secretary of Labor, thereby making her the first woman ever appointed to a federal cabinet post (1933).
- In California, reformer Dr. Francis Townsend reveals his proposal for a pension plan for senior citizens that would provide the aged poor with a monthly allowance and help stabilize the nation's economy (1934).
- President Franklin Delano Roosevelt authorizes the Works Progress Administration (WPA), a major employment program that focuses on large industrial projects using a highly skilled workforce. The United States Congress also passes the *National Labor Relations Act (Wagner Act)*, which strengthens labor unions (1935).
- President Franklin Delano Roosevelt signs the *Social Security Act*, which dramatically transforms the modern social welfare system structure (1935).
- The United Automobile Workers Union wins its strike against General Motors, the United Steelworkers union is similarly victorious against United Sates Steel Corporation, and several longshoremen's unions along the East and West coasts triumph in their struggles against the shipping industry, thus confirming the increasing influence of the labor union movement for workers' rights (1936).
- President Franklin Delano Roosevelt signs the *Fair Labor Standards Act*, which sets a minimum wage and places a specified limit on the number of hours worked per week (1938).
- President Franklin Delano Roosevelt also authorizes the *Emergency Relief Appropriations Act*, which allocates $3 million to expand the existing and new public works programs (1935).

- Drs. Alton Ochsner and Michael DeBakey first noted the spread of lung cancer in Louisiana and concluded that the cause might be linked to cigarette smoking (1938).
- Concert singer Marian Anderson is denied access to sing in Constitution Hall in Washington, DC by the Daughters of the American Revolution (DAR) simply because she is African American. She sings instead in front of the Lincoln Memorial through the intercession of Eleanor Roosevelt, the president's wife (1939).
- John Steinbeck publishes *The Grapes of Wrath*, a novel that describes rural poverty and displacement during the time of the Midwest *Dust Bowl* (1939).
- Seeking to calm the rising anger of African Americans, President Franklin Delano Roosevelt signs an executive order creating the Fair Employment Practices Commission to investigate charges of discrimination based on race, creed, or national origin in any corporation that is part of the defense industry (1941).
- President Franklin Delano Roosevelt signs *Executive Order 9066*, which empowers the War Department to forcibly intern 110,000 Japanese nationals and Japanese American citizens in Hawaii and along the West Coast of the United States (1942).
- The notorious radical "radio priest" Reverend Charles Coughlin is silenced, and his anti-Semitic weekly newspaper, *Social Justice*, is banned under the principles of the 1917 *Espionage Act* (1942).
- The United States Foreign Affairs Committee reports that, since 1933, more than 600,000 immigrants fleeing Nazi Germany persecution, many of them Jews, have been granted admittance to the United States (1943).
- The United States Congress passes the *Servicemen's Readjustment Act*, more commonly referred to as the *G.I. Bill of Rights*, which provides a variety of resources to veterans, including education and training, low-interest home mortgage loans, job counselling and employment placement (1944).
- American soldiers liberate the concentration camps at Dachau and Buchenwald and assist the survivors with medical help (1945).
- President Harry Truman signs the *National Mental Health Act*, which provides substantial resources for mental health education and research and leads to the creation, in 1949, of the National Institute on Mental Health (NIMH) (1946).
- The *Taft-Hartley Act* diminishes many of the advantages gained by labor unions during the New Deal (1947).
- In the face of resistance from several Southern baseball teams and bigoted baseball fans, African American baseball player Jackie Robinson breaks the "color line" when he signs on to play in the major leagues with the Brooklyn Dodgers (1947).
- Dr. Alfred Kinsey publishes *Sexual Behavior in the Human Male*, based on a survey of the sexual activities of 5,000 men (1948).
- Diplomat Ralph Bunche receives the Nobel Peace Prize for his work trying to resolve the conflict between Arabs and Jews in Israel, thus becoming the first African American to earn that honor (1950).
- The latest census tally reveals the presence of 151 million Americans, 64% of whom reside in urban areas (1950).

Note: For a more reflective and functional use of this list of contemporary social welfare historical events, see Question #5 under the **Questions for Further Research and Discussion** section (below).

Sources:
Daniel, C. (1989). *Chronicle of America*. Mt. Kisco, NY: Chronicle Publications.

Mercer, D. (2000). *Millennium year by year*. New York: Dorling Kindersley Publications.

Social welfare developments 1900–1950. (2011). Retrieved from https://socialwelfare.library.vcu.edu/events/1901-1950/

Primary Text Material

Transcript of *Executive Order 9981*: Desegregation of the Armed Forces (1948)

"Establishing the President's Committee on Equality of Treatment and Opportunity In the Armed Forces.

WHEREAS it is essential that there be maintained in the armed services of the United States the highest standards of democracy, with equality of treatment and opportunity for all those who serve in our country's defense:

NOW THEREFORE, by virtue of the authority vested in me as President of the United States, by the Constitution and the statutes of the United States, and as Commander in Chief of the armed services, it is hereby ordered as follows:

1. *It is hereby declared to be the policy of the President that there shall be equality of treatment and opportunity for all persons in the armed services without regard to race, color, religion or national origin. This policy shall be put into effect as rapidly as possible, having due regard to the time required to effectuate any necessary changes without impairing efficiency or morale.*
2. *There shall be created in the National Military Establishment an advisory committee to be known as the President's Committee on Equality of Treatment and Opportunity in the Armed Services, which shall be composed of seven members to be designated by the President.*
3. *The Committee is authorized on behalf of the President to examine into the rules, procedures and practices of the Armed Services in order to determine in what respect such rules, procedures and practices may be altered or improved with a view to carrying out the policy of this order. The Committee shall confer and advise the Secretary of Defense, the Secretary of the Army, the Secretary of the Navy, and the Secretary of the Air Force, and shall make such recommendations to the President and to said Secretaries as in the judgment of the Committee will effectuate the policy hereof.*

Continued

4. All executive departments and agencies of the Federal Government are authorized and directed to cooperate with the Committee in its work, and to furnish the Committee such information or the services of such persons as the Committee may require in the performance of its duties.
5. When requested by the Committee to do so, persons in the armed services or in any of the executive departments and agencies of the Federal Government shall testify before the Committee and shall make available for use of the Committee such documents and other information as the Committee may require.
6. The Committee shall continue to exist until such time as the President shall terminate its existence by Executive order.

Harry Truman
The White House
July 26, 1948"

Source and full text available at: https://www.ourdocuments.gov/doc.php?flash=false&doc=84.

This media file is in the public domain.

- For copies of official primary documents relating to support for and opposition to the integration of the Armed Forces maintained by the Harry S. Truman Presidential Library and Museum, see https://www.trumanlibrary.org/whistlestop/study_collections/desegregation/large/index.php?action=docs&sortorder=category.
- For a chronology of events surrounding the desegregation of the Armed Services, see https://www.trumanlibrary.org/whistlestop/study_collections/desegregation/large/index.php?action=bg.

Timeline of General Events in History, the Humanities, and Science During This Period (1925–1950)

These general historical events may help you understand more clearly the overall historical context during which the primary document was created.

- Referencing the economic growth of the nation during this period, President-elect Calvin Coolidge announces, "The business of America is business" (1925).
- Industrialist Henry Ford introduces the practice of a 40-hour, five-day workweek in his automobile factories (1926).
- Physics professor Robert Goddard demonstrates his invention, a liquid-fueled rocket capable of climbing into the atmosphere (1926).
- Aspiring author Earnest Hemingway publishes his first novel, *The Sun Also Rises* (1926).

- Aviator Charles Lindbergh pilots his plane, *The Spirit of St. Louis*, 3,600 miles nonstop from New York to Paris in 33.5 hours (1927).
- Filmmaker Walt Disney screens the first cartoon with sound, *Steamboat Willie*, and introduces Mickey Mouse to the American public (1928).
- Cartoonist Chester Gould introduces a new newspaper comic strip that features the character of Dick Tracy, a police officer who tracks and arrests criminals relentlessly (1931).
- Aviator Amelia Earhart completes her solo transatlantic flight, originating in Newfoundland and a landing in Northern Ireland, thus becoming the first woman to do so (1932).
- The Hindenburg, a dirigible offering transatlantic air service and sent by Nazi Germany, partly as a propaganda gesture, explodes in flames in Lakewood, NJ, killing 35 passengers and one crew member (1937).
- Radio announcer Orson Wells and his Mercury Theatre players, dramatically reading sections of H. G. Wells's novel *War of the Worlds*, frighten more than 1 million radio listeners into believing that the earth was actually being invaded by Martians (1938).
- The New York World's Fair, representing 60 nations, opens in New York City with the theme of "The World of Tomorrow" and features color film by Kodak, an experimental television set by NBC, a preview of future autos by General Motors, long-distance telephone calling by AT&T, and a prototype of a futuristic 2036 urban area (1939).
- Following Adolph Hitler's vicious invasion of Poland, Great Britain and France declare war on Germany, with the United States opting to remain neutral (1939).
- Reflective of the nation's increasingly positive view on the economy, Hollywood explodes with new films, some of them classics even today, including *Gone With the Wind*, starring Vivien Leigh and Clark Gable; *The Wizard of Oz*, featuring Judy Garland; John Ford's *Stagecoach*; Disney's *Pinocchio*; *Beau Geste*; and *The Roaring Twenties*, starring James Cagney and Humphrey Bogart; among others (1939–1940).
- President Franklin Delano Roosevelt transforms the nation's industrial base to aid the war effort, then proclaims that the United States must be an "arsenal of democracy" and pledges to assist the Allied forces with military supplies and machinery (1940).
- President Franklin Delano Roosevelt inches closer to war as he announces a plan to provide a billion-dollar "lend-lease" program of war material and aid to the Allies fighting Nazi Germany based on his international Four Freedoms: freedom of speech, freedom to worship God, freedom from want, and freedom from fear (1941).
- Following rising tensions between the United States and Japan over Japan's military actions throughout the Pacific, the United States initiates an embargo on all oil and rice imports to Japan (1941).

- Japan initiates a surprise attack on the American naval base and airfields on Pearl Harbor, Hawaii, prompting the United States to declare war on Japan (1941).
- Following the dictates of their Tripartite Pact with Japan, Germany and Italy declare war on the United States (1941).
- More than 10,000 American-born sons of Japanese immigrants, identified as *nisei*, volunteer to join the American military forces (1942).
- Italian physicist Enrico Fermi, working outdoors at the University of Chicago, creates the first controlled atomic chain reaction of fissionable uranium, thereby launching the United States into the nuclear age (1942).
- In order to support the war effort, the federal government introduces the rationing of some food items while President Roosevelt directs the freezing of wages and prices and mandates a 48-hour week at all defense industry factories (1943).
- Victory in Europe over Nazi Germany is declared (1945).
- The United States unleashes atomic bombs over Hiroshima and Nagasaki, leading Japan to surrender and triggering the end of World War II (1945).
- The United Nations is formed to maintain world peace and security, with five nations—China, France, Great Britain, the Soviet Union, and the United States—assigned a leadership role as permanent members of the Security Council (1945).
- The war-crimes trial for German Nazi officers begins in Nuremberg, Germany (1946).
- The Congressional *House Un-American Activities Committee* investigates suspected Communist infiltration of the Hollywood film industry, resulting in the blacklisting of 10 noted film professionals, mostly screenwriters, by the film industry itself (1947).
- In order to assist Western Europe in its recovery from World War II, the United States launches a massive foreign aid program, the Marshall Plan (1948).
- Despite the United Nations plan to divide Palestine into an Arab and Jewish state with Jerusalem as an international city following the cessation of British control over Palestine, the United States recognizes the independent state of Israel, and war breaks out between Israel and several Arab nations (1948).
- The United States provides economic and military aid to the Republic of South Korea after it is invaded by the Communist North Korean Army (1950).
- A United States senator from Wisconsin, Joe McCarthy, releases his alleged list of Communists who are working in the United States Department of State (1950).

Sources:

Daniel, C. (1989). *Chronicle of America*. Mt. Kisco, NY: Chronicle Publications.

Events of the 20th century. Retrieved from https://en.wikipedia.org/wiki/timeline_of_the_20th_century

Mercer, D. (2000). *Millennium year by year*. New York: Dorling Kindersley Publications.

Questions for Further Research and Discussion

1. Conduct further research on the primary historical documents maintained at the Truman Presidential Library (available at https://www.trumanlibrary.org/whistlestop/study_collections/desegregation/large/index.php?action=docs&sortorder=category) that are supportive of *Executive Order 9981*. Compose a summary of the reasons provided for being in favor of the integration of the Armed Services.
2. Conduct further research on the primary historical documents maintained at the Truman Presidential Library (available at https://www.trumanlibrary.org/whistlestop/study_collections/desegregation/large/index.php?action=docs&sortorder=category) that are in opposition to *Executive Order 9981*. Compose a summary of the reasons provided for being opposed to the integration of the Armed Services.
3. After completing further research into the reactions of the various armed services (i.e., Air Force, Army, Navy, and Marines), outline the rationale that each branch offered for either agreeing or disagreeing with *Executive Order 9981*. How credible are the objections, in your estimation?
4. Based on the primary documentary material presented here, as well as other material you discover in the **Additional Selected References** at the end of this chapter, what additional federal policy or policies do you believe should have been developed or changed at that time? Describe those policies in detail. Recall that a policy could be either *legislative* (i.e., a law), *judicial* (i.e., a court decision), or *administrative* (i.e., an executive or organizational policy) in nature.
5. Select three events appearing under the **Linkage to Social Welfare** section (above), conduct further Internet research regarding them, then conclude whether you believe there exists any plausible relationship between *Executive Order 9981* and the events you have chosen. Use the analytical model presented in Appendix 1 of this book, or develop your own analytical model, to draw these conclusions.
6. Select one book from the **Additional Selected References** list at the end of this chapter. Briefly read through it, then summarize the main points contained in the book. Identify your own personal reaction to this book.

Additional Selected References

Axelrod, A. (2007). *Political history of America's wars*. Washington, DC: Congressional Quarterly Press.

Bristol, D. W., & Stur, H. M. (Eds.). (2017). *Integrating the U.S. military: Race, gender, and sexual orientation since World War II*. Baltimore: Johns Hopkins Press.

Brown, H. H., & Bordner, M. S. (2017). *Keep your airspeed up: The story of a Tuskegee airman*. Tuscaloosa, AL: University of Alabama Press.

Green, M. C. (2010). *Black Yanks in the Pacific: Race in the making of American military empire after World War II*. Ithaca, NY: Cornell University Press.

Gropman, A.L. (1986). *The Air Force integrates, 1949–1964*. Montgomery, AL: Office of Air Force History.

James, R. (2013). *The double V: How wars, protest, and Harry Truman desegregated America's military*. New York: Bloomsbury Press.

MacGregor, M. J. (1981). *Integration of the Armed Forces, 1940–1965*. Washington, DC: US Government Printing Office.

Mjagkij, N. (2011). *Loyalty in time of trial: The African American experience during World War I*. Lanham, MD: Rowman & Littlefield Publishers, Inc.

Mershon, S., & Schlossman, S. (2002). *Foxholes and color lines: Desegregating the U.S. Armed Forces*. Baltimore: Johns Hopkins University.

Osur, A. M., & Air Force History and Museums Program (U.S.). (2000). *Separate and unequal: Race relations in the AAF during World War II*. Washington, DC: Airforce History & Museums Program.

Taylor, J. E. (2013). *Freedom to serve: Truman, civil rights, and Executive Order 9981*. New York: Routledge.

Credits

Fig. 21.1: Source: https://commons.wikimedia.org/wiki/File:Tuskegee_airmen_2.jpg.
Fig. 21.2: Source: http://www.loc.gov/pictures/item/89714974/.

Chapter 22

Separate and Not Equal

Brown v. Board of Education of Topeka (1954)

Introduction

Spurred on by court decisions, such as in *Plessy v. Ferguson* (1896), and despite earlier victories, such as the *13th Amendment* (1865) of the *United States Constitution* abolishing slavery and the *14th Amendment* (1868) granting African American men the right to vote, discrimination, forced segregation, and lynching of African Americans continued unabated after the Civil War well into the early 20th century. By the 1930s, the Legal Defense and Education Fund of the National Association for the Advancement of Colored People (NAACP), led by their attorney, Thurgood Marshall, turned to the courts to abolish the so-called *Jim Crow* laws. The NAACP concentrated its efforts on overturning the most notoriously oppressive Jim Crow practices that endured within the field of public education of children.

Brown v. Board of Education, passed by the Supreme Court in 1954, is technically an aggregate term used to describe five separate cases that successfully challenged the racial segregation of children within the nation's public-school systems. The actual Brown v. Board of Education case was preceded by four others: Briggs v. Elliott (1952), Davis v. County School Board of Prince Edward County, Virginia (1952), Gebhart v. Belton (1952) and Bolling v. Sharpe (1954).

The specific details of *Brown v. Board of Education* are meaningfully reflective of the conditions under which African American children struggled in public schools in 1950s America. Oliver Brown, a parent, filed a class-action suit against the Board of Education of Topeka, Kansas, because his daughter was prohibited from enrolling in her local all-white public school class. The case wound through the federal court system and was eventually placed on the docket of the United States Supreme Court. Interestingly, in Kansas, all junior high schools and high schools had been fully integrated since 1941 in

FIGURE 22.1   The Warren Supreme Court, 1953.

all their educational and sports activities and, furthermore, the Kansas law upholding racial segregation in public schools applied only to elementary schools.

In his argument before the Supreme Court, Marshall reasoned that African American children and white children were not being equally educated within the nation's public-school system and that fact was a violation of the *equal protection clause* of the *14th Amendment*. A secondary argument, based on the latest social science research, asserted that a segregated public-school environment harmfully affected African American children to the point that they felt inferior to white children. This social science research included: the groundbreaking 1940s research by African American psychologists Kenneth and Mamie Clark involving children's attitudes on race through the use of dolls of different races; Gunnar Myrdal's 1944 book *An American Dilemma: The Negro Problem and Modern Democracy*; and the 1950 United Nations report *The Race Question*, which dismissed the Nazi regime's contention that racial differences had been scientifically proven.

Over the next two-year time period, aided by the leadership of newly appointed Chief Justice Earl Warren, the Supreme Court finally declared in 1954, in a 9–0 decision, that segregated public schools were inherently unconstitutional. Anticipating wide resistance from the governors of the Southern states, the Supreme Court specifically ordered the attorneys general in every state to develop a plan for the prompt implementation of fully integrated state public school systems.

Initially, many school districts across the South simply ignored the *Brown v. Board of Education* decision. One dramatic example of resistance to integration was the position adopted by Arkansas Governor Orval Faubus in 1957 involving the Little Rock, Arkansas, school district. Governor Faubus ordered the Arkansas National Guard to patrol the front of Little Rock Central High School to prevent nine African American students (eventually referred to as the "Little Rock Nine") from entering on the first day of school. In response, President Dwight Eisenhower purposely nationalized the Arkansas National Guard, ordered them to stand down, then directed federal troops from the 101st Airborne Division from nearby Fort Campbell to escort the students under guard into the school.

There were other examples of resistance to public school integration. In 1963, civil rights leader Medgar Evers appealed to the federal court to desegregate the Jackson, Mississippi, public schools. He was murdered for this action, and his killer was not convicted until 1994. Also in 1963, Alabama Governor George Wallace personally stood at the entrance to the University of Alabama to prevent two African American students from enrolling at the university. Governor Wallace retreated only after President John Kennedy nationalized the Alabama National Guard and ordered the National Guard General Henry Graham to escort the two students into the university.

Despite the enormous positive impact that *Brown v. Board of Education* has had over the following decades, tragically there still exists in America a pattern of schools that are effectively still segregated by race and offer unequal levels of education. This phenomenon is currently due to harsh realities such as community zoning laws, residential housing patterns that lead to "white flight" to suburban areas, and levels of local funding based on real estate values that affect the quality of school buildings, teachers' salaries, the availability of educational technology to teachers and students, and the amount of available educational books and supplies.

FIGURE 22.2   Thurgood Marshall.

In summary, *Brown v, Board of Education* essentially overturned the 1896 *Plessy v. Ferguson* decision that allowed states to maintain segregation by race in public education. Moreover, *Brown v, Board of Education* uncovered the fallacy inherent in the principle of *separate but equal* in public education and, in so doing, created a precedent that all public facilities, such as busses, trains, and airplanes, as well as public employment, should be fully integrated regardless of race, creed, or national origin. It appears to be no accident of history that one year after *Brown v. Board of Education*, Rosa Parks refused to vacate her seat in the white section of a public bus in Montgomery, Alabama, thus leading to her arrest and the launching of the Montgomery Bus Boycott. At that point in time, it is no exaggeration to assume that a new active phase of the civil rights movement across America had begun.

- Further information and exhibits concerning *Brown v. Board of Education* can be viewed at the National Park Service National Historic Site in Kansas, available at https://www.nps.gov/brvb/learn/historyculture/index.htm.

Internet Sources for the Content of This Introduction Include:

http://www.uscourts.gov/educational-resources/educational-activities/history-brown-v-board-education-re-enactment

http://www.history.com/topics/black-history/brown-v-board-of-education-of-topeka

https://en.wikipedia.org/wiki/brown_v._board_of_education
https://www.oyez.org/cases/1940-1955/347us483
http://www.history.com/topics/black-history/brown-v-board-of-education-of-topeka
https://www.theatlantic.com/education/archive/2014/04/two-milestones-in-education/361222/

Linkage to Social Welfare History (1950–1975)

Social welfare historical events for this time period include the following:

- United Nations diplomat Ralph Bunche is awarded the Nobel Peace Prize for his work mediating conflicts between Arabs and Jews in the Middle East, thus becoming the first African American to receive such an honor (1950).
- Social scientists David Riesman, Nathan Glazer, and Reuel Denney publish *The Lonely Crowd*, a study of how Americans are not overly interested in conformity with their fellow citizens (1950).
- Over the veto of President Harry Truman, the Congress passes the *Immigration and Naturalization Act* (also known as the McCarran–Walter Act), restricting the number of immigrants and redefining the criteria for admission to the United States (1952).
- Sexuality becomes public, with Marilyn Monroe starring in the publication of *Playboy* magazine and the release of films such as *The Moon Is Blue* (1953).
- The scourge of the childhood disease polio is eradicated in the United States with the introduction of a vaccine developed by Dr. Jonas Salk at the University of Pennsylvania (1954).
- Rosa Parks, seated in the white section of a Montgomery, Alabama, bus, refuses to give up her seat to a white man and is arrested, thus launching the Montgomery Bus Boycott partly led by the local Christian pastor, the Reverend Martin Luther King Jr. (1955).
- Following the merger of several allied groups, the National Association of Social Workers (NASW) is formally established (1955).
- The Count Basie Orchestra becomes the first African American musical group to play in the famous Starlight Room at the Waldorf Astoria hotel in New York City (1957).
- Under the protection of federal troops and federalized Arkansas National Guardsmen, and in defiance of Arkansas Governor Orval Faubus, nine African American students are escorted into Little Rock Central High School through crowds of angry whites opposing school integration (1957).
- Economist John Kenneth Galbraith publishes *The Affluent Society*, which outlines the wide income disparities in America and calls for greater public resources for those who are disadvantaged (1958).
- The novel *Lady Chatterley's Lover* is publicly banned after being judged as obscene by the United States Postal Service (1959).

- Four African American students stage a nonviolent "sit-in" by refusing to move from their seats at the Woolworth's lunch counter in Greensboro, North Carolina (1960).
- The Food and Drug Administration approves the sale and use of the first contraceptive pill for women (1960).
- CBS television announcer Edward R. Murrow narrates the shocking exposé of the oppressive and dangerous working conditions of migrant agricultural workers in the film *Harvest of Shame* (1960).
- An integrated bus full of members of the Congress of Racial Equality (CORE) travels through Southern states testing the local segregation laws, with the result of the "Freedom Riders" being viciously attacked and arrested along the way. In one instance, Attorney General Robert Kennedy sends in 600 federal marshals to restore order in Montgomery, Alabama (1961).
- In *Engel v. Vitale*, the Supreme Court declares that the recitation of school-sponsored nondenominational prayer in public schools violates the establishment clause of the *First Amendment* to the *United States Constitution* (1962).
- Under the protection of federal marshals, college student James Meredith becomes the first African American student to enroll in the University of Mississippi (1962).
- Michael Harrington publishes *The Other America*, which dramatically exposes the widespread presence of poverty across both urban and rural America (1962).
- While in jail for leading a civil rights demonstration, Reverend Martin Luther King composes his *Letter from the Birmingham Jail*, which clarifies his commitment to nonviolent civil disobedience (1963).
- Singer and songwriter Bob Dylan captivates the audience in Newport, Rhode Island, with his songs of protest, such as *A Hard Rain's A-Gonna Fall, Talkin' John Birch Society Blues*, and *Blowin' in the Wind* (1963).
- Before a crowd of more than 200,000 civil rights proponents, standing in front of the Lincoln Memorial in Washington, DC, Reverend King delivers his celebrated "I Have a Dream" speech (1963).
- After extensive study by medical experts, the surgeon general of the United States declares that cigarettes are the main cause of lung cancer and bronchitis (1964).
- President Lyndon Johnson signs the *Civil Rights Act*, which bans racial discrimination in public accommodations, union activity, employment, and federally funded projects (1964).
- In order to engage in a "War on Poverty," President Johnson signs the *Economic Opportunity Act* (1964).
- In the State of the Union address, President Johnson proposes the development of a "Great Society," which focuses on eradicating poverty and racial injustice (1965).
- President Johnson signs the *Voting Rights Act*, which protects all people, particularly minorities, in the exercise of their constitutional right to vote (1965).
- Reacting to reports of police brutality, African American residents of Watts, a neighborhood in Los Angeles, riot for several days, resulting in 34 deaths,

more than 1,000 injuries, 4,000 arrests, and property damage of approximately $40 million (1965).
- President Johnson signs a series of noteworthy social welfare legislation, including the *Older Americans Act*, the *Elementary and Secondary Education Act* (ESEA), and the Medicare (Title XVIII) and Medicaid (Title XIX) amendments to the *Social Security Act* (1965).
- In the face of opposition from conservative religious and political leaders, the Department of Health, Education, and Welfare plans to spend $3.1 million on providing family planning services to low-income families (1966).
- In *Miranda v. Arizona*, the United States Supreme Court affirms the right of anyone arrested by police authorities to be told of their rights to remain silent and to be provided with a lawyer (1966).
- President Johnson signs the *Child Nutrition Act*, which provides federal funds to feed children from low-income families (1966).
- Detroit, similar to other American cities this summer, experiences bitter race riots due to unemployment, substandard housing, and general despair, resulting in the loss of life, injuries, and property damage of several hundred million dollars (1967).
- Reverend Martin Luther King, who is in Memphis, Tennessee, to assist with the strike of local garbage collectors, is assassinated at his motel. Riots break out in Chicago and other cities across the nation (1968).
- At the Olympics ceremony in Mexico City, African American medalists Tommie Smith and John Carlos, protesting the treatment of African Americans, accept their medals for the 200-meter dash by standing with their right black-gloved hands held aloft in a fist during the playing of *The Star-Spangled Banner* (1968).
- President Richard Nixon proposes his *Family Assistance Plan*, an innovative approach to public assistance that would essentially grant a guaranteed annual income to economically fragile families, but the plan is rejected by the United States Congress (1969).
- The Supreme Court allows the use of bussing and redistricting as valid tactics to attain greater racial integration in public school systems across the nation (1971).
- Journalists Gloria Steinem and Letty Cottin Pogrebin begin publishing a new feminist magazine simply titled *Ms.* (1972).
- The American Indian Movement, headed by Dennis Banks and Russell Means, suffers a setback with the forced removal of protestors at Wounded Knee, South Dakota (1973).
- The Supreme Court, invoking the principle of privacy, decides in *Roe v. Wade* that women have a constitutional right to terminate a pregnancy, with certain limits (1973).
- Court-ordered bussing to attain better racial integration within the Boston public school system causes disruptions and violence from white parents who oppose integrated bussing (1974).

- President Gerald Ford signs into law the *Housing and Community Development Act*, which creates the Community Development Block Grant program and the Section 8 Housing Choice Voucher program (1974).
- The United States Commission on Civil Rights reports that Southern public-school districts have achieved a higher rate of racial integration than have their Northern state counterparts (1975).

Note: For a more reflective and functional use of this list of contemporary social welfare historical events, see Question #5 under the **Questions for Further Research and Discussion** section (below).

Sources:

Daniel, C. (1989). *Chronicle of America*. Mt. Kisco, NY: Chronicle Publications.
Mercer, D. (2000). *Millennium year by year*. New York: Dorling Kindersley Publications.
Social welfare developments 1900–1950. (2011). Retrieved from https://socialwelfare.library.vcu.edu/events/1951-2000/

Primary Text Material

Brown v. Board of Education (1954)

"... Segregation of white and colored children in public schools has a detrimental effect upon the colored children. The impact is greater when it has the sanction of the law, for the policy of separating the races is usually interpreted as denoting the inferiority of the negro group. A sense of inferiority affects the motivation of a child to learn. Segregation with the sanction of law, therefore, has a tendency to [retard] the educational and mental development of negro children and to deprive them of some of the benefits they would receive in a racial[ly] integrated school system.

Whatever may have been the extent of psychological knowledge at the time of Plessy v. Ferguson, this finding is amply supported by modern authority. Any language in Plessy v. Ferguson contrary to this finding is rejected.

We conclude that, in the field of public education, the doctrine of "separate but equal" has no place. Separate educational facilities are inherently unequal. Therefore, we hold that the plaintiffs and others similarly situated for whom the actions have been brought are, by reason of the segregation complained of, deprived of the equal protection of the laws guaranteed by the Fourteenth Amendment. This disposition makes unnecessary any discussion whether such segregation also violates the Due Process Clause of the Fourteenth Amendment..."

Continued

> Source and full text available at https://www.ourdocuments.gov/doc.php?flash=false&doc=87&page=transcript.
>
> This media file is in the public domain.
>
> - Other primary historical documents relating to *Brown v. Board of Education* can be found in the Eisenhower Presidential Library in Kansas, available at https://eisenhower.archives.gov/research/online_documents/civil_rights_brown_v_boe.html.

Timeline of General Events in History, the Humanities, and Science During This Period (1950–1975)

These general historical events may help you understand more clearly the overall historical context during which the primary document was created.

- Wisconsin Senator Joseph McCarthy claims he has a "list" of more than 200 known subversive Communist agents working within the U.S. State Department, thus igniting a period of fierce anti-Communist investigations within the federal government (1950).
- North Korea crosses the 38th parallel line and invades South Korea, prompting the beginning of United States involvement in the Korean War (1950).
- The first formal credit card is launched by the Diners Club in cardboard format with a list of the 28 participating restaurants on the back (1950).
- Maine Republican Senator Margaret Chase Smith, the first woman elected to serve in both Houses of Congress, denounces the discrediting of individuals and fear tactics used by fellow-Republican, Wisconsin Senator Joseph McCarthy (1950).
- The United States detonates its first thermonuclear device, referred to as the "H-bomb," which is more destructive than the atomic bomb used to end World War II (1952).
- Accused Russian spies Julius and Ethel Rosenberg are executed for espionage at Sing Sing Prison in New York, amid controversy over their innocence (1953).
- The Eisenhower administration proposes constructing a massive federal interstate highway system to connect individuals and "farm-to-table" enterprises across the nation (1954).
- President Eisenhower pledges support to South Vietnam in its battle against insurgent Communist forces and authorizes the sending of military advisers there (1955).
- Amid the growing popularity of performers such as Bill Haley and The Comets, Little Richard, Bo Diddley, Fats Domino, and Chuck Berry, some critics denounce the new rock 'n' roll music genre, claiming it to be just as dangerous as drugs for teenagers (1955).

- Musician Leonard Bernstein opens his innovative musical play on a theme of ethnic diversity, *West Side Story*, on the Broadway stage (1957).
- American Airlines announces the first regular same-day air service between New York City and Los Angeles (1959).
- Alaska and Hawai'i become the 49th and 50th states in the nation (1959).
- Massachusetts Senator John F. Kennedy, who is Catholic, is elected president of the United States (1960).
- In President John F. Kennedy's inaugural address, he delivers his legendary "Ask not what your country can do for you—ask what you can do for your country" speech (1961).
- As part of his New Frontier initiative, President Kennedy establishes the Peace Corps, whose unpaid volunteers serve to assist the advancement of under-developed nations (1961).
- Lieutenant John Glenn becomes the first American to reach orbital flight around the earth after his *Friendship 7* blasts off from Cape Canaveral, Florida (1962).
- President John F. Kennedy is murdered by assassin Harvey Lee Oswald in Dallas, Texas (1963).
- The musical group The Beatles make their first American appearance in New York City (1964).
- With more than 500,000 American troops on the ground, the Vietnam War increases in intensity and the loss of lives (1965).
- The Hollywood film *The Graduate*, starring Dustin Hoffman, challenges the young generation to question whether conformity to the older generation's expectations of them is truly worth the emotional price they will pay (1967).
- Israel defeats Egypt and other Arab allies in the Six-Day War, allowing it to fully occupy the entire city of Jerusalem, half of which had been under the control of Jordan before the war (1967).
- In a radical departure from past precedent for journalists, CBS News anchor Walter Cronkite denounces the War in Vietnam as hopeless and immoral (1968).
- Presidential candidate, Senator Robert Kennedy is assassinated at the end of a Democratic campaign rally at the Ambassador Hotel in Los Angeles (1968).
- The Democratic Party, thoroughly divided into doves and hawks over the Vietnam War, holds its Democratic National Convention in Chicago and elects Hubert Humphrey over Eugene McCarthy as its candidate against Richard Nixon for president. Peaceful protests outside the convention center turn into anti-war riots, and allegations are launched against the police for unnecessary brutality (1968).
- *The Smothers Brothers Comedy Hour* on CBS is canceled due to the allegation that much of Tommy and Dick Smothers' humor is anti-Vietnam War and disrespectful of governmental authority (1969).
- The Reverends Daniel and Philip Berrigan, along with members of the Catonsville Nine, are convicted in state court of destroying Selective Service draft records in Catonsville, Maryland (1969).

- With the transmitted words "Houston, Tranquility Base here. The Eagle has landed," astronaut Neil Armstrong reports to the world that he and fellow astronaut Edwin Aldrin Jr. have successfully landed on the moon (1969).
- The so-called Woodstock Nation of more than 400,000 music fans, advocating peace, drugs, and casual sex, meet for an iconic music festival on Max Yasgur's farm outside Woodstock, New York (1969).
- Washington, DC is the site for the largest anti-war demonstration of more than 250,000 people in American history. The protestors march from the Capitol to the Washington Monument, while other anti-war demonstrations take place at many universities because of their alleged financial connections with the Department of Defense (1969).
- Four unarmed students at Kent State University in Ohio die from shots fired by the Ohio National Guard during a student anti-war demonstration on campus (1970).
- Student strikes against the Vietnam War at more than 450 colleges and universities across America lead to canceled classes and disrupted commencement activities (1970).
- Citing the principle of the *First Amendment*, the Supreme Court ends the suspension of publication sought by the Nixon White House and decreed that the *New York Times*, the *Washington Post*, and other newspapers can continue to publish the full story behind *The Pentagon Papers*, which revealed that Defense Secretary McNamara questioned the progression and the likely success of the Vietnam War (1971).
- The Vietnam War technically ends with the signing of a cease-fire agreement by representatives of Vietnam and the United States (1973).
- Reacting to the threat of impeachment due to his reaction to the Watergate conflict, President Richard Nixon resigns from office in disgrace. Vice President Gerald Ford assumes the presidency and, within a month, pardons former President Nixon of all crimes committed (1974).
- Following the unconditional surrender of the South Vietnamese military to the Communist Viet Cong army, the last American troops, along with several thousand South Vietnamese allies, are evacuated by helicopter, under duress, from Saigon (1975).

Sources:
Daniel, C. (1989). *Chronicle of America*. Mt. Kisco, NY: Chronicle Publications.
Events of the 20th century. Retrieved from https://en.wikipedia.org/wiki/timeline_of_the_20th_century
Mercer, D. (2000). *Millennium year by year*. New York: Dorling Kindersley Publications.

Questions for Further Research and Discussion

1. Read the entire *Brown v. Board of Education* decision, then summarize the rationale behind their final ruling as provided by the justices.

2. Choose one of the Supreme Court cases, listed above, involving education and race that preceded *Brown v. Board of Education*. Conduct further research on it, then summarize the facts of the case and indicate how you believe it influenced the outcome of *Brown v. Board of Education*. Be specific in your discussion of influence.
3. Conduct further research on the aftermath of *Brown v. Board of Education* by focusing on one of the following subsequent developments: the Little Rock Nine, Civil Rights leader Medgar Evers, Governor George Wallace and the University of Alabama, or "white flight" in Northern cities.
4. Based on the primary documentary material presented here, as well as other material you discover in the **Additional Selected References** at the end of this chapter, what additional federal policy or policies do you believe should have been developed or changed at that time? Describe those policies in detail. Recall that a policy could be either *legislative* (i.e., a law), *judicial* (i.e., a court decision), or *administrative* (i.e., an executive or organizational policy) in nature.
5. Select three events appearing under the **Linkage to Social Welfare** section (above), conduct further Internet research regarding them, then conclude whether you believe there exists any plausible relationship between the *Brown v. Board of Education* decision and the events you have chosen. Use the analytical model presented in Appendix 1 of this book, or develop your own analytical model, to draw these conclusions.
6. Select one book from the **Additional Selected References** list at the end of this chapter. Briefly read through it, then summarize the main points contained in the book. Identify your own personal reaction to this book.

Additional Selected References

Anderson, J., & Byrne, D. N. (2004). *The unfinished agenda of Brown v. Board of Education*. Hoboken, NJ: J. Wiley & Sons.

Balkin, J. M., & Ackerman, B. A. (2002). *What Brown v. Board of Education should have said: The nation's top legal experts rewrite America's landmark civil rights decision*. New York: New York University Press.

Byrne, D. N., Williams, J., & Thurgood Marshall Scholarship Fund. (2005). *Brown v. Board of Education: Its impact on public education, 1954–2004*. Brooklyn, NY: Word For Word Pub. Co.

Cottrol, R. J., Diamond, R. T., & Ware, L. (2003). *Brown v. Board of Education: Caste, culture, and the constitution*. Lawrence, KS: University Press of Kansas.

Gold, S. D. (2005). *Brown v. Board of Education: Separate but equal?* New York: Benchmark Books.

Hill, W. B., Chestnut, T. M., & United States. (2004). *Federal records pertaining to Brown v. Board of Education of Topeka, Kansas (1954)*. Washington, DC: National Archives and Records Administration.

Martin, W. E. (1998). *Brown v. Board of Education: A brief history with documents*. Boston: Bedford/St. Martin's.

Rountree, C. (2004). *Brown v. Board of Education at fifty: A rhetorical perspective*. Lanham, MD: Lexington Books.

Patterson, J. T. (2001). *Brown v. Board of Education: A civil rights milestone and its troubled legacy*. Oxford: Oxford University Press.

Rubin, S. G. (2016). *Brown v. Board of Education: A fight for simple justice*. New York: Holiday House.

United States. (2001). *Brown v. Board of Education 50th Anniversary Commission*. Washington, DC: United States Government Printing Office.

Credits

Fig. 22.1: Source: https://commons.wikimedia.org/wiki/File:Warren_Supreme_Court.jpg.

Fig. 22.2: Source: https://commons.wikimedia.org/wiki/File:Thurgoodmarshall1967.jpg.

Chapter 23

Oppression of Migrant Workers

Harvest of Shame (1960)

Introduction

Following the introduction of large-scale industrial conglomerates within the agricultural sector in the 1950s, there emerged a new class of exploited and marginalized people: the rural migrant worker. These mostly African American workers toiled under severe working conditions and inhospitable living conditions as they harvested the nation's fruits and vegetables. Typically, their employment was seasonal, their pay was minimal, their workday was long, they had no access to overtime pay or collective bargaining benefits, and their housing, sanitary facilities, and communal facilities could charitably be considered "substandard." Some commentators have even described the circumstances that migrant workers had to endure in the 1950s as comparable to modern slavery.

Historically, the federal government did try to protect workers' rights. President Franklin Delano Roosevelt in 1938, for example, supported the passage of the *Fair Labor Standards Act* (FLSA), which required the payment of a minimum wage, overtime benefits, as well as child labor protections throughout private industries and in federal, state, and local public employment. However, in order to secure the votes of Southern Democrats at the time, the law specifically excluded migrant workers from receiving any of the new benefits.

In an attempt to expose this scar on American society, the CBS television network in 1960 introduced *Harvest of Shame*, a documentary produced and written by Fred W. Friendly and David Lowe. The award-winning narrator, Edward R. Murrow, presented the facts and images collected, mainly by Lowe and his technical team, through on-site interviews over a nine-month period with African American and white migrant workers and through visits to labor camps in New Jersey, North Carolina, and Florida. *Harvest of Shame* was one installment in the longer CBS television series *CBS Reports*, which chronicled several other major economic, political, and social movements. Years before,

FIGURE 23.1   Journalist Edward R. Murrow.

through CBS Radio News, Murrow had investigated the struggles of migrant workers in Virginia's apple orchards, so he was keenly aware of the need to further document though television how these man-made challenges existed throughout the entire agricultural field.

Migrant agricultural workers toiled in mostly hot and humid conditions for an average of 136 days per year for which they received an annual compensation of $900, which computes to only $6.62 per day. Pay was allocated on a "piecework" system, meaning that a day's pay depended on the amount of agricultural product (e.g., heads of lettuce, apples, strawberries, etc.) collected, carried to a waiting truck, and then counted. Additionally, pay was directly related to the wholesale price of the agricultural product they picked, which could vary day by day, thus causing further economic uncertainty in migrant workers' lives.

The scheduled first showing of *Harvest of Shame* shortly after Thanksgiving in 1960 was intentional. The goal was to expose Americans across the nation to the austere truths that lay behind the bounty of food they bought and consumed each day. The shock and distress that *Harvest of Shame* generated, at least initially, did indeed surpass the intentions of the film's producers.

The film received criticism, however, even from some agricultural workers, for minor factual errors and for several false impressions that were generated without proper context.

A few members of Congress and some farm owners complained that the documentary was unfairly biased against the agricultural industry as a whole and, furthermore, that it exaggerated how a small minority of farm owners might have abused their workers. On a more positive note, the film helped to move forward in Congress federal legislation that enhanced health services for migrant workers and enriched educational services for their children.

Two years after the publication of *Harvest of Shame*, noted union organizer Caesar Chavez founded the National Farm Workers Association, which later became the United Farm Workers (UFW), in conjunction with migrant advocate Delores Huerta. During the 1960s, the UFW promoted migrant workers' rights to collective bargaining, adequate compensation, and protection of their health and safety while working.

Most migrant agricultural workers today are Latinos from Mexico, Central America, and South America, many of whom are undocumented. The average migrant farm worker now receives approximately $10,000 annually, and the hiring process remains an early morning "shape-up" by crew bosses in empty parking lots across rural America, just like in the original *Harvest of Shame* documentary. Furthermore, though stricter labor laws protecting migrant workers are in effect today, the appalling reality is that many migrant workers are still being cheated out of their rightful wages, are suffering from pesticide burns and heat emergencies, and are being subjected to child labor law violations and unsanitary living conditions, as well as widespread sexual harassment and abuse. Universal oversight and enforcement by federal authorities have been lacking due to budget cuts and rampant inattention by both Democratic and Republican administrations.

Even though many migrant workers are protected by the UFW union through negotiated contracts with farm owners, the UFW covers only California, Washington State, and eastern Oregon, and not all migrant workers are UFW union members. Further complicating the situation is the fact that nonunion migrant workers are employed under conditions set by farm labor contractors who negotiate with farm owners and, thus, act as middlemen between owners and workers. Unfortunately, not all farm labor contractors follow the laws and established standards that are necessary for equitable pay and safe working conditions. Furthermore, farm labor contractors tend to underbid one another in order to win contracts, which leads to the inevitable poor pay and minimal protections for migrant farm workers.

The day after the screening of *Harvest of Shame*, the *New York Times* described that it revealed in "uncompromising" terms the "filth, despair,

FIGURE 23.2 Migrants weed sugar beets for $2 an hour.

and grinding poverty" experienced day after day by migrant agricultural workers in 1960s America. Tragically, if *Harvest of Shame* were to be revised with current data in 2018, as the UFW union did in 2008, the results would undoubtedly be shockingly similar.

- To view a sample workday schedule for a migrant worker picking tomatoes on an Immokalee, Florida, farm, see a report compiled by the Coalition of Immokalee Workers (CIW) in 2011 on page 2 at http://www.ciw-online.org/Resources/tools/general/12Facts&Figures.pdf.

Internet Sources for the Content of This Introduction Include:
https://www.cbsnews.com/news/harvest-of-shame-50-years-later/
https://www.npr.org/2014/05/31/317364146/in-confronting-poverty-harvest-of-shame-reaped-praise-and-criticism
https://www.theatlantic.com/national/archive/2012/11/for-migrant-workers-still-the-harvest-and-the-shame/265457/
http://billmoyers.com/2013/07/19/watch-edward-r-murrows-harvest-of-shame/
https://en.wikipedia.org/wiki/harvest_of_shame

Linkage to Social Welfare History (1950–1975)

Social welfare historical events for this time period include the following:

- United Nations diplomat Ralph Bunche is awarded the Nobel Peace Prize for his work mediating conflicts between Arabs and Jews in the Middle East, thus becoming the first African American to receive such an honor (1950).
- Social scientists David Riesman, Nathan Glazer, and Reuel Denney publish *The Lonely Crowd*, a study of how Americans are not overly interested in conformity with their fellow citizens (1950).
- Over the veto of President Harry Truman, the Congress passes the *Immigration and Naturalization Act* (also known as the McCarran–Walter Act), restricting the number of immigrants and redefining the criteria for admission to the United States (1952).
- Sexuality becomes public, with Marilyn Monroe starring in the publication of *Playboy* magazine and the release of films such as *The Moon Is Blue* (1953).
- The scourge of the childhood disease polio is eradicated in the United States with the introduction of a vaccine developed by Dr. Jonas Salk at the University of Pennsylvania (1954).
- The United States Supreme Court, in *Brown v. Board of Education*, effectively ends racial segregation in public schools across the nation (1954).
- Rosa Parks, seated in the white section of a Montgomery, Alabama, bus, refuses to give up her seat to a white man and is arrested, thus launching the Montgomery

Bus Boycott partly led by the local Christian pastor, the Reverend Martin Luther King Jr. (1955).
- Following the merger of several allied groups, the National Association of Social Workers (NASW) is formally established (1955).
- The Count Basie Orchestra becomes the first African American musical group to play in the famous Starlight Room at the Waldorf Astoria hotel in New York City (1957).
- Under the protection of federal troops and federalized Arkansas National Guardsmen, and in defiance of Arkansas Governor Orval Faubus, nine African American students are escorted into Little Rock Central High School through crowds of angry whites opposing school integration (1957).
- Economist John Kenneth Galbraith publishes *The Affluent Society*, which outlines the wide income disparities in America and calls for greater public resources for those who are disadvantaged (1958).
- The novel *Lady Chatterley's Lover* is publicly banned after being judged as obscene by the United States Postal Service (1959).
- Four African American students stage a non-violent "sit-in" by refusing to move from their seats at the Woolworth's lunch counter in Greensboro, North Carolina (1960).
- The Food and Drug Administration approves the sale and use of the first contraceptive pill for women (1960).
- An integrated bus full of members of the Congress of Racial Equality (CORE) travels through Southern states testing the local segregation laws, with the result of the "Freedom Riders" being viciously attacked and arrested along the way. In one instance, Attorney General Robert Kennedy sends in 600 federal marshals to restore order in Montgomery, Alabama (1961).
- In *Engel v. Vitale*, the Supreme Court declares that the recitation of school-sponsored nondenominational prayer in public schools violates the establishment clause of the *First Amendment* to the United States Constitution (1962).
- Under the protection of federal marshals, college student James Meredith becomes the first African American student to enroll in the University of Mississippi (1962).
- Michael Harrington publishes *The Other America*, which dramatically exposes the widespread presence of poverty across both urban and rural America (1962).
- While in jail for leading a civil rights demonstration, Reverend King composes his *Letter from the Birmingham Jail*, which clarifies his commitment to nonviolent civil disobedience (1963).
- Singer and songwriter Bob Dylan captivates the audience in Newport, Rhode Island, with his songs of protest, such as *A Hard Rain's A-Gonna Fall, Talkin' John Birch Society Blues*, and *Blowin' in the Wind* (1963).
- Before a crowd of more than 200,000 civil rights proponents, standing in front of the Lincoln Memorial in Washington, DC, Reverend King delivers his celebrated "I Have a Dream" speech (1963).

- After extensive study by medical experts, the surgeon general of the United States declares that cigarettes are the main cause of lung cancer and bronchitis (1964).
- President Lyndon Johnson signs the *Civil Rights Act*, which bans racial discrimination in public accommodations, union activity, employment, and federally funded projects (1964).
- In order to engage in a "War on Poverty," President Johnson signs the *Economic Opportunity Act* (1964).
- In the State of the Union address, President Johnson proposes the development of a "Great Society," which focuses on eradicating poverty and racial injustice (1965).
- President Johnson signs the *Voting Rights Act*, which protects all people, particularly minorities, in the exercise of their constitutional right to vote (1965).
- Reacting to reports of police brutality, African American residents of Watts, a neighborhood in Los Angeles, riot for several days, resulting in 34 deaths, more than 1,000 injuries, 4,000 arrests, and property damage of approximately $40 million (1965).
- President Johnson signs a series of noteworthy social welfare legislation, including the *Older Americans Act*, the *Elementary and Secondary Education Act* (ESEA), and the Medicare (Title XVIII) and Medicaid (Title XIX) amendments to the *Social Security Act* (1965).
- In the face of opposition from conservative religious and political leaders, the Department of Health, Education, and Welfare plans to spend $3.1 million on providing family planning services to low-income families (1966).
- In *Miranda v. Arizona*, the United States Supreme Court affirms the right of anyone arrested by police authorities to be told of their rights to remain silent and to be provided with a lawyer (1966).
- President Johnson signs the *Child Nutrition Act*, which provides federal funds to feed children from low-income families (1966).
- Detroit, similar to other American cities this summer, experiences bitter race riots due to unemployment, substandard housing, and general despair, resulting in the loss of life, injuries, and property damage of several hundred million dollars (1967).
- Reverend King, who is in Memphis, Tennessee, to assist with the strike of local garbage collectors, is assassinated at his motel. Riots break out in Chicago and other cities across the nation (1968).
- At the Olympics ceremony in Mexico City, African American medalists Tommie Smith and John Carlos, protesting the treatment of African Americans, accept their medals for the 200-meter dash by standing with their right black-gloved hands held aloft in a fist during the playing of *The Star-Spangled Banner* (1968).
- President Richard Nixon proposes his *Family Assistance Plan*, an innovative approach to public assistance that would essentially grant a guaranteed annual income to economically fragile families, but the plan is rejected by the United States Congress (1969).

- The Supreme Court allows the use of bussing and redistricting as valid tactics to attain greater racial integration in public school systems across the nation (1971).
- Journalists Gloria Steinem and Letty Cottin Pogrebin begin publishing a new feminist magazine simply titled *Ms.* (1972).
- The American Indian Movement, headed by Dennis Banks and Russell Means, suffers a setback with the forced removal of protestors at Wounded Knee, South Dakota (1973).
- The Supreme Court, invoking the principle of privacy, decides in *Roe v. Wade* that women have a constitutional right to terminate a pregnancy (1973).
- Court-ordered bussing to attain better racial integration within the Boston public school system causes disruptions and violence from white parents who oppose integrated bussing (1974).
- President Gerald Ford signs into law the *Housing and Community Development Act*, which creates the Community Development Block Grant program and the Section 8 Housing Choice Voucher program (1974).
- The United States Commission on Civil Rights reports that Southern public school districts have achieved a higher rate of racial integration than have their Northern state counterparts (1975).

Note: For a more reflective and functional use of this list of contemporary social welfare historical events, see Question #5 under the **Questions for Further Research and Discussion** section (below).

Sources:
Daniel, C. (1989). *Chronicle of America.* Mt. Kisco, NY: Chronicle Publications.
Mercer, D. (2000). *Millennium year by year.* New York: Dorling Kindersley Publications.
Social welfare developments 1900–1950. (2011). Retrieved from https://socialwelfare.library.vcu.edu/events/1901-1950/

Primary Text Material

Harvest of Shame (1960)

In the opening scene of *Harvest of Shame*, with images of the recruitment of African American day laborers to harvest crops, CBS news commentator Edward R. Murrow states:

"This scene is not taking place in the Congo. It has nothing to do with Johannesburg or Cape Town. It is not Nyasaland or Nigeria. This is Florida. These are citizens of the United States, 1960. This is a shape-up for migrant workers. The hawkers are chanting the going piece rate at the various fields. This

Continued

is the way the humans who harvest the food for the best-fed people in the world get hired. One farmer looked at this and said, "We used to own our slaves; now we just rent them . . ."

At the end of the film, Murrow mentions several recommendations made to Congress by the federal *Committee on Migratory Labor* to improve the working and living conditions of migrant laborers. He concludes his documentary by noting:

"There will of course be opposition to these recommendations: too much government interference, too expensive, socialism. The migrants have no lobby. Only an enlightened, aroused, and perhaps angered public opinion can do anything about the migrants. The people you have seen have the strength to harvest your fruit and vegetables. They do not have the strength to influence legislation. Maybe we do."

Source: Friendly, F. W. (Director and Writer), Lowe, D. (Writer), & Murrow, E. R. (News Commentator). (1960). *Harvest of shame* [Television broadcast]. New York: CBS Reports.

- To view the original full-length broadcast of *Harvest of Shame*, see https://www.youtube.com/watch?v=yJTVF_dya7E.
- Also available at https://www.npr.org/2014/05/31/317364146/in-confronting-poverty-harvest-of-shame-reaped-praise-and-criticism.
- For an intriguing view of the troubles still facing many modern agricultural workers, see *California's Harvest of Shame*, produced in 2008 by the UFW union, available at https://vimeo.com/1551798?pg=embed&sec=1551798.

Timeline of General Events in History, the Humanities, and Science During This Period (1950–1975)

These general historical events may help you understand more clearly the overall historical context during which the primary document was created.

- Wisconsin Senator Joseph McCarthy claims he has a "list" of more than 200 known subversive Communist agents working within the U.S. State Department, thus igniting a period of fierce anti-Communist investigations within the federal government (1950).
- North Korea crosses the 38th parallel line and invades South Korea, prompting the beginning of United States involvement in the Korean War (1950).
- The first formal credit card is launched by the Diners Club in cardboard format with a list of 28 the participating restaurants on the back (1950).
- Maine Republican Senator Margaret Chase Smith, the first woman elected to serve in both Houses of Congress, denounces the discrediting of individuals and fear tactics used by fellow-Republican, Wisconsin Senator Joseph McCarthy (1950).

- The United States detonates its first thermonuclear device, referred to as the "H-bomb," which is more destructive than the atomic bomb used to end World War II (1952).
- Accused Russian spies Julius and Ethel Rosenberg are executed for espionage at Sing Sing Prison in New York, amid controversy over their innocence (1953).
- The Eisenhower administration proposes constructing a massive federal interstate highway system to connect individuals and "farm-to-table" enterprises across the nation (1954).
- President Eisenhower pledges support to South Vietnam in its battle against insurgent Communist forces and authorizes the sending of military advisers there (1955).
- Amid the growing popularity of performers such as Bill Haley and His Comets, Little Richard, Bo Diddley, Fats Domino, and Chuck Berry, some critics denounce the new rock 'n' roll music genre, claiming it to be just as dangerous as drugs for teenagers (1955).
- Musician Leonard Bernstein opens his innovative musical play on a theme of ethnic diversity, *West Side Story*, on the Broadway stage (1957).
- American Airlines announces the first regular same-day air service between New York City and Los Angeles (1959).
- Alaska and Hawaii become the 49th and 50th states in the nation (1959).
- Massachusetts Senator John Kennedy, who is Catholic, is elected president of the United States (1960).
- In President Kennedy's inaugural address, he delivers his legendary "Ask not what your country can do for you—ask what you can do for your country" speech (1961).
- As part of his New Frontier initiative, President Kennedy establishes the Peace Corps, whose unpaid volunteers serve to assist the advancement of underdeveloped nations (1961).
- Lieutenant John Glenn becomes the first American to reach orbital flight around the earth after his *Friendship 7* blasts off from Cape Canaveral, Florida (1962).
- President Kennedy is murdered by assassin Harvey Lee Oswald in Dallas, Texas (1963).
- The musical group The Beatles make their first American appearance in New York City (1964).
- With more than 500,000 American troops on the ground, the Vietnam War increases in intensity and the loss of lives (1965).
- The Hollywood film *The Graduate*, starring Dustin Hoffman, challenges the young generation to question whether conformity to their older generation's expectations of them is truly worth the emotional price they will pay (1967).
- Israel defeats Egypt and other Arab allies in the Six-Day War, allowing it to fully occupy the city of Jerusalem, half of which had been under the control of Jordan (1967).

- In a radical departure from past precedent for journalists, CBS News anchor Walter Cronkite denounces the War in Vietnam as hopeless and immoral (1968).
- Presidential Candidate Senator Robert Kennedy is assassinated at the end of a Democratic campaign rally at the Ambassador Hotel in Los Angeles (1968).
- The Democratic Party, thoroughly divided into doves and hawks over the Vietnam War, holds its Democratic National Convention in Chicago and elects Hubert Humphrey over Eugene McCarthy as its candidate against Richard Nixon for president. Peaceful protests outside the convention center turn into anti-war riots, and allegations are launched against the police for unnecessary brutality (1968).
- *The Smothers Brothers Comedy Hour* on CBS is canceled due to the allegation that much of Tommy and Dick Smothers' humor is anti-Vietnam War and disrespectful of governmental authority (1969).
- The Reverends Daniel and Philip Berrigan, along with members of the Catonsville Nine, are convicted in state court of destroying Selective Service draft records in Catonsville, Maryland (1969).
- With the transmitted words "Houston, Tranquility Base here. The Eagle has landed," astronaut Neil Armstrong reports to the world that he and fellow astronaut Edwin Aldrin Jr. have successfully landed on the moon (1969).
- The so-called Woodstock Nation of more than 400,000 music fans, advocating peace, drugs, and casual sex, meet for an iconic festival on Max Yasgur's farm outside Woodstock, New York (1969).
- Washington, DC is the site for the largest anti-war demonstration of more than 250,000 people in American history. The protestors march from the Capitol to the Washington Monument, while other anti-war demonstrations take at place at many universities because of their alleged financial connections with the Department of Defense (1969).
- Four unarmed students at Kent State University in Ohio die from shots fired by the Ohio National Guard during a student anti-war demonstration on campus (1970).
- Student strikes against the Vietnam War at more than 450 colleges and universities across America lead to canceled classes and disrupted commencement activities (1970).
- Citing the principle of the *First Amendment*, the Supreme Court ends the suspension of publication sought by the Nixon White House and decreed that the *New York Times*, the *Washington Post*, and other newspapers can continue to publish the full story behind *The Pentagon Papers*, which revealed that Defense Secretary McNamara questioned the progression and the likely success of the Vietnam War (1971).
- The Vietnam War technically ends with the signing of a cease-fire agreement by representatives of Vietnam and the United States (1973).
- Reacting to the threat of impeachment due to his reaction to the Watergate conflict, President Richard Nixon resigns from office in disgrace. Vice President Gerald

Ford assumes the presidency, and, within a month, pardons former President Nixon of all crimes committed (1974).
+ Following the unconditional surrender of the South Vietnamese military to the Viet Cong army, the last American troops, along with several thousand South Vietnamese allies, are evacuated by helicopter, under duress, from Saigon (1975).

Sources:
Daniel, C. (1989). *Chronicle of America*. Mt. Kisco, NY: Chronicle Publications.
Events of the 20th century. https://en.wikipedia.org/wiki/timeline_of_the_20th_century
Mercer, D. (2000). *Millennium year by year*. New York: Dorling Kindersley Publications.

Questions for Further Research and Discussion

1. Using the URLs listed above, first view the entire original documentary, *Harvest of Shame*, then follow up with the shorter *California's Harvest of Shame* produced in 2008. List the issues raised in both documentaries, and indicate if any concerns are still problematic for migrant agricultural workers in our present society.
2. Choose either journalist Edward R. Murrow or union organizer Caesar Chavez, then conduct further research on their lives and accomplishments. Summarize your findings, emphasizing their contributions to social justice generally as well as specifically to the case of migrant agricultural workers.
3. Search the Internet for any special programs or services that are being offered to assist migrant agricultural workers in your own state of residence or region of the country. Summarize what you have discovered, noting any policy or program needs that should be added.
4. Based on the primary documentary material presented here, as well as other material you discover in the **Additional Selected References** at the end of this chapter, what other federal policy or policies do you believe should have been developed or changed at that time? Describe those policies in detail. Recall that a policy could be either *legislative* (i.e., a law), *judicial* (i.e., a court decision), or *administrative* (i.e., an executive or organizational policy) in nature.
5. Select three events appearing under the **Linkage to Social Welfare** section (above), conduct further Internet research regarding them, then conclude whether you believe there exists any plausible relationship between *Harvest of Shame* and the events you have chosen. Use the analytical model presented in Appendix 1 of this book, or develop your own analytical model, to draw these conclusions.
6. Select one book from the **Additional Selected References** list at the end of this chapter. Briefly read through it, then summarize the main points contained in the book. Identify your own personal reaction to this book.

Additional Selected References

Coles, R. (1970). *Uprooted children: The early life of migrant farm workers.* Pittsburgh: University of Pittsburgh Press.

Finkelstein, N. H. (1997). *With heroic truth: The life of Edward R. Murrow.* New York: Clarion Books.

Goldfarb, R. L. (1981). *Migrant farm workers: A caste of despair.* Ames: Iowa State University Press.

Gonzales, D. (1996). *Cesar Chavez: Leader for migrant farm workers.* Springfield, NJ: Enslow Publishers.

Hovius, C. (2006). *Latino migrant workers: America's harvesters.* Philadelphia: Mason Crest Publishers.

Kendrick, A. (1969). *Prime time: The life of Edward R. Murrow.* Boston: Little, Brown and Company.

Mahalingam, R., & McCarthy, C. (2000). *Multicultural curriculum: New directions for social theory, practice, and policy.* New York: Routledge.

Persico, J. E. (1988). *Edward R. Murrow: An American original.* New York: McGraw-Hill.

Shipler, D. K. (2005). *The working poor: Invisible in America.* New York: Vintage Books.

Street, R. S. (2004). *Photographing farmworkers in California.* Stanford, CA: Stanford University Press.

United States Commission on Civil Rights. (1983). *Migrant workers on Maryland's Eastern Shore.* Washington, DC: U.S. Commission on Civil Rights.

Credits

Fig. 23.1: Source: https://commons.wikimedia.org/wiki/File:LBJ_with_Edward_R._Murrow_Dec_1963.jpg.

Fig. 23.2: Source: http://www.fdrlibrary.marist.edu/archives/collections/franklin/?p=digitallibrary/digitalcontent&id=4155.

Chapter 24

Songs of Protest

"This Land Is Your Land," "Blowin' in the Wind," "I Ain't Marching Anymore," "Eve of Destruction," and "We Shall Overcome" (1940–1964)

Introduction

Every recent decade seems to unveil its own type of music and prominent lyricists and performers who write and record songs for radio, television, film, and the consumer market. The 1960s, however, emerge as an era when an abundance of music was produced with the goal of inducing societal change, particularly around problems such as segregation, poverty, and war.

This is not to assume that the 1960s were all about protest and change. Indeed, there are classic 1960s songs about love (e.g., "Suzanne" by Leonard Cohen, "Unchained Melody" by the Righteous Brothers, "(You Make Me Feel Like) A Natural Woman" by Aretha Franklin, or "When a Man Loves a Woman" by Percy Sledge); loneliness (e.g., "Eleanor Rigby" by The Beatles); interracial love (e.g., "Brown Eyed Girl" by Van Morrison); anguish from love (e.g. "Ring of Fire" by Johnny Cash) and happiness (e.g., "Good Vibrations" by The Beach Boys, "Here Comes the Sun" by The Beatles, and "Turn! Turn! Turn!" by The Byrds).

Many other prominent songs of the 1960s, however, exhibited a definite "edge" in their lyrics and even in their musical arrangements. Although no individual song or cluster of songs directly led to a specific piece of revised federal legislation, a new Supreme Court decision, or any administrative policy or program change, some songs did expose a deep division in the nation about social problems. They also initiated compelling discussions between the young and those of a more advanced age, between conservatives and progressives, and between those favoring free expression and those who would silence all public dissent. Whether or not these forces did indeed silently motivate individual legislators to promote new legislation, individual judges to stand for or against some court decision, or administrators to initiate or abandon some policy or program remains an open question. It seems logical, however, that protest songs actually can affect change, however subtly and inaudibly.

What follows is a selection of a representative few, but certainly not all, of the musical compositions that tried to shake the moral consciences of Americans so they would be able to see the injustice of poverty and racial segregation, as well as the futility of a senseless war in Vietnam.

"This Land Is Your Land" by Woody Guthrie (1940)

Although the song was composed in 1940—two decades before the 1960s—the message underlying "This Land Is Your Land" has such an enduring quality and timeliness about it that the song continued to be performed throughout the 1960s and, undoubtedly, served as an inspiration for many later musical artists. Based on an earlier gospel tune, "This Land Is Your Land" was originally written by Woody Guthrie in 1940 but not recorded until 1944 when Guthrie was on leave in New York City from the United States Merchant Marines. According to Guthrie himself, he composed it because he was irritated with the constant playing of the nationalistic song "God Bless America," performed by the prominent American singer Kate Smith, over the radio. In his youth, Guthrie traveled across America, staying in labor camps with migrant workers during the Dust Bowl and Great Depression. He experienced, personally and deeply, the despair and humiliation of poor Americans as they grappled with an unyielding economy and faced an uncertain future. What he did not witness was the rosy vision of a country blessed by a benevolent God as portrayed by Smith.

Two verses of the original draft of the song were omitted from the original recording due to feared political pressure. One verse was about the dominance of private property over available public lands, and the other had to do with people lining up at the local relief office. The publisher feared that these verses would be interpreted as Marxist in theme and, thus, the entire song would be banned from the radio. During the 1960s, "This Land Is Your Land" was rerecorded by Guthrie's son, Arlo Guthrie, with all of the original verses included.

Recognized at the time as staunchly progressive in his political views, Guthrie fought against injustices in the economic system and the ill treatment of minorities and immigrants. In the 1950s, he struggled against the anti-Communist furor and character assassinations instigated by Senator Joseph McCarthy of Wisconsin. His guitar was notoriously blazoned with a panel that read: This Guitar Kills Fascists.

FIGURE 24.1   Woody Guthrie holding guitar.

Guthrie is nationally known as one of the most influential forces in the entire American folk tradition. He has inspired many later musicians such as Bono, Ani DiFranco, Bob Dylan, and Bruce Springsteen. "This Land Is Your Land" is even considered by some to be an alternative national anthem for America.

Internet Sources for the Content of This Part of the Introduction Include:
https://www.npr.org/2000/07/03/1076186/this-land-is-your-land
http://www.woodyguthrie.org/index.htm
http://www.themomi.org/museum/guthrie/index_800.html
https://folkways.si.edu/woodrow-wilson-woody-guthrie/american-folk-history/music/article/smithsonian

"Blowin' in the Wind" by Bob Dylan (1962)

According to Bob Dylan himself, he wrote "Blowin' in the Wind" in just 10 minutes as he sat in a café in the Greenwich Village neighborhood of New York City. The song quickly became the "voice" of the civil rights movement, especially once it was performed by folk trio Peter, Paul, and Mary in front of the Lincoln Memorial in Washington, DC in August 1963, moments before civil rights leader Reverend Martin Luther King Jr. delivered his enduring "I Have a Dream" speech. Because it mentions war-related terms such as *cannonball* and *white dove*, "Blowin' in the Wind" was also adopted as a cherished song of the anti-war peace movement of the 1960s.

FIGURE 24.2   Civil rights march on Washington with vocalists Joan Baez and Bob Dylan.

The connotation behind of the phrase "... the answer, my friend, is blowin' in the wind..." remains open to speculation, and Dylan has refused to discuss its meaning publicly. Some have suggested that it means humanity already possesses the answers to social problems but those answers are flying around, like the wind, and no one has yet grasped them. Others conclude that the phrase means there are no answers, so we are searching frantically for something that will always be elusive. The true meaning, it seems, depends on one's own subjective analysis.

Internet Sources for the Content of This Part of the Introduction Include:
https://www.npr.org/2000/10/21/1112840/blowin-in-the-wind
https://en.wikipedia.org/wiki/blowin%27_in_the_wind
http://www.songfacts.com/detail.php?id=1669
https://www.snopes.com/music/songs/blowin.asp
http://bob-dylan.org.uk/archives/9

"I Ain't Marching Anymore" by Phil Ochs (1964)

During his short 10-year musical career, Phil Ochs composed and performed eight songs, all with a radical viewpoint. "I Ain't Marching Anymore" stands unquestionably as his most famous. His brief life ended in 1976 by suicide, resulting from severe bouts with depression and paranoia.

"I Ain't Marching Anymore" became synonymous with the anti-war protest movement throughout the 1960s. The song includes a lyrical history of the many wars fought by the United States during its relatively short duration as a nation, starting with the War of 1812; progressing through the battles against Native Americans throughout the 19th century; continuing on to the Mexican-American War, the Civil War, World War I, and World War II; and ending with a denunciation of the greediness of corporate America highlighted by the colonization of Cuba and the expansion of missile development by the so-called military industrial complex.

"I Ain't Marching Anymore" never reached the same level of notoriety or acceptance as did other protest songs, but it is apparent the Ochs knew the history of the United States very well, and he was able to point out a deadly pattern of violence that seems endemic to American culture. For that audacity, he was tracked by the Federal Bureau of Investigation (FBI) and his songs were banned by several radio stations because of their alleged antigovernment bias. In 1968, Ochs performed "I Ain't Marching Anymore" outside the Democratic National Convention in support of the protests against the Vietnam War and urged his audience to burn their military draft cards to show solidarity with the dissenters outside and inside the convention hall.

Internet Sources for the Content of This Part of the Introduction Include:
https://consequenceofsound.net/2009/01/rock-history-101-phil-ochss-i-aint-marching-anymore/
https://en.wikipedia.org/wiki/i_ain%27t_marching_anymore

https://en.wikipedia.org/wiki/phil_ochs

https://www.washingtonpost.com/posteverything/wp/2017/01/24/why-phil-ochs-is-the-obscure-60s-folk-singer-america-needs-in-2017/?utm_term=.d97d403e700a

"Eve of Destruction" by B. F. Sloan, Performed by Barry McGuire (1964)

Troubled by the assassination of President John Kennedy in 1963, songwriter B. F. Sloan felt compelled to write "Eve of Destruction" in 1964. The song encompasses issues such as the Vietnam War, civil rights, congressional inaction, the Cuban Missile Crisis, and the fear of worldwide nuclear destruction. Sloan noted that he was influenced musically by both Woody Guthrie and Bob Dylan. "Eve of Destruction" has been most notably performed by Barry McGuire, a former member of the folk musical group The New Christy Minstrels.

As with so many other protest songs, many radio stations initially refused to play "Eve of Destruction," assuming that its lyrics were dangerously antigovernment. The song continued to gain a wide popular audience and was sung at many anti-Vietnam War demonstrations during the 1960s. The response from political conservatives was swift and direct, and they responded almost immediately with pro-government songs such as "The Dawn of Correction" by The Spokesmen and "The Ballad of the Green Berets" by Barry Sadler.

Internet Sources for the Content of This Part of the Introduction Include:

http://www.songfacts.com/detail.php?id=799

https://www.rollingstone.com/music/lists/readers-poll-the-10-best-protest-songs-of-all-time-20141203/barry-mcguire-eve-of-destruction-20141203

https://en.wikipedia.org/wiki/eve_of_destruction_(song)

https://en.wikipedia.org/wiki/barry_mcguire

https://www.allmusic.com/artist/barry-mcguire-mn0000787011/biography

"We Shall Overcome" Copyrighted by Guy Carawan, Frank Hamilton, Zilphia Horton, and Pete Seeger (1963)

Representing the African American folk tradition with its deep roots in spiritual melodies during the early decades of the 20th century, an earlier version of "We Shall Overcome" was first used as a protest song in 1945 by South Carolina tobacco workers during their strike for better pay and working conditions. By the later 1950s, the civil rights movement adopted the song, and it was soon an integral part of civil rights marches, sit-ins, and other massive rallies. Its usage even spread to other countries, such as Northern Ireland during demonstrations against the British government, South Africa during marches against the white apartheid government, and Israel during Palestinian rallies against the Israeli government.

Based on the religious hymn "O Sanctissima," the song, with the original title "I'll Overcome Someday," was first published by Reverend Charles Tindley in Philadelphia in 1900, and it soon became popular in African American churches throughout the South. It was copyrighted in 1963 with the new title "We Shall Overcome" by Guy Carawan, Frank Hamilton, Zilphia Horton, and Pete Seeger. As clearly expressed in the lyrics, the

FIGURE 24.3 Pete Seeger, American folk singer.

song has long been intimately associated with resistance to racial oppression along with the validation of the entire civil rights movement.

In a very emotional performance, Joan Baez sang "We Shall Overcome" on the steps of the Lincoln Memorial during the civil rights March on Washington in 1963. President Lyndon Johnson used the phrase "we shall overcome" when addressing the Congress in March 1968 following the "Bloody Sunday" attack on civil rights activists during their march from Selma to Montgomery, Alabama. It is also reported that Reverend Martin Luther King Jr. used the phrase in his last sermon preached before his assassination in 1968 in Memphis, Tennessee.

Internet Sources for the Content of This Part of the Introduction Include:
https://en.wikipedia.org/wiki/we_shall_overcome
http://www.loc.gov/teachers/lyrical/songs/overcome.html
http://www.songfacts.com/detail.php?id=9390

- For a history of "We Shall Overcome" as related by Pete Seeger, see: https://www.youtube.com/watch?v=N-FmQEFFFko

As mentioned above, these five songs are simply a sample of the larger number of creative protest songs composed during the turbulent decade of the 1960s. Even though these particular songs are not, strictly speaking, social policies in and of themselves, they are songs that appear to have positively influenced some people to continue to advocate for social change. Consequently, when Americans advocate for a cause they believe is just, that means that they organize, attend rallies, write letters, make telephone calls, appear and speak up at legislative hearings, and, most crucially, vote. Therefore, it does not seem too much of an exaggeration to propose that songs, and other creative expressions of protest, can truly influence legislation, court decisions, and organizational strategies.

Linkage to Social Welfare History (1950–1975)

Social welfare historical events for this time period include the following:

- United Nations diplomat Ralph Bunche is awarded the Nobel Peace Prize for his work mediating conflicts between Arabs and Jews in the Middle East, thus becoming the first African American to receive such an honor (1950).

- Social scientists David Riesman, Nathan Glazer, and Reuel Denney publish *The Lonely Crowd*, a study of how Americans are not overly interested in conformity with their fellow citizens (1950).
- Over the veto of President Harry Truman, the Congress passes the *Immigration and Naturalization Act* (also known as the McCarran–Walter Act), restricting the number of immigrants and redefining the criteria for admission to the United States (1952).
- Sexuality becomes public, with Marilyn Monroe starring in the publication of *Playboy* magazine and the release of films such as *The Moon Is Blue* (1953).
- The scourge of the childhood disease polio is eradicated in the United States with the introduction of a vaccine developed by Dr. Jonas Salk at the University of Pennsylvania (1954).
- The United States Supreme Court, in *Brown v. Board of Education*, effectively ends racial segregation in public schools across the nation (1954).
- Rosa Parks, seated in the white section of a Montgomery, Alabama, bus, refuses to give up her seat to a white man and is arrested, thus launching the Montgomery Bus Boycott partly led by the local Christian pastor, the Reverend Martin Luther King Jr. (1955).
- Following the merger of several allied groups, the National Association of Social Workers (NASW) is formally established (1955).
- The Count Basie Orchestra becomes the first African American musical group to play in the famous Starlight Room at the Waldorf Astoria hotel in New York City (1957).
- Under the protection of federal troops and federalized Arkansas National Guardsmen, and in defiance of Arkansas Governor Orval Faubus, nine African American students are escorted into Little Rock Central High School through crowds of angry whites opposing school integration (1957).
- Economist John Kenneth Galbraith publishes *The Affluent Society*, which outlines the wide income disparities in America and calls for greater public resources for those who are disadvantaged (1958).
- The novel *Lady Chatterley's Lover* is publicly banned after being judged as obscene by the United States Postal Service (1959).
- Four African American students stage a nonviolent "sit-in" by refusing to move from their seats at the Woolworth's lunch counter in Greensboro, North Carolina (1960).
- The Food and Drug Administration approves the sale and use of the first contraceptive pill for women (1960).
- CBS television announcer Edward R. Murrow narrates the shocking exposé of the oppressive and dangerous working conditions of migrant agricultural workers in the film *Harvest of Shame* (1960).
- An integrated bus full of members of the Congress of Racial Equality (CORE) travels through Southern states testing the local segregation laws, with the result

of the "Freedom Riders" being viciously attacked and arrested along the way. In one instance, Attorney General Robert Kennedy sends in 600 federal marshals to restore order in Montgomery, Alabama (1961).
- In *Engel v. Vitale*, the Supreme Court declares that the recitation of school-sponsored nondenominational prayer in public schools violates the establishment clause of the *First Amendment* to the *United States Constitution* (1962).
- Under the protection of federal marshals, college student James Meredith becomes the first African American student to enroll in the University of Mississippi (1962).
- Michael Harrington publishes *The Other America*, which dramatically exposes the widespread presence of poverty across both urban and rural America (1962).
- While in jail for leading a civil rights demonstration, Reverend King composes his *Letter from the Birmingham Jail*, which clarifies his commitment to nonviolent civil disobedience (1963).
- Singer and songwriter Bob Dylan captivates the audience in Newport, Rhode Island, with his songs of protest, such as *A Hard Rain's A-Gonna Fall*, *Talkin' John Birch Society Blues*, and *Blowin' in the Wind* (1963).
- Before a crowd of more than 200,000 civil rights proponents, standing in front of the Lincoln Memorial in Washington, DC, Reverend King delivers his celebrated "I Have a Dream" speech (1963).
- After extensive study by medical experts, the surgeon general of the United States declares that cigarettes are the main cause of lung cancer and bronchitis (1964).
- President Lyndon Johnson signs the *Civil Rights Act*, which bans racial discrimination in public accommodations, union activity, employment, and federally funded projects (1964).
- In order to engage in a "War on Poverty," President Johnson signs the *Economic Opportunity Act* (1964).
- In the State of the Union address, President Johnson proposes the development of a "Great Society," which focuses on eradicating poverty and racial injustice (1965).
- President Johnson signs the *Voting Rights Act*, which protects all people, particularly minorities, in the exercise of their constitutional right to vote (1965).
- Reacting to reports of police brutality, African American residents of Watts, a neighborhood in Los Angeles, riot for several days, resulting in 34 deaths, more than 1,000 injuries, 4,000 arrests, and property damage of approximately $40 million (1965).
- President Johnson signs a series of noteworthy social welfare legislation, including the *Older Americans Act*, the *Elementary and Secondary Education Act* (ESEA), and the Medicare (Title XVIII) and Medicaid (Title XIX) amendments to the *Social Security Act* (1965).
- In the face of opposition from conservative religious and political leaders, the Department of Health, Education, and Welfare plans to spend $3.1 million on providing family planning services to low-income families (1966).

- In *Miranda v. Arizona*, the United States Supreme Court affirms the right of anyone arrested by police authorities to be told of their rights to remain silent and to be provided with a lawyer (1966).
- President Johnson signs the *Child Nutrition Act*, which provides federal funds to feed children from low-income families (1966).
- Detroit, similar to other American cities this summer, experiences bitter race riots due to unemployment, substandard housing, and general despair, resulting in the loss of life, injuries, and property damage of several hundred million dollars (1967).
- Reverend Martin Luther King, who is in Memphis, Tennessee, to assist with the strike of local garbage collectors, is assassinated at his motel. Riots break out in Chicago and other cities across the nation (1968).
- At the Olympics ceremony in Mexico City, African American medalists Tommie Smith and John Carlos, protesting the treatment of African Americans, accept their medals for the 200-meter dash by standing with their right black-gloved hands held aloft in a fist during the playing of "The Star-Spangled Banner" (1968).
- President Richard Nixon proposes his *Family Assistance Plan*, an innovative approach to public assistance that would essentially grant a guaranteed annual income to economically fragile families, but the plan is rejected by the United States Congress (1969).
- The Supreme Court allows the use of bussing and redistricting as valid tactics to attain greater racial integration in public school systems across the nation (1971).
- Journalists Gloria Steinem and Letty Cottin Pogrebin begin publishing a new feminist magazine simply titled *Ms.* (1972).
- The American Indian Movement, headed by Dennis Banks and Russell Means, suffers a setback with the forced removal of protestors at Wounded Knee, South Dakota (1973).
- The Supreme Court, invoking the principle of privacy, decides in *Roe v. Wade* that women have a constitutional right to terminate a pregnancy (1973).
- Court-ordered bussing to attain better racial integration within the Boston public school system causes disruptions and violence from white parents who oppose integrated bussing (1974).
- President Gerald Ford signs into law the *Housing and Community Development Act*, which creates the Community Development Block Grant program and the Section 8 Housing Choice Voucher program (1974).
- The United States Commission on Civil Rights reports that Southern public-school districts have achieved a higher rate of racial integration than have their Northern state counterparts (1975).

Note: For a more reflective and functional use of this list of contemporary social welfare historical events, see Question #5 under the **Questions for Further Research and Discussion** section (below).

Sources:
Daniel, C. (1989). *Chronicle of America*. Mt. Kisco, NY: Chronicle Publications.
Mercer, D. (2000). *Millennium year by year*. New York: Dorling Kindersley Publications.
Social welfare developments 1951–2000. (2011). Retrieved from https://socialwelfare.library.vcu.edu/events/1951-2000/

Primary Text Material

"This Land Is Your Land"

"... By the relief office I seen my people;
   As they stood there hungry..."

Complete lyrics for "This Land Is Your Land" by Woody Guthrie available at http://www.woodyguthrie.org/Lyrics/This_Land.htm.

Musical performance of "This Land Is Your Land" by Woody Guthrie available at https://www.youtube.com/watch?v=wxiMrvDbq3s.

"Blowin' in the Wind"

"... Yes, and how many deaths will it take 'til he knows
   That too many people have died?..."

Complete lyrics by Bob Dylan and musical performance of "Blowin' in the Wind" by Bob Dylan available at: https://genius.com/Bob-dylan-blowin-in-the-wind-lyrics.

"I Ain't Marching Anymore"

"... It's always the old to lead us to the war
   It's always the young to fall
   Now look at all we've won with the saber and the gun..."

Complete lyrics and musical performance of "I Ain't Marching Anymore" by Phil Ochs available at https://genius.com/Phil-ochs-i-aint-marching-anymore-lyrics.

"Eve of Destruction"

"... Handful of Senators don't pass legislation,
   And marches alone can't bring integration

> *When human respect is disintegratin'*
> *This whole crazy world is just too frustratin'..."*

Complete lyrics for "Eve of Destruction" by B. F. Sloan available at https://genius.com/barry-mcguire-eve-of-destruction-lyrics.

Musical performance of "Eve of Destruction" by Barry McGuire, including dramatic film clips, available at https://www.youtube.com/watch?v=qfZVu0alU0I.

"We Shall Overcome"

> *"We shall overcome, we shall overcome*
> *We shall overcome some day*
> *Oh, deep in my heart, I do believe*
> *We shall overcome some day..."*

Complete lyrics for "We Shall Overcome" by Guy Carawan, Frank Hamilton, Zilphia Horton, and Pete Seeger available at https://www.negrospirituals.com/songs/we_shall_overcome.htm.

Musical performance of "We Shall Overcome" by Joan Baez available at https://www.youtube.com/watch?v=RkNsEH1GD7Q.

Timeline of General Events in History, the Humanities, and Science During This Period (1950–1975)

These general historical events may help you understand more clearly the overall historical context during which the primary document was created.

- Wisconsin Senator Joseph McCarthy claims he has a "list" of more than 200 known subversive Communist agents working within the U.S. State Department, thus igniting a period of fierce anti-Communist investigations within the federal government (1950).
- North Korea crosses the 38th parallel line and invades South Korea, promoting the beginning of United States involvement in the Korean War (1950).
- The first formal credit card is launched by the Diners Club in cardboard format with a list of the 28 participating restaurants on the back (1950).
- Maine Republican Senator Margaret Chase Smith, the first woman elected to both Houses of Congress, denounces the discrediting of individuals and fear tactics used by fellow-Republican Senator, Wisconsin Senator Joseph McCarthy (1950).

- The United States detonates its first thermonuclear device, referred to as the "H-bomb," which is more destructive than the atomic bomb used to end World War II (1952).
- Accused Russian spies Julius and Ethel Rosenberg are executed for espionage at Sing Sing Prison in New York, amid controversy over their innocence (1953).
- The Eisenhower administration proposes constructing a massive federal interstate highway system to connect individuals and "farm-to-table" enterprises across the nation (1954).
- President Eisenhower pledges support to South Vietnam in its battle against insurgent Communist forces and authorizes the sending of military advisers there (1955).
- Amid the growing popularity of performers such as Bill Haley and His Comets, Little Richard, Bo Diddley, Fats Domino, and Chuck Berry, some critics denounce the new rock 'n roll music genre, claiming it to be just as dangerous as drugs for teenagers (1955).
- Musician Leonard Bernstein opens his innovative musical play on a theme of ethnic diversity, *West Side Story*, on the Broadway stage (1957).
- American Airlines announces the first regular same-day air service between New York City and Los Angeles (1959).
- Alaska and Hawaii become the 49th and 50th states in the nation (1959).
- Massachusetts Senator John Kennedy, who is Catholic, is elected president of the United States (1960).
- In President Kennedy's inaugural address, he delivers his legendary "Ask not what your country can do for you—ask what you can do for your country" speech (1961).
- As part of his New Frontier initiative, President Kennedy establishes the Peace Corps, whose unpaid volunteers serve to assist the advancement of underdeveloped nations (1961).
- Lieutenant John Glenn becomes the first American to reach orbital flight around the earth after his *Friendship 7* blasts off from Cape Canaveral, Florida (1962).
- President Kennedy is murdered by assassin Harvey Lee Oswald in Dallas, Texas (1963).
- The musical group The Beatles make their first American appearance in New York City (1964).
- With more than 500,000 American troops on the ground, the Vietnam War increases in intensity and the loss of lives (1965).
- The Hollywood film *The Graduate*, starring Dustin Hoffman, challenges the young generation to question whether conformity to their older generation's expectations of them is truly worth the emotional price they will pay (1967).
- Israel defeats Egypt and other Arab allies in the Six-Day War, allowing it to fully occupy the entire city of Jerusalem, half of which had been under the control of Jordan before the war (1967).

- In a radical departure from past precedent for journalists, CBS News anchor Walter Cronkite denounces the War in Vietnam as hopeless and immoral (1968).
- Presidential Candidate Senator Robert Kennedy is assassinated at the end of a Democratic campaign rally at the Ambassador Hotel in Los Angeles (1968).
- The Democratic Party, thoroughly divided into doves and hawks over the Vietnam War, holds its Democratic National Convention in Chicago and elects Hubert Humphrey over Eugene McCarthy as its candidate against Richard Nixon for president. Peaceful protests outside the convention center turn into anti-war riots, and allegations are launched against the police for unnecessary brutality (1968).
- *The Smothers Brothers Comedy Hour* on CBS is canceled due to the allegation that much of Tommy and Dick Smothers' humor is anti-Vietnam War and disrespectful of governmental authority (1969).
- The Reverends Daniel and Philip Berrigan, along with members of the Catonsville Nine, are convicted in state court of destroying Selective Service draft records in Catonsville, Maryland (1969).
- With the transmitted words "Houston, Tranquility Base here. The Eagle has landed," astronaut Neil Armstrong reports to the world that he and fellow astronaut Edwin Aldrin Jr. have successfully landed on the moon (1969).
- The so-called Woodstock Nation of more than 400,000 music fans, advocating peace, drugs, and casual sex, meet for an iconic festival on Max Yasgur's farm outside Woodstock, New York (1969).
- Washington, DC is the site for the largest anti-war demonstration of more than 250,000 people in American history. The protestors march from the Capitol to the Washington Monument, while other anti-war demonstrations take at place at many universities because of their alleged financial connections with the Department of Defense (1969).
- Four unarmed students at Kent State University in Ohio die from shots fired by the Ohio National Guard during a student anti-war demonstration on campus (1970).
- Student strikes against the Vietnam War at more than 450 colleges and universities across America lead to canceled classes and disrupted commencement activities (1970).
- Citing the principle of the *First Amendment*, the Supreme Court ends the suspension of publication sought by the Nixon White House and decreed that the *New York Times*, the *Washington Post*, and other newspapers can continue to publish the full story behind *The Pentagon Papers*, which revealed that Defense Secretary McNamara questioned the progression and the likely success of the Vietnam War (1971).
- The Vietnam War technically ends with the signing of a cease-fire agreement by representatives of Vietnam and the United States (1973).
- Reacting to the threat of impeachment due to his reaction to the Watergate conflict, President Richard Nixon resigns from office in disgrace. Vice President Gerald Ford assumes the presidency, and, within a month, pardons former President Nixon of all crimes committed (1974).

- Following the unconditional surrender of the South Vietnamese military to the Viet Cong army, the last American troops, along with several thousand South Vietnamese allies, are evacuated by helicopter, under duress, from Saigon (1975).

Sources:

Daniel, C. (1989). *Chronicle of America*. Mt. Kisco, NY: Chronicle Publications.

Events of the 20th century. Retrieved from https://en.wikipedia.org/wiki/timeline_of_the_20th_century

Mercer, D. (2000). *Millennium year by year*. New York: Dorling Kindersley Publications.

Questions for Further Research and Discussion

1. Read the complete lyrics and view the YouTube presentations of performances of these five protest songs. Then list all of the major social welfare values and attitudes that you see and hear exhibited in these songs and performances.
2. Select one of the major musical artists of the 1960s who produced protest songs. Then conduct further research on their lives and motivations in writing such protests against the evils in society through their eyes. Summarize your results.
3. Select what you believe to be the top five current songs in your region of the country. Through further Internet research, find a copy of the complete lyrics and view a performance of each of the top five songs. Do any of the lyrics for any of the current songs portray some level of protest against any current social conditions? State, in your opinion, why protest songs are or are not being created today.
4. Based on the original musical lyrics presented here, as well as other material you discover in the **Additional Selected References** at the end of this chapter, what additional federal policy or policies do you believe should have been developed or changed at that time? Describe those policies in detail. Recall that a policy could be either *legislative* (i.e., a law), *judicial* (i.e., a court decision), or *administrative* (i.e., an executive or organizational policy) in nature.
5. Select three events appearing under the **Linkage to Social Welfare** section (above), conduct further Internet research regarding them, then conclude whether you believe there exists any plausible relationship between the protest songs of the 1960s and the events you have chosen. Use the analytical model presented in Appendix 1 of this book, or develop your own analytical model, to draw these conclusions.
6. Select one book from the **Additional Selected References** list at the end of this chapter. Briefly read through it, then summarize the main points contained in the book. Identify your own personal reaction to this book.

Additional Selected References

Archive of Folk Song (U.S.). (1974). *A brief list of material relating to freedom songs of the civil rights movement.* Washington, DC: The Archive.

Blecha, P. (2004). *Taboo tunes. A history of banned bands and censored songs.* Ontario, Canada: Backbeat Books.

Carawan, G., & Carawan, C. (Eds). (1968). *Freedom is a constant struggle.* Minneapolis, MN: Oak Publications.

Carter, D. C. (2009). *The music has gone out of the movement: Civil rights and the Johnson administration, 1965–1968.* Chapel Hill: University of North Carolina Press.

Chapman, R. (1992). *Selling the sixties: The pirates and pop music radio.* New York: Routledge.

Cohen, D. (1999). *Phil Ochs: A bio-bibliography.* Westport, CT: Greenwood Press.

Dean, M. (2003). *Rock 'n' roll gold rush: A singles un-cyclopedia.* New York: Algora Publishing.

Kutschke, B., & Norton, B. (2013). *Music and protest in 1968.* New York: Cambridge University Press.

Martinelli, D. (2017). *Give peace a chant: Popular music, politics, and social protest.* Champaign, IL: Springer.

Redmond, S. L. (2014). *Anthem: Social movements and the sound of solidarity in the African diaspora.* New York: New York University Press.

Schumacher, M. (1996). *There but for fortune: The life of Phil Ochs.* New York: Hyperion.

Tsesis, A. (2008). *We shall overcome: A history of civil rights and the law.* New Haven: Yale University Press.

Credits

Fig. 24.1: Source: https://commons.wikimedia.org/wiki/File:Woody_Guthrie_NYWTS.jpg.
Fig. 24.2: Source: https://commons.wikimedia.org/wiki/File:Joan_Baez_Bob_Dylan.jpg.
Fig. 24.3: Source: https://commons.wikimedia.org/wiki/File:Pete_Seeger_NYWTS.jpg.

Chapter 25

The War on Poverty

Economic Opportunity Act, PL 88–452 (1964)

Introduction

Historians generally note three distinct influences behind the development of the *Economic Opportunity Act* of 1964. First was the publication of Michael Harrington's 1962 *The Other America*, which unmasked the appalling conditions of millions of Americans; second was the startling discoveries by then-Attorney General Robert Kennedy during his visits to decaying rural areas, urban poverty-stricken neighborhoods, and Native American reservations; and finally was the 1964 report of the President's Council of Economic Advisers, which showed that 20% of all American families fell below the official poverty index of an annual income of $3,000 for a family of four. Furthermore, the Council's report noted that a full 50% of all non-white families fell below the official poverty index.

This combination of formal and informal testimonies led to the creation of a task force headed by Sargent Shriver, President John Kennedy's brother-in-law, which was charged to design an appropriate governmental response to the shameful conditions that so many people were forced to endure. The result of the task force's efforts was federal legislation: the *Economic Opportunity Act* of 1964. Quickly passed by Congress and signed into law by President Lyndon Johnson, the *Economic Opportunity Act* created the authority and financial resources for the so-called "War on Poverty," which was itself a major foundational piece of the Great Society that the Johnson administration was promoting. Overall, the most unique aspect of the *Economic Opportunity Act* was that it did not focus on a massive transfer of financial resources from the federal government but rather concentrated on maximizing new opportunities for people in poverty and facilitating physical and psychological access to those opportunities.

FIGURE 25.1   President Lyndon Johnson signs the Economic Opportunity Act.

The Great Society was an extensive package of legislation enacted during the Johnson administration that redirected the nation on a more progressive path, similar to the comprehensive efforts of President Franklin Delano Roosevelt in his New Deal programs in the 1930s. The Great Society efforts in the 1960s included the *Civil Rights Act* (1964), the *Wilderness Act* (1964), the *National Endowment for the Humanities Act* (1965), the *Immigration and Nationality Act* (1965), the *Elementary and Secondary Education Act* (ESEA) (1965), the additions of Medicare and Medicaid to the original *Social Security Act* (1965), the creation of the Department of Housing and Urban Development (1965), the *Model Cities Program* (1966), the *Voting Rights Act* (1965), and the *Fair Housing Act* (1968).

The *Economic Opportunity Act* itself formally established a federal Office of Economic Opportunity (OEO) to ensure full implementation of the law's components. The director of the OEO was made responsible for the overall coordination of all antipoverty programs funded under the law and organized by both public and nonprofit entities. To assist with this wide management oversight, the law also established an ongoing Economic Opportunity Council of respected experts in their field. In order to maintain some level of state involvement and cooperation, the law likewise mandated the establishment of a local Office of Economic Development in each state under the direct supervision of the governor's office.

There were 11 main programs instituted under the *Economic Opportunity Act*, namely:

Assistance for Migrant Agricultural Employees – Funded state and local governments and nonprofit agencies for outreach services to migrant workers who needed assistance with housing, education, or child welfare.

Adult Basic Education – Provided grants to local neighborhood educational agencies to offer basic reading and writing competencies to adults to assist them in their search for employment.

Employment Investment Incentives – Offered small loans (as much as $25,000) to individuals who wished to be entrepreneurs and start their own small businesses.

Financial Assistance for Rural Families – Financed the distribution of small grants to rural families whose annual income fell below $2,500 annually.

Job Corps – Established residential centers in nonurban areas to provide basic education and work training skills for disadvantaged youths ages 16 to 21.

Neighborhood Youth Corps – Provided job training and employment in poor local neighborhoods for youth ages 16 to 21.

Urban and Rural Community Action – Arranged for technical and financial resources to be distributed to local public and nonprofit agencies with the goal of eradicating poverty. This program required the "maximum feasible

FIGURE 25.2   Job Corps training camp at Catoctin, Maryland.

participation" of neighborhood or area residents in the planning, development, and operations of any community action effort. Several notable examples of community action programs (CAP) were Head Start, Upward Bound, Neighborhood Legal Services, and Foster Grandparents.

Voluntary Assistance to Needy Children – Generated a national public relations campaign to encourage adults to provide voluntary services to needy children in communities throughout the nation.

Volunteers in Service to America (VISTA) – Created a national replica of the international Peace Corps program designed to enlist volunteer adults to assist local public and nonprofit agencies in their efforts to eradicate poverty.

Work Experience – Sponsored demonstration or pilot programs that offered work experience opportunities for unemployed adults so they could care for their families.

Work Study Programs – Arranged for grants to colleges and universities and part-time employment on campus for college students from low-income families.

Pro and con arguments relating to the final effectiveness of the *Economic Opportunity Act* and the success or failure of the War on Poverty continue even to the present day. In summary, these varying opinions can be summarized as follows:

> Despite its stated mandate, the federal OEO and the Economic Opportunity Council failed to adequately coordinate all of the antipoverty programs because

FIGURE 25.3   Operation Head Start at Webb School.

they were too actively involved in directly operating specific programs, such as the Job Corps program.

Funding was not at a realistic level given the broad set of goals and objectives.

Funding was not closely monitored, which instigated unacceptable levels of inefficiency, corruption, and waste.

Financial resources were funneled strictly to cities and some rural areas, resulting in tensions between local mayors and state government officials.

The focus of the War on Poverty should have been on equal *results* for all people and not simply on such a vague principle as equal *opportunity*.

There existed only minimal job-related programs for adults, especially adult men.

Launching such an expansive endeavor called the "War on Poverty," with the implication that a complex social and economic condition could be easily "defeated," was naïve and ill-conceived.

Finally, the lack of adequate funding and total commitment to the War on Poverty was weakened, and even blocked, by the realities of this nation's involvement in a real, destructive, and expensive war in Vietnam.

Although certain program units funded by the original *Economic Opportunity Act* still exist today and are administered by various parts of the federal bureaucracy (e.g., Head Start, Volunteers in Service to America (VISTA), Job Corps, Upward Bound, and Foster Grandparents), the *Economic Opportunity Act* itself was slowly dismantled during the first year of the Nixon administration, starting in 1969. It was eventually repealed in 1981 by the Reagan administration and replaced by the existing Community Services Block Grant (CSBG) program, which is administered by individual states.

- For a video recording of President Johnson's State of the Union speech delivered to Congress in which he announced the War on Poverty and the Great Society, see https://www.youtube.com/watch?v=znQKueSDpvI.

Internet Sources for the Content of This Introduction Include:

http://wps.prenhall.com/wps/media/objects/751/769950/documents_library/eoa1964.htm
https://business.laws.com/economic-opportunity-act
http://www.encyclopedia.com/social-sciences-and-law/economics-business-and-labor/economics-terms-and-concepts/economic-0
http://www.ushistory.org/us/56e.asp
http://www.cafca.org/history
http://www.pbs.org/johngardner/chapters/4c.html
https://www.ncbi.nlm.nih.gov/pmc/articles/PMC4266933/
https://en.wikipedia.org/wiki/economic_opportunity_act_of_1964
https://en.wikipedia.org/wiki/great_society

Linkage to Social Welfare History (1950–1975)

Social welfare historical events for this time period include the following:

- United Nations diplomat Ralph Bunche is awarded the Nobel Peace Prize for his work mediating conflicts between Arabs and Jews in the Middle East, thus becoming the first African American to receive such an honor (1950).
- Social scientists David Riesman, Nathan Glazer, and Reuel Denney publish *The Lonely Crowd*, a study of how Americans are not overly interested in conformity with their fellow citizens (1950).
- Over the veto of President Harry Truman, the Congress passes the *Immigration and Naturalization Act* (also known as the McCarran–Walter Act), restricting the number of immigrants and redefining the criteria for admission to the United States (1952).
- Sexuality becomes public, with Marilyn Monroe starring in the publication of *Playboy* magazine and the release of films such as *The Moon Is Blue* (1953).
- The scourge of the childhood disease polio is eradicated in the United States with the introduction of a vaccine developed by Dr. Jonas Salk at the University of Pennsylvania (1954).
- The United States Supreme Court, in *Brown v. Board of Education*, effectively ends racial segregation in public schools across the nation (1954).
- Rosa Parks, seated in the white section of a Montgomery, Alabama, bus, refuses to give up her seat to a white man and is arrested, thus launching the Montgomery Bus Boycott partly led by the local Christian pastor, the Reverend Martin Luther King Jr. (1955).
- The Count Basie Orchestra becomes the first African American musical group to play in the famous Starlight Room at the Waldorf Astoria hotel in New York City (1957).
- Under the protection of federal troops and federalized Arkansas National Guardsmen, and in defiance of Arkansas Governor Orval Faubus, nine African American students are escorted into Little Rock Central High School through crowds of angry whites opposing school integration (1957).
- Economist John Kenneth Galbraith publishes *The Affluent Society*, which outlines the wide income disparities in America and calls for greater public resources for those who are disadvantaged (1958).
- The novel *Lady Chatterley's Lover* is publicly banned after being judged as obscene by the United States Postal Service (1959).
- Four African American students stage a nonviolent "sit-in" by refusing to move from their seats at the Woolworth's lunch counter in Greensboro, North Carolina (1960).
- The Food and Drug Administration approves the sale and use of the first contraceptive pill for women (1960).
- CBS television announcer Edward R. Murrow narrates the shocking exposé of the oppressive and dangerous working conditions of migrant agricultural workers in the film *Harvest of Shame* (1960).

- An integrated bus full of members of the Congress of Racial Equality (CORE) travels through Southern states testing the local segregation laws, with the result of the "Freedom Riders" being viciously attacked and arrested along the way. In one instance, Attorney General Robert Kennedy sends in 600 federal marshals to restore order in Montgomery, Alabama (1961).
- In *Engel v. Vitale*, the Supreme Court declares that the recitation of school-sponsored nondenominational prayer in public schools violates the establishment clause of the *First Amendment* to the *United States Constitution* (1962).
- Under the protection of federal marshals, college student James Meredith becomes the first African American student to enroll in the University of Mississippi (1962).
- Michael Harrington publishes *The Other America*, which dramatically exposes the widespread presence of poverty across both urban and rural America (1962).
- While in jail for leading a civil rights demonstration, Reverend King composes his *Letter from the Birmingham Jail*, which clarifies his commitment to nonviolent civil disobedience (1963).
- Singer and songwriter Bob Dylan captivates the audience in Newport, Rhode Island, with his songs of protest, such as *A Hard Rain's A-Gonna Fall, Talkin' John Birch Society Blues*, and *Blowin' in the Wind* (1963).
- Before a crowd of more than 200,000 civil rights proponents, standing in front of the Lincoln Memorial in Washington, DC, Reverend King delivers his celebrated "I Have a Dream" speech (1963).
- After extensive study by medical experts, the surgeon general of the United States declares that cigarettes are the main cause of lung cancer and bronchitis (1964).
- President Lyndon Johnson signs the *Civil Rights Act*, which bans racial discrimination in public accommodations, union activity, employment, and federally funded projects (1964).
- In the State of the Union address, President Johnson proposes the development of a "Great Society," which focuses on eradicating poverty and racial injustice (1965).
- President Johnson signs the *Voting Rights Act*, which protects all people, particularly minorities, in the exercise of their constitutional right to vote (1965).
- Reacting to reports of police brutality, African American residents of Watts, a neighborhood in Los Angeles, riot for several days, resulting in 34 deaths, more than 1,000 injuries, 4,000 arrests, and property damage of approximately $40 million (1965).
- President Johnson signs a series of noteworthy social welfare legislation, including the *Older Americans Act*, the *Elementary and Secondary Education Act* (ESEA), and the Medicare (Title XVIII) and Medicaid (Title XIX) amendments to the *Social Security Act* (1965).
- In the face of opposition from conservative religious and political leaders, the Department of Health, Education, and Welfare plans to spend $3.1 million on providing family planning services to low-income families (1966).

- In *Miranda v. Arizona*, the United States Supreme Court affirms the right of anyone arrested by police authorities to be told of their rights to remain silent and to be provided with a lawyer (1966).
- President Johnson signs the *Child Nutrition Act*, which provides federal funds to feed children from low-income families (1966).
- Detroit, similar to other American cities this summer, experiences bitter race riots due to unemployment, substandard housing, and general despair, resulting in the loss of life, injuries, and property damage of several hundred million dollars (1967).
- Reverend King, who is in Memphis, Tennessee, to assist with the strike of local garbage collectors, is assassinated at his motel. Riots break out in Chicago and other cities across the nation (1968).
- At the Olympics ceremony in Mexico City, African American medalists Tommie Smith and John Carlos, protesting the treatment of African Americans, accept their medals for the 200-meter dash by standing with their right black-gloved hands held aloft in a fist during the playing of *The Star-Spangled Banner* (1968).
- President Richard Nixon proposes his *Family Assistance Plan*, an innovative approach to public assistance that would essentially grant a guaranteed annual income to economically fragile families, but the plan is rejected by the United States Congress (1969).
- The Supreme Court allows the use of bussing and redistricting as valid tactics to attain greater racial integration in public school systems across the nation (1971).
- Journalists Gloria Steinem and Letty Cottin Pogrebin begin publishing a new feminist magazine simply titled *Ms.* (1972).
- The American Indian Movement, headed by Dennis Banks and Russell Means, suffers a setback with the forced removal of protestors at Wounded Knee, South Dakota (1973).
- The Supreme Court, invoking the principle of privacy, decides in *Roe v. Wade* that women have a constitutional right to terminate a pregnancy (1973).
- Court-ordered bussing to attain better racial integration within the Boston public school system causes disruptions and violence from white parents who oppose integrated bussing (1974).
- President Gerald Ford signs into law the *Housing and Community Development Act*, which creates the Community Development Block Grant program and the Section 8 Housing Choice Voucher program (1974).
- The United States Commission on Civil Rights reports that Southern public-school districts have achieved a higher rate of racial integration than have their Northern state counterparts (1975).

Note: For a more reflective and functional use of this list of contemporary social welfare historical events, see Question #5 under the **Questions for Further Research and Discussion** section (below).

Sources:

Daniel, C. (1989). *Chronicle of America*. Mt. Kisco, NY: Chronicle Publications.

Mercer, D. (2000). *Millennium year by year*. New York: Dorling Kindersley Publications.

Social welfare developments 1951–2000. (2011). Retrieved from https://socialwelfare.library.vcu.edu/events/1951-2000/

Primary Text Material

The Economic Opportunity Act of 1964

"... *TITLE II—URBAN AND RURAL COMMUNITY ACTION PROGRAMS*

PART A—GENERAL COMMUNITY ACTION PROGRAMS STATEMENT OF PURPOSE

SEC. 201. *The purpose of this part is to provide stimulation and incentive for urban and rural communities to mobilize their resources to combat poverty through community action programs.*

COMMUNITY ACTION PROGRAMS

SEC.202. *(a) The term "community action program" means a program—*

(1) which mobilizes and utilizes resources, public or private, of any urban or rural, or combined urban and rural, geographical area (referred to in this part as a "community"), including but not limited to a State, metropolitan area, county, city, town, multicity unit, or multicounty unit in an attack on poverty;

(2) which provides services, assistance, and other activities of sufficient scope and size to give promise of progress toward elimination of poverty or a cause or causes of poverty through developing employment opportunities, improving human performance, motivation, and productivity, or bettering the conditions under which people live, learn, and work;

(3) which is developed, conducted, and administered with the maximum feasible participation of residents of the areas and members of the groups served; and

(4) which is conducted, administered, or coordinated by a public or private nonprofit agency (other than a political party), or a combination thereof...

... *TITLE III—SPECIAL PROGRAMS TO COMBAT POVERTY IN RURAL AREAS*

STATEMENT OF PURPOSE

SEC. 301. *It is the purpose of this title to meet some of the special problems of rural poverty and thereby to raise and maintain the income and living standards of low-income rural families and migrant agricultural employees and their families.*

PART A—AUTHORITY TO MAKE GRANTS AND LOANS

SEC. 302. *(a) The Director is authorized to make—*

(1) loans having a maximum maturity of 15 years and in amounts not exceeding $2,500 in the aggregate to any low income rural family where, in the

Continued

judgment of the Director, such loans have a reasonable possibility of effecting a permanent increase in the income of such families by assisting or permitting them to—

(A) acquire or improve real estate or reduce encumbrances or erect improvements thereon,

(B) operate or improve the operation of farms not larger than family sized, including but not limited to the purchase of feed, seed, fertilizer, livestock, poultry, and equipment, or

(C) participate in cooperative associations; and/or to finance nonagricultural enterprises which will enable such families to supplement their income.

(b) Loans under this section shall be made only if the family is not qualified to obtain such funds by loan under other Federal programs . . .

. . . TITLE VI—ADMINISTRATION AND COORDINATION . . .

SEC. 603. (a) The Director is authorized to recruit, select, train, and—

(1) upon request of State or local agencies or private nonprofit organizations, refer volunteers to perform duties in furtherance of programs combating poverty at a State or local level; and

(2) in cooperation with other Federal, State, or local agencies involved, assign volunteers to work (A) in meeting the health, education, welfare, or related needs of Indians living on reservations, of migratory workers and their families, or of residents of the District of Columbia, the Commonwealth of Puerto Rico, Guam, American Samoa, the Virgin Islands, or the Trust Territory of the Pacific Islands; (B) in the care and rehabilitation of the mentally ill or mentally retarded under treatment at nonprofit mental health or mental retardation facilities assisted in their construction or operation by Federal funds; and (C) in furtherance of programs or activities authorized or supported under title I or II of this Act . . ."

Source and full text available at https://www.gpo.gov/fdsys/pkg/STATUTE-78/pdf/STATUTE-78-Pg508.pdf.

Timeline of General Events in History, the Humanities, and Science During This Period (1950–1975)

These general historical events may help you understand more clearly the overall historical context during which the primary document was created.

- Wisconsin Senator Joseph McCarthy claims he has a "list" of more than 200 known subversive Communist agents working within the U.S. State Department, thus igniting a period of fierce anti-Communist investigations within the federal government (1950).
- North Korea crosses the 38th parallel line and invades South Korea, prompting the beginning of United States involvement in the Korean War (1950).

- The first formal credit card is launched by the Diners Club in cardboard format with a list of the 28 participating restaurants on the back (1950).
- Maine Republican Senator Margaret Chase Smith, the first woman elected to serve in both Houses of Congress denounces the discrediting of individuals and fear tactics used by fellow-Republican, Wisconsin Senator Joseph McCarthy (1950).
- The United States detonates its first thermonuclear device, referred to as the "H-bomb," which is more destructive than the atomic bomb used to end World War II (1952).
- Accused Russian spies Julius and Ethel Rosenberg are executed for espionage at Sing Sing Prison in New York, amid controversy over their innocence (1953).
- The Eisenhower administration proposes constructing a massive federal interstate highway system to connect individuals and "farm-to-table" enterprises across the nation (1954).
- President Eisenhower pledges support to South Vietnam in its battle against insurgent Communist forces and authorizes the sending of military advisers there (1955).
- Amid the growing popularity of performers such as Bill Haley and His Comets, Little Richard, Bo Diddley, Fats Domino, and Chuck Berry, some critics denounce the new rock 'n' roll music genre, claiming it to be just as dangerous as drugs for teenagers (1955).
- Musician Leonard Bernstein opens his innovative musical play on a theme of ethnic diversity, *West Side Story*, on the Broadway stage (1957).
- American Airlines announces the first regular same-day air service between New York City and Los Angeles (1959).
- Alaska and Hawaii become the 49th and 50th states in the nation (1959).
- Massachusetts Senator John Kennedy, who is Catholic, is elected president of the United States (1960).
- In President Kennedy's inaugural address, he delivers his legendary "Ask not what your country can do for you—ask what you can do for your country" speech (1961).
- As part of his New Frontier initiative, President Kennedy establishes the Peace Corps, whose unpaid volunteers serve to assist the advancement of underdeveloped nations (1961).
- Lieutenant John Glenn becomes the first American to reach orbital flight around the earth after his *Friendship 7* blasts off from Cape Canaveral, Florida (1962).
- President Kennedy is murdered by assassin Harvey Lee Oswald in Dallas, Texas (1963).
- The musical group The Beatles make their first American appearance in New York City (1964).
- With more than 500,000 American troops on the ground, the Vietnam War increases in intensity and the loss of lives (1965).
- The Hollywood film *The Graduate*, starring Dustin Hoffman, challenges the young generation to question whether conformity to their older generation's expectations of them is truly worth the emotional price they will pay (1967).

- Israel defeats Egypt and other Arab allies in the Six-Day War, allowing it to fully occupy the city of Jerusalem, half of which had been under the control of Jordan (1967).
- In a radical departure from past precedent for journalists, CBS News anchor Walter Cronkite denounces the War in Vietnam as hopeless and immoral (1968).
- Senator Robert Kennedy is assassinated at the end of a Democratic campaign rally at the Ambassador Hotel in Los Angeles (1968).
- The Democratic Party, thoroughly divided into doves and hawks over the Vietnam War, holds its Democratic National Convention in Chicago and elects Hubert Humphrey over Eugene McCarthy as its candidate against Richard Nixon for president. Peaceful protests outside the convention center turn into anti-war riots and allegations are launched against the police for unnecessary brutality (1968).
- *The Smothers Brothers Comedy Hour* on CBS is canceled due to the allegation that much of Tommy and Dick Smothers' humor is anti-Vietnam War and disrespectful of governmental authority (1969).
- The Reverends Daniel and Philip Berrigan, along with members of the Catonsville Nine, are convicted in state court of destroying Selective Service draft records in Catonsville, Maryland (1969).
- With the transmitted words "Houston, Tranquility Base here. The Eagle has landed," astronaut Neil Armstrong reports to the world that he and fellow astronaut Edwin Aldrin Jr. have successfully landed on the moon (1969).
- The so-called Woodstock Nation of more than 400,000 music fans, advocating peace, drugs, and casual sex, meet for an iconic festival on Max Yasgur's farm outside Woodstock, New York (1969).
- Washington, DC is the site for the largest anti-war demonstration of more than 250,000 people in American history. The protestors march from the Capitol to the Washington Monument, while other anti-war demonstrations take at place at many universities because of their alleged financial connections with the Department of Defense (1969).
- Four unarmed students at Kent State University in Ohio die from shots fired by the Ohio National Guard during a student anti-war demonstration on campus (1970).
- Student strikes against the Vietnam War at more than 450 colleges and universities across America lead to canceled classes and disrupted commencement activities (1970).
- Citing the principle of the *First Amendment*, the Supreme Court ends the suspension of publication sought by the Nixon White House and decreed that the *New York Times*, the *Washington Post*, and other newspapers can continue to publish the full story behind *The Pentagon Papers*, which revealed that Defense Secretary McNamara questioned the progression and the likely success of the Vietnam War (1971).
- The Vietnam War technically ends with the signing of a cease-fire agreement by representatives of Vietnam and the United States (1973).

- Reacting to the threat of impeachment due to his reaction to the Watergate conflict, President Richard Nixon resigns from office in disgrace. Vice President Gerald Ford assumes the presidency, and, within a month, pardons former President Nixon of all crimes committed (1974).
- Following the unconditional surrender of the South Vietnamese military to the Viet Cong army, the last American troops, along with several thousand South Vietnamese allies, are evacuated by helicopter, under duress, from Saigon (1975).

Sources:

Daniel, C. (1989). *Chronicle of America*. Mt. Kisco, NY: Chronicle Publications.
Events of the 20th century. https://en.wikipedia.org/wiki/timeline_of_the_20th_century
Mercer, D. (2000). *Millennium year by year*. New York: Dorling Kindersley Publications.

Questions for Further Research and Discussion

1. Skim through the entire text of the *Economic Opportunity Act*, then summarize the values and attitudes toward poverty that you find in the text. Note whether these values and attitudes are still current in current society. Why or why not?
2. Choose one of the other programs listed under the Great Society of the Johnson administration listed above. Conduct further research on that program, then summarize what you have discovered.
3. Conduct further Internet research on the community action programs (CAP) that were funded under the *Economic Opportunity Act*. Summarize why some of them became so controversial that they were eventually eliminated. Provide specific examples of your findings.
4. Based on the primary documentary material presented here, as well as other material you discover in the **Additional Selected References** at the end of this chapter, what additional federal policy or policies do you believe should have been developed or changed at that time? Describe those policies in detail. Recall that a policy could be either *legislative* (i.e., a law), *judicial* (i.e., a court decision), or *administrative* (i.e., an executive or organizational policy) in nature.
5. Select three events appearing under the **Linkage to Social Welfare** section (above), conduct further Internet research regarding them, then conclude whether you believe there exists any plausible relationship between the *Economic Opportunity Act* and the events you have chosen. Use the analytical model presented in Appendix 1 of this book, or develop your own analytical model, to draw these conclusions.
6. Select one book from the **Additional Selected References** list at the end of this chapter. Briefly read through it, then summarize the main points contained in the book. Identify your own personal reaction to this book.

Additional Selected References

Bailey, M. J., & Danziger, S. (Eds.). (2013). *Legacies of the War on Poverty*. New York: Russell Sage Foundation.

Farmbry, K. (Ed.). (2014). *The war on poverty: A retrospective*. Lanham, MD: Lexington Books.

Harrington, M. (1963). *The other America: Poverty in the United States*. New York: The Macmillan Company.

Harrington, M. (1984). *The new American poverty*. New York: Viking Penguin.

Kershaw, J. A. (970). *Government against poverty*. Washington, DC: Brookings Institution.

Moynihan, D. P. (1969). *Maximum feasible misunderstanding*. New York: The Free Press.

Orleck, A., & Hazirjian, L. G. (2011). *The war on poverty: A new grassroots history, 1964—1980*. Athens: University of Georgia Press.

Stricker, F. (2007). *Why America lost the war on poverty—and how to win it*. Chapel Hill: University of North Carolina Press.

Sundquist, J. L. (1969). *On fighting poverty*. New York: Basic Books.

United States. (1964). *Economic Opportunity Act of 1964: Hearings before the Subcommittee on the War on Poverty Program of the Committee on Education and Labor, House of Representatives, Eighty-eighth Congress, second session, on H. R. 10440, a bill to mobilize the human and financial resources of the nation to combat poverty in the United States*. Washington, DC: United States Government Printing Office.

Credits

Fig. 25.1: Source: http://www.lbjlibrary.net/collections/photo-archive.html.

Fig. 25.2: Source: http://www.loc.gov/pictures/item/2016647260/.

Fig. 25.3: Source: http://www.loc.gov/pictures/item/2016647284/.

Chapter 26

Discrimination Further Challenged

The *Civil Rights Act* (1964) and the *Voting Rights Act* (1965)

Introduction

The *Civil Rights Act* of 1964

Initially proposed by President John Kennedy, then advanced by President Lyndon Johnson after President Kennedy's assassination, the *Civil Rights Act* of 1964 endures as a monumental piece of federal legislation that countered racial segregation and oppression in the United States. As an overview, this law prohibited the segregation of people based on their race, color, religion, sex, or national origin in all public activities. Furthermore, it outlawed discrimination on the same bases in all forms of employment.

Following the end of the Civil War in 1865, slavery was prohibited across America and African American males received the right to vote. However, in Southern states (mostly), the oppression of African American men and women continued relentlessly. African Americans were constrained by the notorious *Jim Crow* laws that continued to enforce racial segregation policies in business, education, religion, transportation, and social interactions. Access to voting was also essentially blocked by abusive strategies such as literacy tests, tests of moral character, requirement for land ownership, a "grandfather clause" that required proof that one's grandfather voted in the past, poll taxes, physical intimidation at polling places, risk of employment loss if voting rights were pursued, as well as the underlying threat of lynching by the ever-vigilant Ku Klux Klan for any kind of civil disobedience to the dictates of white Southern society.

These deplorable conditions for African American citizens endured well into the 20th century. President Harry Truman did, however, desegregate the Armed Services following World War II and was a vocal advocate against racial segregation and the activities of the Ku Klux Klan. Soon after that, in

FIGURE 26.1   President Lyndon Johnson signs the Civil Rights Act of 1964.

1957, President Dwight D. Eisenhower established a Commission on Civil Rights to study the issue of race relations in the United States and, as a result of that Commission's findings, a Civil Rights Division was established within the United States Department of Justice. These, unfortunately, were only small steps taken to eradicate the massive, long-standing, and institutionalized oppression of African Americans.

There were a series of events and movements during this period that began to raise many Americans' consciousness about race relations and social justice. In 1961, for example, integrated groups of civil rights activists, named "Freedom Riders," literally rode interstate busses throughout Southern states in order to highlight the refusal of many Southern areas to desegregate public busses, despite several court cases that ruled to the contrary. The horrendous 1963 bombing of the 16th Street Baptist Church in Birmingham, Alabama, in which four young African American girls were killed, also shook the nation for its cruelty and senselessness. Activist groups such as the Southern Christian Leadership Conference (SCLC) and the Student Nonviolent Coordinating Committee (SNCC) were formed and focused the nation's attention during this period on the racial injustices being committed daily.

Probably the most determining factor that led to the passage of the *Civil Rights Act* of 1964 was the civil rights demonstrations in Birmingham, Alabama, in the spring of 1963. During a series of demonstrations, orchestrated initially by Reverend Martin Luther King Jr., peaceful marchers were set upon by snarling police dogs, high-pressure water cannons, and officers wielding police clubs. Graphic pictures and news accounts appeared in newspapers and on television across the nation, and the Kennedy administration had to intervene to help restore order.

After overcoming a long filibuster by senators from Southern states, the final law declared that any type of physical segregation based on race, color, religion, sex, or national origin was illegal in all places of public accommodation. This included, among other environments, courthouses, parks, places of worship, bus stations and busses, train stations and trains, restaurants, theaters, concerts, hotels, and even water fountains.

The *Civil Rights Act* of 1964 further prohibited discrimination in all aspects of employment, including hiring, firing, promoting, training, harassment, pay scales, and benefit packages. Finally, the law created the establishment of the Equal Employment Opportunity Commission (EEOC) to administer the law and to process any complaints of nonconformity. Over time, the "sex" category was expanded to include pregnancy, gender identity, or sexual orientation; the "age" category was specified to be "40 or older;" and a new category, "disability," was added.

- For a brief, three-minute visual summary of the development of the *Civil Rights Act* of 1964, see http://www.history.com/topics/black-history/civil-rights-act.

Internet Sources for the Content of This Part of the Introduction Include:
https://www.nps.gov/articles/civil-rights-act.htm
https://www.archives.gov/education/lessons/civil-rights-ac
http://www.crf-usa.org/black-history-month/the-civil-rights-act-of-1964
https://en.wikipedia.org/wiki/civil_rights_act_of_1964

The *Voting Rights Act* of 1965
One year after the passage of the *Civil Rights Act* of 1964, Congress passed the *Voting Rights Act* of 1965. Similar to the enactment of the civil rights legislation, there were precipitating events that prompted the passage of this act. Specifically, what caught the nation's attention were murders of three young voting rights activists—James Earl Chaney, Andrew Goodman, and Michael Schwerner—in Philadelphia, Mississippi, sometime between June and August 1964, as well as the violent police attacks with tear gas and clubs, once again on peaceful demonstrators who were crossing the Edmund Pettus Bridge in Selma, Alabama, in March 1965 during a lawful march for equal voting rights. These two events apparently prompted President Johnson and Congress to overcome many Southern state legislators' resistance to any type of voting rights legislation.

As passed, the *Voting Rights Law* of 1965 prohibited the nationwide use of literacy tests that were commonly introduced as a means to prove African Americans were ineligible to vote. A so-called "literacy test" could involve impediments such as handing an African American voter a passage in Spanish or Greek and demanding an oral reading and translation or requiring that African American voters sign their names on a piece of

FIGURE 26.2 President Lyndon B. Johnson meets with Reverend Martin Luther King Jr. at the signing of the Voting Rights Act of 1965.

kitchen wax paper using a ballpoint pen. Successfully passing these outrageous literacy tests became impossible even for most college graduates.

The use of poll taxes for the same purpose of denying the right to vote were, unfortunately, not directly banned by this legislation. Instead, the United States Attorney General was commissioned to challenge the constitutionality of their use in federal court whenever and wherever they were discovered to be in effect. The attorney general was also authorized, in Section 5 of the *Voting Rights Act* of 1965, to monitor and administer, on a continuing basis, the voting procedures of any county where discriminatory patterns of voting rights had been uncovered. Specifically, that meant that in any area of the country that had a notorious history of discrimination involving voting rights, the attorney general must be contacted and must provide prior approval (i.e., preclearance) to any planned changes in any policy or procedure that impacted voting eligibility as well as the entire voting process itself. Finally, the *Voting Rights Act* of 1965 expanded full voting rights to any United States citizen who did not speak fluent English at the time of voting.

The consequences of the *Voting Rights Act* of 1965, both positive and negative, quickly became apparent. By 1968, for example, reports indicate that 60% of African American adults eligible to vote had been successfully registered. Other outcomes include: a marked increase in the number of African Americans elected to public office; a realignment of the Democratic and Republican political parties in the South, with many conservatives switching affiliation from Democrat to Republican; and the beginning of patterns of racial gerrymandering in which state voting district lines were changed so as to cluster African Americans together in a few districts, thereby diminishing the power of their vote.

In the 2013 the United States Supreme Court decision in *Shelby County v. Holder*, the Justices, with a 5–4 vote, weakened somewhat the strict requirements for preclearance of any changes identified in Section 5 of the *Voting Rights Act* of 1965. This landmark Supreme Court action abolished the formula upon which a state would be required to seek the attorney general's preapproval for any changes to voting rights laws. In essence, this means that the Supreme Court decided that no state can be required to seek preclearance for any variations on voting practices merely because that state has a history of discrimination. The attorney general, however, still holds the authority to actively pursue any alleged violation of the original *Voting Rights Act* of 1965, but that oversight process is no longer automatic because of past discriminatory practices.

+ For a short video summary of the *Voting Rights Act* of 1965, see: http://www.history.com/topics/black-history/voting-rights-act

Internet Sources for the Content of This Part of the Introduction Include:

http://www.history.com/topics/black-history/voting-rights-act
https://www.justice.gov/crt/history-federal-voting-rights-laws
http://civilrights.findlaw.com/other-constitutional-rights/the-voting-rights-act-of-1965-overview.html
https://en.wikipedia.org/wiki/voting_rights_act_of_1965
http://www.nytimes.com/interactive/2013/06/25/us/annotated-supreme-court-decision-on-voting-rights-act.html
https://en.wikipedia.org/wiki/shelby_county_v._holder

Linkage to Social Welfare History (1950-1975)

Social welfare historical events for this time period include the following:

+ United Nations diplomat Ralph Bunche is awarded the Nobel Peace Prize for his work mediating conflicts between Arabs and Jews in the Middle East, thus becoming the first African American to receive such an honor (1950).
+ Social scientists David Riesman, Nathan Glazer, and Reuel Denney publish *The Lonely Crowd*, a study of how Americans are not overly interested in conformity with their fellow citizens (1950).
+ Over the veto of President Harry Truman, the Congress passes the *Immigration and Naturalization Act* (also known as the McCarran–Walter Act), restricting the number of immigrants and redefining the criteria for admission to the United States (1952).

- Sexuality becomes public, with Marilyn Monroe starring in the publication of *Playboy* magazine and the release of films such as *The Moon Is Blue* (1953).
- The scourge of the childhood disease polio is eradicated in the United States with the introduction of a vaccine developed by Dr. Jonas Salk at the University of Pennsylvania (1954).
- The United States Supreme Court, in *Brown v. Board of Education*, effectively ends racial segregation in public schools across the nation (1954).
- Rosa Parks, seated in the white section of a Montgomery, Alabama, bus, refuses to give up her seat to a white man and is arrested, thus launching the Montgomery Bus Boycott partly led by the local Christian pastor, the Reverend Martin Luther King Jr. (1955).
- Following the merger of several allied groups, the National Association of Social Workers (NASW) is formally established (1955).
- The Count Basie Orchestra becomes the first African American musical group to play in the famous Starlight Room at the Waldorf Astoria hotel in New York City (1957).
- Under the protection of federal troops and federalized Arkansas National Guardsmen, and in defiance of Arkansas Governor Orval Faubus, nine African American students are escorted into Little Rock Central High School through crowds of angry whites opposing school integration (1957).
- Economist John Kenneth Galbraith publishes *The Affluent Society*, which outlines the wide income disparities in America and calls for greater public resources for those who are disadvantaged (1958).
- The novel *Lady Chatterley's Lover* is publicly banned after being judged as obscene by the United States Postal Service (1959).
- Four African American students stage a nonviolent "sit-in" by refusing to move from their seats at the Woolworth's lunch counter in Greensboro, North Carolina (1960).
- The Food and Drug Administration approves the sale and use of the first contraceptive pill for women (1960).
- CBS television announcer Edward R. Murrow narrates the shocking exposé of the oppressive and dangerous working conditions of migrant agricultural workers in the film *Harvest of Shame* (1960).
- An integrated bus full of members of the Congress of Racial Equality (CORE) travels through Southern states testing the local segregation laws, with the result of the "Freedom Riders" being viciously attacked and arrested along the way. In one instance, Attorney General Robert Kennedy sends in 600 federal marshals to restore order in Montgomery, Alabama (1961).
- In *Engel v. Vitale*, the Supreme Court declares that the recitation of school-sponsored nondenominational prayer in public schools violates the establishment clause of the *First Amendment* to the *United States Constitution* (1962).

- Under the protection of federal marshals, college student James Meredith becomes the first African American student to enroll in the University of Mississippi (1962).
- Michael Harrington publishes *The Other America*, which dramatically exposes the widespread presence of poverty across both urban and rural America (1962).
- While in jail for leading a civil rights demonstration, Reverend King composes his *Letter from the Birmingham Jail*, which clarifies his commitment to nonviolent civil disobedience (1963).
- Singer and songwriter Bob Dylan captivates the audience in Newport, Rhode Island, with his songs of protest, such as *A Hard Rain's A-Gonna Fall*, *Talkin' John Birch Society Blues*, and *Blowin' in the Wind* (1963).
- Before a crowd of more than 200,000 civil rights proponents, while standing in front of the Lincoln Memorial in Washington, DC, Reverend King delivers his celebrated "I Have a Dream" speech (1963).
- After extensive study by medical experts, the surgeon general of the United States declares that cigarettes are the main cause of lung cancer and bronchitis (1964).
- In order to engage in a "War on Poverty" President Lyndon Johnson signs the *Economic Opportunity Act* (1964).
- In the State of the Union address, President Johnson proposes the development of a "Great Society," which focuses on eradicating poverty and racial injustice (1965).
- Reacting to reports of police brutality, African American residents of Watts, a neighborhood in Los Angeles, riot for several days, resulting in 34 deaths, more than 1,000 injuries, 4,000 arrests, and property damage of approximately $40 million (1965).
- President Johnson signs a series of noteworthy social welfare legislation, including the *Older Americans Act*, the *Elementary and Secondary Education Act* (ESEA), and the Medicare (Title XVIII) and Medicaid (Title XIX) amendments to the *Social Security Act* (1965).
- In the face of opposition from conservative religious and political leaders, the Department of Health, Education, and Welfare plans to spend $3.1 million on providing family planning services to low-income families (1966).
- In *Miranda v. Arizona*, the United States Supreme Court affirms the right of anyone arrested by police authorities to be told of their rights to remain silent and to be provided with a lawyer (1966).
- President Johnson signs the *Child Nutrition Act*, which provides federal funds to feed children from low-income families (1966).
- Detroit, similar to other American cities this summer, experiences bitter race riots due to unemployment, substandard housing, and general despair, resulting in the loss of life, injuries, and property damage of several hundred million dollars (1967).
- Reverend King, who is in Memphis, Tennessee, to assist with the strike of local garbage collectors, is assassinated at his motel. Riots break out in Chicago and other cities across the nation (1968).

- At the Olympics ceremony in Mexico City, African American medalists Tommie Smith and John Carlos, protesting the treatment of African Americans, accept their medals for the 200-meter dash by standing with their right black-gloved hands held aloft in a fist during the playing of *The Star-Spangled Banner* (1968).
- President Richard Nixon proposes his *Family Assistance Plan*, an innovative approach to public assistance that would essentially grant a guaranteed annual income to economically fragile families, but the plan is rejected by the United States Congress (1969).
- The Supreme Court allows the use of bussing and redistricting as valid tactics to attain greater racial integration in public school systems across the nation (1971).
- Journalists Gloria Steinem and Letty Cottin Pogrebin begin publishing a new feminist magazine simply titled *Ms.* (1972).
- The American Indian Movement, headed by Dennis Banks and Russell Means, suffers a setback with the forced removal of protestors at Wounded Knee, South Dakota (1973).
- The Supreme Court, invoking the principle of privacy, decides in *Roe v. Wade* that women have a constitutional right to terminate a pregnancy (1973).
- Court-ordered bussing to attain better racial integration within the Boston public school system causes disruptions and violence from white parents who oppose integrated bussing (1974).
- President Gerald Ford signs into law the *Housing and Community Development Act*, which creates the Community Development Block Grant program and the Section 8 Housing Choice Voucher program (1974).
- The United States Commission on Civil Rights reports that Southern public-school districts have achieved a higher rate of racial integration than have their Northern state counterparts (1975).

Note: For a more reflective and functional use of this list of contemporary social welfare historical events, see Question #5 under the **Questions for Further Research and Discussion** section (below).

Sources:

Daniel, C. (1989). *Chronicle of America*. Mt. Kisco, NY: Chronicle Publications.

Mercer, D. (2000). *Millennium year by year*. New York: Dorling Kindersley Publications.

Social welfare developments 1951–2000. (2011). Retrieved from https://socialwelfare.library.vcu.edu/events/1951-2000/

> **Primary Text Material**

The *Civil Rights Act* of 1964

"... TITLE II—INJUNCTIVE RELIEF AGAINST DISCRIMINATION IN PLACES OF PUBLIC ACCOMMODATION

SEC. 201. (a) All persons shall be entitled to the full and equal enjoyment of the goods, services, facilities, and privileges, advantages, and accommodations of any place of public accommodation, as defined in this section, without discrimination or segregation on the ground of race, color, religion, or national origin . . .

TITLE IV—DESEGREGATION OF PUBLIC EDUCATION DEFINITIONS

SEC. 401. As used in this title—

(a) "Commissioner" means the Commissioner of Education.

(b) "Desegregation" means the assignment of students to public schools and within such schools without regard to their race, color, religion, or national origin, but "desegregation" shall not mean the assignment of students to public schools in order to overcome racial imbalance . . .

TITLE VII—EQUAL EMPLOYMENT OPPORTUNITY DEFINITIONS

SEC. 701. For the purposes of this title—

(a) The term "person" includes one or more individuals, labor unions, partnerships, associations, corporations, legal representatives, mutual companies, joint-stock companies, trusts, unincorporated organizations, trustees, trustees in bankruptcy, or receivers . . .

DISCRIMINATION BECAUSE OF RACE, COLOR, RELIGION, SEX, OR NATIONAL ORIGIN

SEC. 703. (a) It shall be an unlawful employment practice for an employer—

(1) to fail or refuse to hire or to discharge any individual, or otherwise to discriminate against any individual with respect to his compensation, terms, conditions, or privileges of employment, because of such individual's race, color, religion, sex, or national origin; or

(2) to limit, segregate, or classify his employees in any way which would deprive or tend to deprive any individual of employment opportunities or otherwise adversely affect his status as an employee, because of such individual's race, color, religion, sex, or national origin.

(b) It shall be an unlawful employment practice for an employment agency to fail or refuse to refer for employment, or otherwise to discriminate against, any individual because of his race, color, religion, sex, or national origin, or to classify or refer for employment any individual on the basis of his race, color, religion, sex, or national origin . . ."

Source and full text available at https://www.ourdocuments.gov/doc.php?flash=false&doc=97&page=transcript.

Continued

> ### The *Voting Rights Act* of 1965
>
> ... SEC. 2. No voting qualification or prerequisite to voting, or standard, practice, or procedure shall be imposed or applied by any State or political subdivision to deny or abridge the right of any citizen of the United States to vote on account of race or color.
>
> SEC. 3. (a) Whenever the Attorney General institutes a proceeding under any statute to enforce the guarantees of the fifteenth amendment in any State or political subdivision the court shall authorize the appointment of Federal examiners by the United States Civil Service Commission in accordance with section 6 to serve for such period of time and for such political subdivisions as the court shall determine is appropriate to enforce the guarantees of the fifteenth amendment (1) as part of any interlocutory order if the court determines that the appointment of such examiners is necessary to enforce such guarantees or (2) as part of any final judgment if the court finds that violations of the fifteenth amendment justifying equitable relief have occurred in such State or subdivision: Provided, That the court need not authorize the appointment of examiners if any incidents of denial or abridgement of the right to vote on account of race or color (1) have been few in number and have been promptly and effectively corrected by State or local action, (2) the continuing effect of such incidents has been eliminated, and (3) there is no reasonable probability of their recurrence in the future ... "
>
> Source and full text available at https://www.ourdocuments.gov/doc.php?flash=false&doc=100&page=transcript.

Timeline of General Events in History, the Humanities, and Science During This Period (1950–1975)

These general historical events may help you understand more clearly the overall historical context during which the primary document was created.

- Wisconsin Senator Joseph McCarthy claims he has a "list" of more than 200 known subversive Communists agents working within the U.S. State Department, thus igniting a period of fierce anti-Communist investigations within the federal government (1950).
- North Korea crosses the 38th parallel line and invades South Korea, prompting the beginning of United States involvement in the Korean War (1950).
- The first formal credit card is launched by the Diners Club in cardboard format with a list of the 28 participating restaurants listed on the back (1950).
- Maine Republican Senator Margaret Chase Smith, the first woman elected to serve in both Houses of Congress, denounces the discrediting of individuals and fear tactics used by fellow-Republican, Wisconsin Senator Joseph McCarthy (1950).

- The United States detonates its first thermonuclear device, referred to as the "H-bomb," which is more destructive than the atomic bomb used to end World War II (1952).
- Accused Russian spies Julius and Ethel Rosenberg are executed for espionage at Sing Sing Prison in New York, amid controversy over their innocence (1953).
- The Eisenhower administration proposes constructing a massive federal interstate highway system to connect individuals and "farm-to-table" enterprises across the nation (1954).
- President Eisenhower pledges support to South Vietnam in its battle against insurgent Communist forces and authorizes the sending of military advisers there (1955).
- Amid the growing popularity of performers such as Bill Haley and His Comets, Little Richard, Bo Diddley, Fats Domino, and Chuck Berry, some critics denounce the new rock 'n' roll music genre, claiming it to be just as dangerous as drugs for teenagers (1955).
- Musician Leonard Bernstein opens his innovative musical play on a theme of ethnic diversity, *West Side Story*, on the Broadway stage (1957).
- American Airlines announces that the first regular same-day air service between New York City and Los Angeles (1959).
- Alaska and Hawaii become the 49th and 50th states in the nation (1959).
- Massachusetts Senator John Kennedy, who is Catholic, is elected president of the United States (1960).
- In President Kennedy's inaugural address, he delivers his legendary "Ask not what your country can do for you—ask what you can do for your country" speech (1961).
- As part of his New Frontier initiative, President Kennedy establishes the Peace Corps, whose unpaid volunteers serve to assist the advancement of underdeveloped nations (1961).
- Lieutenant John Glenn becomes the first American to reach orbital flight around the earth after his *Friendship 7* blasts off from Cape Canaveral, Florida (1962).
- President Kennedy is murdered by assassin Harvey Lee Oswald in Dallas, Texas (1963).
- The musical group The Beatles make their first American appearance in New York City (1964).
- With more than 500,000 American troops on the ground, the Vietnam War increases in intensity and the loss of lives (1965).
- The Hollywood film *The Graduate*, starring Dustin Hoffman, challenges the young generation to question whether conformity to their older generation's expectations of them is truly worth the emotional price they will pay (1967).
- Israel defeats Egypt and other Arab allies in the Six-Day War, allowing it to fully occupy the entire city of Jerusalem, half of which had been under the control of Jordan (1967).

- In a radical departure from past precedent for journalists, CBS News anchor Walter Cronkite denounces the War in Vietnam as hopeless and immoral (1968).
- Senator Robert Kennedy is assassinated at the end of a Democratic campaign rally at the Ambassador Hotel in Los Angeles (1968).
- The Democratic Party, thoroughly divided into doves and hawks over the Vietnam War, holds its Democratic National Convention in Chicago and elects Hubert Humphrey over Eugene McCarthy as its candidate against Richard Nixon for president. Peaceful protests outside the convention center turn into anti-war riots, and allegations are launched against the police for unnecessary brutality (1968).
- *The Smothers Brothers Comedy Hour* on CBS is canceled due to the allegation that much of Tommy and Dick Smothers' humor is anti-Vietnam War and disrespectful of governmental authority (1969).
- The Reverends Daniel and Philip Berrigan, along with members of the Catonsville Nine, are convicted in state court of destroying Selective Service draft records in Catonsville, Maryland (1969).
- With the transmitted words "Houston, Tranquility Base here. The Eagle has landed," astronaut Neil Armstrong reports to the world that he and fellow astronaut Edwin Aldrin Jr. have successfully landed on the moon (1969).
- The so-called Woodstock Nation of more than 400,000 music fans, advocating peace, drugs, and casual sex, meet for an iconic festival on Max Yasgur's farm outside Woodstock, New York (1969).
- Washington, DC is the site for the largest anti-war demonstration of more than 250,000 people in American history. The protestors march from the Capitol to the Washington Monument, while other anti-war demonstrations take at place at many universities because of their alleged financial connections with the Department of Defense (1969).
- Four unarmed students at Kent State University in Ohio die from shots fired by the Ohio National Guard during a student anti-war demonstration on campus (1970).
- Student strikes against the Vietnam War at more than 450 colleges and universities across America lead to canceled classes and disrupted commencement activities (1970).
- Citing the principle of the *First Amendment*, the Supreme Court ends the suspension of publication sought by the Nixon White House and decreed that the *New York Times*, the *Washington Post*, and other newspapers can continue to publish the full story behind *The Pentagon Papers*, which revealed that Defense Secretary McNamara questioned the progression and the likely success of the Vietnam War (1971).
- The Vietnam War technically ends with the signing of a cease-fire agreement by representatives of Vietnam and the United States (1973).
- Reacting to the threat of impeachment due to his reaction to the Watergate conflict, President Richard Nixon resigns from office in disgrace. Vice President Gerald Ford assumes the presidency, and, within a month, pardons former President Nixon of all crimes committed (1974).

- Following the unconditional surrender of the South Vietnamese military to the Viet Cong army, the last American troops, along with several thousand South Vietnamese allies, are evacuated by helicopter, under duress, from Saigon (1975).

Sources:

Daniel, C. (1989). *Chronicle of America*. Mt. Kisco, NY: Chronicle Publications.
Events of the 20th century. https://en.wikipedia.org/wiki/timeline_of_the_20th_century
Mercer, D. (2000). *Millennium year by year*. New York: Dorling Kindersley Publications.

Questions for Further Research and Discussion

1. Skim through the entire text of either the *Civil Rights Act* or the *Voting Rights Act*, then summarize your reactions, whether negative or positive, to the facts and attitudes being presented.
2. Conduct further research on the later reauthorizations and developments (i.e., after 1964) of the *Civil Rights Act*, then summarize what those later changes did to the original law.
3. Conduct further research on the later reauthorizations and developments (i.e., after 1965) of the *Voting Rights Act*, then summarize what those later changes did to the original law.
4. Based on the primary documentary material presented here, as well as other material you discover in the **Additional Selected References** at the end of this chapter, what other federal policy or policies do you believe should have been developed or changed at that time? Describe those policies in detail. Recall that a policy could be either *legislative* (i.e., a law), *judicial* (i.e., a court decision), or *administrative* (i.e., an executive or organizational policy) in nature.
5. Select three events appearing under the **Linkage to Social Welfare** section (above), conduct further Internet research regarding them, then conclude whether you believe there exists any plausible relationship between the *Civil Rights Act* and/or the *Voting Rights Act* and the events you have chosen. Use the analytical model presented in Appendix 1 of this book, or develop your own analytical model, to draw these conclusions.
6. Select one book from the **Additional Selected References** list at the end of this chapter. Briefly read through it, then summarize the main points contained in the book. Identify your own personal reaction to this book.

Additional Selected References

Ball, H., Krane, D., & Lauth, T. P. (1982). *Compromised compliance: Implementation of the 1965 Voting Rights Act*. Westport, CT: Greenwood Press.

Garrow, D. J. (1978). *Protest at Selma: Martin Luther King Jr. and the Voting Rights Act of 1965.* New Haven, CT: Yale University Press.

Grofman, B. (2000). *Legacies of the 1964 Civil Rights Act.* Charlottesville, VA: University Press of Virginia.

Gold, S. D. (2011). *The Civil Rights Act of 1964.* New York: Marshall Cavendish Benchmark.

Hudson, D. M. (1998). *Along racial lines: Consequences of the 1965 Voting Rights Act.* New York: Peter Lang Publishing Group.

Landsberg, B. K. (2007). *Free at last to vote: The Alabama origins of the 1965 Voting Rights Act.* Lawrence, KS: University Press of Kansas.

Loevy, R. D. (1997). *The Civil Rights Act of 1964: The passage of the law that ended racial segregation.* New York: State University of the New York Press.

Mayer, R. (Ed.). (2004). *The Civil Rights Act of 1964.* San Diego: Greenhaven Publishing.

Purdum, T. S. (2014). *An idea whose time has come: Two presidents, two parties, and the battle for the Civil Rights Act of 1964.* New York: Henry Holt and Company.

U.S. Nuclear Regulatory Commission. (2009). *Your rights under Title VI of the Civil Rights Act of 1964.* Washington, DC: U.S. Nuclear Regulatory Commission. Available at http://purl.fdlp.gov/GPO/gpo81280

Zeitz, J. (2018). *Building the great society: Inside Lyndon Johnson's White House.* New York: Viking.

Credits

Fig. 26.1: Source: https://commons.wikimedia.org/wiki/File:Civil_Rights_Act_signing_LBJ.jpg.

Fig. 26.2: Source: https://commons.wikimedia.org/wiki/File:Lyndon_Johnson_and_Martin_Luther_King,_Jr._-_Voting_Rights_Act.jpg.

Chapter 27

Equality in Juvenile Justice

In re[1] *Gault*, 387 U.S. 1 (1967)

Introduction

In Colonial America and up through most of the 19th century, the American court system was based primarily on English Law principles. This heritage assumed a distinction only between those classified as "infants" and those classified as "adults" in terms of culpability for committing crimes and receiving a punitive sentence for these illegal acts. "Infants" were generally assumed to be anyone 7 years or age and younger, and it was commonly accepted that they could not be held responsible before any court for criminal activity. "Adults" were defined as anyone 14 years of age and older who would be responsible for any unlawful act and, therefore, subject to conviction and punishment for crimes. Young people between 7 and 14 years of age were in a "gray zone" of responsibility, but it was universally assumed that, depending on the situation, they still could be tried as adults and convicted of crimes, thereby unofficially placing them in the "adult" category. Youth between 7 and 14, then, could even be sentenced to death after being convicted of murder.

Changes gradually began to surface in some large urban areas during the 19th century. Social reformers in New York City, for example, established a House of Refuge for adolescent offenders in 1825. In Chicago, child welfare advocates opened the Chicago Reform School in 1855. This new model quickly spread to several other states by the end of the century. Other innovations in juvenile justice, such as out-of-home placements and probation, augmented the reform school model. These new progressive institutions allowed for the separation of youthful offenders into their own specialized facilities,

---

[1] *In re* is a formal legal term that means simply "concerning," "in reference to," or "in the matter of."

thereby separating them from adult offenders. The motivation for treating adolescents in these facilities was rehabilitative and therapeutic rather than punitive as it was in adult facilities.

The environment dramatically changed in 1899 with the opening of the first separate juvenile court in Chicago. Its establishment was initiated by philanthropist Lucy Flower, working with social reformers such as Jane Addams and Julia Lathrop and others who were concerned that too many children were being treated by the criminal courts a "mini-adults" and subjected to harsh punishments. Other states quickly established similar juvenile courts that removed children and adolescents from the criminal court system and placed over them a blanket of protection and oversight by court officials and human services personnel. However, what started in 1899 as a well-intentioned innovation in child welfare became a system that too often led to an oppressive bureaucracy that denied some basic rights to adolescent offenders by the 1960s. And thus emerged the *Gault* Supreme Court decision in 1967.

FIGURE 27.1   A proposed "cure" for juvenile delinquency in the slums is planned housing.

Gerald Gault was a 15-year-old teenager living with his family in Phoenix, Arizona. On June 8, 1964, Gault and a friend, Ronald Lewis, were accused by a neighbor, Mrs. Cook, of making an obscene telephone call to her. In her words, Gault "talked dirty to me." Following her complaint to the Gila County Sheriff's Office, both Gault and Lewis were arrested and transferred to the local children's detention center. Gault was already on probationary status for his presence during a robbery by another friend of a woman's wallet.

At the time of his arrest, both of Gault's parents were at work. The arresting officer did not try to contact either of them, nor did the officer leave a note at their home explaining the arrest. Once the parents learned of their son's arrest from Lewis's parents, they went to the children's detention center, where they were told an informal hearing would be held the next day. They were not provided with a petition for arrest, nor was any lawyer present.

At the hearing, Mrs. Cook was not present, no transcript was made of the proceedings, and no one was sworn in under oath to testify. The judge simply heard testimony from the Sheriff's Office and then questioned Gault, who denied the charge and indicated that his friend, Lewis, had actually made the telephone call to Mrs. Cook from his home telephone. There arose differences of opinion as to what exactly was said at this informal hearing. Gault was then remanded to the Gila County juvenile center. He was released three days later, without any explanation, and a formal hearing was set for June 15, 1964.

At this second hearing, again Mrs. Cook was not present, no transcript was recorded, no lawyer was present, and conflicts continued over what was said. Following this hearing, a probation officer filed a report alleging that Gault made the obscene telephone call.

For this offense, Gault was charged with being a juvenile delinquent and committed to the Arizona State Industrial School until his 21st birthday. The crime of making obscene telephone calls, if committed by an adult, would have resulted in a maximum sentence of two months in jail and a $50 fine.

Because Arizona law did not allow any appeal of a juvenile court decision, Gault's parents appealed the decision to the Superior Court of Arizona and then to the Arizona Supreme Court by filing a *habeas corpus* petition.[1] This type of petition contested the constitutionality of the juvenile court decision on the basis that it denied Gault the basic principles guaranteed by the due process clause of the *Fifth* and *Fourteenth Amendments* to the *United States Constitution*. Both Arizona courts dismissed the *habeas corpus* petition, so the parents then appealed the case to the United States Supreme Court. While these events unfolded, Gault remained in the Arizona State Industrial School.

The United States Supreme Court decided, with an 8–1 majority, on March 18, 1967, that the decision of the Arizona juvenile court was a violation of the *Fourteenth Amendment* to the *United States Constitution*. Justice Abe Fortas wrote the majority opinion for

---

1 *Habeas corpus* is a formal legal term that means, literally, "you have the body."

FIGURE 27.2   Supreme Court Justice Abe Fortas.

the court, and Justice Potter Stewart added the only dissenting opinion. Explicitly, the Supreme Court declared that Gault and his parents were denied:

- Adequate notification of specific charges
- Information as to his right to an attorney
- The ability to confront and cross-examine the complainant at a formal hearing
- The safeguards to prevent self-incrimination
- The right to a full transcript of the proceedings
- The right to an appellate review

In summary, the United States Supreme Court decided that the *Fourteenth Amendment* applies equally to juvenile defendants as it does to adults. This ruling has had a profound practical effect on how juvenile court cases are processed as well as how juvenile offenders receive social services when they are placed on an aftercare status in their home communities. This ruling severely limited the power of youth probation and youth parole officers to return a youthful offender to a secure facility, such as a youth detention center, training center, or reform school with simply an internal administrative hearing involving agency personnel. As a result of *In re Gault*, any formal attempt to remove a youth who is under aftercare supervision from his or her community now demands a full judicial hearing in a local family court with parents, defense counsel, and a judge present.

In a 2007 National Public Radio interview featuring Gault himself, it was reported that Gault, upon his release from the Arizona State Industrial School, finished high school and worked successfully in several types of employment into his young adulthood. He then spent 23 years in military service and was pursuing a teaching certificate at the time of his interview.

Internet Sources for the Content of This Introduction:

http://www.uscourts.gov/educational-resources/educational-activities/facts-and-case-summary-re-gault

https://www.oyez.org/cases/1966/116

https://supreme.justia.com/cases/federal/us/387/1/case.html

https://www.americanbar.org/publications/insights_on_law_andsociety/16/winter2016/lessonplan_inregault.html

https://en.wikipedia.org/wiki/in_re_gault

https://www.npr.org/templates/story/story.php?storyid=10279166

https://www.americanbar.org/content/dam/aba/migrated/publiced/features/dyjpart1.authcheckdam.pdf

FIGURE 27.3   Supreme Court Justice Potter Stewart.

Linkage to Social Welfare History (1950–1975)

Social welfare historical events for this time period include the following:

- United Nations diplomat Ralph Bunche is awarded the Nobel Peace Prize for his work mediating conflicts between Arabs and Jews in the Middle East, thus becoming the first African American to receive such an honor (1950).
- Social scientists David Riesman, Nathan Glazer, and Reuel Denney publish *The Lonely Crowd*, a study of how Americans are not overly interested in conformity with their fellow citizens (1950).
- Over the veto of President Harry Truman, the Congress passes the *Immigration and Naturalization Act* (also known as the McCarran–Walter Act), restricting the number of immigrants and redefining the criteria for admission to the United States (1952).
- Sexuality becomes public, with Marilyn Monroe starring in the publication of *Playboy* magazine and the release of films such as *The Moon Is Blue* (1953).
- The scourge of the childhood disease polio is eradicated in the United States with the introduction of a vaccine developed by Dr. Jonas Salk at the University of Pennsylvania (1954).
- The United States Supreme Court, in *Brown v. Board of Education*, effectively ends racial segregation in public schools across the nation (1954).
- Rosa Parks, seated in the white section of a Montgomery, Alabama, bus, refuses to give up her seat to a white man and is arrested, thus launching the Montgomery

- Bus Boycott partly led by the local Christian pastor, the Reverend Martin Luther King Jr. (1955).
- Following the merger of several allied groups, the National Association of Social Workers (NASW) is formally established (1955).
- The Count Basie Orchestra becomes the first African American musical group to play in the famous Starlight Room at the Waldorf Astoria hotel in New York City (1957).
- Under the protection of federal troops and federalized Arkansas National Guardsmen, and in defiance of Arkansas Governor Orval Faubus, nine African American students are escorted into Little Rock Central High School through crowds of angry whites opposing school integration (1957).
- Economist John Kenneth Galbraith publishes *The Affluent Society*, which outlines the wide income disparities in America and calls for greater public resources for those who are disadvantaged (1958).
- The novel *Lady Chatterley's Lover* is publicly banned after being judged as obscene by the United States Postal Service (1959).
- Four African American students stage a non-violent "sit-in" by refusing to move from their seats at the Woolworth's lunch counter in Greensboro, North Carolina (1960).
- The Food and Drug Administration approves the sale and use of the first contraceptive pill for women (1960).
- CBS television announcer Edward R. Murrow narrates the shocking exposé of the oppressive and dangerous working conditions of migrant agricultural workers in the film *Harvest of Shame* (1960).
- An integrated bus full of members of the Congress of Racial Equality (CORE) travels through Southern states testing the local segregation laws, with the result of the "Freedom Riders" being viciously attacked and arrested along the way. In one instance, Attorney General Robert Kennedy sends in 600 federal marshals to restore order in Montgomery, Alabama (1961).
- In *Engel v. Vitale*, the Supreme Court declares that the recitation of school-sponsored nondenominational prayer in public schools violates the establishment clause of the *First Amendment* to the *United States Constitution* (1962).
- Under the protection of federal marshals, college student James Meredith becomes the first African American student to enroll in the University of Mississippi (1962).
- Michael Harrington publishes *The Other America*, which dramatically exposes the widespread presence of poverty across both urban and rural America (1962).
- While in jail for leading a civil rights demonstration, Reverend Martin Luther King composes his *Letter from the Birmingham Jail*, which clarifies his commitment to nonviolent civil disobedience (1963).
- Singer and songwriter Bob Dylan captivates the audience in Newport, Rhode Island, with his songs of protest, such as *A Hard Rain's A-Gonna Fall, Talkin' John Birch Society Blues*, and *Blowin' in the Wind* (1963).

- Before a crowd of more than 200,000 civil rights proponents, standing in front of the Lincoln Memorial in Washington, DC, Reverend King delivers his celebrated "I Have a Dream" speech (1963).
- After extensive study by medical experts, the surgeon general of the United States declares that cigarettes are the main cause of lung cancer and bronchitis (1964).
- President Lyndon Johnson signs the *Civil Rights Act*, which bans racial discrimination in public accommodations, union activity, employment, and federally funded projects (1964).
- In order to engage in a "War on Poverty," President Johnson signs the *Economic Opportunity Act* (1964).
- In the State of the Union address, President Johnson proposes the development of a "Great Society," which focuses on eradicating poverty and racial injustice (1965).
- President Johnson signs the *Voting Rights Act*, which protects all people, particularly minorities, in the exercise of their constitutional right to vote (1965).
- Reacting to reports of police brutality, African American residents of Watts, a neighborhood in Los Angeles, riot for several days, resulting in 34 deaths, more than 1,000 injuries, 4,000 arrests, and property damage of approximately $40 million (1965).
- President Johnson signs a series of noteworthy social welfare legislation, including the *Older Americans Act*, the *Elementary and Secondary Education Act* (ESEA), and the Medicare (Title XVIII) and Medicaid (Title XIX) amendments to the *Social Security Act* (1965).
- In the face of opposition from conservative religious and political leaders, the Department of Health, Education, and Welfare plans to spend $3.1 million on providing family planning services to low-income families (1966).
- In *Miranda v. Arizona*, the United States Supreme Court affirms the right of anyone arrested by police authorities to be told of their rights to remain silent and to be provided with a lawyer (1966).
- President Johnson signs the *Child Nutrition Act*, which provides federal funds to feed children from low-income families (1966).
- Detroit, similar to other American cities this summer, experiences bitter race riots due to unemployment, substandard housing, and general despair, resulting in the loss of life, injuries, and property damage of several hundred million dollars (1967).
- Reverend Martin Luther King, who is in Memphis, Tennessee, to assist with the strike of local garbage collectors, is assassinated at his motel. Riots break out in Chicago and other cities across the nation (1968).
- At the Olympics ceremony in Mexico City, African American medalists Tommie Smith and John Carlos, protesting the treatment of African Americans, accept their medals for the 200-meter dash by standing with their right black-gloved hands held aloft in a fist during the playing of *The Star-Spangled Banner* (1968).
- President Richard Nixon proposes his *Family Assistance Plan*, an innovative approach to public assistance that would essentially grant a guaranteed annual

income to economically fragile families, but the plan is rejected by the United States Congress (1969).
- The Supreme Court allows the use of bussing and redistricting as valid tactics to attain greater racial integration in public school systems across the nation (1971).
- Journalists Gloria Steinem and Letty Cottin Pogrebin begin publishing a new feminist magazine simply titled *Ms.* (1972).
- The American Indian Movement, headed by Dennis Banks and Russell Means, suffers a setback with the forced removal of protestors at Wounded Knee, South Dakota (1973).
- The Supreme Court, invoking the principle of privacy, decides in *Roe v. Wade* that women have a constitutional right to terminate a pregnancy (1973).
- Court-ordered bussing to attain better racial integration within the Boston public school system causes disruptions and violence from white parents who oppose integrated bussing (1974).
- President Gerald Ford signs into law the *Housing and Community Development Act*, which creates the Community Development Block Grant program and the Section 8 Housing Choice Voucher program (1974).
- The United States Commission on Civil Rights reports that Southern public-school districts have achieved a higher rate of racial integration than have their Northern state counterparts (1975).

Note: For a more reflective and functional use of this list of contemporary social welfare historical events, see Question #5 under the **Questions for Further Research and Discussion** section (below).

Sources:

Daniel, C. (1989). *Chronicle of America*. Mt. Kisco, NY: Chronicle Publications.
Mercer, D. (2000). *Millennium year by year*. New York: Dorling Kindersley Publications.
Social welfare developments 1951–2000. (2011). Retrieved from https://socialwelfare.library.vcu.edu/events/1951-2000/

Primary Text Material

In re Gault (1967)

"U.S. Supreme Court
In re Gault, 387 U.S. 1 (1967)
In re Gault
No. 116
Argued December 6, 1966

Decided May 15, 1967
387 U.S. 1
APPEAL FROM THE SUPREME COURT OF ARIZONA
Syllabus

Appellants' 15-year-old son, Gerald Gault, was taken into custody as the result of a complaint that he had made lewd telephone calls. After hearings before a juvenile court judge, Gerald was ordered committed to the State Industrial School as a juvenile delinquent until he should reach majority. Appellants brought a habeas corpus action in the state courts to challenge the constitutionality of the Arizona Juvenile Code and the procedure actually used in Gerald's case, on the ground of denial of various procedural due process rights. The State Supreme Court affirmed dismissal of the writ. Agreeing that the constitutional guarantee of due process applies to proceedings in which juveniles are charged as delinquents, the court held that the Arizona Juvenile Code impliedly includes the requirements of due process in delinquency proceedings, and that such due process requirements were not offended by the procedure leading to Gerald's commitment.

Held:

... 2. Due process requires, in such proceedings, that adequate written notice be afforded the child and his parents or guardian. Such notice must inform them "of the specific issues that they must meet," and must be given "at the earliest practicable time, and, in any event, sufficiently in advance of the hearing to permit preparation." Notice here was neither timely nor adequately specific, nor was there waiver of the right to constitutionally adequate notice ...

3. In such proceedings, the child and his parents must be advised of their right to be represented by counsel and, if they are unable to afford counsel, that counsel will be appointed to represent the child. Mrs. Gault's statement at the habeas corpus hearing that she had known she could employ counsel, is not "an intentional relinquishment or abandonment of a fully known right ..."

4. The constitutional privilege against self-incrimination is applicable in such proceedings:

"an admission by the juvenile may [not] be used against him in the absence of clear and unequivocal evidence that the admission was made with knowledge that he was not obliged to speak and would not be penalized for remaining silent."

"[T]he availability of the privilege does not turn upon the type of proceeding in which its protection is invoked, but upon the nature of the statement or admission and the exposure which it invites . . . . [J]uvenile proceedings to determine 'delinquency,' which may lead to commitment to a state institution, must be regarded as 'criminal' for purposes of the privilege against self-incrimination."

Furthermore, experience has shown that "admissions and confessions by juveniles require special caution" as to their reliability and voluntariness, and "[i]t would indeed be surprising if the privilege against self-incrimination were available to hardened criminals, but not to children."

Continued

> *"[S]pecial problems may arise with respect to waiver of the privilege by or on behalf of children, and . . . there may well be some differences in technique—but not in principle—depending upon the age of the child and the presence and competence of parents. . . . If counsel was not present for some permissible reason when an admission was obtained, the greatest care must be taken to assure that the admission was voluntary . . ."*
>
> Gerald's admissions did not measure up to these standards, and could not properly be used as a basis for the judgment against him . . .
>
> 5. Absent a valid confession, a juvenile in such proceedings must be afforded the rights of confrontation and sworn testimony of witnesses available for cross-examination . . .
>
> 6. Other questions raised by appellants, including the absence of provision for appellate review of a delinquency adjudication, and a transcript of the proceedings, are not ruled upon.
>
> 99 Ariz. 181, 407 P.2d 760, reversed and remanded.
>
> MR. JUSTICE FORTAS delivered the opinion of the Court . . ."
>
> Source and full text available at https://supreme.justia.com/cases/federal/us/387/1/case.html.

Timeline of General Events in History, the Humanities, and Science During This Period (1950-1975)

These general historical events may help you understand more clearly the overall historical context during which the primary document was created.

Wisconsin Senator Joseph McCarthy claims he has a "list" of more than 200 known subversive Communists agents working within the U.S. State Department, thus igniting a period of fierce anti-Communist investigations within the federal government (1950).

- North Korea crosses the 38th parallel line and invades South Korea, prompting the beginning of United States involvement in the Korean War (1950).
- The first formal credit card is launched by the Diners Club in cardboard format with a list of the 28 participating restaurants listed on the back (1950).
- Maine Republican Senator Margaret Chase Smith, the first woman elected to serve in both Houses of Congress, denounces the discrediting of individuals and fear tactics used by fellow-Republican, Wisconsin Senator Joseph McCarthy (1950).
- The United States detonates its first thermonuclear device, referred to as the "H-bomb," which is more destructive than the atomic bomb used to end World War II (1952).
- Accused Russian spies Julius and Ethel Rosenberg are executed for espionage at Sing Sing Prison in New York, amid controversy over their innocence (1953).

- The Eisenhower administration proposes constructing a massive federal interstate highway system to connect individuals and "farm-to-table" enterprises across the nation (1954).
- President Eisenhower pledges support to South Vietnam in its battle against insurgent Communist forces and authorizes the sending of military advisers there (1955).
- Amid the growing popularity of performers such as Bill Haley and His Comets, Little Richard, Bo Diddley, Fats Domino, and Chuck Berry, some critics denounce the new rock 'n' roll music genre, claiming it to be just as dangerous as drugs for teenagers (1955).
- Musician Leonard Bernstein opens his innovative musical play on a theme of ethnic diversity, *West Side Story*, on the Broadway stage (1957).
- American Airlines announces that the first regular same-day air service between New York City and Los Angeles (1959).
- Alaska and Hawaii become the 49th and 50th states in the nation (1959).
- Massachusetts Senator John Kennedy, who is Catholic, is elected president of the United States (1960).
- In President Kennedy's inaugural address, he delivers his legendary "Ask not what your country can do for you—ask what you can do for your country" speech (1961).
- As part of his New Frontier initiative, President John Kennedy establishes the Peace Corps, whose unpaid volunteers serve to assist the advancement of underdeveloped nations (1961).
- Lieutenant John Glenn becomes the first American to reach orbital flight around the earth after his *Friendship 7* blasts off from Cape Canaveral, Florida (1962).
- President Kennedy is murdered by assassin Harvey Lee Oswald in Dallas, Texas (1963).
- The musical group the Beatles make their first American appearance in New York City (1964).
- With more than 500,000 American troops on the ground, the Vietnam War increases in intensity and the loss of lives (1965).
- The Hollywood film *The Graduate*, starring Dustin Hoffman, challenges the young generation to question whether conformity to their older generation's expectations of them is truly worth the emotional price they will pay (1967).
- Israel defeats Egypt and other Arab allies in the Six-Day War, allowing it to fully occupy the city of Jerusalem, half of which had been under the control of Jordan (1967).
- In a radical departure from past precedent for journalists, CBS News anchor Walter Cronkite denounces the War in Vietnam as hopeless and immoral (1968).
- Senator Robert Kennedy is assassinated at the end of a Democratic campaign rally at the Ambassador Hotel in Los Angeles (1968).
- The Democratic Party, thoroughly divided into doves and hawks over the Vietnam War, holds its Democratic National Convention in Chicago and elects

Hubert Humphrey over Eugene McCarthy as its candidate against Richard Nixon for president. Peaceful protests outside the convention center turn into anti-war riots and allegations are launched against the police for unnecessary brutality (1968).

- *The Smothers Brothers Comedy Hour* on CBS is canceled due to the allegation that much of Tommy and Dick Smothers' humor is anti-Vietnam War and disrespectful of governmental authority (1969).
- The Reverends Daniel and Philip Berrigan, along with members of the Catonsville Nine, are convicted in state court of destroying Selective Service draft records in Catonsville, Maryland (1969).
- With the transmitted words "Houston, Tranquility Base here. The Eagle has landed" astronaut Neil Armstrong reports to the world that he and fellow astronaut Edwin Aldrin Jr. have successfully landed on the moon (1969).
- The so-called Woodstock Nation of more than 400,000 music fans, advocating peace, drugs and casual sex, meet for an iconic festival on Max Yasgur's farm outside Woodstock, New York (1969).
- Washington, DC is the site for the largest anti-war demonstration of more than 250,000 people in American history. The protestors march from the Capitol to the Washington Monument, while other anti-war demonstrations take at place at many universities because of their alleged financial connections with the Department of Defense (1969).
- Four unarmed students at Kent State University in Ohio die from shots fired by the Ohio National Guard during a student anti-war demonstration on campus (1970).
- Student strikes against the Vietnam War at more than 450 colleges and universities across America lead to canceled classes and disrupted commencement activities (1970).
- Citing the principle of the *First Amendment*, the Supreme Court ends the suspension of publication sought by the Nixon White House and decreed that the *New York Times*, the *Washington Post*, and other newspapers can continue to publish the full story behind *The Pentagon Papers*, which revealed that Defense Secretary McNamara questioned the progression and the likely success of the Vietnam War (1971).
- The Vietnam War technically ends with the signing of a cease-fire agreement by representatives of Vietnam and the United States (1973).
- Reacting to the threat of impeachment due to his reaction to the Watergate conflict, President Richard Nixon resigns from office in disgrace. Vice President Gerald Ford assumes the presidency, and, within a month, pardons former President Nixon of all crimes committed (1974).
- Following the unconditional surrender of the South Vietnamese military to the Viet Cong army, the last American troops, along with several thousand South Vietnamese allies, are evacuated by helicopter, under duress, from Saigon (1975).

Sources:

Daniel, C. (1989). *Chronicle of America*. Mt. Kisco, NY: Chronicle Publications.

Events of the 20th century. Retrieved from https://en.wikipedia.org/wiki/timeline_of_the_20th_century

Mercer, D. (2000). *Millennium year by year*. New York: Dorling Kindersley Publications.

Questions for Further Research and Discussion

1. Read the full text of *In re Gault* at https://supreme.justia.com/cases/federal/us/387/1/case.html, and summarize the dissenting opinion as offered by Justice Potter Stewart at the end of the decision. What is your personal opinion regarding Justice Potter's argument?
2. The *In re Gault* Supreme Court decision clearly limits the well-respected child welfare doctrine of *parens patriae*, which holds that the state can step in as guardian and protector of children who are in some vulnerable position and to whom the family is not able or willing to provide support. Conduct further research on the doctrine of *parens patriae*, then summarize its strengths and challenges as related to the field of child and family welfare.
3. Interview a small number of social workers who are employed in some type of juvenile justice agency or institution, and try to determine their thoughts about the effects, both positive and negative, of the *In re Gault* decision on their professional interactions with juvenile defendants. Then summarize what you have learned.
4. Based on the primary documentary material presented here, as well as other material you discover in the **Additional Selected References** at the end of this chapter, what other federal policy or policies do you believe should have been developed or changed at that time? Describe those policies in detail. Recall that a policy could be either *legislative* (i.e., a law), *judicial* (i.e., a court decision), or *administrative* (i.e., an executive or organizational policy) in nature.
5. Select three events appearing under the **Linkage to Social Welfare** section (above), conduct further Internet research regarding them, then conclude whether you believe there exists any plausible relationship between the *In re Gault* Supreme Court decision and the events you have chosen. Use the analytical model presented in Appendix 1 of this book, or develop your own analytical model, to draw these conclusions.
6. Select one book from the **Additional Selected References** list at the end of this chapter. Briefly read through it, then summarize the main points contained in the book. Identify your own personal reaction to this book.

Additional Selected References

Agnew, R., & Brezina, T. (2015). *Juvenile delinquency: Causes and control*. New York: Oxford University Press.

Dowd, N. E. (2015). *A new juvenile justice system: Total reform for a broken system.* New York: New York University Press.

Feld, B. C. (2017). *The evolution of the juvenile court: Race, politics, and the criminalizing of juvenile justice.* New York: New York University Press.

Feld, B. C., & Bishop, D. M. (2012). *The Oxford handbook of juvenile crime and juvenile justice.* Oxford: Oxford University Press.

Getis, V. (2000). *The juvenile court and the progressives.* Urbana, IL: University of Illinois Press.

Gold, S. D. (1995). *In re Gault (1967): Juvenile justice.* New York: Twenty-first Century Books.

Gold, S. D. (2008). *In re Gault: Do minors have the same rights as adults?* New York: Marshall Cavendish Benchmark.

Tanenhaus, D. S. (2011). *The constitutional rights of children: In re Gault and juvenile justice.* Lawrence, KS: University Press of Kansas.

Tanenhaus, D. S., & Zimring, F. E. (Eds.). (2014). *Choosing the future for American juvenile justice.* New York: New York University Press.

United States. (2016). *Protecting the civil rights of students in the juvenile justice system.* Washington, DC: U.S. Department of Education, Office for Civil Rights.

Wilkerson, A. E. (1973). *The rights of children: Emergent concepts in law and society.* Philadelphia: Temple University Press.

Credits

Fig. 27.1: Source: http://www.loc.gov/pictures/item/98518316/.

Fig. 27.2: Source: https://prologuepiecesofhistory.files.wordpress.com/2016/11/b466-28.jpg.

Fig. 27.3: Source: https://commons.wikimedia.org/wiki/File:US_Supreme_Court_Justice_Potter_Stewart_-_1976_official_portrait.jpg.

Chapter 28

Legal Access to Abortion

Roe v. Wade, 410 U.S. 113 (1973)

Introduction

Throughout the history of the United States, during those decades when medical abortions were illegal except to save the life of the mother, there have always existed a number of doctors, nurses, midwives, and other medical practitioners who risked fines, loss of their professional licenses, and even imprisonment in order to provide abortion services to women seeking to end their pregnancies. Tragically, some of these medical workers were incompetent due to lack of training, unsafe surgical procedures or environments, or callous inattention. As a consequence, many women died or were left permanently damaged from botched medical procedures or self-induced abortions. Data from the 1960s, for example, suggest that illegal abortions in the United States comprised approximately one-sixth of all deaths attributed to pregnancy and births. This untenable situation changed completely in 1973.

Jane Roe was a fictitious name used by the plaintiff, Norma McCorvey, a single Texas woman who had two previous children and was trying to terminate her third pregnancy. Because Texas law at the time of her suit declared abortion a felony crime except in cases when the mother's life was in danger, Roe sued Henry Wade, the district attorney of Dallas County, Texas, for relief from the punishment for a felony crime. The rationale submitted by Roe's lawyers to the federal District Court for the Northern District of Texas was twofold: The right to an abortion already existed under the principle of the right to privacy as established by the United States Supreme Court in *Griswold v. Connecticut* (1965) and this right to privacy over medical conditions was implicit in the *due process* clause of the *Fourteenth Amendment* to the *United States Constitution*. The Texas District Court found in favor of Roe and agreed that the Texas abortion ban violated the right to privacy established in the *Ninth*

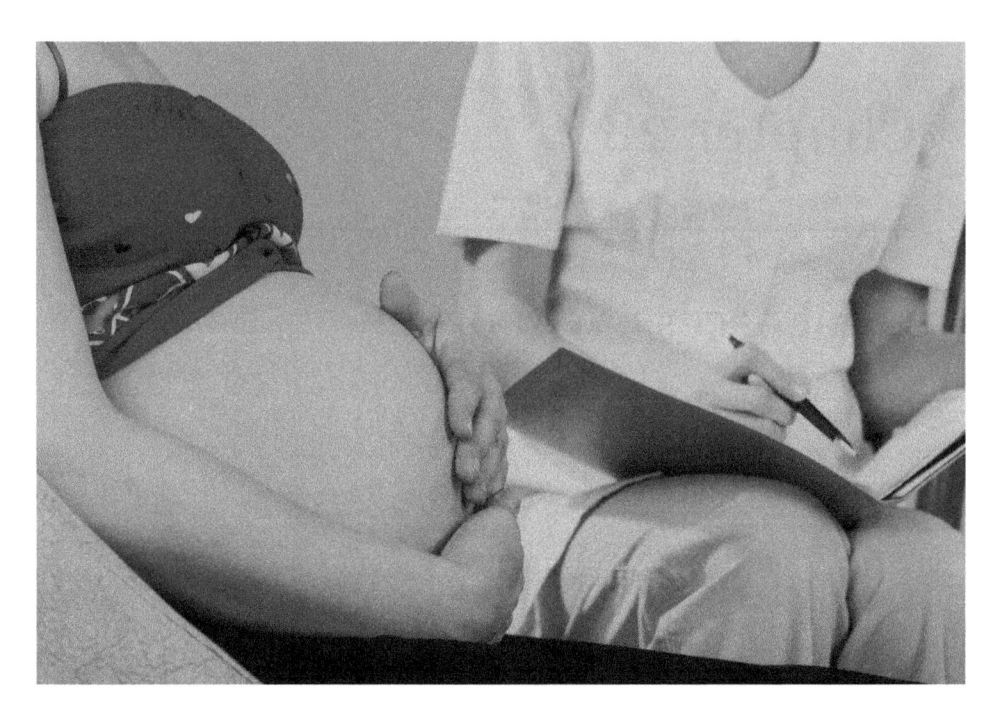

FIGURE 28.1   Prenatal medical exam.

Amendment to the *United States Constitution*. The Dallas County district attorney then appealed that District Court opinion to the United States Supreme Court.

In a 7–2 opinion, with Justice Harry Blackmun composing the majority position, and Justices Byron White and William Rehnquist dissenting, the United States Supreme Court found that women have a fundamental right to privacy under the *United States Constitution* and, furthermore, that right extends to the right to make their own medical decisions, including the right to terminate a pregnancy. Roe requested the right to abort the fetus at any point during her entire pregnancy. The Supreme Court, however, refused to progress to that level of freedom, declaring instead that the state did have an interest in protecting the overall health of the mother as well as an interest in providing for the future growth of society. Three levels of involvement were delineated: In the first trimester of a pregnancy, a woman has an absolute right to terminate her pregnancy; during the second trimester, the state has an interest in preservation of a woman's life and, thus, may set reasonable limitations in allowing abortions; in the third trimester—when the fetus is assumed to be viable—the state has a compelling interest in prohibiting abortions except when there is a danger to the mother's life. In this last trimester situation, the fetus is to be protected once it has attained capability and could exist on its own outside the mother's womb.

Before the Supreme Court rendered its decision, Roe delivered her baby and subsequently placed that baby up for adoption. Over time, Roe had a change of heart due to her religious conversion and became a vocal anti-abortion rights advocate. In 2003, she tried unsuccessfully to have her original court case in the Texas District Court overturned on the basis that abortion could cause serious psychological harm to the mother. Roe's appeal was eventually denied by a three-judge panel in the 5th United States Court of Appeals.

The *Roe v. Wade* decision has never been repealed, but there have been many attempts to add restrictions, both locally and nationally, with varying results. In *Planned Parenthood v. Casey* (1992), for example, the Supreme Court affirmed that any restrictions placed on abortions that caused any "undue burdens" on the woman were unconstitutional. In 1972, the United States Congress passed the *Hyde Amendment*, which prohibits the use of federal money in the Medicaid program to pay for abortions, except in the case of rape, incest, or to save the life of the mother. Several years later, in *Gonzales v. Carhart* (2007), the Supreme Court upheld the constitutionality of the federal *Partial-Birth Abortion Ban Act* (2003), which prohibits one extremely rare abortion procedure that includes the intact dilation and evacuation of the fetus. Furthermore, in *Whole Woman's Health v. Hellerstedt* (2016), the Supreme Court struck down the Texas law that requires all abortion facilities to maintain the same medical standards as a mobile surgical center and that all physicians performing abortions possess admitting privileges at a local hospital.

FIGURE 28.2 Supreme Court Justice Harry Blackmun.

Due to the ongoing tensions between the anti-abortion rights and the pro-abortion rights movements across America, there continue to be a number of endeavors at the state level to add restrictions to the legal right of a woman to have an abortion. These challenges to the law tend to appear as either: requiring parental consent or notification for minors seeking an abortion; ensuring spousal consent or notification before any abortion; forcing abortions to be performed in hospitals; denying state funding for abortions; mandating long waiting periods before an abortion; and requiring that women read and view pro-life materials before having an abortion.

Interestingly, the legal principle of the individual's right to privacy, as clearly established in *Roe v. Wade*, has expanded and spread to other legal contexts. Since 1973, this principle has been applied defensively in cases involving sex workers, members of the gay and lesbian communities, actors and actresses appearing in pornography films, couples living together outside of a legal marriage, the protection of personal information, and individuals involved with the right to die movement.

In essence, when the Supreme Court decided in favor of Roe, it thereby invalidated any state statute that had prohibited abortions within the first trimester of the pregnancy. Thus began a conflict of values and moral ethics among Americans that continues to our present day.

- For a 90-minute C-SPAN overview with two attorneys discussing the *Roe v. Wade* case, see https://www.c-span.org/video/?327721-1/supreme-court-landmark-case-roe-v-wade.

Internet Sources for the Content of This Introduction Include:

https://commons.wikimedia.org/wiki/file:hoact21.jpg
http://caselaw.findlaw.com/us-supreme-court/410/113.html
https://www.plannedparenthoodaction.org/issues/abortion/roe-v-wade
https://www.britannica.com/event/roe-v-wade
https://www.cnn.com/2013/11/04/us/roe-v-wade-fast-facts/index.html
https://www.nytimes.com/2018/01/21/opinion/roe-v-wade-abortion.html
https://en.wikipedia.org/wiki/roe_v._wade

Linkage to Social Welfare History (1950–1975)

Social welfare historical events for this time period include the following:

- United Nations diplomat Ralph Bunche is awarded the Nobel Peace Prize for his work mediating conflicts between Arabs and Jews in the Middle East, thus becoming the first African American to receive such an honor (1950).
- Social scientists David Riesman, Nathan Glazer, and Reuel Denney publish *The Lonely Crowd*, a study of how Americans are not overly interested in conformity with their fellow citizens (1950).
- Over the veto of President Harry Truman, the Congress passes the *Immigration and Naturalization Act* (also known as the McCarran–Walter Act), restricting the number of immigrants and redefining the criteria for admission to the United States (1952).
- Sexuality becomes public, with Marilyn Monroe starring in the publication of *Playboy* magazine and the release of films such as *The Moon Is Blue* (1953).
- The scourge of the childhood disease polio is eradicated in the United States with the introduction of a vaccine developed by Dr. Jonas Salk at the University of Pennsylvania (1954).
- The United States Supreme Court, in *Brown v. Board of Education*, effectively ends racial segregation in public schools across the nation (1954).
- Rosa Parks, seated in the white section of a Montgomery, Alabama, bus, refuses to give up her seat to a white man and is arrested, thus launching the Montgomery Bus Boycott partly led by the local Christian pastor, the Reverend Martin Luther King Jr. (1955).
- Following the merger of several allied groups, the National Association of Social Workers (NASW) is formally established (1955).
- The Count Basie Orchestra becomes the first African American musical group to play in the famous Starlight Room at the Waldorf Astoria hotel in New York City (1957).

- Under the protection of federal troops and federalized Arkansas National Guardsmen, and in defiance of Arkansas Governor Orval Faubus, nine African American students are escorted into Little Rock Central High School through crowds of angry whites opposing school integration (1957).
- Economist John Kenneth Galbraith publishes *The Affluent Society*, which outlines the wide income disparities in America and calls for greater public resources for those who are disadvantaged (1958).
- The novel *Lady Chatterley's Lover* is publicly banned after being judged as obscene by the United States Postal Service (1959).
- Four African American students stage a non-violent "sit-in" by refusing to move from their seats at the Woolworth's lunch counter in Greensboro, North Carolina (1960).
- The Food and Drug Administration approves the sale and use of the first contraceptive pill for women (1960).
- CBS television announcer Edward R. Murrow narrates the shocking exposé of the oppressive and dangerous working conditions of migrant agricultural workers in the film *Harvest of Shame* (1960).
- An integrated bus full of members of the Congress of Racial Equality (CORE) travels through Southern states testing the local segregation laws, with the result of the "Freedom Riders" being viciously attacked and arrested along the way. In one instance, Attorney General Robert Kennedy sends in 600 federal marshals to restore order in Montgomery, Alabama (1961).
- In *Engel v. Vitale*, the Supreme Court declares that the recitation of school-sponsored nondenominational prayer in public schools violates the establishment clause of the *First Amendment* to the *United States Constitution* (1962).
- Under the protection of federal marshals, college student James Meredith becomes the first African American student to enroll in the University of Mississippi (1962).
- Michael Harrington publishes *The Other America*, which dramatically exposes the widespread presence of poverty across both urban and rural America (1962).
- While in jail for leading a civil rights demonstration, Reverend King composes his *Letter from the Birmingham Jail*, which clarifies his commitment to nonviolent civil disobedience (1963).
- Singer and songwriter Bob Dylan captivates the audience in Newport, Rhode Island, with his songs of protest, such as *A Hard Rain's A-Gonna Fall*, *Talkin' John Birch Society Blues*, and *Blowin' in the Wind* (1963).
- Before a crowd of more than 200,000 civil rights proponents, standing in front of the Lincoln Memorial in Washington, DC, Reverend King delivers his celebrated "I Have a Dream" speech (1963).
- After extensive study by medical experts, the surgeon general of the United States declares that cigarettes are the main cause of lung cancer and bronchitis (1964).

- President Lyndon Johnson signs the *Civil Rights Act*, which bans racial discrimination in public accommodations, union activity, employment, and federally funded projects (1964).
- In order to engage in a "War on Poverty," President Johnson signs the *Economic Opportunity Act* (1964).
- In the State of the Union address, President Johnson proposes the development of a "Great Society," which focuses on eradicating poverty and racial injustice (1965).
- President Johnson signs the *Voting Rights Act*, which protects all people, particularly minorities, in the exercise of their constitutional right to vote (1965).
- Reacting to reports of police brutality, African American residents of Watts, a neighborhood in Los Angeles, rioted for several days, resulting in 34 deaths, more than 1,000 injuries, 4,000 arrests, and property damage of approximately $40 million (1965).
- President Johnson signs a series of noteworthy social welfare legislation, including the *Older Americans Act*, the *Elementary and Secondary Education Act* (ESEA), and the Medicare (Title XVIII) and Medicaid (Title XIX) amendments to the *Social Security Act* (1965).
- In the face of opposition from conservative religious and political leaders, the Department of Health, Education, and Welfare plans to spend $3.1 million on providing family planning services to low-income families (1966).
- In *Miranda v. Arizona*, the United States Supreme Court affirms the right of anyone arrested by police authorities to be told of their rights to remain silent and to be provided with a lawyer (1966).
- President Johnson signs the *Child Nutrition Act*, which provides federal funds to feed children from low-income families (1966).
- Detroit, similar to other American cities this summer, experiences bitter race riots due to unemployment, substandard housing, and general despair, resulting in the loss of life, injuries, and property damage of several hundred million dollars (1967).
- Reverend King, who is in Memphis, Tennessee, to assist with the strike of local garbage collectors, is assassinated at his motel. Riots break out in Chicago and other cities across the nation (1968).
- At the Olympics ceremony in Mexico City, African American medalists Tommie Smith and John Carlos, protesting the treatment of African Americans, accept their medals for the 200-meter dash by standing with their right black-gloved hands held aloft in a fist during the playing of *The Star-Spangled Banner* (1968).
- President Richard Nixon proposes his *Family Assistance Plan*, an innovative approach to public assistance that would essentially grant a guaranteed annual income to economically fragile families, but the plan is rejected by the United States Congress (1969).
- The Supreme Court allows the use of bussing and redistricting as valid tactics to attain greater racial integration in public school systems across the nation (1971).

- Journalists Gloria Steinem and Letty Cottin Pogrebin begin publishing a new feminist magazine simply titled *Ms.* (1972).
- The American Indian Movement, headed by Dennis Banks and Russell Means, suffers a setback with the forced removal of protestors at Wounded Knee, South Dakota (1973).
- Court-ordered bussing to attain better racial integration within the Boston public school system causes disruptions and violence from white parents who oppose integrated bussing (1974).
- President Gerald Ford signs into law the *Housing and Community Development Act*, which creates the Community Development Block Grant program and the Section 8 Housing Choice Voucher program (1974).
- The United States Commission on Civil Rights reports that Southern public-school districts have achieved a higher rate of racial integration than have their Northern state counterparts (1975).

Note: For a more reflective and functional use of this list of contemporary social welfare historical events, see Question #5 under the **Questions for Further Research and Discussion** section (below).

Sources:

Daniel, C. (1989). *Chronicle of America*. Mt. Kisco, NY: Chronicle Publications.

Mercer, D. (2000). *Millennium year by year*. New York: Dorling Kindersley Publications.

Social welfare developments 1951–2000. (2011). Retrieved from https://socialwelfare.library.vcu.edu/events/1951-2000/

Primary Text Material

Roe v. Wade (1973)

"United States Supreme Court
ROE v. WADE (1973)
No. 70-18
Argued: December 13, 1971
Decided: January 22, 1973

A pregnant single woman (Roe) brought a class action challenging the constitutionality of the Texas criminal abortion laws, which proscribe procuring or attempting an abortion except on medical advice for the purpose of saving the mother's life. A licensed physician (Hallford), who had two state abortion prosecutions pending against him, was permitted to intervene. A childless married

Continued

couple (the Does), the wife not being pregnant, separately attacked the laws, basing alleged injury on the future possibilities of contraceptive failure, pregnancy, unpreparedness for parenthood, and impairment of the wife's health. A three-judge District Court, which consolidated the actions, held that Roe and Hallford, and members of their classes, had standing to sue and presented justiciable controversies. Ruling that declaratory, though not injunctive, relief was warranted, the court declared the abortion statutes void as vague and overbroadly infringing those plaintiffs' Ninth and Fourteenth Amendment rights. The court ruled the Does' complaint not justiciable. Appellants directly appealed to this Court on the injunctive rulings, and appellee cross-appealed from the District Court's grant of declaratory relief to Roe and Hallford. Held . . .

MR. JUSTICE BLACKMUN delivered the opinion of the Court.

This Texas federal appeal and its Georgia companion, Doe v. Bolton present constitutional challenges to state criminal abortion legislation. The Texas statutes under attack here are typical of those that have been in effect in many States for approximately a century. The Georgia statutes, in contrast, have a modern cast and are a legislative product that, to an extent at least, obviously reflects the influences of recent attitudinal change, of advancing medical knowledge and techniques, and of new thinking about an old issue.

We forthwith acknowledge our awareness of the sensitive and emotional nature of the abortion controversy, of the vigorous opposing views, even among physicians, and of the deep and seemingly absolute convictions that the subject inspires. One's philosophy, one's experiences, one's exposure to the raw edges of human existence, one's religious training, one's attitudes toward life and family and their values, and the moral standards one establishes and seeks to observe, are all likely to influence and to color one's thinking and conclusions about abortion.

In addition, population growth, pollution, poverty, and racial overtones tend to complicate and not to simplify the problem.

Our task, of course, is to resolve the issue by constitutional measurement, free of emotion and of predilection . . .

. . . XI

To summarize and to repeat:

1. A state criminal abortion statute of the current Texas type, that excepts from criminality only a life-saving procedure on behalf of the mother, without regard to pregnancy stage and without recognition of the other interests involved, is violative of the Due Process Clause of the Fourteenth Amendment.

(a) For the stage prior to approximately the end of the first trimester, the abortion decision and its effectuation must be left to the medical judgment of the pregnant woman's attending physician.

(b) For the stage subsequent to approximately the end of the first trimester, the State, in promoting its interest in the health of the mother, may, if it chooses, regulate the abortion procedure in ways that are reasonably related to maternal health.

> *(c) For the stage subsequent to viability, the State in promoting its interest in the potentiality of human life [410 U.S. 113, 165] may, if it chooses, regulate, and even proscribe, abortion except where it is necessary, in appropriate medical judgment, for the preservation of the life or health of the mother.*
>
> *2. The State may define the term "physician," as it has been employed in the preceding paragraphs of this Part XI of this opinion, to mean only a physician currently licensed by the State and may proscribe any abortion by a person who is not a physician as so defined.*
>
> *In Doe v. Bolton, post, p. 179, procedural requirements contained in one of the modern abortion statutes are considered. That opinion and this one, of course, are to be read together.*
>
> *This holding, we feel, is consistent with the relative weights of the respective interests involved, with the lessons and examples of medical and legal history, with the lenity of the common law, and with the demands of the profound problems of the present day. The decision leaves the State free to place increasing restrictions on abortion as the period of pregnancy lengthens, so long as those restrictions are tailored to the recognized state interests. The decision vindicates the right of the physician to administer medical treatment according to his professional judgment up to the points where important [410 U.S. 113, 166] state interests provide compelling justifications for intervention. Up to those points, the abortion decision in all its aspects is inherently, and primarily, a medical decision, and basic responsibility for it must rest with the physician. If an individual practitioner abuses the privilege of exercising proper medical judgment, the usual remedies, judicial and intra-professional, are available . . ."*
>
> Source and full text available at http://caselaw.findlaw.com/us-supreme-court/410/113.html.

Timeline of General Events in History, the Humanities, and Science During This Period (1950–1975)

These general historical events may help you understand more clearly the overall historical context during which the primary document was created.

- Wisconsin Senator Joseph McCarthy claims he has a "list" of more than 200 known subversive Communists agents working within the U.S. State Department, thus igniting a period of fierce anti-Communist investigations within the federal government (1950).
- North Korea crosses the 38th parallel line and invades South Korea, prompting the beginning of United States involvement in the Korean War (1950).
- The first formal credit card is launched by the Diners Club in cardboard format with a list of the 28 participating restaurants listed on the back (1950).

- Maine Republican Senator Margaret Chase Smith, the first woman elected to serve in both Houses of Congress, denounces the discrediting of individuals and fear tactics used by fellow-Republican, Wisconsin Senator Joseph McCarthy (1950).
- The United States detonates its first thermonuclear device, referred to as the "H-bomb," which is more destructive than the atomic bomb used to end World War II (1952).
- Accused Russian spies Julius and Ethel Rosenberg are executed for espionage at Sing Sing Prison in New York, amid controversy over their innocence (1953).
- The Eisenhower administration proposes constructing a massive federal interstate highway system to connect individuals and "farm-to-table" enterprises across the nation (1954).
- President Eisenhower pledges support to South Vietnam in its battle against insurgent Communist forces and authorizes the sending of military advisers there (1955).
- Amid the growing popularity of performers such as Bill Haley and His Comets, Little Richard, Bo Diddley, Fats Domino, and Chuck Berry, some critics denounce the new rock 'n' roll music genre, claiming it to be just as dangerous as drugs for teenagers (1955).
- Musician Leonard Bernstein opens his innovative musical play on a theme of ethnic diversity, *West Side Story*, on the Broadway stage (1957).
- American Airlines announces that the first regular same-day air service between New York City and Los Angeles (1959).
- Alaska and Hawaii become the 49th and 50th states in the nation (1959).
- Massachusetts Senator John Kennedy, who is Catholic, is elected president of the United States (1960).
- In President Kennedy's inaugural address, he delivers his legendary "Ask not what your country can do for you—ask what you can do for your country" speech (1961).
- As part of his New Frontier initiative, President Kennedy establishes the Peace Corps, whose unpaid volunteers serve to assist the advancement of underdeveloped nations (1961).
- Lieutenant John Glenn becomes the first American to reach orbital flight around the earth after his *Friendship 7* blasts off from Cape Canaveral, Florida (1962).
- President Kennedy is murdered by assassin Harvey Lee Oswald in Dallas, Texas (1963).
- The musical group The Beatles make their first American appearance in New York City (1964).
- With more than 500,000 American troops on the ground, the Vietnam War increases in intensity and the loss of lives (1965).
- The Hollywood film *The Graduate*, starring Dustin Hoffman, challenges the young generation to question whether conformity to their older generation's expectations of them is truly worth the emotional price they will pay (1967).

- Israel defeats Egypt and other Arab allies in the Six-Day War, allowing it to fully occupy the entire city of Jerusalem, half of which had been under the control of Jordan (1967).
- In a radical departure from past precedent for journalists, CBS News anchor Walter Cronkite denounces the War in Vietnam as hopeless and immoral (1968).
- Senator Robert Kennedy is assassinated at the end of a Democratic campaign rally at the Ambassador Hotel in Los Angeles (1968).
- The Democratic Party, thoroughly divided into doves and hawks over the Vietnam War, holds its Democratic National Convention in Chicago and elects Hubert Humphrey over Eugene McCarthy as its candidate against Richard Nixon for president. Peaceful protests outside the convention center turn into anti-war riots and allegations are launched against the police for unnecessary brutality (1968).
- *The Smothers Brothers Comedy Hour* on CBS is canceled due to the allegation that much of Tommy and Dick Smothers' humor is anti-Vietnam War and disrespectful of governmental authority (1969).
- The Reverends Daniel and Philip Berrigan, along with members of the Catonsville Nine, are convicted in state court of destroying Selective Service draft records in Catonsville, Maryland (1969).
- With the transmitted words "Houston, Tranquility Base here. The Eagle has landed" astronaut Neil Armstrong reports to the world that he and fellow astronaut Edwin Aldrin Jr. have successfully landed on the moon (1969).
- The so-called Woodstock Nation of more than 400,000 music fans, advocating peace, drugs and casual sex, meet for an iconic festival on Max Yasgur's farm outside Woodstock, New York (1969).
- Washington, DC is the site for the largest anti-war demonstration of more than 250,000 people in American history. The protestors march from the Capitol to the Washington Monument, while other anti-war demonstrations take at place at many universities because of their alleged financial connections with the Department of Defense (1969).
- Four unarmed students at Kent State University in Ohio die from shots fired by the Ohio National Guard during a student anti-war demonstration on campus (1970).
- Student strikes against the Vietnam War at more than 450 colleges and universities across America lead to canceled classes and disrupted commencement activities (1970).
- Citing the principle of the *First Amendment*, the Supreme Court ends the suspension of publication sought by the Nixon White House and decreed that the *New York Times*, the *Washington Post*, and other newspapers can continue to publish the full story behind *The Pentagon Papers*, which revealed that Defense Secretary McNamara questioned the progression and the likely success of the Vietnam War (1971).
- The Vietnam War technically ends with the signing of a cease-fire agreement by representatives of Vietnam and the United States (1973).

- Reacting to the threat of impeachment due to his reaction to the Watergate conflict, President Richard Nixon resigns from office in disgrace. Vice President Gerald Ford assumes the presidency, and, within a month, pardons former President Nixon of all crimes committed (1974).
- Following the unconditional surrender of the South Vietnamese military to the Viet Cong army, the last American troops, along with several thousand South Vietnamese allies, are evacuated by helicopter, under duress, from Saigon (1975).

Sources:

Daniel, C. (1989). *Chronicle of America*. Mt. Kisco, NY: Chronicle Publications.

Events of the 20th century. Retrieved from https://en.wikipedia.org/wiki/rimeline_of_ the_20th_century

Mercer, D. (2000). *Millennium year by year*. New York: Dorling Kindersley Publications.

Questions for Further Research and Discussion

1. Read briefly through the entire *Roe v. Wade* decision available at http://caselaw.findlaw.com/us-supreme-court/410/113.html. At the end of the document, focus on Justice William Rehnquist's dissenting opinion, then summarize his position on why abortion should be illegal. Finally, summarize your own thoughts on the subject.
2. Conduct further research specifically on what major Christian, Hindu, Jewish, and Muslim religious organizations believe about abortion. Summarize your results and identify any patterns of thought you may identify.
3. Focusing on an international perspective, choose two countries located in different parts of the world (e.g., Asia and South America, Europe and Africa, or some other combination). Conduct further Internet research on each country's national abortion policies, then summarize what you discover. How do your two countries' abortion policies compare to each other and to the policy in the United States?
4. Based on the primary documentary material presented here, as well as other material you discover in the **Additional Selected References** at the end of this chapter, what other federal policy or policies do you believe should have been developed or changed at that time? Describe those policies in detail. Recall that a policy could be either *legislative* (i.e., a law), *judicial* (i.e., a court decision), or *administrative* (i.e., an executive or organizational policy) in nature.
5. Select three events appearing under the **Linkage to Social Welfare** section (above), conduct further Internet research regarding them, then conclude whether you believe there exists any plausible relationship between the *Roe v. Wade* Supreme Court decision and the events you have chosen. Use the analytical model presented in Appendix 1 of this book, or develop your own analytical model, to draw these conclusions.

6. Select one book from the **Additional Selected References** list at the end of this chapter. Briefly read through it, then summarize the main points contained in the book. Identify your own personal reaction to this book.

Additional Selected References

Critchlow, D. T. (1996). *The politics of abortion and birth control in historical perspective.* University Park, PA: Pennsylvania State University Press.

Faux, M. (1988). *Roe v. Wade: The untold story of the landmark Supreme Court decision that made abortion legal.* New York: Macmillan.

Forsythe, C. D. (2013). *Abuse of discretion: The inside story of Roe v. Wade.* New York: Encounter Books.

Garrow, D. J. (1998). *Liberty and sexuality: The right to privacy and the making of Roe v. Wade.* Berkeley: University of California Press.

Gold, S. D. (2005). *Roe v. Wade: A woman's choice.* Tarrytown, NY: Benchmark Books.

Greenhouse, L., & Siegel, R. B. (2010). *Before Roe v. Wade: Voices that shaped the abortion debate before the Supreme Court's ruling.* New York: Kaplan Publishing.

Herda, D. J. (1994). Roe v. Wade: *The abortion question.* Hillside, NJ: Enslow Publishers.

Hull, N. E. H., & Hoffer, P. C. (2001). *Roe v. Wade: The abortion rights controversy in American history.* Lawrence, KS: University Press of Kansas.

Joffe, C. E. (1995). *Doctors of conscience: The struggle to provide abortion before and after Roe v. Wade.* Boston: Beacon Press.

McCorvey, N., & Meisler, A. (1994). *I am Roe: My life, Roe v. Wade, and freedom of choice.* New York: Harper Collins Publishers.

Rubin, E. R. (1982). *Abortion, politics, and the courts: Roe v. Wade and its aftermath.* Westport, CT: Greenwood Press.

Solinger, R. (1992). *Wake up little Susie: Single pregnancy and race before Roe v. Wade.* New York: Routledge.

Stevens, L. A. (1996). *The case of Roe v. Wade.* New York: G.P. Putnam's Sons.

Williams, D. K. (2016). *Defenders of the unborn: The pro-life movement before Roe v. Wade.* New York: Oxford University Press.

Credits

Fig. 28.1: Copyright © 2011 Depositphotos/IuriiSokolov.

Fig. 28.2: Source: https://upload.wikimedia.org/wikipedia/commons/b/b8/US_Supreme_Court_Justice_Harry_Blackmun.jpg.

Chapter 29

Adoption and Foster Care for Native Americans

Indian Child Welfare Act, PL 95–608 (1978)

Introduction

During the early stages of our nation's history, when people and institutions stretched westward from the East Coast and Midwest regions, native tribes experienced intense pressure to assimilate into the community life and cultural practices of the dominant white society. To assist with this wholesale accommodation, the federal government launched a series of Indian boarding schools near native reservations. These schools' overt mission was to concentrate on the next generation—the young children—and purposively immerse them in the cultural artifacts and routines of white society that would enable them to suppress their Indian heritage and assume a new cultural identity capable of functioning within the uniquely new, post-Revolutionary, American, Judeo-Christian environment. The Indian boarding school undertaking was undoubtedly a part of the widely accepted 19th century belief that our nation had a *Manifest Destiny* from its God to conquer the entire Western frontier and homogenize all peoples into one idealized American nation.

In general, Indian boarding schools were designed to instruct the Indian children to value private property, inculcate the goal of gaining material wealth, and embrace the ideal of a stable monogamous marriage. Explicitly, the native students were forced to wear non-native clothing, served the same food as their white instructors ate, taught to speak English exclusively, and received formal education in the arts, science, humanities, and citizenship. Most intentionally, the Indian children were converted by persuasion into the Christian religion. Indian girls learned basic homemaking skills of cooking and cleaning, whereas Indian boys were trained to be blacksmiths, carpenters, and farmers. To reinforce the total assimilation process, native children were forbidden to speak among themselves in their tribal languages. This governmental approach

FIGURE 29.1   Native American graduates of the Carlisle Boarding School, Carlisle, Pennsylvania.

started as day schools either on or near tribal reservations. Over time, many new schools evolved as residential programs and were located at long distances from the reservations and, thus, from the children's families. By the 1880s, there were 60 schools nationwide educating approximately 6,200 Indian children.

Over time, several factors coalesced and led to the physical removal of many Indian children from their biological families, including:

- A lack of culturally sensitive state standards used by human service workers to assess the competency of native families to care for their children
- Clear violations of the legal principle of *due process* during many custody hearings for Indian children and their immediate families
- The lack of social service agencies managed by Indian administrators who would be able to advocate for the special needs of Indian children
- Generous funding incentives to non-Indian social service agencies to remove native children for placement in non-Indian foster care homes
- Poor economic and social conditions that were clearly observable on many Native American reservations

To further exacerbate the situation, during the 1950s and 1960s, the federal government collaborated with the Child Welfare League of America and other national child welfare organizations in a deliberate, national effort to remove Indian children from abusive or otherwise inappropriate home situations and place them, perhaps too freely, into non-Indian foster care and adoptive homes. During this period, members of the Church of Jesus Christ of Latter-Day Saints—Mormons—also operated their Indian Placement Program throughout the Western states and Alaska, which included the adoption and foster care of many Indian children by non-Indian Mormon families. Typically, Indian children, more so than most non-Indian children, come from large extended families of grandparents, uncles, aunts, and cousins who live in close proximity to one another. Indian children are also imbued with a deep and unique tribal identity that includes rich cultural overlays of language, food, and social interactions.

Unwittingly, and certainly with the best of intentions, these non-Indian child welfare organizations and churches interpreted the basic child welfare principle of "in the best interests of the child" too narrowly, and in so doing, they minimized the multilayered cultural, family, and tribal aspects that contribute to Indian children's identities. As a result, a number of Indian children who were placed in non-Indian homes suffered inevitable social problems such as poor self-image, disruptive social behavior, depression, substance abuse, and suicide. By the late 1960s, due undoubtedly to societal unrest over civil rights, the Vietnam War, and the outcry from indigenous groups within the African American, Latino, and especially the Native American communities, the federal government began to emphasize native tribal self-determination. Most prominently, this new federal initiative included granting wide-ranging autonomy over many services formerly provided by non-Indian entities.

In 1978, the United States Congress passed the *Indian Child Welfare Act (ICWA)*, which concentrated on American Indian and Alaska native children, with the stated dual goal to ". . . protect the best interests of Indian children and to promote the stability and security of Indian tribes and families . . . ." At this point in American history, it was estimated that between 25% and 35% of Indian children were being removed from their immediate family homes, and of that number, approximately 85% were placed with non-Indian families at a distance from their own extended families, tribes, and communities. *ICWA* formally inaugurated a set of federal regulations involving all state custody proceedings that involve an Indian child who is a member of any federally recognized tribe or is eligible for membership in any federally recognized tribe.

On a programmatic basis, *ICWA* established minimum child welfare standards for permanent adoption, voluntary termination of parental rights, involuntary termination of parental rights, removal from the family home, and foster care placement. *ICWA* regulations, however, do not encompass child custody hearings that are part of a divorce proceeding, nor does it cover any court procedures involving Indian children accused of juvenile delinquency in which an act, if committed by an adult, would be a crime. In terms of jurisdiction, *ICWA* mandated that an Indian tribe have *exclusive* jurisdiction over an Indian child living on tribal land but only *concurrent* jurisdiction—with state child welfare officials—if the child is not residing on tribal land.

Current research indicates that Indian and Alaskan native families are four times as likely as non-Indian families to have a child removed from the home by state child welfare authorities. The most pressing problem today, as identified by the federal Bureau of

FIGURE 29.2 Three Indian children and a baby.

Indian Affairs (BIA) and other Native American advocacy groups, is that the application of the original intent and regulations of *ICWA* is inconsistent across state lines, with the result that there are significant gaps in the protection of native children and their access to appropriate foster care and adoption placements. That raises the obvious modern challenge to the professional community to continue to search for further developments in *ICWA* implementation so that Indian children are fully protected and helped, when needed, by culturally sensitive social services staff and organizations.

Internet Sources for the Content of This Introduction Include:

https://www.bia.gov/sites/bia.gov/files/assets/bia/ois/pdf/idc2-056831.pdf

https://www.nicwa.org/about-icwa/

https://www.narf.org/nill/documents/icwa/ch1.html

http://www.un.org/esa/socdev/unpfii/documents/the%20indian%20child%20welfare%20act.v3.pdf

http://www.nativepartnership.org/site/pageserver?pagename=airc_hist_boardingschools

Linkage to Social Welfare History (1975-2000)

Social welfare historical events for this time period include the following:

- The United States Commission on Civil Rights reports that Southern public-school districts have achieved a higher rate of racial integration than have their Northern state counterparts (1975).
- The ABC television miniseries based on Alex Haley's *Roots*, which covers seven generations of an African American family and their rise from slavery, is reported to have received the highest viewer response in television's history (1977).
- Abandoning the principle of "when medically necessary," the United States Congress restricts the payment of federal funds for abortion under Medicaid to only those women who are physically sick or victims of rape or incest (1977).
- Insisting on the principle of "equal pay for equal play," tennis star Billie Jean King champions equality for women within the professional sports environment (1978).
- In San Francisco, Harvey Milk, the first openly gay public official, is assassinated by fellow-supervisor Dan White, who professed himself to be a guardian of morality (1978).
- In *Regents of the University of California v. Bakke*, the United States Supreme Court upholds the practice of using race as a consideration in college admissions and also declares the use of racial quotas in college admissions to be unconstitutional (1978).
- The United States Commission on Civil Rights announces that 46% of all minority students still attend segregated public schools, 25 years after the *Brown v. Board of Education* decision (1979).
- Amid shareholder controversy, the Chrysler Corporation invites United Auto Workers President Douglas Fraser to become a member of its board of directors (1979).
- Justice Sandra Day O'Connor is sworn in as the first woman appointed to the United States Supreme Court (1981).
- Following a number of deaths among the homosexual and Haitian immigrant communities from an unknown illness, the American Cancer Institute identifies the malady as the acquired immune deficiency syndrome (AIDS) (1981).
- The United States Census Bureau reports that the poverty rate has reached a new high of 34% for African Americans, 26% for Hispanics, and 11% for whites

for a total average of 14% of all Americans, the largest percentage increase since 1967 (1982).
- At the University of Utah Hospital, doctors successfully implant the first artificial heart into patient Barney Clark (1982).
- Harold Washington is elected as the first African American mayor of Chicago (1983).
- The birthday of Reverend Martin Luther King Jr. is proclaimed as a national holiday following congressional action and approval by President Ronald Reagan (1983).
- Geraldine Ferraro (D-NY), is chosen as the first female vice-presidential candidate by a major political party (1984).
- National attention is turned to the growing problem of homelessness across America, estimated to number between 350,000 to 1,000,000 with only an estimated 91,000 beds available for the homeless (1985).
- Following a vote of 6–3, in a case involving an New York City sheet-metal workers union, the United States Supreme Court reinforces the use of affirmative action strategies to correct past discriminatory actions leveled against minority populations (1986).
- Both public health and law enforcement officials note the alarming rise in the abuse of crack, which is an inexpensive derivative of cocaine, throughout urban, inner-city America (1988).
- The United States Congress passes the *Civil Liberties Act*, which provides compensation to Japanese Americans who were incarcerated or suffered economic losses during the oppressive actions of the federal government during World War II (1988).
- President George H. W. Bush signs the *Americans with Disabilities Act* (ADA), which prohibits any discrimination against individuals with disabilities in employment, housing, education, public accommodations, and telecommunications. Furthermore, the federal law requires that individuals with disabilities be provided with reasonable adaptations in employment and education, as well as accessibility resources in all public accommodations (1990).
- Following a contentious set of hearings in which Anita Hill, a former employee of Supreme Court nominee Clarence Thomas, accuses him of sexual harassment, the Senate confirms him as a Justice of the United States Supreme Court (1991).
- President Bill Clinton enacts the notorious *Don't Ask, Don't Tell* military policy that excludes gay, lesbian, and bisexual individuals from military service (1993).
- President Bill Clinton signs into law the *Personal Responsibility and Work Opportunity Reconciliation Act* (PRWORA), which turns out to be a controversial attempt at modern welfare reform. Among other changes, this federal law abolishes the Aid to Families with Dependent Children (AFDC) program and replaces it with

the time-limited, more restrictive Temporary Assistance for Needy Families (TANF) program (1996).

Note: For a more reflective and functional use of this list of contemporary social welfare historical events, see Question #5 under the **Questions for Further Research and Discussion** section (below).

Sources:
Daniel, C. (1989). *Chronicle of America*. Mt. Kisco, NY: Chronicle Publications.
Mercer, D. (2000). *Millennium year by year*. New York: Dorling Kindersley Publications.
Social welfare developments 1951–2000. (2011). Retrieved from https://socialwelfare.library.vcu.edu/events/1951-2000/

Primary Text Material

Indian Child Welfare Act (1978)

"... Sec. 2. [25 U.S.C. 1901] Recognizing the special relationship between the United States and the Indian tribes and their members and the Federal responsibility to Indian people, the Congress finds—

(1) that clause 3, section 8, article I of the United States Constitution provides that "The Congress shall have Power to regulate Commerce with Indian tribes" and, through this and other constitutional authority, Congress has plenary power over Indian affairs;

(2) that Congress, through statutes, treaties, and the general course of dealing with Indian tribes, has assumed the responsibility for the protection and preservation of Indian tribes and their resources;

(3) that there is no resource that is more vital to the continued existence and integrity of Indian tribes than their children and that the United States has a direct interest, as trustee, in protecting Indian children who are members of or are eligible for membership in an Indian tribe;

(4) that an alarmingly high percentage of Indian families are broken up by the removal, often unwarranted, of their children from them by nontribal public and private agencies and that an alarmingly high percentage of such children are placed in non-Indian foster and adoptive homes and institutions; and

(5) that the States, exercising their recognized jurisdiction over Indian child custody proceedings through administrative and judicial bodies, have often failed to recognize the essential tribal relations of Indian people and the cultural and social standards prevailing in Indian communities and families.

Sec. 3. [25 U.S.C. 1902] The Congress hereby declares that it is the policy of this Nation to protect the best interests of Indian children and to promote

Continued

the stability and security of Indian tribes and families by the establishment of minimum Federal standards for the removal of Indian children from their families and the placement of such children in foster or adoptive homes which will reflect the unique values of Indian culture, and by providing for assistance to Indian tribes in the operation of child and family service programs...

Title I—CHILD CUSTODY PROCEEDINGS

... Sec. 105. [25 U.S.C. 1915] (a) In any adoptive placement of an Indian child under State law, a preference shall be given, in the absence of good cause to the contrary, to a placement with (1) a member of the child's extended family; (2) other members of the Indian child's tribe; or (3) other Indian families.

(b) Any child accepted for foster care or preadoptive placement shall be placed in the least restrictive setting which most approximates a family and in which his special needs, if any, may be met. The child shall also be placed within reasonable proximity to his or her home, taking into account any special needs of the child. In any foster care or preadoptive placement, a preference shall be given, in the absence of good cause to the contrary, to a placement with—

(i) a member of the Indian child's extended family;

(ii) a foster home licensed, approved, or specified by the Indian child's tribe;

(iii) an Indian foster home licensed or approved by an authorized non-Indian licensing authority; or

(iv) an institution for children approved by an Indian tribe or operated by an Indian organization which has a program suitable to meet the Indian child's needs...

Sec. 107. [25 U.S.C. 1917] Upon application by an Indian individual who has reached the age of eighteen and who was the subject of an adoptive placement, the court which entered the final decree shall inform such individual of the tribal affiliation, if any, of the individual's biological parents and provide such other information as may be necessary to protect any rights flowing from the individual's tribal relationship.

Title II—INDIAN CHILD AND FAMILY PROGRAMS

Sec. 201. [25 U.S.C. 1931] (a) The Secretary is authorized to make grants to Indian tribes and organizations in the establishment and operation of Indian child and family service programs on or near reservations and in the preparation and implementation of child welfare codes. The objective of every Indian child and family service program shall be to prevent the breakup of Indian families and, in particular, to insure that the permanent removal of an Indian child from the custody of his parent or Indian custodian shall be a last resort. Such child and family service programs may include, but are not limited to—

(1) a system for licensing or otherwise regulating Indian foster and adoptive homes;

> (2) the operation and maintenance of facilities for the counseling and treatment of Indian families and for the temporary custody of Indian children;
>
> (3) family assistance, including homemaker and home counselors, day care, afterschool care, and employment, recreational activities, and respite care;
>
> (4) home improvement programs;
>
> (5) the employment of professional and other trained personnel to assist the tribal court in the disposition of domestic relations and child welfare matters;
>
> (6) education and training of Indians, including tribal court judges and staff, in skills relating to child and family assistance and service programs;
>
> (7) a subsidy program under which Indian adoptive children may be provided support comparable to that for which they would be eligible as foster children, taking into account the appropriate State standards of support for maintenance and medical needs; and
>
> (8) guidance, legal representation, and advice to Indian families involved in tribal, State, or Federal child custody proceedings . . ."
>
> Source and full text available at https://www.ssa.gov/OP_Home/comp2/F095-608.html.

Timeline of General Events in History, the Humanities, and Science During This Period (1975-2000)

These general historical events may help you understand more clearly the overall historical context during which the primary document was created.

- Following the unconditional surrender of the South Vietnamese military to the Viet Cong army, the last American troops, along with several thousand South Vietnamese allies, are evacuated by helicopter, under duress, from Saigon (1975).
- Engineers Steve Jobs and Steve Wozniak introduce a new line of personal computers from their recently established company called Apple (1976).
- The United States celebrates the 200th year of independence from Great Britain (1976).
- Democratic Party nominee Jimmy Carter is elected president of the United States after defeating Republican President Gerald Ford (1976).
- President Jimmy Carter grants amnesty to all Vietnam Ward draft dodgers, excluding anyone convicted of violence or desertion from a military unit (1977).
- Popular Hollywood movies produced at this time include *Saturday Night Fever*, *Annie Hall*, *Close Encounters of the Third Kind*, and the beginning of George Lucas' *Star Wars* series (1977).
- President Jimmy Carter successfully negotiates a peace agreement between President Anwar el-Sadat of Egypt and Prime Minister Menachem Begin of Israel (1979).

- More than 500 Iranian students and activists attack and occupy the American Embassy in Tehran, holding 52 American personnel hostages (1979).
- Minutes after Ronald Reagan is inaugurated as president of the United States, Iran frees the 52 American hostages being held in captivity (1981).
- The International Business Machines Corporation (IBM) launches its first personal computer line for office and home use (1981).
- As a result of a seven-year antitrust suit against the American Telephone & Telegraph (AT&T) company, more than two-thirds of its assets are sold, leaving AT&T with additional financial resources, a smaller infrastructure, and the freedom to pursue new avenues of innovation within the growing telecommunications industry (1982).
- The Disney Corporation opens a new futuristic exhibit, the Experimental Prototype Community of Tomorrow (EPCOT), at Disney World in Florida (1982).
- Two hundred forty-one United States Marines are killed in an Islamic terrorist bombing of Marine headquarters in Beirut, Lebanon (1983).
- President Reagan and Vice President George H. W. Bush successfully win reelection over Democratic candidates Walter Mondale and Geraldine Ferraro (1984).
- After having lost 16,000 troops since 1980, the Soviets leave Afghanistan in the hands of the successful Afghan guerrilla forces (1988).
- The Berlin Wall, the iconic symbol of Communist rule in Western Europe, is destroyed after the Communist East German government opens the border gates and allows East Germans to enter West Berlin and freedom (1989).
- The executive president of the Union of Soviet Socialist Republics (USSR), Mikhail Gorbachev, resigns under pressure from the 11 leaders of the former Soviet republics, thus ending the formal existence of the USSR (1991).
- Facilitated by the government of Norway and President Bill Clinton, Yasser Arafat, the chairman of the Palestine Liberation Organization (PLO), and Yitzhak Rabin, the prime minister of Israel, sign a peace agreement providing a measure of Palestinian autonomy in the West Bank and Gaza Strip (1993).
- Experiencing a destructive terrorist attack on the United States, the New York World Trade Center shakes from a bomb that explodes in an underground garage in the twin-tower building (1993).
- Islamic extremists led by Osama bin Laden and his organization, al Qaeda, bomb American embassies in Nairobi, Kenya, and Dar es Salaam, Tanzania, killing more than 250 and injuring more than 5,500, most of whom are African citizens (1998).
- Brokered by the former United States Senator from Maine, George Mitchell, the historic Good Friday Peace Accord is signed by British-ruled Northern Ireland and the independent Republic of Ireland (1998).
- The *Euro* is introduced throughout most European countries as the common currency (1999).

- Following a Florida court challenge, the United States Supreme Court, in *Bush v. Gore*, decides in favor of Republican Texas Governor George W. Bush, as President of the United States. (2000).

Sources:

Daniel, C. (1989). *Chronicle of America*. Mt. Kisco, NY: Chronicle Publications.

Events of the 20th century. Retrieved from https://en.wikipedia.org/wiki/timeline_of_the_20th_century

Mercer, D. (2000). *Millennium year by year*. New York: Dorling Kindersley Publications.

Questions for Further Research and Discussion

1. Study in greater detail the full text of the *Indian Child Welfare Act*, then summarize the specific components of this federal act that indicate a clear cultural sensitivity to the unique needs of Indian children and their families.
2. Refer to the list of Indian boarding schools at the end of the Wikipedia article available at https://en.wikipedia.org/wiki/american_indian_boarding_schools. Then choose one school from the list, conduct further Internet research on its history and operations, and finally, summarize the facts and impressions you uncover about that school.
3. Review the latest 2016 revision of the *Indian Child Welfare Act* available at https://www.bia.gov/bia/ois/dhs/icwa. Use the Quick Reference Sheets on Active Efforts, for State Agencies, and for State Courts, then summarize the enhanced procedures used to define "active efforts" as well as specific requirements for state agencies and state courts in cases involving the custody of Indian and native children.
4. Based on the primary documentary material presented here, as well as other material you discover in the **Additional Selected References** at the end of this chapter, what other federal policy or policies do you believe should have been developed or changed at that time? Describe those policies in detail. Recall that a policy could be either *legislative* (i.e., a law), *judicial* (i.e., a court decision), or *administrative* (i.e., an executive or organizational policy) in nature.
5. Select three events appearing under the **Linkage to Social Welfare** section (above), conduct further Internet research regarding them, then conclude whether you believe there exists any plausible relationship between the *Indian Child Welfare Act* and the events you have chosen. Use the analytical model presented in Appendix 1 of this book, or develop your own analytical model, to draw these conclusions.
6. Select one book from the **Additional Selected References** list at the end of this chapter. Briefly read through it, then summarize the main points contained in the book. Identify your own personal reaction to this book.

Additional Selected References

Canby, W. C., Jr. (2004). *American Indian law in a nutshell*. Eagan, MN: West Publishing.

Federal Law Enforcement Training Centers. (2016). *Indian law handbook*. Artesia, NM: Homeland Security, Federal Law Enforcement Training Centers, Office of Chief Counsel, Artesia Legal Division.

Fletcher, M. L. M., Singel, W. T., & Fort, K. E. (Eds.). (2009). *Facing the future: The Indian Child Welfare Act at 30*. Lansing, MI: Michigan State University Press.

Goldstein, J., Freud, A., & Solnit, A. J. (1979). *Beyond the best interests of the child* (2nd ed.). New York: Simon & Schuster.

Jacobs, M. D. (2014). *A generation removed: The fostering and adoption of indigenous children in the postwar world*. Lincoln, NE: University of Nebraska Press.

Jones, B. J., Tilden, M. C., & Gaines-Stoner, K. (2008). *The Indian Child Welfare Act handbook: A legal guide to the custody and adoption of Native American children*. Chicago, IL: American Bar Association.

Jones, W. L. (1995). *The Indian Child Welfare Act handbook: A legal guide to the custody and adoption of Native American children*. Chicago, IL: Section on Family Law, American Bar Association.

Josephy, A. M., Nagel, J., & Johnson, T. R. (1999). *Red power: the American Indians' fight for freedom* (2nd ed.). Lincoln, NE: University of Nebraska Press.

National Council of Juvenile and Family Court Judges. (2013). *The Indian Child Welfare Act facts and fiction: A legal guide to the custody and adoption of Native American children*. Reno, NV: National Council of Juvenile and Family Court Judges.

Pevar, S. L. (2012). *The rights of Indians and tribes*. Oxford: Oxford University Press.

Richland, J. B., & Deer, S. (2016). *Introduction to tribal legal studies*. Lanham, MD: Rowman & Littlefield.

Wilkins, A. (2016). *Fostering state-tribal collaboration: An Indian law primer*. Lanham, MD: Rowman & Littlefield.

Credits

Fig. 29.1: Source: https://commons.wikimedia.org/wiki/File:1890s_Carlisle_Boarding_School_Graduates_PA.jpg.

Fig. 29.2: Source: https://commons.wikimedia.org/wiki/File:Three_Indian_children_and_a_baby_-_NARA_-_297496.jpg.

Chapter 30

Modern Welfare Reform

Personal Responsibility and Work Opportunity Reconciliation Act, PL 104–193 (1996)

Introduction

The story of modern welfare reform technically begins with a brief return to the days of the Great Depression in the late 1920s and the 1930s in America. As previously discussed in Chapter 18 of this book, the 1935 *Social Security Act* launched a major realignment within the social welfare system in this country by defining some problems, such as poverty and family and child welfare, as national challenges that demanded rigorous federal responses. The premier program enacted under the *Social Security Act* for children was the Aid to Dependent Children (ADC) program, later expanded as the Aid to Families with Dependent Children (AFDC) program. This means-tested family support effort faced almost immediate resistance from the politically conservative community on the accusation that it was theoretically ill-conceived, wasted financial resources, and created a system of intergenerational dependency that, ironically, served only to hurt poor families rather than to support them. This negative attitude against most forms of public assistance endured over the next six decades leading up to the administration of President Bill Clinton toward the end of the 20th century.

One of the many contentious issues that roiled through the Clinton administration was a demand for some kind of welfare reform. The President faced a Republican-led Congress that had made welfare reform one of the components of its notorious *Contract with America*, which was a published wish-list of conservative Republican priorities. As a practical move, President Bill Clinton openly cooperated with the reform initiative, especially since he himself, in his 1991 campaign speech, had promised to "... end welfare as we have come to know it ...." Concerns about the effectiveness of the existing Aid to Families with Dependent Children (AFDC) program, as well as the viability of several

FIGURE 30.1 A poor mother and her children during the Great Depression, Elm Grove, Oklahoma.

other safety net social programs, and accusations that these programs were unwittingly trapping poor people in a "cycle of poverty," dominated much of the political conversations between progressives and conservatives. Both the administrations of Presidents Richard Nixon and Jimmy Carter, each with distinctive approaches, had initiated welfare reform legislation, but neither achieved sufficient congressional support. Exacerbating the already contentious situation for President Clinton was the economic recession that lasted from 1989 through 1994, resulting in a 33% increase in the number of households eligible for AFDC. It is an understatement to note that by the mid-1990s, most of the nation was ready for some type of adjustment within the social welfare system.

Technically speaking, the *Personal Responsibility and Work Opportunity Reconciliation Act* (PRWORA) simply repealed the AFDC section of the original 1935 *Social Security Act*. Most notably, *PRWORA* ended AFDC as a categorical entitlement program and replaced it with a new, time-limited, work-focused program: Temporary Assistance to Needy Families (TANF), with an emphasis on the first word—*temporary*. The new TANF program would be managed by states and funded with a fixed annual block grant allocation based on population size. Although general federal guidelines existed, each state could determine the precise eligibility requirements for receiving cash benefits under the TANF program. *PRWORA* also imposed a new citizenship rule on beneficiaries by excluding non-citizens from many of the federally funded social programs. Although the federal government did increase financial support for child care, it also lowered allocations for food stamps, Supplemental Security Income (SSI), and child nutrition programs.

According to this new welfare reform legislation, several significant changes were instituted for families who were threatened with severe economic instability due to unemployment, underemployment, lack of education and marketable work skills, substance abuse, or acute emotional and psychological struggles. The major highlights of these modifications include:

Block grant allocations – States could spend as much as 30% of their federal block grant resources on child care, child protection, or other family-related social services.

Child care – States received mandatory block grant financial resources based on population figures, but states were also provided with greater responsibility to adjust their individual child care programs according to local conditions and values.

Child support enforcement – States were required to enhance their child support services so that financially dependent families could receive appropriate economic resources from the absent parent, typically the father. Any unwed mother receiving TANF benefits was required to identify the father of her child or receive a 25% reduction in cash benefits.

Food stamps (its name was changed to **Supplemental Nutritional Assistance Program** or **SNAP** in 2008 to avoid harmful stigma) – There were previously established national standards of eligibility so families in poverty could access food supplementation resources, but states were empowered to tailor their individual food supplementation programs according to local conditions and values.

Medicaid – States were expected to provide Medicaid services to any family who would be eligible for AFDC resources at the time *PRWORA* was enacted.

TANF – Financial assistance to families was now limited to five years from the date of acceptance into the program. Also included within the first two years of assistance was a work, volunteer, or skills training component, which could include formal education at the discretion of the individual state. Legal immigrants who are non-citizens, except for asylum seekers, were prohibited from receiving TANF benefits during the first five years of residence in the United States. In fact, legal immigrants were excluded from collecting any federal welfare benefit or accessing any non-cash social service during their first five years in the country. Furthermore, unwed teenage mothers could not receive TANF benefits independently but were required to stay in school and reside with at least one adult family member. Finally, single mothers with children younger than 6 years of age would not be penalized if they could not find appropriate work opportunities.

FIGURE 30.2 President Bill Clinton.

Vouchers – States were forbidden to provide any type of non-cash vouchers (e.g., food vouchers, clothing vouchers, rent vouchers, etc.) to any *PRWORA* family after the completion of their five-year period of receiving financial support.

Since the passage of *PRWORA*, legislators on both sides of the political spectrum, social science researchers, and social welfare advocates have debated whether the law's effectiveness has truly altered the substance of this nation's safety net for families living in poverty. Although this debate still continues to the present day, there are several program evaluation issues that should be considered, namely:

- A number of TANF recipients did, in fact, secure full-time work but still received prorated federal benefits due to the low wages they received.
- When asked, most mothers preferred to stay home to raise their young children rather than seek employment or training.
- During the period following 1996, the United States entered a robust economic cycle that created many jobs and new training opportunities in the private sector that were unrelated to the available TANF resources.
- Not all states used the *PRWORA* resources to implement training for recipient family members.
- Most of the families receiving TANF funds continued to need resources from other social welfare programs (such as food stamps and disability payments available under the Social Security program) in order to survive, especially in urban centers.
- It appears that some families were removed from the TANF program as a budgetary strategy rather than as an indication of success.
- Many of those families with extensive and chronic social problems had to resort to homeless shelters once their five-year time limit had elapsed.
- States had the authority to drastically change the requirements and procedures of the former AFDC program with very mixed results for individuals and families.
- Many social scientists charge that *PRWORA* was based on a flawed theory that all poor people were inherently lazy, sexually overactive, overweight, and ignorant about issues like child care, nutrition, and family economics.
- The time pressure in TANF to secure employment led inevitably to many situations of underemployment.

- To hold the belief that the "success" of any social welfare program can be measured by the amount of reduction in caseload size is overly simplistic, politically partisan, and possibly damaging to people's lives.

In summary, the core purpose of the 1996 *Personal Responsibility and Work Opportunity Reconciliation Act* was to interrupt the perceived widespread cycle of intergenerational welfare dependency that shaped the lives of many families in poverty. The underlying assumption was that if federal government resources could train parents to find and keep meaningful work experiences, then their children would have positive role models of economic self-sufficiency and, thus, move on into their own futures with the motivation to stay in school, become employable, and contribute positively to society. The words are indeed noble and inspiring but the results, to many social welfare officials, remain elusive.

Internet Sources for the Content of This Introduction Include:
http://www.epi.org/publication/webfeatures_viewpoints_tanf_testimony/
https://scholarship.richmond.edu/cgi/viewcontent.cgi?referer=https://www.google.com/&httpsredir=1&article=1028&context=pilr
https://www.justice.gov/ovw/file/883641/download
https://aspe.hhs.gov/report/personal-responsibility-and-work-opportunity-reconciliation-act-1996
https://en.wikipedia.org/wiki/personal_responsibility_and_work_opportunity_act
https://royce.house.gov/uploadedfiles/the%201996%20welfare%20reform%20law.pdf
https://www.ssa.gov/history/tally1996.html
https://nwcitizen.com/oldsite/usa/welfare-reform.html

Linkage to Social Welfare History (1975-2000)

Social welfare historical events for this time period include the following:

- The United States Commission on Civil Rights reports that Southern public-school districts have achieved a higher rate of racial integration than have their Northern state counterparts (1975).
- The ABC television miniseries based on Alex Haley's *Roots*, which covers seven generations of an African American family and their rise from slavery, is reported to have received the highest viewer response in television's history (1977).
- Abandoning the principle of "when medically necessary," the United States Congress restricts the payment of federal funds for abortion under Medicaid to only those women who are physically sick or victims of rape or incest (1977).
- Insisting on the principle of "equal pay for equal play," tennis star Billie Jean King champions equality for women within the professional sports environment (1978).

- In San Francisco, Harvey Milk, the first openly gay public official, is assassinated by fellow-Supervisor Mayor Dan White, who professed himself to be a guardian of morality (1978).
- In *Regents of the University of California v. Bakke*, the United States Supreme Court upholds the practice of using race as a consideration in college admissions and also declares the use of racial quotas in college admissions to be unconstitutional (1978).
- President Jimmy Carter signs the *Indian Child Welfare Act* into law, thereby granting greater autonomy to Indian tribes in most matters affecting child welfare (1978).
- The United States Commission on Civil Rights announces that 46% of all minority students still attend segregated public schools, 25 years after the *Brown v. Board of Education* decision (1979).
- Amid shareholder controversy, the Chrysler Corporation invites United Auto Workers President Douglas Fraser to become a member of its board of directors (1979).
- Justice Sandra Day O'Connor is sworn in as the first woman appointed to the United States Supreme Court (1981).
- Following a number of deaths among the homosexual and Haitian immigrant communities from an unknown illness, the American Cancer Institute identifies the malady as the acquired immune deficiency syndrome (AIDS) (1981).
- The United States Census Bureau reports that the poverty rate has reached a new high of 34% for African Americans, 26% for Hispanics, and 11% for whites for a total average of 14% of all Americans, the largest percentage increase since 1967 (1982).
- At the University of Utah Hospital, doctors successfully implant the first artificial heart into patient Barney Clark (1982).
- Harold Washington is elected as the first African American mayor of Chicago (1983).
- The birthday of Reverend Martin Luther King Jr. is proclaimed as a national holiday following congressional action and approval by President Ronald Reagan (1983).
- Geraldine Ferraro (D-NY) is chosen as the first female vice-presidential candidate by a major political party (1984).
- National attention is turned to the growing problem of homelessness across America, estimated to number between 350,000 to 1,000,000 with only an estimated 91,000 beds available for the homeless (1985).
- Following a vote of 6–3, in a case involving a New York City sheet metal workers union, the United States Supreme Court reinforces the use of affirmative action strategies to correct past discriminatory actions leveled against minority populations (1986).
- Both public health and law enforcement officials note the alarming rise in the abuse of crack, which is an inexpensive derivative of cocaine, throughout urban, inner-city America (1988).

- The United States Congress passes the *Civil Liberties Act*, which provides compensation to Japanese Americans who were incarcerated or suffered economic losses during the oppressive actions of the federal government during World War II (1988).
- President George H. W. Bush signs the *Americans with Disabilities Act* (ADA), which prohibits any discrimination against individuals with disabilities in employment, housing, education, public accommodations, and telecommunications. Furthermore, the federal law requires that individuals with disabilities be provided with reasonable adaptations in employment and education, as well as accessibility resources in all public accommodations (1990).
- Following a contentious set of hearings in which Anita Hill, a former employee of Supreme Court nominee Clarence Thomas, accuses him of sexual harassment, the Senate confirms him as a Justice of the United States Supreme Court (1991).
- President Bill Clinton enacts the notorious *Don't Ask, Don't Tell* military policy that excludes gay, lesbian, and bisexual individuals from military service (1993).

Note: For a more reflective and functional use of this list of contemporary social welfare historical events, see Question #5 under the **Questions for Further Research and Discussion** section (below).

Sources:

Daniel, C. (1989). *Chronicle of America*. Mt. Kisco, NY: Chronicle Publications.

Mercer, D. (2000). *Millennium year by year*. New York: Dorling Kindersley Publications.

Social welfare developments 1951–2000. (2011). Retrieved from https://socialwelfare.library.vcu.edu/events/1951-2000/

Primary Text Material

Personal Responsibility and Work Opportunity Reconciliation Act (1996)

"... *TITLE I—BLOCK GRANTS FOR TEMPORARY ASSISTANCE FOR NEEDY FAMILIES*

SEC. 101. FINDINGS.

The Congress makes the following findings:

(1) Marriage is the foundation of a successful society.

(2) Marriage is an essential institution of a successful society which promotes the interests of children.

Continued

(3) Promotion of responsible fatherhood and motherhood is integral to successful child rearing and the well-being of children.

(4) In 1992, only 54 percent of single-parent families with children had a child support order established and, of that 54 percent, only about one-half received the full amount due. Of the cases enforced through the public child support enforcement system, only 18 percent of the caseload has a collection.

(5) The number of individuals receiving aid to families with dependent children (in this section referred to as "AFDC") has more than tripled since 1965. More than two-thirds of these recipients are children. Eighty-nine percent of children receiving AFDC benefits now live in homes in which no father is present . . .

(7) An effective strategy to combat teenage pregnancy must address the issue of male responsibility, including statutory rape culpability and prevention. The increase of teenage pregnancies among the youngest girls is particularly severe and is linked to predatory sexual practices by men who are significantly older . . .

(9) Currently 35 percent of children in single-parent homes were born out-of-wedlock, nearly the same percentage as that of children in single-parent homes whose parents are divorced (37 percent). While many parents find themselves, through divorce or tragic circumstances beyond their control, facing the difficult task of raising children alone, nevertheless, the negative consequences of raising children in single-parent homes are well documented as follows:

(A) Only 9 percent of married-couple families with children under 18 years of age have income below the national poverty level. In contrast, 46 percent of female- headed households with children under 18 years of age are below the national poverty level.

(B) Among single-parent families, nearly 1/2 of the mothers who never married received AFDC while only 1/5 of divorced mothers received AFDC.

(C) Children born into families receiving welfare assistance are 3 times more likely to be on welfare when they reach adulthood than children not born into families receiving welfare.

(D) Mothers under 20 years of age are at the greatest risk of bearing low birth weight babies.

(E) The younger the single-parent mother, the less likely she is to finish high school.

(F) Young women who have children before finishing high school are more likely to receive welfare assistance for a longer period of time . . .

PART A—BLOCK GRANTS TO STATES FOR TEMPORARY ASSISTANCE FOR NEEDY FAMILIES

SEC. 401. PURPOSE.

(a) IN GENERAL.—The purpose of this part is to increase the flexibility of States in operating a program designed to—

(1) provide assistance to needy families so that children may be cared for in their own homes or in the homes of relatives;

(2) end the dependence of needy parents on government benefits by promoting job preparation, work, and marriage;

(3) prevent and reduce the incidence of out-of-wedlock pregnancies and establish annual numerical goals for preventing and reducing the incidence of these pregnancies; and

(4) encourage the formation and maintenance of two-parent families.

(b) NO INDIVIDUAL ENTITLEMENT.—This part shall not be interpreted to entitle any individual or family to assistance under any State program funded under this part . . .

. . . (1) OUTLINE OF FAMILY ASSISTANCE PROGRAM.—

(A) GENERAL PROVISIONS.—A written document that outlines how the State intends to do the following:

(i) Conduct a program, designed to serve all political subdivisions in the State (not necessarily in a uniform manner), that provides assistance to needy families with (or expecting) children and provides parents with job preparation, work, and support services to enable them to leave the program and become self-sufficient.

(ii) Require a parent or caretaker receiving assistance under the program to engage in work (as defined by the State) once the State determines the parent or caretaker is ready to engage in work, or once the parent or caretaker has received assistance under the program for 24 months (whether or not consecutive), whichever is earlier.

(iii) Ensure that parents and caretakers receiving assistance under the program engage in work activities in accordance with section 407.

(iv) Take such reasonable steps as the State deems necessary to restrict the use and disclosure of information about individuals and families receiving assistance under the program attributable to funds provided by the Federal Government.

(v) Establish goals and take action to prevent and reduce the incidence of out-of-wedlock pregnancies, with special emphasis on teenage pregnancies, and establish numerical goals for reducing the illegitimacy ratio of the State . . .

Source and full text available at https://www.gpo.gov/fdsys/pkg/PLAW-104publ193/pdf/PLAW-104publ193.pdf or https://www.congress.gov/bill/104th-congress/house-bill/3734.

Timeline of General Events in History, the Humanities, and Science During This Period (1975–2000)

These general historical events may help you understand more clearly the overall historical context during which the primary document was created.

- Following the unconditional surrender of the South Vietnamese military to the Viet Cong army, the last American troops, along with several thousand South Vietnamese allies, are evacuated by helicopter, under duress, from Saigon (1975).

- Engineers Steve Jobs and Steve Wozniak introduce a new line of personal computers from their recently established company called Apple (1976).
- The United States celebrates the 200th year of independence from Great Britain (1976).
- Democratic Party nominee Jimmy Carter is elected president of the United States after defeating Republican President Gerald Ford (1976).
- President Carter grants amnesty to all Vietnam Ward draft dodgers, excluding anyone convicted of violence or desertion from a military unit (1977).
- Popular Hollywood movies produced at this time include *Saturday Night Fever, Annie Hall, Close Encounters of the Third Kind*, and the beginning of George Lucas' *Star Wars* series (1977).
- President Carter successfully negotiates a peace agreement between President Anwar el-Sadat of Egypt and Prime Minister Menachem Begin of Israel (1979).
- More than 500 Iranian students and activists attack and occupy the American Embassy in Tehran, holding 52 American personnel hostages. (1979).
- Minutes after Ronald Reagan is inaugurated as president of the United States, Iran frees the 52 American hostages being held in captivity (1981).
- The International Business Machines Corporation (IBM) launches its first personal computer line for office and home use (1981).
- As a result of a seven-year antitrust suit against the American Telephone & Telegraph (AT&T) company, more than two-thirds of its assets are sold, leaving AT&T with additional financial resources, a smaller infrastructure, and the freedom to pursue new avenues of innovation within the growing telecommunications industry (1982).
- The Disney Corporation opens a new futuristic exhibit, the Experimental Prototype Community of Tomorrow (EPCOT), at Disney World in Florida (1982).
- Two hundred forty-one United States Marines are killed in an Islamic terrorist bombing of Marine headquarters in Beirut, Lebanon (1983).
- President Ronald Reagan and Vice President George H. W. Bush successfully win reelection over Democratic candidates Walter Mondale and Geraldine Ferraro (1984).
- After having lost 16,000 troops since 1980, the Soviets leave Afghanistan in the hands of the successful Afghan guerrilla forces (1988).
- The Berlin Wall, the iconic symbol of Communist rule in Western Europe, is destroyed after the Communist East German government opens the border gates and allows East Germans to enter West Berlin and freedom (1989).
- The executive president of the Union of Soviet Socialist Republics (USSR), Mikhail Gorbachev, resigns under pressure from the 11 leaders of the former Soviet republics, thus ending the formal existence of the USSR (1991).
- Facilitated by the government of Norway and President Bill Clinton, Yasser Arafat, the chairman of the Palestine Liberation Organization (PLO) and Yitzhak Rabin, the prime minister of Israel, sign a peace agreement providing a measure of Palestinian autonomy in the West Bank and Gaza Strip (1993).
- Experiencing a destructive terrorist attack on the United States, the New York World Trade Center shakes from a bomb that exploded in an underground garage in the twin-tower building (1993).

- Islamic extremists led by Osama bin Laden and his organization, al Qaeda, bomb American embassies in Nairobi, Kenya, and Dar es Salaam, Tanzania, killing more than 250 and injuring more than 5,500, most of whom are African citizens (1998).
- Brokered by the former United States Senator from Maine, George Mitchell, the historic Good Friday Peace Accord is signed by British-ruled Northern Ireland and the independent Republic of Ireland (1998).
- The *Euro* is introduced throughout most European countries as the common currency (1999).
- Following a Florida court challenge, the United States Supreme Court, in *Bush v. Gore*, decides in favor of Republican Texas Governor George W. Bush as President of the United States (2000).

Sources:

Daniel, C. (1989). *Chronicle of America*. Mt. Kisco, NY: Chronicle Publications.

Events of the 20th century. Retrieved from https://en.wikipedia.org/wiki/timeline_of_the_20th_century

Mercer, D. (2000). *Millennium year by year*. New York: Dorling Kindersley Publications.

Questions for Further Research and Discussion

1. As with most federal legislation, there have been many changes to the *Personal Responsibility and Work Opportunity Reconciliation Act* introduced by succeeding Congresses since 1996. Through further Internet research, determine what the major changes to the law have been, then list them in order of importance.
2. Contact, by email and/or telephone, the public social agency that is responsible for cash programs affecting children and families in your own state. That agency may be called the Department of Human Services, Department Social Services, Department of Family and Child Welfare, or some other similar name. Then summarize the range of cash, in-kind, and personal social service programs available to low-income families in your state.
3. Conduct further Internet research specifically on the later effects of the *Personal Responsibility and Work Opportunity Reconciliation Act* on individuals and families as the law was implemented into the early 2000s. Then summarize what you discovered were both the accomplishments and the challenges contained in the law.
4. Based on the primary documentary material presented here, as well as other material you discover in the **Additional Selected References** at the end of this chapter, what other federal policy or policies do you believe should have been developed or changed at that time? Describe those policies in detail. Recall that a policy could be either *legislative* (i.e., a law), *judicial* (i.e., a court decision), or *administrative* (i.e., an executive or organizational policy) in nature.
5. Select three events appearing under the **Linkage to Social Welfare** section (above), conduct further Internet research regarding them, then conclude whether

you believe there exists any plausible relationship between the *Personal Responsibility and Work Opportunity Reconciliation Act* and the events you have chosen. Use the analytical model presented in Appendix 1 of this book, or develop your own analytical model, to draw these conclusions.

6. Select one book from the **Additional Selected References** list at the end of this chapter. Briefly read through it, then summarize the main points contained in the book. Identify your own personal reaction to this book.

Additional Selected References

Albelda, R., & Withorn, A. (Eds.). (2002). *Lost ground: Welfare reform, poverty, and beyond*. Brooklyn, NY: South End Press.

Bane, M. J., & Ellwood, D. T. (1994). *Welfare realities: From rhetoric to reform*. Cambridge, MA: Harvard University Press.

Brauner, S., & Loprest, P. (1999). *Where are they now? What States' studies of people who left welfare tell us*. Washington, DC: The Urban Institute.

Greenberg, M., & Savner, S. (1996). *A detailed summary of key provisions of the Temporary Assistance for Needy Families Block Grant of H.R. 3734: The Personal Responsibility and Work Opportunity Reconciliation Act of 1996*. Washington, DC: Center for Law and Social Policy.

Haskins, R. (2006). *Work over welfare: The inside story of the 1996 welfare reform law*. Washington, DC: Brookings Institution Press.

Hays, S. (2003). *Flat broke with children: Women in the age of welfare reform*. Oxford: Oxford University Press.

Lennon, M. C., & Corbett, T. (2003). *Policy into action: Implementation research and welfare reform*. Washington, DC: Urban Institute Press.

Morgen, S., Acker, J., & Weigt, J. M. (2010). *Stretched thin: Poor families, welfare work, and welfare reform*. Ithaca: Cornell University Press.

Reese, E. (2011). *They say cut back, we say fight back! Welfare activism in an era of retrenchment*. New York: Russell Sage Foundation.

Riccucci, N. M. (2005). *How management matters: Street-level bureaucrats and welfare reform*. Washington, DC: Georgetown University Press.

Tanner, M. (2003). *The poverty of welfare: Helping others in civil society*. Washington, DC: Cato Institute.

United States Commission on Civil Rights & United States Commission on Civil Rights. (2000). *The Personal Responsibility and Work Opportunity Reconciliation Act of 1996: An examination of its impact on legal immigrants and refugees in Rhode Island*. Washington, DC: U.S. Commission on Civil Rights, Eastern Regional Office.

Credits

Fig. 30.1: Source: https://commons.wikimedia.org/wiki/File:Poor_mother_and_children,_Oklahoma,_1936_by_Dorothea_Lange.jpg.

Fig. 30.2: Source: http://www.loc.gov/pictures/item/93505822/.

Chapter 31

Modern Health Care Reform

The *Patient Protection and Affordable Care Act* (2010) and Recent Developments (2018)

Introduction

According to available statistics, in 2010, approximately 48 million (18.2%) of non-elderly Americans were not covered by any health insurance policy, either as an employment benefit or purchased as individual coverage from private health insurance companies. It was within this context that President Barack Obama, aided by a Democratic-controlled House of Representatives and Senate, successfully passed the *Patient Protection and Affordable Care Act* (*ACA*) in 2010.

By 2016, the number of non-elderly, uninsured individuals dropped to approximately 27 million Americans (10.3%), most of whom were individuals and families with limited economic resources, though not officially considered "poor." Most of those who are legally considered "poor" do possess health insurance coverage. In fact, anyone receiving federal public assistance (e.g., TANF, SNAP, SSI, etc.) is typically covered by the Medicaid health insurance program for their health needs. Furthermore, every American age 65 and older, regardless of income status, and any individual receiving disability benefits under the *Social Security* program is covered by the Medicare health insurance program.

In essence, the *ACA* is a long and intricate piece of federal legislation that was somewhat problematic in its initiation due to a series of technical glitches and has faced a multiyear assault from the conservative right because it clearly attempts to radically reform the entire American health care system. This reform effort includes several very progressive goals, such as extending health care insurance coverage to millions of uninsured Americans; lowering health costs and increasing efficiency in the system; implementing a spirit of *shared responsibility* for health care, in which all individuals would pool some of their

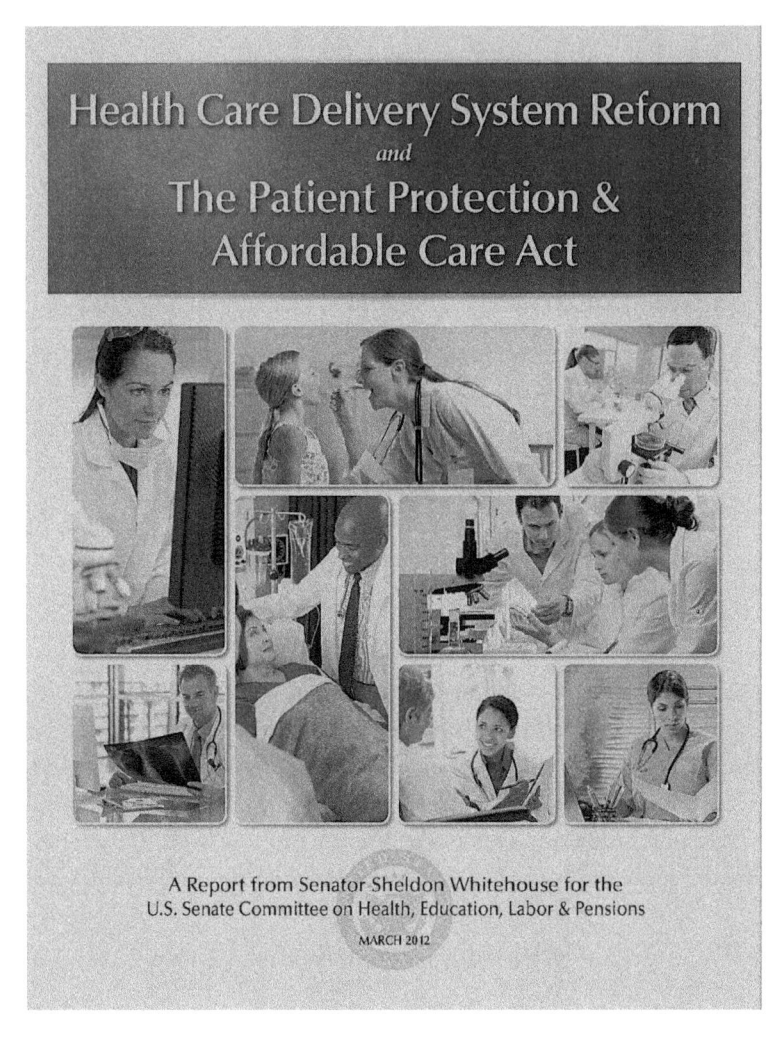

FIGURE 31.1 Health care delivery system and the Patient Protection and Affordable Care Act.

resources, thereby reducing costs for those who need to pay for health care at a particular point in their lives; and insisting that every private health insurance policy contain a list of minimum coverage requirements.

One of the most prominent components of the *ACA* calls for the inclusion in any health insurance policy drawn up under the new law a list of what are identified as 10 essential health benefits, which include:

- Outpatient care
- Hospital emergency services
- Inpatient hospital care
- Maternity and newborn care, plus contraceptives and breastfeeding services
- Mental health services and addiction treatment

- Pharmaceutical drugs prescribed by a physician
- Rehabilitation services and devices
- Laboratory services
- Prevention services, wellness services, and chronic disease treatment
- Pediatric services for infants and children

The *ACA* contains nine distinct titles, or sections, that address several areas for reform within the health insurance system in place in 2010. These titles, along with a brief summary of what each encompasses, follows here.

Title I: Quality, affordable health care for all Americans
This section, the longest and most notable, eliminated annual and lifetime limits on health benefits; prevented private, for-profit health insurance companies from cancelling (except for fraud or deception) a health insurance policy retroactively (i.e., after an illness arose) because of some minor technicality; abolished the use of pre-existing conditions to refuse coverage; allowed dependents to be covered by parent's health insurance policy until age 26; facilitated the use of similar policy language so consumers could understand coverage across several offers; placed limits on administrative costs of health insurance providers; allowed a consumer appeals process in cases of denial of coverage; created a government-sponsored Internet portal where health providers could advertise insurance coverage plans for each state; created health care exchanges available in each state where consumers could purchase health policies directly; provided subsidized tax credits to families earning between 100% and 400% of the official federal poverty level (FPL); and, finally, authorized what has been called the *individual mandate*, a rule that requires every American citizen to obtain minimum essential health insurance coverage or pay a fine that is scheduled to increase annually for nonconformance.

Title II: Role of public programs
This title expanded Medicaid coverage to all individuals and families earning up to 133% of the FPL, with the federal government reimbursing the states for most, but not all, of the increased health insurance coverage. It also provided additional financial support for the nationwide Children's Health Insurance Program (CHIP). In a 2012 decision, the United States Supreme Court restricted the mandatory requirement for states to expand their Medicaid programs so that the expansion is now voluntary on the state's part.

Title III: Improving the quality and efficiency of health care
This section linked state reimbursements for Medicaid to documented evidence of quality performance and outcomes for several health conditions, such as heart disease, major surgeries, and pneumonia; encouraged the development of pilot programs nationally that focus on patient care models; and mandated

FIGURE 31.2 President Barack Obama signing the Patient Protection and Affordable Care Act at the White House.

drug companies to provide 50% discounts on brand-name medications paid for under Part D of the original Medicare legislation.

Title IV: Prevention of chronic disease and improving public health

This title introduced a new commitment and financial resources to encourage a national emphasis on promoting better community health for all Americans and preventing the spread of disease and increased access to preventive services for all clinical areas of concern.

Title V: Health care workforce

This section encouraged the improvements in the recruitment, training, and retention of health care workers; provided grants to states for health workforce research and future planning; and facilitated the increase in the number of health care workers by improving the federal student loan program for anyone interested in health care delivery.

Title VI: Transparency and program integrity

This section created a greater transparency throughout the health care system by providing consumers with information on topics such as physician-owned hospitals, the use of gifts to medical personnel by drug manufacturer, and the ownership of nursing homes.

Title VII: Improving access to innovative medical therapies

In this title, patients were offered greater access to new technology and new pharmaceuticals, especially those designed for children and for the underserved communities.

Title VIII: Community living assistance services and supports

This section explored the formation of a voluntary, self-funded program to respond to the need for long-term care, especially for the elderly.

Title IX: Revenue provisions
This final title introduced an excise tax (referred to as the *Cadillac tax*) on expensive, employer-provided health insurance plans that far exceed the minimum health coverage requirements of the *ACA*; mandated an annual flat fee of a total of $2 billion on medical device manufacturers allocated across all manufacturers and based on each one's percentage of market share; introduced a small excise tax on voluntary cosmetic surgery procedures; and, finally, limited the amounts of compensation to the executive staff of all health insurance companies.

Negative reaction to the *ACA* has been swift and enduring. Almost immediately after its enactment in 2010, Congressional Republicans started engaging in an unrelenting campaign to repeal and replace the *ACA*, which they disdainfully referred to as "Obamacare." Despite more than 70 attempts in Congress to abort the *ACA*, it has endured since its inception. Republicans seem to all agree on repealing the *ACA* but have been unable to agree on the concrete details of its replacement. Democrats, generally, have tried over this period to adjust several elements of the law which admittedly need changing, but their repair efforts have been met with stern resistance from their conservative colleagues.

Since the successful election and 2017 inauguration of President Donald Trump, with the assistance of a strong Republican majority in the House of Representatives and a slim Republican edge in the Senate, several initiatives have weakened the full effect of the *ACA* as originally intended. The Trump administration's 2017 *Tax Cuts and Jobs Act*, for example, contains the repeal of the *individual mandate* provision of the *ACA*. This could have a major destabilizing effect throughout the private health insurance market because there will undoubtedly be a smaller pool of covered individuals and fewer insurance resources available to disburse when needed. In turn, this situation will inevitably lead to an increase in premiums for those still enrolled, those who most probably will be people who are older, sicker, and most vulnerable to price increases. With this elimination of a penalty for not purchasing health insurance, the Congressional Budget Office estimates that approximately 13 million individuals will be without health insurance in future years.

Other Republican strategies to undermine distinct sections of the *ACA* include: allowing health insurance companies to sell individual policies across state lines as a means of increasing competition; lowering premium costs by removing the mandated 10 essential health benefits from insurance plans, even though those plans will then offer inferior benefits to consumers; decreasing the eligibility for *Medicaid* from 138% of the FPL down to 100%; ending cost-sharing arrangements with health insurance companies, thus guaranteeing further increases in insurance premiums for consumers; allowing low-cost, short-term health insurance policies to be sold, thus limiting coverage and avoiding the requirement for the inclusion of the 10 essential health benefits; permitting health insurance companies to charge seniors as much as five times more than young clients, which is an increase from the three times limit under the original *ACA*; and, finally, adding a work requirement for Medicaid recipients, even though Medicaid is a health insurance instrument used by people when they are sick and is not directly connected to the work environment.

Beyond the government, some religious groups, such as the Roman Catholic Church, as well as conservative Jewish and Protestant congregations, have been somewhat successful in their negative reactions to the *ACA*'s coverage of contraceptives, some of which these religious organizations claim will cause abortions and, therefore, violate their moral beliefs. Several for-profit lay organizations and small businesses have also used this moral argument as a tactic to avoid offering contraceptive insurance coverage to their employees.

The future of the *ACA* and whether it will be expanded with the addition of necessary changes or further weakened, and perhaps even repealed, remains essentially a political question to be answered by Democratic, Independent, and Republican legislators at both the state and federal levels. The ultimate task going forward for all American citizens, however, is to decide in the voting booth what kind of health care system is consistent with their view of American values. Is health care a universal right for all, just as fresh air and clean water and a secure environment can be considered a common right? Or is heath care to be secured through the marketplace, managed by the rules of supply and demand with varying prices and benefits based on a person's financial resources? Or is some feasible combination possible? Whatever the future produces for the health care system in the United States, it is clear that social workers, along with other medical and human service professionals, will be impacted in their daily interactions with their clients and their communities.

Internet Sources for the Content of This Introduction Include:

https://www.kff.org/health-reform/fact-sheet/summary-of-the-affordable-care-act/
https://www.dpc.senate.gov/healthreformbill/healthbill04.pdf
https://obamacarefacts.com/affordablecareact-summary/
http://accountablecaredoctors.org/american-healthcare-whats-the-problem/?gclid=EAIaIQob-ChMIzema96C62QIVDLXACh2ZzwkNEAMYASAAEgKAiPD_BwE
https://en.wikipedia.org/wiki/patient_protection_and_affordable_care_act
https://www.kff.org/uninsured/fact-sheet/key-facts-about-the-uninsured-population/

Linkage to Social Welfare History (2000–2018)

Social welfare historical events for this time period include the following:

- A working model of the human genome is published, thus launching a new area of genetic understanding and discovery (2001).
- In an effort to reform the education system by establishing measurable goals, President George W. Bush signs the *No Child Left Behind Act* into law (2002).

- Democratic Representative Nancy Pelosi of California is elected as the first woman to become speaker of the United States House of Representatives (2007).
- Democratic Senator Barack Obama is elected as the first African American president of the United States (2008).
- Attorney Sonia Sotomayor is confirmed as the first Latina associate justice of the United States Supreme Court (2009).
- The United States Congress passes the *Don't Ask, Don't Tell Repeal Act*, which removes restrictions formerly placed on gay, lesbian, and bisexual individuals in the military service (2010).
- The world population reportedly reaches more than 7 billion individuals (2011).
- In Obergefell v. Hodges, the United States Supreme Court declares that gay marriage must be recognized as legal in all 50 states (2015).
- By the end of President Barack Obama's two terms as president, the Republican majority in Congress has attempted more than 70 times to repeal the *ACA* but is unsuccessful each time (2016).
- Republican nominee Donald Trump, running on a platform that is outwardly anti-immigrant, racially insensitive, and misogynistic, is elected president of the United States and carries with him a Republican majority in both the House of Representatives and the Senate (2016).
- President Donald Trump signs the *Tax Cuts and Jobs Act*, which, among other things, repeals the *individual mandate* provision of the *ACA*, thereby creating new financial constraints for private health insurance companies in their coverage of individuals and families with limited economic means (2017).
- In response to a series of credible accusations of sexual harassment and assault against women by powerful men in politics, business, the arts, and television, the #MeToo movement spreads quickly and widely over social media platforms (2017).
- Despite promises to the contrary, President Trump and the Republican-controlled Congress fail to protect the more than 700,000 young people brought into the United States without legal papers by their parents and who have been protected until now by the Obama administration's 2012 *Deferred Action for Childhood Arrivals* (*DACA*) program (2018).

Note: For a more reflective and functional use of this list of contemporary social welfare historical events, see Question #5 under the **Questions for Further Research and Discussion** section (below).

Sources:

Timeline of United States history (1990–present). Retrieved from https://en.wikipedia.org/wiki/timeline_of_united_states_history_(1990–present)

The Guardian. Decade timeline, 2000–2009. Retrieved from https://www.theguardian.com/world/2009/oct/17/decade-timeline-what-happened-when

Timeline of the 21st century. Retrieved from https://en.wikipedia.org/wiki/timeline_of_the_21st_century

Primary Text Material

Patient Protection and Affordable Care Act (2010)

"... Subpart II—Improving Coverage
'SEC. 2711. NO LIFETIME OR ANNUAL LIMITS.
(a) IN GENERAL.—A group health plan and a health insurance issuer offering group or individual health insurance coverage may not establish—
(1) lifetime limits on the dollar value of benefits for any participant or beneficiary; or
(2) unreasonable annual limits . . . on the dollar value of benefits for any participant or beneficiary . . .

SEC. 2712. PROHIBITION ON RESCISSIONS.
A group health plan and a health insurance issuer offering group or individual health insurance coverage shall not rescind such plan or coverage with respect to an enrollee once the enrollee is covered under such plan or coverage involved, except that this section shall not apply to a covered individual who has performed an act or practice that constitutes fraud or makes an intentional misrepresentation of material fact as prohibited by the terms of the plan or coverage. Such plan or coverage may not be cancelled except with prior notice to the enrollee, and only as permitted under section 2702(c) or 2742(b).

SEC. 2713. COVERAGE OF PREVENTIVE HEALTH SERVICES.
(a) IN GENERAL.—A group health plan and a health insurance issuer offering group or individual health insurance coverage shall, at a minimum provide coverage for and shall not impose any cost sharing requirements for—
(1) evidence-based items or services that have in effect a rating of 'A' or 'B' in the current recommendations of the United States Preventive Services Task Force;
(2) immunizations that have in effect a recommendation from the Advisory Committee on Immunization Practices of the Centers for Disease Control and Prevention with respect to the individual involved; and
(3) with respect to infants, children, and adolescents, evidence-informed preventive care and screenings provided for in the comprehensive guidelines supported by the Health Resources and Services Administration.
(4) with respect to women, such additional preventive care and screenings not described in paragraph (1) as provided for in comprehensive guidelines supported by the Health Resources and Services Administration for purposes of this paragraph.

> *(5) for the purposes of this Act, and for the purposes of any other provision of law, the current recommendations of the United States Preventive Service Task Force regarding breast cancer screening, mammography, and prevention shall be considered the most current other than those issued in or around November 2009.*
>
> *Nothing in this subsection shall be construed to prohibit a plan or issuer from providing coverage for services in addition to those recommended by United States Preventive Services Task Force or to deny coverage for services that are not recommended by such Task Force . . ."*
>
> Source and full text available at https://www.gpo.gov/fdsys/pkg/PLAW-111publ148/pdf/PLAW-111publ148.pdf.

Timeline of General Events in History, the Humanities, and Science During This Period (2000-2018)

These general historical events may help you understand more clearly the overall historical context during which the primary document was created.

- Timothy McVeigh is executed as an American terrorist because of his involvement in the 1995 bombing of a federal building in Oklahoma City (2001).
- On September 11, radical Islamist terrorists hijack a series of planes and crash them into the World Trade Center in New York City, the Pentagon in Virginia, and an open field in Shanksville, Pennsylvania, killing a total of 2,996 and injuring more than 6,000 people (2001).
- In response to the 9/11 attacks on the United States, President George W. Bush declares a "War on Terror" (2001).
- One month after the 9/11 attacks, United States military forces invade Afghanistan (2001).
- The United States, joined by the United Kingdom, Australia, and Poland, invade Iraq and capture Iraqi President Saddam Hussein (2003).
- The space shuttle *Columbia* is destroyed, with no survivors, upon reentry at the end of its mission (2003).
- Facebook, a new social media networking tool developed by Harvard student Mark Zuckerberg, is officially launched (2004).
- Hurricane Katrina ravishes New Orleans and nearby coastal areas, causing major flooding and killing nearly 2,000 people. The Bush administration is criticized for its limited and uncoordinated federal relief response (2005).
- Following a new definition of a planet by the International Astronomical Union, Pluto is no longer considered one of the planets orbiting the earth's sun (2006).
- The Apple company releases its first *iPhone*, which basically functions as a handheld computer (2007).

- Within a global context, stock markets are devalued, leading to a worldwide economic recession (2008).
- A new politically conservative group, the Tea Party, begins a series of public protests that advocate for small government, fiscal constraint, personal freedoms, and a strict, originalist view of the *United States Constitution* (2009).
- An explosion at the *Deepwater Horizon* oil installation in the Gulf of Mexico produces the largest oil spill in United States history, thus creating major environmental damage to coastal areas (2010).
- Terrorist leader Osama bin Laden is killed by United States military forces in Pakistan (2011).
- Hurricane Sandy devastates areas along the East Coast and causes extensive property damage, especially to the New Jersey Shore and New York City (2012).
- Sandy Hook Elementary school in Newtown, Connecticut, becomes another statistic in a long history of school shootings, resulting in the deaths of 20 young children and six educational staff members (2012).
- The *Higgs boson*, which is the most elemental unit in the field particle physics, also called the "God particle," is discovered (2012).
- Security analyst Edward Snowden releases thousands of classified documents that reveal widespread surveillance of American citizens by the United States National Security Agency (2013).
- At the United Nations Climate Change Conference in Paris, 196 countries agree to limit the amount of global greenhouse emissions each produce (2015).
- Following the shooting and deaths of 15 students and two educational staff at the Marjory Stoneman Douglas High School in Parkland, Florida, at the hands of a disturbed former student with an AR-15 assault rifle, high school students in many communities across the United States begin to advocate with words and actions for sensible gun reform legislation (2018).

Sources:

Timeline of United States history (1990–present). Retrieved from https://en.wikipedia.org/wiki/timeline_of_united_states_history_(1990–present)

The Guardian. Decade timeline, 2000–2009. Retrieved from https://www.theguardian.com/world/2009/oct/17/decade-timeline-what-happened-when

Timeline of the 21st century. Retrieved from https://en.wikipedia.org/wiki/timeline_of_the_21st_century

Questions for Further Research and Discussion

1. The *Patient Protection and Affordable Care Act* is quite a lengthy document, so access it at the website provided above, then skim through the nine titles quickly and look for words and phrases that indicate values or

attitudes underlying what is written. After that, summarize what you have discovered.

2. The latest information regarding the *Patient Protection and Affordable Care Act* can be accessed online at healthcare.gov. Go to that site, study what is offered, then summarize the types of explicit information that is available to the American public.
3. Search online for your own state's *Affordable Care Act Marketplace*, where individual health insurance plans for your state will be listed. Briefly skim through the different plan offerings, looking for commonalities and differences among the insurance companies. Then summarize what you have discovered and include specific examples.
4. Based on the primary documentary material presented here, as well as other material you discover in the **Additional Selected References** at the end of this chapter, what other federal policy or policies do you believe should have been developed or changed at that time? Describe those policies in detail. Recall that a policy could be either *legislative* (i.e., a law), *judicial* (i.e., a court decision), or *administrative* (i.e., an executive or organizational policy) in nature.
5. Select three events appearing under the **Linkage to Social Welfare** section (above), conduct further Internet research regarding them, then conclude whether you believe there exists any plausible relationship between the *Patient Protection and Affordable Care Act* and the events you have chosen. Use the analytical model presented in Appendix 1 of this book, or develop your own analytical model, to draw these conclusions.
6. Select one book from the **Additional Selected References** list at the end of this chapter. Briefly read through it, then summarize the main points contained in the book. Identify your own personal reaction to this book.

Additional Selected References

Amadeo, K. (2015). *The ultimate Obamacare handbook: A definitive guide to the benefits, rights, responsibilities, and potential pitfalls of the Affordable Care Act*. New York: Skyhorse Publishing.

Aurbach, D., Heaton, P., & Brantley, I. (2014). *How will the Patient Protection and Affordable Care Act affect insurance liability costs?* Santa Monica, CA: Rand Corporation.

Béland, D., Rocco, P., & Waddan, A. (2016). *Obamacare wars: Federalism, state politics, and the Affordable Care Act*. Lawrence, KS: University of Kansas Press.

Brill, S. (2015). *America's bitter pill: Money, politics, backroom deals, and the fight to fix our broken healthcare system*. New York: Random House.

Goldsmith, F. (2015). *Libraries and the Affordable Care Act: Helping the community understand health-care options*. Chicago: American Library Association.

Fritzsche, K., Masi, S., & United States. (2017). *How repealing portions of the Affordable Care Act would affect health insurance coverage and premiums*. Washington, DC: Congressional Budget Office.

Malani, A., & Schill, M. H. (2015). *The future of healthcare reform in the United States*. Chicago: University of Chicago Press.

National Council on Disability (U.S.). (2016). *The Impact of the Affordable Care Act on people with disabilities: A 2015 status report*. Washington, DC: National Council on Disability.

National Council on Disability (U.S.). (2016). *Monitoring and enforcing the Affordable Care Act: A roadmap for people with disabilities*. Washington, DC: National Council on Disability.

Powers, J. S. (Ed.). (2014). *Healthcare changes and the Affordable Care Act: A physician call to action*. Champaign, IL: Springer.

Selker, H. P., & Wasser, J. S. (Eds.). (2014). *The Affordable Care Act as a national experiment: Health policy innovations and lessons*. New York: Springer.

Vardell, E., & Medical Library Association. (2015). *The Medical Library Association guide to answering questions about the Affordable Care Act*. Lanham, MD: Rowman & Littlefield.

Credits

Fig. 31.1: Source: https://commons.wikimedia.org/wiki/File:Health_Care_Delivery_System_Reform_and_The_Patient_Protection_%26_Affodable_Care_Act.pdf.

Fig. 31.2: Source: https://commons.wikimedia.org/wiki/File:Obama_signs_health_care-20100323.jpg.

Appendix

Analytical Model: Linkage of Social Welfare History Event and Primary Document

Relevant Social Welfare History Event:

Primary Document Name:

Timing: Did the social welfare historical event occur
   before _____ or
   after _____ the primary document was composed?

Direction: Between the event and the primary document, was there a
   direct relationship (i.e., strong, obvious) _____ or
   indirect relationship (i.e., weak, unforeseen) _____ or
   tangential relationship (i.e., virtually nonexistent, vague) _____ or
   no relationship (i.e., not logically present) _____?

Effect: Considering the outcome of the relationship between the historical event and the primary document, was that outcome, in your judgement,
   positive (i.e., constructive, enhancing, progressive) _____ or
   negative (i.e., harmful, damaging, regressive) _____ or
   neutral (i.e., indistinct, detached, balanced) _____?

Comments:

Documents/vf/2018

Index

A

Abbot Institute, 85
Abbott, Edith, 156
Abbott, Grace, 156
abortion
    legal access to, 321–324
    Roe v. Wade (1973), 321–324
An Act Declaring the Rights and Liberties of the Subject and Settling the Succession of the Crown, 13. *See also* English Bill of Rights
Addams, Jane, 155–157, 160–162, 308
adoption
    for Native Americans, 335–339
    "orphan trains," 44, 54, 65
Adult Basic Education, 281
adults, defined, 307
The Affluent Society (Galbraith), 242, 255, 269, 284, 298, 312, 325
African Americans
    and education, 239–241
    lynching of, 239
    oppression of, 293
    police brutality, 243–244
    in U.S. armed forces, 227–229
Aid to Dependent Children (ADC), 192, 347
Aid to Families with Dependent Children (AFDC), 192, 347–348
America and Americans (Steinbeck), 205
American Bill of Rights, 13
American Civil Liberties Union (ACLU), 156, 179
An American Dilemma: The Negro Problem and Modern Democracy (Myrdal), 240
American Revolution, 11, 21, 229
America's foundational documents
    Articles of Confederation, 21–22, 28
    Bill of Rights, 21–25, 27–28
    Constitution of the United States, 21–25
    Declaration of Independence, 21–22, 28, 52, 167
Anthony, Susan B., 167–168
Appeal to Reason, 143
Arawak tribe, 2, 5–6
Arthur, Chester, 98
Articles of Confederation, 21–22, 28
Assistance for Migrant Agricultural Employees, 281
Atlanta Compromise, 130
Aunt Phillis's Cabin; Or, Southern Life as It Is (Eastman), 43

B

"The Ballad of the Green Berets," 267
Battle of Bull Run, Virginia, 61
Battle of Fort Pillow, 62
The Beach Boys, 263
The Beatles, 247, 259, 263, 274, 289, 303
Bell, John, 178
Bill of Rights, 21–25, 27–28
Birth of a Nation, 74, 135, 147, 159, 171
Black History Month, 33
Black Lives Matter Movement, 33
Blackmun, Harry, 322
Blackwell, Henry, 167
block grant allocations, 349
"Bloody Sunday" attack, 268
Blow, Peter, 51
"Blowin' in the Wind," 243, 255, 265–266, 270, 272, 285, 299, 312, 325
Boleyn, Anne, 13
Bolling v. Sharpe, 239
Bono, 265
Boston (Sinclair), 144
Briggs v. Elliott, 239
Brotherhood of Sleeping Car Porters, 227

Brown, Henry, 120
Brown, John, 32
Brown, Oliver, 239
"Brown Eyed Girl," 263
Brown v. Board of Education of Topeka (1954), 64, 74, 120, 239–241, 245–246, 254, 269, 284, 298, 311, 324, 339, 352
Buck, Carrie, 178
Buck v. Bell, 177–180, 183–184
Bureau of Indian Affairs (BIA), 337–338
Butler, Nicholas Murray, 157
The Byrds, 263

C

Carawan, Guy, 267–268
Carter, Jimmy, 348
Cash, Johnny, 263
Catholicism, 4
Catholics, 11, 74, 135, 148, 160
CBS Reports, 251
Central Pacific Railroad, 95–96
A Century of Dishonor: A sketch of the United States government's dealings with some Indian tribes (Jackson), 86, 88, 91–92
Chaney, James Earl, 295
Charity Organization Society (COS), 157
Chavez, Caesar, 253
child care, and welfare reform legislation, 349
Children's Bureau, 156
child support enforcement, 349
Child Welfare League of America, 336
Chinese Exclusion Act, 97–98, 102, 216
Chinese immigrants, 95–98
Christianity, 43, 75
Civil Rights Act of 1964, 75, 256, 270, 280, 293–296, 301, 313, 326
Civil Rights March, 132
Civil Rights Movement, 33, 64, 75
Civil War, 32, 43, 51–53, 61, 63, 73, 119, 129, 168
Civil Works Administration (CWA), 190
The Clansman (Dixon), 74
Clark, Kenneth, 240
Clark, Mamie, 240
Cleveland, Grover, 87
Clinton, Bill, 347–348, 350
Columbus, Christopher, 1–8
　describing Native Peoples, 1–2

Commission on Civil Rights, 294
Committee on Equality of Treatment and Opportunity, 228
Community Services Block Grant (CSBG) program, 283
Congress of Racial Equality (CORE), 243, 255, 269, 285, 298, 312, 325
Constitution of the United States, 21–25, 120, 169
Continental Congress, 21
Contract with America, 347
Covey, Edward, 31
Cozans, Philip, 43
The Crisis, 131
Criswell, Robert, 43
Cronkite, Walter, 331
Cup of Gold (Steinbeck), 203

D

Darrow, Clarence, 144
Darwin, Charles, 177
Davis v. County School Board of Prince Edward County, Virginia, 239
Dawes Act, 88
"The Dawn of Correction," 267
Day-Lewis, Daniel, 144
Declaration of Independence, 21–22, 28, 52, 167
Declaration of Sentiments and Resolutions, 172–173
Department of Housing and Urban Development, 280
The Devastation of the Indies, A Brief Account (Las Casas), 4
Dewey, John, 156
Dickens, Charles, 108, 155
Dickenson, Emily, 85
DiFranco, Ani, 265
discrimination, 95–104
　Civil Rights Act of 1964, 293–295, 301
　Voting Rights Act of 1965, 296–297, 302
Dixon, Thomas, 74
Dobbs, Alice, 178
Dobbs, John, 178
Douglass, Frederick, 31, 167
The Douglass Monthly, 32
Dragon's Teeth (Sinclair), 145
Du Bois, W.E.B., 121, 137–139
Dyer Anti-Lynching Bill, 135, 148, 172

Dylan, Bob, 243, 255, 265–266, 270, 272, 285, 299, 312, 325

E

Eastman, Mary Henderson, 43
East of Eden (Steinbeck), 205
Economic Opportunity Act, 279–283, 287–288, 299, 313, 326
  main programs under, 281–282
education
  Adult Basic Education, 281
  and African Americans, 239–241
Edwards, Harry Stillwell, 43
Eisenhower, Dwight, 240, 294
"Eleanor Rigby," 263
Elementary and Secondary Education Act (ESEA), 244, 256, 270, 280, 285, 299, 313, 326
Elizabethan Poor Laws, 11–19
Emancipation Proclamation, 61–64, 67–68, 75, 129
Emergency Banking Act, 190
Emerson, Ralph Waldo, 85
Employment Investment Incentives, 281
Encyclopedia Africana project, 132
End Poverty in California (EPIC) movement, 145
Engel v. Vitale, 243, 255, 270, 285, 298, 312, 325
English Anglican Church, 11
English Bill of Rights, 11. *See also* An Act Declaring the Rights and Liberties of the Subject and Settling the Succession of the Crown
Equal Employment Opportunity Commission (EEOC), 295
equality
  call for, 61–71
  setback for, 51–59
equality for all, 73–82
Evacuation Claims Act, 217
The Evening Sun, 107
"Eve of Destruction," 267, 272–273
Evers, Medgar, 241
Executive Order 9066, 215–218, 222–223. *See also* Japanese Relocation Order
Executive Order 9981, 227–229, 233–234

F

Fair Housing Act, 280

Fair Labor Standards Act (FLSA), 182, 195, 208, 220, 231, 251
Farm Credit Administration (FCA), 192
Farm Security Administration, 190
Faubus, Orval, 240
Federal Bureau of Investigation (FBI), 156
Federal Deposit Insurance Commission (FDIC), 192
Federal Emergency Relief Administration (FERA), 190
Federal Housing Administration (FHA), 192
The Federalist Papers, 22
Ferguson, John, 120, 121
Ferguson, Phoebe, 121
Fifth Amendment, 309
Financial Assistance for Rural Families, 281
First Amendment, 243, 248, 255, 260, 270, 285, 290, 298, 304, 312, 318, 325, 331
Fiske, Deborah Vinal, 85
Fiske, Nathan, 85
Flivver King (Sinclair), 145
Flower, Lucy, 308
Fonda, Henry, 205
Food and Drug Act, 144
Food and Drug Administration, 243, 255, 269, 284, 298, 312, 325
food health and safety, 143–153
food stamps, 349
forced sterilizations, 177–187
Ford, Henry, 145
Ford, John, 205
Fort Pillow Massacre, 62
foster care
  for Native Americans, 335–339
  "orphan trains," 44, 54, 65
Fourteenth Amendment, 239, 240, 309–310, 321
Franklin, Aretha, 263
Franklin, Benjamin, 22, 86
Frederick Douglass' Paper, 32
Freedmen's Bureau, 119, 121, 132
freedom, call for, 61–71
"Freedom Riders," 294
Friendly, Fred W., 251
The Fugitive Slave Act, 42

G

Galbraith, John Kenneth, 242, 255, 269, 284, 298, 312, 325
Galton, Sir Francis, 177

Gangs of New York, 107
Garrison, William, 31
Gault, Gerald, 308–310
Geary Act, 98
Gebhart v. Belton, 239
Glorious Revolution, 11
"God Bless America," 264
Gold Rush in California, 95
Gonzales v. Carhart, 323
Goodman, Andrew, 295
"Good Vibrations," 263
Graham, Henry, 241
The Grapes of Wrath, 203–206, 209–211
Great Depression, 145
    introduction, 189–193
    and Social Security Act, 189–192
Great Famine, 33
Great Society, 243, 256, 270, 279–280, 283, 285, 299, 313, 326
Griffith, D. W., 74
Griswold v. Connecticut, 321
gross domestic product (GDP), 190
Guthrie, Arlo, 264
Guthrie, Woody, 264–265

H

habeas corpus petition, 309
Haley, Alex, 339, 351
Hamilton, Alexander, 22–23
Hamilton, Frank, 267–268
"A Hard Rain's A-Gonna Fall," 243, 255, 270, 285, 299, 312, 325
Harlan, John Marshall, 120, 126
Harrington, Michael, 243, 255, 270, 279, 285, 299, 312, 325
Harvest of Shame, 251–254, 257–258
Hayes, Rutherford B., 119
health care reforms
    modern, 359–364
    Patient Protection and Affordable Care Act (2010), 359–364, 366–367
    recent developments, 359–364
Helicon Hall, 144
Hentz, Caroline Lee, 42
"Here Comes the Sun," 263
historical events
    1492–1600, 7–8
    1600–1750, 18–19
    1750–1800, 28–29
    1800–1850, 38–39
    1850–1875, 47–48, 57–58, 69–70, 80–81
    1875–1900, 92–93, 102–103, 115, 126–127
    1900–1925, 139–141, 150–152, 162–164, 173–175
    1925–1950, 184–186, 198–200, 211–213, 223–225, 234–236
    1950–1975, 246–248, 258–261, 273–276, 288–291, 302–305, 316–318, 329–332
    1975–2000, 343–345, 355–357
    2000–2018, 367–368
The History of the Standard Oil Company (Tarbell), 110, 144
Hitler, Adolph, 145, 177
Holmes, Oliver Wendell, 85, 179
Hoover, Herbert, 181, 189, 194, 207, 219–220, 230–231
Horton, Zilphia, 267–268
How the Other Half Lives: Studies Among the Tenements of New York (Riis), 107–111, 114
Hull, Charles Jerald, 155
Hull House, 155–156, 157
Hull House Museum, 156
humanities (general events)
    1492–1600, 7–8
    1600–1750, 18–19
    1750–1800, 28–29
    1800–1850, 38–39
    1850–1875, 47–48, 57–58, 69–70, 80–81
    1875–1900, 92–93, 102–103, 115, 126–127
    1900–1925, 139–141, 150–152, 162–164, 173–175
    1925–1950, 184–186, 198–200, 211–213, 223–225, 234–236
    1950–1975, 246–248, 258–261, 273–276, 288–291, 302–305, 316–318, 329–332
    1975–2000, 343–345, 355–357
    2000–2018, 367–368
Hunt, Edward, 85
Hyde Amendment, 323

I

"I Ain't Marching Anymore," 266, 272
"I Have a Dream" speech, 243, 255, 265, 270, 285, 299, 313, 325
Immigration Act, 98
Immigration and Nationality Act, 280
Immigration and Naturalization Act, 242, 254

Indian Child Welfare Act (ICWA), 335–339, 341–343
In Dubious Battle (Steinbeck), 203
infants, defined, 307
In Ole Virginia (Page), 43
In re Gault (1967), 307–311, 314–316
Intercollegiate Socialist Society, 144
Irish Home Rule movement, 33
Islam, 1, 4

J

Jackson, H. H., 91–92
Jackson, Robert, 217
Jackson, William, 85
James II, King of England, 11, 13
Japanese Relocation Order, 215–218, 222–223
The Jazz Singer, 180, 194, 207, 219, 230
Jews, 1, 4, 74
Jim Crow laws, 33, 239, 293
Job Corps, 281
Johnson, Lyndon, 98, 205, 243, 268, 271, 285–286
  Civil Rights Act, 256, 270, 293–296, 313, 326
  Economic Opportunity Act, 279, 299, 313, 326
  social welfare legislations signed by, 244
  Voting Rights Act, 243, 326
Jolson, Al, 180, 194, 207, 219, 230
Journal of Arthur Stirling, 144
Judaism, 1, 4
The Jungle (Sinclair), 110, 143–145, 148–150
juvenile justice
  equality in, 307–311
  In re Gault (1967), 307–311, 314–316

K

Katyal, Neal, 217
Kelley, Florence, 144, 156
Kennedy, John, 241
  assassination of, 247, 267, 274, 289, 293, 303, 317, 330
  elected as U.S. President, 259, 289, 330
Kennedy, John Pendleton, 43
Kennedy, Robert, 255, 275, 279, 298, 312, 317, 325
  assassination of, 247, 304, 331
Keynesian economics, 189
King, Martin Luther, Jr., 242–244, 255, 265, 268–269, 271, 284, 294–295
  Letter from the Birmingham Jail, 243, 255, 270, 285, 299, 312, 325
King Coal (Sinclair), 144
King Ferdinand, 1, 4
King Midas (Sinclair), 144
Korean War, 228
Korematsu, Fred, 216–217
Korematsu v. United States, 216–218
Ku Klux Klan, 32, 73–75, 78–80, 194, 206, 219, 230, 293

L

Lady Chatterley's Lover, 242, 255, 269, 284, 298, 312, 325
Lady of the Lake (Scott), 31
Las Casas, Bartolomé de, 4
Lathrop, Julia, 156, 308
Law of Settlement and Removal, 13
Letter from the Birmingham Jail, 243, 255, 270, 285, 299, 312, 325
Lewis, Ronald, 309
life, of slave, 31–39
The Life and Times of Frederick Douglass (Douglass), 32
Lincoln, Abraham, 32, 52–53, 61–64, 75, 129, 155
linkage to social welfare history, 5–7
"literacy test," 295
Little Eva, The Flower of the South (Cozans), 43
London, Jack, 144
The Long Valley (Steinbeck), 203
Louisiana Supreme Court, 120
Lowe, David, 251
lynching of African Americans, 239

M

Madison, James, 22–23
Magnuson Act, 98
"managed market economy," 189
Manifest Destiny, 86, 335
The Marbeau Cousins (Edwards), 43
Marshall, Thurgood, 239–240
McCarthy, Eugene, 247, 260, 275, 290, 304, 318, 331
McCarthy, Joseph, 186, 200, 213, 225, 236, 246, 258, 264, 273, 289, 302, 316, 329–330
McClellan, George, 61
McCorvey, Norma, 321
McGuire, Barry, 267
Medicaid, 190, 192, 244, 256, 270, 280, 285, 299, 313, 326, 349, 363

Medicare, 190, 192, 244, 256, 270, 280, 285, 299, 313, 326, 359, 362
Merrimac, 61
Mexican-American War, 87, 266
migrant agricultural workers, 251–254
    Harvest of Shame, 251–254
    oppression of, 251–254
"mini-adults," 308
Minor v. Happersett, 169
Missouri Supreme Court, 52
Model Cities Program, 280
modern welfare reform, 347–351
Monitor, 61
Monroe, Marilyn, 242, 254
Montgomery Bus Boycott, 241, 242, 269, 284, 298, 324
Morrison, Van, 263
Mott, Lucretia, 167
Murray, Anna, 31
Murrow, Edward R., 251–252
Muslims, 1, 4, 98
My Bondage and My Freedom (Douglass), 32
Myrdal, Gunnar, 240

N

Narrative of the Life of Frederick Douglass, An American Slave (Douglass), 32, 36–37
National Association for the Advancement of Colored People (NAACP), 121, 131, 227
    Legal Defense and Education Fund, 239
National Association of Social Workers (NASW), 242, 255, 269, 298, 312, 324
National Conference on Charities and Corrections, 156
National Conference on Social Welfare, 156
National Endowment for the Humanities Act, 280
National Farm Workers Association, 253
National Historic Landmark sites, 218
National Origins Act, 98
National Public Radio, 310
National Recovery Administration (NRA), 190
National Urban League, 227
Native Americans
    adoption for, 335–339
    foster care for, 335–339
    Indian Child Welfare Act (ICWA), 337–338
    oppression of, 85–94
    reservations, 279

Native Peoples
    Columbus, Christopher and, 1–2
    eyewitness account of Spanish cruelty toward, 4–5
Nazi Party, 177
Neighborhood Youth Corps, 281
The New Christy Minstrels, 267
New Deal, 181, 183, 189–192, 194–196, 207, 209, 220–221, 231–232, 280
New Deal programs, 145
New National Era, 32
New Testament, 53
New York Herald Tribune, 205
New-York Tribune, 107
Niagara Movement, 121, 131
Ninth Amendment, 321–322
Nixon, Richard, 348
non-cash vouchers, 350
Nordic Vikings explorations, 5
The North Star, 32
Nuremberg War Criminal Trials, 179

O

The Oaths, Signs, Ceremonies, and Objects of the Ku Klux Klan: A Full Exposé, 74
"Obamacare." See Patient Protection and Affordable Care Act (ACA)
Ochs, Phil, 266
O'Connell, Daniel, 33
Office of Economic Opportunity (OEO), 280
Of Mice and Men (Steinbeck), 203
Oil! (Sinclair), 144
oppression of Native Americans, 85–94
"orphan trains," 44, 54, 65
"O Sanctissima," 267
Oswald, Harvey Lee, 247, 259, 274, 289, 303, 317, 330
The Other America (Harrington), 243, 255, 270, 279, 285, 299, 312, 325

P

Page, Thomas Nelson, 43
pan-Africanism, 132
Parks, Rosa, 241, 242, 254, 269, 284, 298, 311
Parnell, Charles Stewart, 33
Partial-Birth Abortion Ban Act, 323
The Pastures of Heaven (Steinbeck), 203
Patient Protection and Affordable Care Act (ACA), 359–364, 366–367
Pearl Harbor attack, 215

Perkins, Frances, 156
Personal Responsibility and Work Opportunity Reconciliation Act (PRWORA), 347–351, 353–355
The Philadelphia Negro (Du Bois), 131
Pitts, Helen, 33
Planned Parenthood v. Casey, 323
Planter's Northern Bride (Hentz), 42
Plessy, Homer, 119–120, 121
Plessy, Keith, 121
Plessy and Ferguson Foundation, 121
Plessy v. Ferguson, 74, 119–121, 125, 239, 241
poverty
    early views of, 11–20
    urban, 107–116
prejudice, 95–104
Priddy, Albert, 178
Public Law 506, 215
Public Proclamation No. 21, 217

Q
Queen Isabella, 1, 4

R
The Race Question, 240
racial equality, 227–229, 233–234
racial segregation, 119–128
racism, 41–49
    two views of, 129–141
Railroad Retirement Act, 190
Ramona (Jackson), 87
Randolph, Philip, 227
Reconstruction Act, 45, 55, 77
Reconstruction Period, 119
Red Pony books (Steinbeck), 203
Rehnquist, William, 322
Revolutionary War, 167
Righteous Brothers, 263
Riis, Jacob, 107–111, 114
"Ring of Fire," 263
Robinson, Harriet, 51
Rockefeller, John D., 110
Rodrigo de Escobedo, 2
Roe v. Wade (1973), 321–324
Roosevelt, Eleanor, 205
Roosevelt, Franklin Delano, 145, 156, 189, 229
    Executive Order 9066, 215–218, 222–223
    Fair Labor Standards Act (FLSA), 251
    New Deal programs, 280
Roosevelt, Theodore, 86, 108, 130
Roots (Haley), 339, 351
Rukus, Jurgis, 144

S
Sadler, Barry, 267
Sandford, John, 52
Schwerner, Michael, 295
science (general events)
    1492–1600, 7–8
    1600–1750, 18–19
    1750–1800, 28–29
    1800–1850, 38–39
    1850–1875, 47–48, 57–58, 69–70, 80–81
    1875–1900, 92–93, 102–103, 115, 126–127
    1900–1925, 139–141, 150–152, 162–164, 173–175
    1925–1950, 184–186, 198–200, 211–213, 223–225, 234–236
    1950–1975, 246–248, 258–261, 273–276, 288–291, 302–305, 316–318, 329–332
    1975–2000, 343–345, 355–357
    2000–2018, 367–368
scientific racism, 108
Scorsese, Martin, 107
Scott, Dred, 51–53
Scott, Sir Walter, 31
Scott v. Sandford, 51–53, 56–57
Securities Act of 1933, 190
Securities and Exchange Commission (SEC), 192
Seeger, Pete, 267–268
Separate Car Act, 119
setback for equality, 51–59
Settlement House Movement, 155–164
The Shame of Cities (Steffens), 110, 144
Shelby County v. Holder, 297
Simms, William Gilmore, 43
Sinclair, Upton, 110, 143–145, 148–150
slave
    life of, 31–39
slavery, 22, 31–39, 51–53, 120
    abolishment of, 293
    Emancipation Proclamation and, 62–63
Sledge, Percy, 263
Sloan, B. F., 267
Smith, Kate, 264
Social Security Act (1935), 197–198

and Great Depression, 189–192
permanent pension system, 190
programs, 192
Social Security Act (1965), 244, 256, 270, 280, 285, 299, 313, 326
Social Security Administration, 192
Social Security disability insurance, 192
social welfare historical events
1600-1750, 15–16
1750-1800, 25–26
1800-1850, 33–36
1850-1875, 43–46, 54–56, 65–67, 76–78
1875-1900, 88–91, 99–101, 111–113, 122–124
1900-1925, 133–135, 146–148, 158–160, 170–172
1925-1950, 180–183, 194–196, 206–209, 219–221, 230–232
1950-1975, 242–245, 254–257, 268–271, 284–286, 297–300, 311–314, 324–327
1975-2000, 339–341, 351–353
2000-2018, 364–365
songs of protest
"Blowin' in the Wind," 265–266
"Eve of Destruction," 267
"I Ain't Marching Anymore," 266
introduction, 263–264
"This Land Is Your Land," 264–265
"We Shall Overcome," 267–268
The Souls of Black Folk: Essays and Sketches (Du Bois), 132, 137–139
Southern Christian Leadership Conference (SCLC), 294
Spanish Inquisition, 4
The Spokesmen, 267
Springsteen, Bruce, 265
Standing Bear, Chief of Ponca tribe, 85–86
Stanton, Elizabeth Cady, 32, 167–168
Starr, Ellen, 155
Steffens, Lincoln, 110, 144
Steinbeck, John, 182, 195, 221, 232
early career, 203
The Grapes of Wrath, 203–206, 209–211
introduction, 203
Presidential Medal of Freedom, 205

Stock Market Crash of 1929, 189
Stone, Lucy, 167
Stowe, Calvin, 41
Stowe, Harriet Beecher, 41–43, 85, 87
Student Nonviolent Coordinating Committee (SNCC), 294
Supplemental Nutritional Assistance Program (SNAP), 349
Supplemental Security Income (SSI), 192, 349
The Suppression of the African Slave Trade to the United States of America, 1638–1870, 131
The Swallow Barn (Kennedy), 43
The Sword and the Distaff (Simms), 43

T
Taft, William Howard, 130, 156
"Talkin' John Birch Society Blues," 243, 255, 270, 285, 299, 312, 325
Tarbell, Ida, 110, 144
Tax Cuts and Jobs Act, 363
Temporary Assistance to Needy Families (TANF), 192, 348–349
Tennessee Valley Authority (TVA), 192
There Will Be Blood, 144
13th Amendment, 239
"This Land Is Your Land," 264–265, 272
Tindley, Charles, 267
To a God Unknown (Steinbeck), 203
Tortilla Flat (Steinbeck), 203
Tourgée, Albion, 119
Travels with Charley in Search of America (Steinbeck), 205
Trotter, William, 121
Truman, Harry, 64, 217, 227
Executive Order 9981, 227–229, 233–234
veto of, 242, 254
Trump, Donald, 98, 363
Truth, Sojourner, 167
Tudor Queen Elizabeth I, 13
"Turn! Turn! Turn!", 263
21st Amendment, 195, 207, 220, 231
Twenty Years at Hull House (Addams), 155–157, 160–162

U
"Unchained Melody," 263
Uncle Tom's Cabin (Stowe), 42, 87

"Uncle Tom's Cabin" Contrasted with Buckingham Hall, the Planter's Home (Criswell), 43, 46–47
unemployment insurance, 192
Union Pacific Railroad, 95
United Farm Workers (UFW), 253–254
United Nations, 240
United States
    armed services, integration of, 227–229, 233–234
    Department of Justice Civil Rights Division, 294
United States Congress, 29, 58, 66–67, 69, 78, 81, 135, 140, 148, 160, 163, 169, 182, 195, 196, 208, 217, 220, 231–232, 256, 286, 300
    Reconstruction Act, 45, 55, 77
    Revolutionary War Pension Act, 34
United States Constitution, 13, 24, 51–52, 195, 207, 220, 231, 239, 243, 255, 270, 285, 298, 309–310, 312, 321–322, 325
United States Housing Authority, 190
United States Supreme Court, 52, 53, 74, 120, 168
University of Illinois, 156
Up from Slavery: An Autobiography (Washington), 136–137
Urban and Rural Community Action, 281–282
urban poverty, 107–116

V

Veterans Administration (VA), 227
Vietnam War, 247–248, 259–260, 266–267, 274–275, 289–290, 303–304, 317–318, 330–331, 337
Virginia Eugenical Sterilization Act, 178
Voluntary Assistance to Needy Children, 282
Volunteers in Service to America (VISTA), 282
voting equality for women, 167–176
Voting Rights Act of 1965, 75, 243, 256, 270, 280, 285, 295–297, 302, 313, 326

W

Wagner Act, 190
Wallace, George, 241
Warner, Mark, 179
War of 1812, 229, 266
War on Poverty, 279–283
Warren, Earl, 240

Washington, Booker T., 132, 136–137
Washington, Booker Taliaferro, 129
Washington, George, 22
"We Shall Overcome," 267–268, 273
"When a Man Loves a Woman," 263
White, Byron, 322
Whole Woman's Health v. Hellerstedt, 323
Wilderness Act, 280
Wilson, Woodrow, 157, 169
The Winter of Our Discontent (Steinbeck), 205
women
    and abortion services, 321
    freedom of, 24
    voting equality for, 167–176
    voting rights for, 156
Women's International League for Peace and Freedom, 156
work experience opportunities, 282
Works Progress Administration (WPA), 190
Work Study Programs, 282
World War I, 131, 157, 169, 266
World War II, 98, 179, 200, 205, 213, 216–218, 224–225, 227–228, 236, 259, 266, 274, 289, 293, 303, 316, 330, 340, 353

Y

"(You Make Me Feel Like) A Natural Woman," 263

Z

Zanuck, Darryl, 205

CPSIA information can be obtained
at www.ICGtesting.com
Printed in the USA
LVHW100741060121
675689LV00005B/28